The Dictionary of
Magic and Mystery

The Dictionary of Magic and Mystery

The definitive guide
to the mysterious, the magical
and the supernatural

Compiled by Mélusine Draco

**MOON
BOOKS**

Winchester, UK
Washington, USA

First published by Moon Books, 2012
O-Books is an imprint of John Hunt Publishing Ltd.,
Laurel House, Station Approach, Alresford, Hants, SO24 9JH, UK
office1@o-books.net
www.o-books.com

For distributor details and how to order please visit the 'Ordering' section on our website.

Text copyright: Mélusine Draco 2010

ISBN: 978-1-84694-462-8

A CIP catalogue record for this book is available from the British Library.

Design: DKD
Printed in the UK by CPI Antony Rowe
Printed in the USA by Offset Paperback Mfrs, Inc

We operate a distinctive and ethical publishing philosophy in all
areas of our business, from our global network of authors to
production and worldwide distribution.

Contents

Author Biography

Writing as Mélusine Draco, the author has been a magical and spiritual instructor for over 20 years, and writer of numerous popular books including *Liber Ægyptius: The Book of Egyptian Magic*; *The Egyptian Book of Days, The Hollow Tree*, an elementary guide to Qabalah; *The Thelemic Handbook; A Witch's Treasury of the Countryside; Root & Branch: British Magical Tree Lore* and *Starchild: A Rediscovery of Stellar Wisdom*. Her highly individualistic teaching methods, as used in her latest Traditional Witchcraft series, draw on historical sources, supported by academic texts and current archeological findings. *The Dictionary of Magic & Mystery* is the result of 10 years work that was originally compiled for purely personal use.

Her latest titles *Traditional Witchcraft for Urban Living; Traditional Witchcraft for the Seashore; Traditional Witchcraft for Fields and Hedgerows; Traditional Witchcraft for Woods and Forests* and *The Dictionary of Magic & Mystery* are published by O-Books

"The most beautiful thing we can experience is the mysterious – it is the source of all true art and science.
Albert Einstein

Introduction

Every good reference book is both a product and a reflection of its time. *The Dictionary of Magic & Mystery* is not just another compendium or dictionary of occultism: it is a jumping-off point for further research. Here, the reader will find the ancient and modern interpretation for magical and mystical terms, together with explanations for the differences between the varied (and often conflicting) approaches to magic. You will also find both the common, the regional, and the obscure, because even popular usage can often distill the true essence from original meaning. There are historical and archeological references that are essential in helping to put the past into perspective, whether we are talking about witchcraft, ritual magic, or the different paths and traditions from the East. Added to all this information are some of the sacred sites that are associated with our pagan past; together with thumbnail sketches of the well-known (and sometimes dubious) personalities who have been associated with the pursuit of magical knowledge throughout the centuries.

To thoroughly understand what magic is all about, whether from the perspective of the village wise-woman or the high-powered ceremonial magician, we *have* to know the true history of the path we wish to follow. These are paths that have been beset with persecution and ridicule; both physical and mental anguish; hardship and deprivation. To understand where we now stand, we need to walk in the footsteps of those who have gone before and learn from their experiences, their failures and their triumphs. We also need a basic grounding in Classical subjects because we cannot hope to plug in to the here-and-now and expect instant enlightenment, or become a witch or magician in twelve easy lessons!

Paradoxically, although there are now more books on occultism (in its widest sense) in publication than ever before, the contents are by no means guaranteed to be accurate, or even penned by someone with a knowledgeable, *working* background in the subject on which they write. Sadly, even mainstream editors have little *practical* experience in the subjects they are commissioning and, as a result, the genre of 'mind, body and spirit' publishing is awash with books and magazine articles by those who are merely regurgitating information, often taken from questionable sources, blended with hefty dollops of contemporary Orientalism.

As that invaluable encyclopedia, *Man, Myth & Magic*, pointed out back in the 1970s, at the roots of mythology and magic is a kind of thinking which is certainly not random, and which has its own curious logic. Where metaphor, sigla and ceremony convey the intangible and bring the supernatural into the natural world, by making connections between things that outwardly and rationally are not connected at all. And magic is all about understanding these analogies, allegories and symbols. *The Dictionary of Magic & Mystery* attempts to put this way of thinking into some kind of perspective for the serious student.

For example: The 16th century ritual magician would have had a firm grounding in the Classics in their original language, i.e. Hebrew, Latin and Greek, not to mention a working knowledge of European history, mathematics, astronomy and alchemy. By the 19th century, Adepts of the occult sciences were adding the Eastern influences of Tantra, yoga, meditation techniques and the karmic philosophy of reincarnation. Traditional ritual magic texts are governed by this broad spectrum of learning under the guise of Magical Correspondences and, unless this method of working is fully understood, then the results will be a long time in coming for the striving *magus adeptus*.

By contrast, the natural witch or cunning-man would have developed an instinctive knowledge of ancestral and natural history, weather lore and folk medicine. And by studying the popular versions of our native folklore and superstitions, we can glimpse behind the Victorian obsession with the 'Devil and all his works' when it came to compiling their collections, and grasp the fact that most of these protective charms were originally witches' spells culled for popular use. Modern witches need to develop the discipline of cultivating the powers of seeing and interacting with Nature, or we will not be able to read the 'signs' when they appear.

Like the Universe itself, magic is a living, expanding thing and to become a successful magical practitioner, we must learn to grow magically and intellectually in tandem with these developments. Modern paganism is now permeated with Oriental influences (reiki, feng shui, I Ching, etc) and it also helps to have a nodding acquaintance with modern astronomy, astrophysics, archeology and anthropology to help us to understand where everything fits within the Laws of Correspondence.

Remember: *Fact has nothing to do with belief; that the ancients believed, is all we need to know. And even if we think we are no longer susceptible to the powers of the Old Gods, we only have to look through ancient Egyptian, Greek, Roman, Celtic or Viking eyes to see them.*

So, some may ask, why can't we just abandon the use of these ancient symbols? The experienced magical practitioner understands that contact with these 'old energies' can be attained more completely through symbols that are so ancient that they are buried deep within the storehouse of our collective unconsciousness. The alternatives – intellectual formulae and symbols of mathematics and science – have been evolved too recently to serve as direct conduits. The magician or mystic uses the more direct paths, which long ago were mapped out in the shadowlands of what Carl Jung referred to as the racial or universal subconscious.

Many of the books referred to in this text are now out of print, but the tracking down and acquisition of such rare volumes should be viewed as part of the magical learning process. These are included simply because they remain the best explanation of the subject (or the most controversial), even though there may be dozens of other more recent titles in print. Others reflect the publishing viewpoint of their time and, as such, offer an insight into the limited availability of good source material during the early 1960s and 1970s; remembering that the last Witchcraft Act wasn't repealed until 1951.

Some titles offer a basic introduction to a subject, while others may need to stay on the shelf until the moment of enlightenment, when the scales fall from the seeker's eyes and they are ready to receive the wisdom from the printed page. Surprisingly, perhaps, there are also a handful of fictional titles here, since many of these contain more than just a grain of magical truth. The search for such treasures should be looked upon as part of the magical quest, for seeking out such 'truths' should never be as simple as taking down a book from a shelf.

Mélusine Draco

A

A∴A∴: *Argentinum Astrum*, the Order of the Silver Star was the name of the magickal Order of the Great White Brotherhood (of Adepts) founded by Aleister **Crowley**. The triangle of dots indicates that the Order is a secret society connected with the ancient Mysteries. The reference is to Sothis-Sirius, the Star of the Shadow. Crowley's own magical encyclopedia, *The Equinox*, remains the finest source material of A∴A∴ philosophy and magickal teaching.

Abbots Bromley: The scene of the annual Horn Dance, which takes place on the first Sunday after 4th September. It starts at dawn outside the village church, makes a 20-mile circuit of the local farms where the dancers are welcomed as the bearers of good luck, and finishes with a final performance in the main street in the afternoon. No one knows how old the dance is, but its closest parallels are believed to be the ritual dances of primitive societies, reaching back to the Stone Age. The reindeer antlers themselves are at least 1000 years old. SOURCE: *Folklore, Myths & Customs of Britain*, Marc Alexander; *Folklore, Myths & Legends of Britain*, compiled by Reader's Digest.

Abiegnus: The mystic mountain of the **Rosicrucians**, symbolizing **Initiation**.

Abominor: *'I pray that the* (omen or ill-luck) *may be averted'* and used when mentioning anything unlucky. A simple figure of speech to avert ill-luck, similar to touching wood.

Aborigine Tradition: The beliefs and culture of the Australian Aboriginal people lie in remote antiquity and, like many so-called 'primitive' societies, focuses strongly on **Nature** and **Ancestor** Worship. Even those who have lived among them for decades remain almost in total ignorance of the ways of the Bushmen and so the source material available only gives a superficial overview of this extremely ancient culture. It is one of the oldest living religions in the world, although tribal differences make a general description almost impossible.

Abracadabra: A magical word of great power that gave rise to the medieval protective spell, meaning: *'Hurt me not!'* Originally a Qabalistic charm constructed from the initials of the Hebrew words AB (father), BEN (son), and RUACH ACADASCH (Holy Spirit). It was considered to be an antidote for all ailments; the word was written on parchment and suspended from the neck by a linen thread in the triangular format.

ABRACADABRA
ABRACADABR
ABRACADAB
ABRACADA
ABRACAD
ABRACA
ABRAC
ABRA
ABR
AB
A

Abracax: The Persian Supreme Being and in Greek notation it stands for

365, as Abracax was said to preside over the 365 virtues, one of which is supposed to prevail on each day of the year. Abracax Stones were carried as **Talismans**, having the name engraved on them, or the symbolic forms combining a fowl's head, a serpent's body and human limbs.

Abrahadabra: Not to be confused with the above, this is the formula of the **Great Work**. SOURCE: *The Magical Revival*, Kenneth Grant.

Abramelin the Mage: A 15th century Jewish magus whose Qabalistic writings have influenced generations of magicians, including Samuel MacGregor-**Mathers**, a leading figure of the **Golden Dawn** and later Aleister Crowley. An 18th century manuscript written in French and located in the Bibliothèque de l'Arsenal in Paris, it is alleged to be a translation of a Hebrew original of 1458; Mathers' translation, *The Book of the Sacred Magic of Abra-Melin the Mage*, remains in print to the present day. There is an occult superstition that those who follow Abramelin will sooner or later come to a sticky end.

Abyss: [Qabalah] The gulf between the real and the unreal. 'Crossing the Abyss' is the most critical step taken on the magical/mystical path and a magician's personal attainment is dependant upon the successful crossing. This symbolizes the 'desert of arid human intellection' and only those who have been magically trained to cope with the aftermath should attempt the crossing.

Academy: [Greek] Originally a grove of olive trees near Athens where Plato and his successors taught, his school of philosophy was known as the Academy. Plato was buried near the grove. Now used to denote a specialist school for higher study or teaching and recently adopted by some occult factions.

Acca Lārentia: An early Italian goddess of the Earth to whom the seed was entrusted. She was worshipped at the *Lārentālia* on 23rd December. SOURCE: *The Roman Book of Days*, Paulina Erina ; *Phases in the Religion of Ancient Rome*, Cyril Bailey.

Accretion Disk: [Astronomy] A disk of material rotating in orbit around a massive object such as a planet or star, or a **Black Hole**. The rings around **Saturn** are an accretion disk.

Acheron: [Greek] The 'River of Sorrows' and one of the five rivers of the underworld or **Hades**.

Aconite: Also known as monkshood or wolfsbane. Its poisonous qualities were ascribed to the foam that dropped from the mouths of the three-headed Cerberus when Hercules dragged him from the Underworld. It was used in various potions and flying ointments, as well as being a remedy for poison, and as a sedative. Ruling planet: **Saturn**.

Acolyte: From the classical Greek/Roman meaning 'follower'. In modern occult terms, an attendant or low-ranking member of a temple or coven who is not an **Initiate**.

Acronymics: The practice of forming magical or spiritually significant words from the initials of a series of words, often used by Qabalists.

Actaeon: Either because he boasted that he was a better hunter than **Artemis**, or because he came upon her bathing, the goddess changed him into a stag;

he was then torn to pieces by his own hounds. A symbolic reversal of fortune: the hunter becomes the hunted.

Acupressure: A variation on Chinese acupuncture called *G-jo* (meaning 'first aid') in which finger pressure replaces needles and achieves results by manipulation. The Japanese form is called **Shiatsu.**

Acupuncture: An ancient Chinese system of healing and preventative medicine, which has been practiced extensively in the West since the 1930s. Needles are inserted into the skin at points that have no apparent connection with the ailment. According to the Chinese texts, there are about a thousand points where needles can produce the required stimulation to relieve or cure disease. This is the oldest known medical system recorded in *The Yellow Emperor's Classic of Internal Medicine* or *Nei Ching*.

Adam Kadmon: According to the Jewish **Qabalah**, this was the first man, an emanation of absolute perfection. He is symbolized by the major axis of ten concentric circles, the sephiroth or ten circles of creation – as primeval man he symbolizes the Universe. On a mystical level he is actually androgynous, and seen in ancient Jewish mysticism as blending with God.

Adder: see **Viper.**

Adder's Tongue: Found growing in the hedgerows and meadows, this fern was used in medieval times for cleansing wounds and as an astringent, healing ointment and salve. **Culpeper** recommended the juice, mixed with the distilled water of horsetail for internal wounds and bruises. The ruling planet is the Moon in **Cancer.**

Adept: Someone completely versed in a particular occult tradition or Path. In classical occult tradition, one who was supposed to have obtained the Elixir of Life and the Philosopher's Stone.

Adeptus Minor: A grade of adeptship within ritual magic.

Adhikari: [Sanskrit] Refers to the state of being spiritually competent; a condition of preparedness for undertaking any form of mystical culture.

Adibuddha: Meaning 'primeval Buddha' and the concept of a **Buddha** who has existed from the beginning of time – an original creator.

Adikalika: [Sanskrit] The primordial (*adi*) black (*kali*) goddess (*ka*). A description of **Kali**, whose symbol is the Night of Time

Adisakti: [Sanskrit] Primordial Power.

Aditi: An Indian goddess whose name means 'infinity' and a form of the Great Mother who embraces all living and being. In later tradition she was seen as the personification of the earth.

Adjuration: In classical demonology, it refers to a form of ritual held around an altar or in a circle, in an attempt to make the Devil, or one of his legions, appear.

Adonai: A name that often appears in magical invocations and inscriptions, which translates as 'Lord'. Son of the star-being and god of light among the Rosicrucians. Sometimes applied to the **Holy Guardian Angel**.

Adraste or **Andraste:** Meaning 'she who is invincible' and the goddess of war in ancient Briton. This was the deity to whom Boudicca of the Iceni (61AD) had captured Roman women sacrificed. A parallel is found in Gaul where the Vicontii had a goddess of war named Andarta.

Adris: Magical stones sensitive to the approach of spirits, i.e. the crystal that responds to the presence of unknown entities.

Adytum: The Holy of Holies, or inner sanctum of Greek and Roman temples, into which the general public were not admitted.

Advaitan Cosmology: By the medieval period in India the Advaitan **Vedanta** (salvation philosophy) had developed an organized '**Cosmology**', based upon the combination of earlier traditions, and the closely related world-view of classical **Hinduism**. SOURCE: *The Penguin Dictionary of Religions*, ed John R. Hinnells.

Aegis: The Greek for 'shield' and a sacred symbol of protection that cannot be violated.

Aelfric: A Benedictine monk of **Cerne Abbas**. Among his numerous works, written in both Latin and Old English, was *Colloquy* (*Nominum Herbarum*), compiled in 995AD and comprising a list of over 200 herbs and trees, several of which are no longer identifiable.

Aeneas: A son of Aphrodite and hero in the Trojan War. The saga of his flight from the ruins of Troy became known to the Romans in the 6th century BC, and soon after he was honored as a *heros*. For the Romans he was the embodiment of the old virtue of *pietas* (piety, reverence for age and tradition), having rescued his lame father and the holy images from the burning city. The emperor Augustus believed his family was descended from this son of the gods.

Aeneid: An epic poem in 12 books by Virgil to celebrate the origin and growth of the Roman Empire; the background is drawn from the legend of Aeneas and his wanderings after the fall of Troy.

Aeon: (1) A vast age or eternity; the largest or a very large division of geological time. (2) A cycle of time denoting a period of approximately 2000 years. There have been three such aeons within historical times: The Aeon of Isis, the Aeon of Osiris, and the present, the Aeon of Horus. (3) Card number XX in Aleister **Crowley's Thoth Tarot**, replacing **Judgement** in the standard Rider-**Waite** deck.

Aerolite: A class of meteorite composed dominantly of silicate material that was revered in Phoenicia and Syria, and still held to be sacred in Islam as is shown by the reverence paid to the black stone of Mecca. Aerolite debris often forms part of the content of amulets.

Aeromancy: Divination using the formation of clouds and other patterns in the skies, and predicting events by wind direction.

Aesir: The main gods of Norse mythology, excluding Freyr, Njord, and other Vanir deities. In the poetic *Edda*, the Aesir are described as builders and craftsmen, playing board-games, establishing law, meeting at their Assembly (the 'Thing') and creating mankind, but who are doomed to perish. In Iceland a new religious sect, the Asatruarmenn ('Believers in the Aesir'), was officially recognized in 1973, the aim of the founders being to restore the ancient rituals of pre-Christian Iceland (Ssee **Northern Tradition, Asatru** and **Vanir**). SOURCE: *The New Believers*, David V. Barrett.

Aeternitas: For the Romans the

personification of eternity, both of the Empire and of the deified emperors. Symbolically represented by the **Phoenix** perpetually rising from the ashes of its own burning, and the serpent biting its own tail (see **Uroboros**) – both illustrating a process that has no beginning and no end.

Aetites: A stone supposedly found in the head, neck or stomach of an eagle and used as a powerful talisman, bringing courage and good fortune to the wearer (see **Animal Concretion**).

Aethyr: A term coined by Dr. John **Dee** to refer to angelic or non-terrestrial abodes; or dimensions of consciousness not normally experienced. Aleister **Crowley's** *The Vision and the Voice* and *Vel Chanokh* are probably the best sources of information.

Afterlife: The general term for a form of spirit life that continues after death. This widespread concept differs from culture to culture, although in modern pagan belief there appears to be a general adoption of the Eastern belief in **Reincarnation** and **Karma**. SOURCE: *Penguin Dictionary of Religions*, ed John R. Hinnells; *Chambers Dictionary of the Unexplained.*

African Witchcraft: There are still many African societies where witchcraft is still a tangible and threatening belief. SOURCE: *Man, Myth & Magic*, ed Richard Cavendish; *Witchcraft & Sorcery*, ed Max Marwick.

Agapé: Greek word for 'love' often used in magical working to refer to higher or spiritual love, as opposed to Eros or sexual love.

Agate: A variety of chalcedony with colored bands or other markings and used as an amulet for protection against snake and insect bites. Also makes the wearer eloquent.

Agathos Daimon: A guardian spirit in Greek mythology that was imagined as a winged serpent that hovered invisibly around a person, and brought good luck to his home.

Aglet or **Aiguillette:** A knotted cord which was believed to cause impotence in men, barrenness in women, and general discord in a marriage. For the spell to be effective the cord should be knotted during the wedding ceremony. It was also used to bind couples in illicit amatory relationships. The belief was recorded in ancient times by both Virgil and Pliny – and was still being taken seriously in the Middle Ages. SOURCE: *A Dictionary of Devils & Demons*, J. Tondriau and R. Villeneuve; *The Encyclopedia of Witches & Witchcraft*, Rosemary Ellen Guiley.

Agni: [Sanskrit for 'fire'] The Vedic god of fire, who carries the sacrificial burnt offerings to the gods. He is the intermediary between mankind and the gods when he appears in the sacrificial fire.

Agnostic: A person who only believes what is knowable, rejecting divine revelation and the doctrine of the Trinity as being 'past human understanding'.

Agonalia: Public games in honor of **Janus** and the guardian deities of Rome; held three times a year in January, May and December.

Agriculture: Plowing, sowing, reaping and other agricultural operations, depended for success on the regularity of **Nature** and the bounty of the gods. Many of the important pagan rituals and customs still reflect the propitiatory rites for a bountiful harvest.

Agrimony: A handful of leaves, fresh or dried, steeped in a pint of boiling water to cure jaundice and diseases of the liver or blood. Keep in the bedroom to aid sleep. Ruling planet: Jupiter in **Cancer.**

Agrippa, Cornelius: Or Henry Cornelius Agrippa von Nettesheim (to give him his assumed title) was born into a noble family in Cologne in 1486. Widely known for his books on magic and occultism in the courts and universities of Western Europe. Like most magicians who followed him, little of Agrippa's work is original thought and he mercilessly plagiarized the writings of both ancient and modern esoteric sources. He nonetheless produced a magical system that indicates a tremendous degree of learning and occult lore, which deals with divine names, natural magic and cosmology. SOURCE: *De Occult Philosopha (Occult Philosophy).*

Ague: An old name for fever, 'the ague' was formerly widespread, and a bewildering variety of cures for it were current well into the 20th century. In addition to numerous herbal cures, the ague was believed to be avoidable, or caused by magical application.

Ahimsa: The principle of non-violence, or non-injury to living creatures and common to **Buddhist** and Jain ethics, based on the belief that violence produces negative **Karma** for the person who inflicts it, with consequent ill-effects in terms of unfavorable re-births. Buddhists take the view that it is the act of killing that is harmful, but not the eating of meat that someone else has killed.

Ahmed, Rollo: A journalist, who caused considerable harm to modern embryonic Wicca with his damaging accusations of black magic and depravity in relation to *any* form of occult practice, in his book *The Black Art,* published in 1936. Although an 'occult adviser' to Dennis Wheatley, most British occultists considered his writing highly suspect and, in many instances, provably inaccurate. It has been suggested that Ahmed belonged to the world of 'occult literature' that existed before real occultists began to write books for genuinely interested seekers.

Ahriman: The Persian god of evil and **Ahura Mazda's** adversary, who counters every act of creation with an act of anti-creation. In **Mithraism** and Zervanism, he is venerated as a god.

Ahura Mazda: [Persian – Wisdom Lord] The name of the one true god as preached by **Zoroaster.**

Aidoneus: The Greek form of the Lord of the Underworld (i.e. **Hades**) – the opposite of **Adonai**, Lord of the Upper World.

Aiguillette: see **Aglet.**

Aikido: [Japanese, *ai,* to harmonize, *ki,* breath, spirit, *dō,* way, doctrine] An evolutionary form of 'spiritual' self-defense originated by Professor Morihei Ueshiba at the turn of the 20th century. SOURCE: *Aikido,* Koichi Tohei.

Ain: [Qabalah] Nothingness. The Void beyond Kether (see **Tree of Life**).

Ain Soph: [Qabalah] No Limit; infinity.

Ain Soph Aur: [Qabalah] Limitless Light. The Void beyond the known Universe represented by the Tree of Life, of which Kether is the most remote outpost.

Air: see **Elemental Air.**

Aiwass: The messenger of unknown extra-terrestrial intelligence, who communicated *The Book of the Law* to Aleister Crowley in 1904. SOURCE: *Confessions of Aleister Crowley,* Aleister Crowley; *The Eye in the Triangle,* Israel Regardie; *The Magical Revival,* Kenneth Grant.

Ajna chakra: [Sanskrit] The occult circle of power usually referred to as the **Third Eye** and located between the eyes.

Akasha: [Sanskrit] Spirit or **Aethyr,** symbolized by a **Black Egg.**

Akashic Records: A Sanskrit variation of the cosmic Book of Life in which are recorded the complete activities of every being that ever lived. They are of particular importance to those of the Eastern religions and philosophies who believe in the concept of **Reincarnation** (see **Anima Mundi**).

Akhira: The Islamic afterlife when, after the Last Judgement, the righteous will be separated from the damned. Paradise is described in physical terms in the Koran as a luxurious garden, with all sorts of physical delights and the vision of God.

AL: Literally 'The' – a term for God. Its Qabalistic value is 31, which is the key number of Aleister **Crowley's** *The Book of the Law;* the *Book* is often referred to as *AL.*

Al Azif: [Arabic] The alleged original title of *The Necronomicon.*

Albertus Magnus: Born in 1205 and regarded by his contemporaries as an alchemist, despite the fact that he was Bishop of Ratisbon. He claimed to have magical control over the weather and is best remembered as having discovered the Philosopher's Stone; he claimed in his work *De Rebus Metallis et Mineralibus* that he had conducted tests on alchemical gold. Several other works of magical practice and superstition have been wrongly attributed to him.

Alchemy: The quest for a substance (the **'Philosopher's Stone'** or **'Elixir of Life'**) that will transform base metals into gold or confer immortality on man, combining spirituality and chemistry. Western alchemy descends from 2nd century **Gnostic** texts on metallurgy, while Chinese alchemy is almost invariably associated with the quest for immortality. In modern practice, alchemy is more an art than a science and its *'most important and most interesting aim is the spiritual transformation of the alchemist himself'.* The term derives from the Arabic *Khem,* an ancient word for Egypt, thus making it the 'art of Egypt' or magic.

Alchemystical: Meaning 'alchemical', an adjective used by the modern alchemist Frater Albertus, to imply a connection with *'mystes'* or initiates, as in the **Eleusinian** Mysteries.

Albigensian Crusade: The annihilation of the **Cathars** of southern France on the charge of heresy in 1209.

Albion: An archaic name for England, from the ancient inhabitants called Albiones. The term Albin was at one time applied to the northern part of Scotland, called by the Romans 'Caledonia' and was the partly inhabited by the Picts.

Alder: The indigenous tribes of Britain regarded the tree as sacred as a sentinel, guarding the realms of Otherworld. It also has strong associations with the **Faere** Folk. **Culpeper** states that the leaves *'gathered while the morning* *dew is on them'*, will rid a bed of fleas. The ruling planet is **Venus**. SOURCE: *Root & Branch: British Magical Tree Lore,* Mélusine Draco.

Alderley Edge: In the woods on this sheer sandstone cliff rising from the Cheshire plain is a wishing well formed by a natural spring that has connections with **Merlin**. It was also an important working site for traditional witches during the 1960s and although the underground caverns have been rendered inaccessible, it remains a 'sacred place' for those belonging to that era.

Alectorius: A stone from a cockerel makes a powerful amulet for power, courage and wealth. To obtain it, lay the body in an anthill for nine days, after which time the stone will be found (see **Animal Concretion)**.

Alectromancy: Forecasting the future through atmospheric or celestial conditions.

Alectryomancy: Divination involving the behavior of animals.

Aleuromancy: Divination through messages baked inside cakes or biscuits, i.e. Chinese fortune cookies.

Alexandrian Library: Founded by Ptolemy II in Egypt, it housed some 700,000 volumes by the 1st century. The library itself was destroyed by fire around 642AD.

Alexandrianism: The Alexandrian school of Greek poets on Roman poetry. Its chief features were 'artificiality, an excessive display of mythological learning, and elaboration of form'.

Alexandrian Tradition: Eventually eclipsed the **Gardnerian** Tradition in popularity under the leadership of Manchester-born Alex **Sanders** and

his wife Maxine during the 1970s. The Alexandrians continued the Gardnerian practice of working naked, or 'sky-clad' and were far more geared-up to cope with the attendant publicity that their leader courted. Alexandrian groups differ from the Gardnerians principally in that they lean far more strongly towards ceremonial magic and foreign influences, although like the Gardnerians, they worship the god and goddess, and observe the same seasonal rituals. *What Witches Do*, by Stewart **Farrar**, is a study of the Alexandrian school of **Wicca**. SOURCE: *King of the Witches*, June Johns; *Maxine - Witch Queen*, Maxine Sanders.

Algol: Bright white star in the constellation of Perseus, widely regarded as evil because a dark star that revolves around it dims its light at intervals and gives the impression of a malevolent winking eye. Called 'Demon's Head' by the Arabs; by the Jews 'Satan's Head' and later **Lilith** – a demon of the night. Classical authors said it was the head of Medusa the Gorgon, hanging from Perseus' belt.

Alim: [Hebrew] The elemental gods.

Alkanet: see Bugloss.

All Hallow Summer: A second summer that sets in around All-Hallows (or St. Luke's summer – St. Luke's Day is 18th October), which is now more popularly referred to as an Indian Summer. Shakespeare uses the term in *Henry IV, i.2 'Farewell, thou latter spring; farewell, All-Hallown Summer!'*

All Hallows Eve (see **Hallowe'en** and **Samhain**): A Scottish tradition claims that those born on All Hallows Eve have the gift of second sight, and commanding powers over spirits.

Allotriophagy: The vomiting or disgorging of strange or foul objects was seen as the result of witchcraft... and produced a memorable scene in the film *The Witches of Eastwick*!

Almanac: Annual publications, produced in large quantities for mass sale, and cheap enough for everyone to afford by the 17th century. They contained a wealth of information, including a calendar, tide tables, moon phases, weather predictions, simplified astrology and predictions for the coming year (see **Old Moore's Almanac**).

Almousin: One of the barbarous or alien names of evocation that appears in an alleged ritual preserved by Eliphas **Levi**.

Alphabets: Some **Grimoires** and so-called demonic texts have preserved secret alphabets and vary according to different traditions and translations. Magical alphabets were frequently made by combining symbols from the Hebrew, runic and other alphabets believed to contain power. The most popular are **Theban**, **Runic** and **Ogham**. SOURCE: *Alchemical Symbols & Secret Alphabets*, C.J.S. Thompson; *The Alphabet*, David Diringer; *Ogham & Coelbren: Keys to the Celtic Mysteries*, Nigel Pennick; *Runes*, Ralph Elliott; *Magic: An Occult Primer*, David Conway.

Alphitomancy: Divination that proves guilt or innocence through the eating of a loaf of barley bread. It was believed the guilty party would choke while swallowing.

Alraun: A talismanic image made from rowan wood.

Altar: The focal point of any magical working and only magical equipment should be placed on it. It has a double origin, as the platform or table on which offerings to a deity were placed, but also sometimes as the throne or home of the deity itself. In ritual magic the perpetual lamp should burn above it, symbolizing the divine presence and to serve as a beacon for those on an astral journey. SOURCE: *Magic: An Occult Primer*, David Conway; *Magick*, Aleister Crowley; *Witches & Witchcraft*, Rosemary Ellen Guiley; *The BM Dictionary of Ancient Egypt*, Shaw & Nicholson.

Altered State of Consciousness: Conditions under which an individual undergoes a range of unusual sensations and experiences.

Alternative Medicine: An umbrella term applied to a wide range of therapeutic or preventive health care that does not follow accepted or conventional medicine. SOURCE: *Chambers Dictionary of the Unexplained*.

Amaranthus: A flower that never fades and used in charms and amulets for fame and long life. Ruling planet: **Saturn**.

Amaterasu: [Japanese – coming from heaven] The sun goddess of **Shinto**, venerated in the shrine at Ise as the divine progenitor of the Japanese imperial family. Her epithet is Omikami: 'great and exalted deity'.

Ambarvalia: A solemn Roman festival of purification of the fields carried out by farmers. The ceremony involved the sacrificial animals being led round the boundaries of the fields that were to be purified. In early times, the principal agricultural deity was **Mars**; in Republican days the deity was **Ceres**, while during Imperial times the earth deity was Dea Dia.

Amber: A yellow-gold, fossilized resin, which since ancient times has been associated with immortality, often included with early 'grave goods', especially pieces with insects or plants preserved inside. Used as a ritual necklace worn by witches of a certain rank. A piece of red amber was considered to be excellent protection against poison, plague and the **Evil Eye**.

Ambergris: A secretion of the intestines of the sperm whale used in the preparation of magical perfumes. Extensively used as an aphrodisiac in the East.

Amenominakanushi: [Japanese – Lord of the bright center of heaven] The supreme divinity of **Shinto**, who plays no part in myth, nor is there any record of a shrine, or place of worship in his honor. Nevertheless, he occupies first place in the list of gods and transcending them all, sits alone on a nine-fold layer of cloud.

Amenti: see **Duat**.

Amerindian Religions: A people that have displayed a vast variety of forms over their 25,000-year history. These have ranged from simple hunting rites, through more elaborate calendric rituals and the war-related cults of the plains, to more contemporary beliefs such as the **Ghost Dance** and **Peyotism**. *'The world of the American Indians was once a rather lonely but free place where humans were close to nature and followed a natural system of belief; the spirits of ancestors, and personification of the forces of nature were the basic units of their religion, and every natural object might have a spirit which could be contacted.'* SOURCE: *500 Nations*, Alvin M. Josephy; *Book of the Hopi*, Frank Waters; *Everyday Life Among the American Indians*, Candy Moulton; *Native American Myth & Legend*, Mike Dixon-Kennedy; *Native American Traditions*, Arthur Versluis; *Native American Wisdom*, comp by Steve McFadden; *North American Indians*, George Catlin; *North American Mythology*, C.A. Burland; *Touch the Earth*, T.C. McLuhan.

Amethyst: A form of rock crystal ranging from deep purple to lilac and white. It is the sacred stone of the priesthood, used to increase spiritual power. Bishops and popes have rings set with amethyst and upon the death of a pope his amethyst ring will be destroyed. It was also prized by Roman matrons because of the superstition that it would prevent their husbands from straying, and keep the wearer free from drunkenness. SOURCE: *Magical Jewels*, Joan Evans; *The Curious Lore of Precious Stones*, George Frederick Kunz.

Amida: The **Buddha** who possesses the properties of immeasurable light and life.

Amidah: The central prayer of the Jewish liturgy, the word meaning 'standing' since the prayer is said standing facing towards Jerusalem.

Ammet: An Egyptian demon that plays a vital role in the **Judgement** of the Dead.

Amniomancy: Method of predicting the future of an individual born with a **Caul** covering their head at birth.

Amrita: [Sanskrit] Ambrosia, nectar, honey, the elixir of immortality, the wine of paradise.

Amulets: Objects charged with magical

protective energies that have been used since ancient times. From the Latin *amuletum*, meaning 'defense', amulets were anything worn about the person as protection from sickness, bad luck or the attentions of malevolent spirits (see **Talismans**). The use of amulets has been universal and can be found in all cultures both ancient and modern. SOURCE: *Amulets & Superstitions*, E.A. Budge; *Magical Jewels*, Joan Evans; *Magic In The Middle Ages*, Richard Kieckhefer; *The BM Dictionary of Ancient Egypt*, Shaw and Nicholson.

Amun: [Egyptian] Almost unknown outside the Theban area at the time of the Old Kingdom, Amun's cult grew to prominence during the great Pharaohs of the 18th Dynasty. He was sometimes represented with the horns of a ram and this led to the later confusion concerning the occult symbol of the 'goat of Mendes' (see **Goat**). The great temple of Amum is located on the eastern bank of the Nile at modern Luxor.

Ana or **Anu:** A Celtic-Irish goddess of the earth and fertility, who was said to be the mother of the gods. Two hills near Killarney in Munster are called *Da Chich Anann* – the two breasts of Ana.

Anagarika: [*an-grarika* = 'non-householder'] The term relates to a person who has left their home to search for the truth about life. It was, and still is, regarded as very honorable in **Buddhist** circles.

Anathema: A denunciation or curse from the Greek 'to place' or 'set up', in allusion to the mythological custom of hanging up in the temple of a patron god something devoted to him. Something set apart for destruction.

Ancestors, The: An important aspect of traditional Old Craft that regularly pays homage to, or calls upon the ancestral spirits of the clan or Coven; akin to **Ancestor Worship**. [SEE PANEL]

Ancestor Worship (see **Death Cults**): Best described as devotion, going beyond veneration, to persons who have died and believing that the dead live on and can affect the lives of later generations. Regular prayers and offerings are made by the descendants and this is still an important element of religious belief in many parts of the world today. SOURCE: *Penguin Dictionary of Religions*, ed John R. Hinnells; *Under the Ancestors' Shadow*, Francis Hsu

Anti-Occult Campaign: A national campaign to outlaw any form of occult practice and New Age or pagan thinking, spearheaded by evangelical and/or establishment bodies. The most recent (1988–94) was countermanded by Judge (now Dame) Elizabeth Butler-Sloss who ruled that there was no evidence to support the numerous allegations of 'satanic child abuse' and the whole fabrication evaporated overnight (see **Satanic Child Abuse Myth**). An earlier campaign had manifested in the 1960s but there were few far-reaching repercussions by comparison to the later, better-orchestrated campaign. SOURCE: *Malleus Satani, the Hammer of Satan*, Suzanne Ruthven.

Anubis: The Egyptian jackal-headed deity who led the dead to the place of judgement (see **Psychopomp**) and often appears in Western ritual magic as a Guide between the worlds. He was the most distinctive of all the Egyptian

The Ancestors in Traditional Witchcraft

The honoring of the dead and venerating their memory is a common root of all religion, with many cultures believing that the dead live on in another dimension, continuing to affect the lives of subsequent generations. This concept of spirit-ancestors is an extremely ancient one, especially when it involves dealing with deceased members of a particular people or clan, and is still widely observed in Japanese Shinto, Chinese Confucianism and among the Australian aboriginal and Amerindian peoples.

In the West, we know from the prehistoric remains of the numerous earthworks that the early people of the British Isles and the Celts honored their ancestors; and the earliest written observations are those of the Roman *Paternalia* (February) and the *Lemuria* (May), which later spread throughout the Empire.

Interaction with these spirit-ancestors as an invisible and powerful presence is also a constant feature of traditional British Old Craft, with the Ancestors remaining important members of the tradition or people they have left behind. In general they are seen as Elders, treated and referred to in much the same way as the most senior of living Elders of a coven or magical group, with additional mystical and/or magical powers. Sometimes they are identified as the Holy Guardian Angel, the Mighty Dead, the Watchers or the Old Ones, who gave magical knowledge to mankind, rather than family or tribal dead. Or, even more ambiguously, 'those who have gone before' – their magical essence distilled into the universal subconscious at different levels.

Reverence for Craft ancestors is part of the ethic of respect for those who have preceded us in life, and their continued presence on the periphery of our consciousness means that they are always with us. And because traditional witchcraft is essentially a practical thing, the Ancestors are called upon to help find solutions to magical problems through divination, path-working and spellcasting. Although witchcraft is *not* a religion, the belief in the ancestral spirits goes hand in hand with a deep reverence for Nature

Once contact has been established, the Ancestors can be relied upon to have the interests of the 'tradition' – and therefore the witch's interests – as their primary concern. This belief reflects the profound importance of kinship in the ordering of pagan society. The Ancestors protect the living, but insist on the maintenance of various customs, and any serious breach of etiquette could result in the removal of their favor.

All Hallows or Samhain is the beginning of the dark, winter half of the year and a time for honoring the Ancestors. This is a somber occasion in the witch's year and certainly not a time for celebration. To use a familiar phrase, 'it is when the veil between the worlds is at its thinnest', and a candle placed at the window can call the Ancestors to come home. Some traditional witches hold a 'Dumb Supper' to mark the occasion, setting an empty place at the table for any wandering ancestral spirit who cares to partake of the offerings.

... And heavy is the tread
Of the living; but the dead
Returning lightly dance...

From pre-Christian times, this darkening time of the year has been associated with ancestral spirits, unquiet ghosts and death. Ritual fires were kindled on hilltops for the purification of the people and the land, but unlike the Bel-fires that were lit at dawn, the Hallow-fires were lit at dusk. Much of what we see in the towns that pass for Hallowe'en rites are imported from America, although this is *not* a time for trick and treating! The festival should be observed as a means of demonstrating pagan unity to outsiders, while at the same time ritually remembering the Ancestors and reinforcing the heritage of traditional witchcraft.

These observations and subsequent teaching of traditional ancestor worship within the practice of witchcraft could play an important role in ensuring the continuity of the 'tradition'.

EXTRACT FROM KICKING OVER THE CAULDRON
MÉLUSINE DRACO

gods and best known for the imposing life-size image found in the tomb of Tutankhamen.

Aossic: The name of a great **Old One**; an extra-terrestrial entity that maintains a link with mundane consciousness. SOURCE: *Nightside of Eden*, Kenneth Grant.

Apantomancy: Divination interpreted by chance encounters with animals (see **Alectryomancy**).

Ape of Thoth: In Thelemic teaching, the shadow or double of **Thoth**, the Egyptian god of magic. The ape being the symbol of the mirror-world or astral plane.

Aphrodisiac: Food or drugs credited with the effect of arousing sexual desire.

Aphrodite: Greek goddess of beauty and love, identified with the Roman **Venus**. Her cult is pre-Greek with probable Eastern origins. Her attribute is the dove.

Apocalypse: (1) From the Greek word meaning 'un-veiling' and apocalyptic literature undertakes to disclose matters inaccessible to normal knowledge, such as the **Mysteries**, often in symbolic language. (2) It later referred to the last book in the New Testament.

Apollo or **Apollon:** A Greek god of many parts, his twin sister was **Artemis** and his son **Asclepius,** the god of healing; he was the first Greek god to be introduced into Italy. The Emperor Augustus saw him as his personal tutelary deity.

Apophis: In Egyptian mythology, the huge serpent god and enemy of Re; eternal and persistently hostile, Apophis represents the primeval forces of chaos.

Apotheosis: Recognition of a human being as a god. For example: Alexander the Great and the Roman Emperors, whose deification influenced the later European belief in the 'divine right of kings'.

Apotropaics: Objects or practices that are believed to have the power to turn away evil, i.e. charms and amulets.

Apparition: Hallucinatory image of a living or dead person, seen in a semi-waking or dream state.

Apple: (1) A particularly sacred tree in European mythology. A 7th century text says that if a man cuts down an apple tree, he must pay a fine of one cow; while in Ireland the penalty was the sacrifice of a living creature. The apple tree represents immortality, eternal youth and happiness in the life after death, which is why the superstition remains to this day. (2) The crab apple is an indigenous tree of Britain and the fruit has been found in a coffin dating from the early Bronze Age. (3) Either cut up or mashed, the apple is used in love potions, and also used in working magically against enemies when cut with a knife. Ruling planet: **Venus**. SOURCE: *The Dictionary of Omens & Superstitions*, Philippa Waring; *Root & Branch*, Mélusine Draco.

Apport: A solid object materializing out of thin air during a séance.

Apsu: Personification of the sweet water ocean lying under the earth, which united with **Tiamat** at the beginning of time.

Aquarius: (1) The Water Carrier is the eleventh sign of the zodiac – 20 January–19 February – and dates back as far as Babylonian times. (2) The constellation contains the Helix Nebula, which, at 450 light years away, is the nearest planetary nebula to **Earth**. The Aquarids is a strong meteor shower that peaks every year on 28th July.

Aquarius, the Age of: The coming of a global age of peace and harmony in a spirit of gentleness and moderation.

Aquilaeus: see **Aetites**.

Aradia, or *Gospel of the Witches:* Translated from the Italian into English by folklorist Charles Godfrey Leland, in 1889. During his travels in Tuscany in the 1880s, Leland encountered a local wise-woman by the name of Maddalena who, claiming to be a hereditary Etruscan witch, provided him with a handwritten document allegedly a copy of the old tenets of witchcraft from the area. *Aradia* is an account of the liaison between **Diana** and **Lucifer**, (which Leland took as proof of witchcraft as an old religion) and the daughter from that union who was hailed as 'the messiah of witches'. Although the Aradian tradition has attracted some modern adherents, particularly in America, contemporary folklore scholars do not accept it as authentic.

Aralez: Beneficent dog-like spirits that lived in heaven, according to Armenian myth. They were gifted with supernatural powers and their specific function was to lick the wounds of those killed or wounded in battle, who then recovered or were resurrected to new life.

Arbor Low: [Derbyshire] A fine example of a henge monument with two entrances in a containing bank, still some 6ft high. Some 50 stones (or their fragments) originally stood upright to form an outer circle and

a central horseshoe. A Bronze Age barrow overlaps the line of the bank and appears to have been constructed partly with re-used material. SOURCE: *The Secret Country,* Janet and Colin Bord.

Arbory Hill: The earliest relics of buildings for human habitation in Britain are those of the Iron Age people who came from the Continent from about 550BC, who were gradually pushed north and west by the invading Romans in the 1st century AD. The fort on Arbory Hill may well have been still inhabited when the Roman legions were passing along their road in the Clyde Valley below.

Arcadia: A mountainous region in the center of the Peloponnese that has many associations with Greek mythology, particularly **Pan**.

Arcana: (1) A secret formula or process. (2) Used to denote the cards of the **Tarot**: the Major Arcana includes 22 cards; the Minor Arcana has 52.

Arcane: That which is secret or mysterious.

Archeoacoustics: The study of the acoustic qualities of prehistoric constructions.

Archangel: According to the Koran there are four archangels. Gabriel, the angel of revelations, who writes down divine decrees; Michael, the champion, who fights the battles of faith; **Azrael**, the angel of death; and Azrafil, who sounds the trumpet of the resurrection. They appear in both Jewish and Christian texts.

Archangel, White or **Dead Nettle:** Valued for the treatment of both internal disorders and external wounds to staunch bleeding. The plant was listed by **Aelfric** and its ruling planet is **Venus**.

Archetype: A phrase coined by psychologist **C.G. Jung** to refer to the collective characteristic of the human unconscious. For example, the Devil, the Mother and the Trickster are universal archetypes that are instantly recognizable to all creeds and cultures.

Archidoxis Magica: That part of the *Philosophia Magna* that encompasses **Paracelsus'** cosmological and spiritual vision of the nature of God and **Creation**.

Arduinna: A localized Gaulish goddess named after the Ardennes. She was a goddess of hunting and identified by the Romans with **Diana**. Her sacred animal was the **Boar**.

Ares: The Greek god of war and identified with the Roman **Mars**. His original homeland was Thrace, but there are few temples dedicated to him in Greece. He was not a popular god and is rarely portrayed in Greek art.

Aretz: Hebrew for the element Earth.

Argei: The Vestal Virgins cast bundles of rushes (in the shape of men bound hand and foot) into the River Tiber on 14th May each year. The rite was thought to be one of purification. There were 27 shrines of these *argei* throughout Rome: the 'lucky' number 27 (thrice nine) occurs frequently in Greek and Roman ritual.

Aries: (1) The famous ram, Chrysomallon, whose golden fleece was stolen by Jason in his Argonautic expedition. It was transported to the stars, and made the first sign of the zodiac – 21 March– 19 April. *'The Vernal signs the Ram begins;/Then comes the Bull; in May the Twins;/ The Crab in June; next Leo shines;/*

And Virgo ends the northern signs.' (2) Aries is the zodiac's first constellation, since the Sun at one time was entering Aries on the day of the vernal equinox – the moment when it crosses from the southern to the northern half of the celestial globe. Because of the Earth's **Precession**, the Sun is now in Pisces at the **Vernal Equinox**.

Arithmancy: see **Numerology**.

Armilustrium: The purification of the Roman army, when the soldiers would be assembled and reviewed in the Circus Maximus on 19th November, and as a military festival it was sacred to **Mars**.

Armomancy: An outdated method of divination to detect a person's psychic abilities.

Aromatherapy: The art and science of using plant oils in medical treatment and has its roots in most ancient healing practices the world over. Natural essences are concentrated in oils extracted from herbs, fruits, flowers and other plants and used to achieve different results. The therapeutic benefits of aromas were widely prescribed in ancient times with a variety of crushed herbs, barks and spices being inhaled for their curative value. SOURCE: *Aromatherapy: An A-Z*, Patricia Davies; *Perfume Power*, Joules Taylor; *Sacred Luxuries: Fragrance, Aromatherapy & Cosmetics in Ancient Egypt*, Lise Manniche.

Arras Witchcraft: In 1459–60 the Inquisition organized a witch hunt at Arras that was one of the earliest in northern France. At this time, just what constituted witchcraft had still not been precisely defined and the Inquisition's conduct was denounced by several bishops of the time; after 1500, few would have dared to criticize. SOURCE: *The Encyclopedia of Witchcraft & Demonology*, Rossell Hope Robbins.

Artemis: Greek goddess of the hunt and sister of **Apollo**, whom the Romans identified with **Diana**. She has many different guises and often her cult overlapped with other goddesses.

Arthurian Legend: The 'real' Arthur is believed to have been a chieftain of the Romano-Britons, who fought against the invading Saxons around 450AD. The Celtic myth of the magic cauldron that subsequently became the Holy Grail expanded the legend that has been built up around him, together with French sources which expanded on the concept of chivalry, and the introduction of the fabled 'Round Table'. SOURCE: *A History of the Kings of England*, Geoffrey of Monmouth; *Morte D'Arthur*, Sir Thomas Malory; *Britain AD*, Francis Pryor.

Arthurian Tradition: A modern revivalist Tradition based on the Grail Quest and the Arthurian legend, and the wealth of material that surrounds the story of Arthur and his Knights of the **Round Table**.

Arrow: The bow was one of the earliest weapons invented by man and the arrow's ability to kill at a distance has given it a place in magic and folklore all over the world, from ancient Egypt to Europe and the Americas. In Britain, prehistoric flint arrowheads were thought to be **Elf-bolts**.

Asa: In Scandinavian mythology, a term of address to all the gods of Gladsheim: as in Asa Odin. Gladsheim ('home of joy') was the largest and most magnificent mansion of the Aesir. It contained 12 seats besides the throne of Alfader, the most ancient and chief of the gods; the great hall was called **Valhalla**.

Asafoetida: An evil-smelling gum, made by drying the juice of the plant *ferula assafoetida* and listed in the **Lemegeton** as a substance used in calling up demons, as its stench is suitable to 'the nature of demons, which stink of hell'. Aleister **Crowley** places it in his list of 'perfumes' in **Liber 777**, to correspond with **Saturn**, The Universe, sulphur and 'all Evil Odors'.

Asana: Special yoga postures designed to influence currents of subtle energy within the human body.

Asatru: see **Aesir, Northern Tradition** and **Vanir**.

Asbestos: The fire-retardant properties of asbestos were known as long ago as 5000 years. It was the ancient Greeks, in awe of the stone that could be woven but not consumed by fire, who gave it the name *asvesto*, meaning inextinguishable. Throughout ancient history, it was renowned as a substance of almost magical properties. SOURCE: *Journeys From the Centre of the Earth*, Iain Stewart.

Ascendant: In casting a horoscope the easternmost star, representing the House of Life, is called the ascendant, because it is in the act of ascending. This is the subject's strongest star, and so long as it is above the horizon their fortune is said to be good. When a person's circumstances begin to improve and things look brighter, it is said that their star is in the ascendant.

Asch: Hebrew for the element of Fire.

Asclepius or **Esclepius:** (1) The son of Apollo and god of medicine, who came to be worshipped as the god of healing, especially at Epidaurus where there is a circular temple to him patterned with caduceus wands. (2) The text known as *Esclepius*, supposedly written by **Hermes Trismegistus**, was that part of the *Corpus Hermeticum*, the body of **Hermetic** writing that remained in circulation right up to the Renaissance after being translated into Latin in the 2nd century AD. (3) Alchemists used the *Esclepius* as a spiritual handbook, a guide to creation and man's creative powers.

Ash: (1) From ancient times the ash has been revered as a sacred tree; it was considered dangerous to cut one down without the appropriate observances. Also known as the 'Tree of the Universe' (see **Yggrasil**). (2) In wort-lore the bark, shoots, leaves and keys are all used in potions and other recipes. The red bud of the ash was believed to avert witchcraft and the Evil Eye if eaten on St. John's Eve. Ruling planet: **Sun.**

Ashes: The residue of fire, and just as fire is regarded magically as something that 'fixes' a spell, or has the power to regenerate and bring new life, so the same properties are associated with ashes. Ashes from a magical working should never be discarded but should be retained in order to reaffirm the magical working at a later date. The only means of disposal is to sprinkle them in running water.

Ashram: A Hindu term for a spiritual center or a retreat where disciples of a guru spend their time meditating and studying spiritual teachings.

Asmodeus: (1) According to Francis Barrett's *Magus*, Asmodeus was originally a demon of rage, who turned into a spirit of lust, whom the magician must summon bare-headed as a mark of respect. (2) According to the **Talmud** he was the 'king of devils'. SOURCE: *Goetia,* Aleister Crowley.

Aspen: One of the most beautiful of Britain's native trees and the source of a great deal of folklore. The bark was used to lower fever and as a remedy for digestive problems. Ruling planet: **Saturn** in **Capricorn.**

Aspergillum (less commonly, **aspergilium** or **aspergil**): An implement used to sprinkle holy water. It comes in two common forms: a brush that is dipped in the water and shaken, and a perforated ball at the end of a short handle

Aspersion: Slander or accuse falsely, i.e. to cast aspersions on a person's character. A common occurrence among magical practitioners.

Ass: Sleeping upon the skin of an ass was believed to keep away devils, witches and nightmares.

Assiah: One of the Four Worlds of the Qabalistic system; the material world.

Astarte or **Asthoreth:** A Middle Eastern great goddess of fertility, motherhood and war. Her cult spread westwards where she was transformed into the male demon Astaroth in later writings. Both images are frequently shown with the figure wearing a pair of bull's horns.

Asteroid: A small body of rock or metal in orbit around the Sun. A type of minor planet. The Asteroid Belt is located between the orbits of Mars and Jupiter.

Astragalomancy: Divination by throwing dice or dominos to determine the future.

Astragyromancy: Divination by the

use of bones, usually vertebra or knucklebones.

Astral Body: The spiritual intelligence supposed to be present in all humans. It may either penetrate the physical body, or be partially or wholly detached from it.

Astral Doorways: Symbols or pictures that can be used in a meditative way to aid astral projection. The 'court' cards of the **Tarot** can be used in this way but the most well-known are the **Tattwas** of the Eastern esoteric traditions used by members of the **Golden Dawn**. SOURCE: *The Complete Rituals of the Golden Dawn*, Israel Regardie

Astral Plane: An altered state of consciousness that admits the astral body to the 'spirit' world, or the alternate dimensions of reality.

Astral Projection: Among occultists it is generally held that in addition to our physical body, we possess another, more subtle one. This is the body inhabited after death, and which we are capable of detaching from the physical body at will, under certain circumstances. Or which spontaneously leaves the physical body, more or less completely, in sleep, trance, coma, or under the influence of anesthetic. It is normally invisible, intangible, impalpable to the senses, and cannot be discovered upon the operating table. Although proof is difficult to obtain there are many who assert they have, on certain occasions, found themselves inhabiting such a body and, on looking back, seen their own physical body asleep on the bed. They are convinced that the experience is real because they can see and feel and handle it. Moreover they are fully conscious at the time… these are

instances of involuntary or spontaneous projection. SOURCE: *Magic: An Occult Primer*, David Conway; *Techniques of High Magic*, Francis King and Stephen Skinner;

Astro-archeology: The science of the alignment of ancient monuments with early astronomy. SOURCE: *Astronomy in Prehistoric Britain and Ireland*, Clive Ruggles; *Starchild*, Mélusine Draco; *Astronomy Before the Telescope*, ed Christopher Walker; *From Stonehenge to Modern Cosmology*, Fred Hoyle; *The Phenomenology of Landscape*, Christopher Tilley.

Astrology: The art of predicting the future or interpreting events and character from the positions of the stars and planets. Originating in Mesopotamia in the 2nd millennium BCE, by the 5th century it had spread throughout the Greek world. The art reached its definitive form during the Roman Empire by c100CE. (See **Zodiac** and **Zodiac-Chinese**.) Popular astrologer Jonathan Cainer points out that *'a lot of what passes today for 'common astrological knowledge' is actually just myth, superstition, invention and embroidery.'* While leading astronomer, Patrick Moore, defines astrology as a superstition of the stars that is a relic of the past. SOURCE: *The Ancient Gods*, E.O. James; *Applied Magic*, Dion Fortune; *The Arkana Dictionary of Astrology*, Fred Gettings; *The Complete Golden Dawn System of Magic*, Israel Regardie; *Guide to the Zodiac*, Jonathan Cainer; *Magic In The Middle Ages*, Richard Kieckhefer; *The New Astrology*, Nicholas Campion and Steve Eddy; *Religion & the Decline of Magic*, Keith Thomas; *The Magical Arts*, Richard Cavendish.

Astromancy: An ancient method of divination by looking at the stars and planets on a clear night.

Astronomy: The study of the celestial bodies and the heavens from all scientific aspects. This is an exact science and its development over the past five millennia has been one of the greatest achievements of human civilization. The **Muse**, Urania, was the Greek patron of astronomy. SOURCE: *Astronomy: Before the Telescope*, ed Christopher Walker; *Astronomy & the Imagination*, Norman Davidson; *Discover the Stars*, Richard Berry; *Encyclopaedia of the Universe*; *Gods in the Sky*, Allan Chapman; *Origins*, John Gribbin & Simon Goodwin; *Prehistoric Astronomy & Ritual*, Aubrey Burl; *Skywatching*, David Levy.

Asura: In Indian mythology, a class of non-human beings who are the enemies of the gods (heavenly beings) and responsible for encouraging evil tendencies.

Ataraxia: (1) A state of mental serenity, calmness and tranquility that is required before attempting to communicate with the spirit world. (2) A drug that produces this effect without inducing sleep.

Atavism: Refers to the incarnation in human or animal form of an ancestral being. According to *Man, Myth & Magic*, in a broader sense, the term atavism is used by occultists to mean the reappearance of characteristics which come from so long ago that they constitute an embodiment of pre-human consciousness, i.e. things that come from the time of creatures half-human and half-beast. One of the greatest visionaries of atavistic

expression was the artist and member of the **Golden Dawn**, Austin Osman **Spare.**

Atavistic Resurgence: The name of the magical formula devised by Austin Osman **Spare** to tap subliminal levels of consciousness in order to re-vitalize dormant superhuman powers. He used symbolic pictures to give visible form to terrifying impulses deep in the mind, claiming that he only had to visualize one of these images for the atavistic desire to surge up. SOURCE: *The Magical Revival*, Kenneth Grant.

Ate: A Greek word for ruin or disaster, personified as a power that disorders the mind, so that the victim cannot tell wrong from right. In the *Iliad* she is a daughter of **Zeus**, goddess of vengeance and mischief.

Athame: (1) The term 'athame' comes from the magic knife described in the *Key of Solomon* and other magical textbooks, used for casting the magic circle. (2) In modern Wiccan ceremonial it is often described as being black-handled and decorated with mystic symbols. In Old Craft, all types of knives are used according to personal preference (see **Knife**).

Atheism: The disbelief in the existence of any god(s), and a belief that matter is eternal, and what we call '**Creation**' is the result of natural laws.

Athena: Tutelary goddess of Athens and Greek goddess of war and wisdom. The Romans identified her with **Minerva.**

Atlantis: A fictional 'lost paradise' that only appears in the writings of the Athenian philosopher Plato (427–348BCE). Despite its allegorical origins, the belief in the reality of the sunken world has permeated occult writing, with many well-known names claiming to have some form of Atlantean connections. SOURCE: *The Atlantis Syndrome*, Paul Jordan; *Critias* and *Timaeus*, Plato.

Atlantis Bookshop: Located in Museum Street, London, this world famous occult bookseller has been supplying esoteric books since 1922.

Atlantis Syndrome: The belief that all magical/mystical wisdom came originally from Atlantis and provided the basic beliefs of all cultures, all over the world. This has been reflected in occult fact and fiction for decades without any reference to Plato's first references to it around 360BC, when the story started as a moral tale about the decline of Athens. The Atlantis story passed into occult fiction and was drawn upon by Dion Fortune for *Sea Priestess* and *Moon Magic*. SOURCE: *The Atlantis Syndrome*, Paul Jordan.

Atma: [Sanskrit] The True Self, as opposed to the illusory personality or ego.

Attribute: A creature, plant or object associated with a particular deity, and often revealing an aspect of that deity's nature (see **Correspondences**).

Atu: House, cell or division. A term used to denote the 22 keys or trumps of *The Book of Thoth*, or Atus of Tahuti, the Egyptian Tarot deck designed by Aleister **Crowley**.

Atum-Re: Re is the name of the ancient Egyptian sun god, sovereign Lord of the sky. Like Atum, his principle sanctuary was at Heliopolis, and from a very early time the priesthood identified the two gods as one. Re was the rising sun that manifested on the primeval **Mound**, while Atum personified the setting sun. Not to be confused with Aten, of the monotheist cult that Akhenaten introduced at El Amarna.

Atziluth: [Hebrew] The archetypal or spirit world.

Augoeides: [Greek] Refers to 'the Holy Guardian Angel' and derives from *augo*, meaning 'the morning light'. It is a term used by **Iamblichus** in his *De Mysteriis* and **Bulwer-Lytton** popularized the concept in his novel *Zanoni*, where he interpreted it as meaning 'the luminous Self or Higher Ego'. Through the **Holy Guardian Angel**, human consciousness is linked with, and can become consciously merged with, cosmic consciousness. Attainment of the knowledge of the Holy Guardian Angel is the foundation of a magician's training and, with the exception of crossing the **Abyss**, is the most critical stage of magical development. SOURCE: *The Eye in the Triangle*, Israel Regardie.

Augur: (1) A person who can foretell the future. (2) In ancient Rome augurs were specifically Imperial spiritualists who divined the future using birds.

Auguries and **Auspices**: see **Divination** and **Omen**.

Aura: In occultism this refers to a luminous appearance seen surrounding all living things. Often described in rainbow colors, which reveal the mental/ physical/ emotional state of an individual, it is related to the aureole or halo surrounding the bodies or heads of figures in religious art. It is said that the aura has five specific layers: the health aura, the vital aura, the karmic aura, the character aura and the spiritual nature aura. The colors and their significance are: pink – affection;

brown-red – passion and the sensual; red – anger or force; orange – pride and ambition; purple – spirituality, occult power and psychic ability; yellow – intellectual ability; blue – religiousness and mysticism; green – jealousy and deceit.

Auspices: see **Divination** and **Omen.**

Auspicia: The *auspicia* (omens) were the special province of the Roman **Augurs** and were sent by **Jupiter,** as the chief state god.

Austrian Witchcraft: The worse period of witchcraft in Austria occurred under the Emperor Rudolf II (1576–1612), and fueled by the Jesuits trying to stop the spread of Protestantism. A secondary period followed at the end of the 17th century as a result of the *Halsgerichtsordnung,* a severe anti-witchcraft code adopted in 1707.

Austromancy: Divination by listening to the sound of the wind and interpreting the messages. In China and Tibet a seashell was held to the ear and the sounds were used to foretell the future or define an omen.

Automatic Writing: Another form of divination by allowing 'the spirits of the ethereal world to direct the writing of one's hand and arm with pencil and paper'. SOURCE: *Book of Divining the Future,* Eva Shaw; *Guide to the Supernatural,* Raymond Buckland.

Automatism: Writing, drawing, painting or musical abilities produced without the control of the conscious mind; unconscious talent attributed to supernatural guidance.

Auto de Fe: 'Act of Faith' commonly used for the burning to death of heretics, but strictly speaking, it was the public ceremony in Spain and Portugal at which the **Inquisition** pronounced judgement on heretics (see **Heresy**). Those condemned to death were handed over to the civil authorities for execution.

Autumnal Equinox: Falls on or around 21st September and signifies the end of harvesting. The Church calendar aligned it with Michaelmas and around this time there were a large number of great fairs and animal sales. An important celebration within traditional witchcraft.

Avalon: The ancient and mythological name for the area around Glastonbury Tor in Somerset, meaning 'Isle of Apples'. In **Arthurian** legend it was said to be where King Arthur resided and was buried.

Avatar: A descent of a deity into a visible human or animal form.

Avebury: An avenue of great megaliths forms a ceremonial approach to the circles of sarsen stones and most of Avebury village lies within the largest prehistoric monument in Europe. The avenue connects Avebury with the Sanctuary, a smaller temple on Overton Down 1½ miles away.

Averse: A term usually applied to negative magical processes.

Avesta: The scriptures of **Zoroastrianism,** traditionally believed to have been revealed in their entirety to Zoroaster. The material was originally transmitted in oral form, writing being considered an 'alien art' and therefore unsuitable for sacred words.

Avidya: [Sanskrit, meaning literally 'non-knowledge', or the lack of understanding of the nature of reality.] The inability to see the true nature of things is regarded in **Buddhist**

tradition as the root of all evil.

Axe: One of the first tools ever invented. The coming of the Iron Age enhanced the magical power of the axe, because the first iron used by man was meteoric in origin. There are various forms of divination that make use of an axe and it is said that to dream of an axe is a warning of danger, either personal, or to a friend. SOURCE: *Book of Divining the Future*, Eva Shaw.

Axinomancy: Axes were traditionally used to find buried treasure, or for finding out where something was hidden.

Axis Mundi or **Cosmic Axis:** An ancient and enduring symbol of what is today referred to as the 'personal universe', i.e. that every man or woman is the center of their own magical universe.

Ayurveda: Developed from the Vedas, India's ancient books of wisdom, Ayurveda combines physical, psychological and spiritual therapies in an approach to health that is as relevant to the modern world as it was to the ancient. Now it has been 'discovered' by Western health practitioners, and, with a celebrity following, is set to 'revolutionize our thinking about nutrition and disease prevention'. SOURCE: *Ayurveda: The Gentle Health System*, Hans H. Rhyner; *Ayurveda: Life, Health & Longevity*, Robert E. Svoboda.

Aza: The evil mother of all demons. The Gnostic concept of the source of all alien energies.

Azande: Considered to be a ground-breaking study of African witchcraft by Professor E.E. Evans-Pritchard during the 1920s. Unfortunately, this anthropological study was used for many years as a prejudicial benchmark by academics and professionals as a reference against the growing interest in the occult and witchcraft in the West. SOURCE: *Witchcraft & Sorcery*, ed Max Marwick.

Azathoth: An entity given great prominence in the **Necronomicon** mythos because it typifies the supreme reflex of **Daath** [Qabalah] in the form of **Aza**.

Azazel or **Azrael:** A name preserved from medieval demonology and in popular **Grimoires**, he is said to be the guardian of the goat. He is the standard-bearer and leader of the Watchers, and sometimes identified with the Angel of Death. In *The Sea Priestess*, Dion Fortune refers to the Fire of Azrael for the purpose of seeing the 'past that was dead'.

Azoth: An alchemical term for the combined essences of the fully polarized power-zones in the human male and female.

Aztec: The master sculptures of the Aztec traditions developed the aesthetic forms of their Toltec predecessors (see **MesoAmerican Religion**).

Azym: A Gateway to the Abyss and, ultimately, the Universe.

an insect hums
you become it
a bird sings
you become it
you're meditating
Paul Reps

B

Ba: The ancient Egyptians believed that each individual person was made up up of five distinct components: the physical body, the *ba*, the **Ka**, the **Name** and the **Shadow**. The *ba* has similarities with the modern concept of the personality, on that it comprised all those non-physical attributes that made one human being unique.

Baal: This ancient Semitic word *ba'l* (owner or lord) was applied to both men and gods to signify ownership: Baal-Samin (god of celestial places); Baal-Shemesh (the sun god). Although the Old Testament attacks Baal worship, the early religion of Israel was strongly influenced by the great fertility god, the upholder of order against chaos. He eventually became demonized and appeared in Collin de Plancy's *Dictionnaire Infernal* with three heads: a cat, a man and a toad.

Baba: An Eastern European fairy-like creature that gradually became a witch in folklore. For example: Baba-Yaga was a White Russian forest-sprite who could travel through the air in an iron kettle with a fiery broom.

Babalon: The name of Aleister **Crowley's** **'Scarlet Woman'**. She is representative of the female principle within a ritual magical application and is chosen for her ability to transmit the solar current and manifest it in oracular and/or tangible form. A name applicable to any woman magically competent to channel and/or transmit psychic forces within ritual magick techniques.

Bacchus: (1) A name of **Dionysus**, the Greek god of fertility, wine and ecstatic dancing, whose worshippers were called Bacchae or Bacchantes. (2) *Bacchae* is the name of a tragedy by Euripides, which shows sympathy for the mystic side of the religion but condemns its extravagancies.

Bacchanalia: The Latin name for the **Mysteries** celebrated in the god Bacchus's honor, originally confined to women. They were banned at Rome in 186BC for their excesses but reintroduced in the 1st century AD.

Bach, Dr. Edward: Qualified as a medical doctor in 1912 and having made a detailed study of bacteriology, immunology and homoeopathy, found a clear connection between chronic disease and negative mental attitudes. As a result, he produced the 'Bach Flower Remedies', which offered people a simple, safe and effective system of healing. SOURCE: *Dictionary of the Bach Flower Remedies*, T.W. Hyne Jones; *A Guide to the Bach Flower Remedies*, Julian Barnard.

Bachwen: Close to the sea in North Wales stands a typical megalithic burial chamber, with uprights and capstone, from which the circular mound has long since disappeared. The unusual feature here is the wealth of 'cup marks' that cover the upper surface of the capping. This type of carving, first introduced at the end of the Neolithic period, is fairly well distributed in northern and western Britain, but is not commonly found in this position in a grave.

Backward Blessing: Muttering a **Curse**. Saying the Lord's Prayer backwards was believed to invoke the Devil.

Bacon, Francis: (1561–1626) A scientist, alchemist, Freemason and visionary who combined magical imagination and reason.

Baculum: A witch's rod, staff, wand or besom used in divination and certain fertility spells.

Badb: Irish goddess of war, the battlefield being referred to as 'the land of Badb'. She often took the form of a crow and at the mythical battle of Mag Tured, it was she who decided the day.

Badger: The flesh, blood and grease of the animal was considered useful for oils, ointments, salves and powders for *'shortness of breath, the cough of the lungs' for the stone, sprained sinews, etc..'* There is a country belief that badgers bury their dead in specially excavated holes away from the set. Badger teeth, claws and fur are powerful amulets for protection against the home.

Bag o' Nails: The name of an ale-house that stood in the Tyburn Road, London. It was originally called *The Bacchanals* with a sign showing Pan and the Satyrs. The name became corrupted and the cloven-hoofed god identified with the Devil. The later inn sign of *The Devil and the Bag o' Nails* was not an uncommon sight in the Midland counties.

Baguette d'Armide: The name for a sorcerer's wand given by the sorceress Armide in Tasso's *Jerusalem Delivered*. Baguette means a rod or wand.

Baha'i: A peace-living and humanitarian religion with no clergy, rites or sacraments. Its main teaching is the 'oneness' of mankind and the unity of all religions.

Bailey, Alice: (1880–1949) British psychic and author who specialized in automatic writing. She founded the Arcane School to study the secret knowledge of the ethereal world.

Balefire: A ritual coven fire (see **Needfire**).

Balai: [French] To be a witch. According to French superstition, all witches had to pass the brooms on which they rode, three times up the chimney between one **Sabbat** and the next.

Balder or **Baldr:** A popular hero of the Norse and Icelandic sagas, and an archetypal **Sacrificial God**.

Bamberg Witchcraft: The slaughter of witches in Germany was greatest in the principalities of Würzberg and Bamberg where 1500 souls were burned in the mid 16th century. The speed of these trials was amazing and Bamberg became synonymous with torture. SOURCE: *The Encyclopedia of Witchcraft & Demonology*, Rossell Hope Robbins.

Banckes' Herbal: The first printed English herbal is an anonymous compilation from various sources, published in 1525 by Richard Banckes. It contains a copy of the famous discourse on the virtues of **Rosemary**, sent by the Countess of Hainault to her daughter Queen Philippa, wife of Edward I.

Banishing: (1) To expel a malevolent or unquiet entity; the correct occult term for '**Exorcism**'. (2) Ritually expel a member from a coven or Tradition.

Ban: To **Curse** in traditional witchcraft.

Bane: Something or someone that is destructive or poisonous, coming from the Anglo-Saxon *bana*, meaning a murderer. The popular term for many plants includes 'bane', i.e. henbane, wolf's bane, etc.

Banshee: One of the household spirits

of certain Scottish Highland or Irish families, who is said to wail at the death of a family member. The word is supposed to be derived from the Old Irish *ben sidhe*, meaning 'a woman of the **Faere Folk**'. The Welsh name is *cyhyraeth*.

Baphomet: Usually represented as a half-goat, half-human figure created by the 19th century magician, Eliphas Lévi, which combined the imagery of the 'Devil' Tarot card and the erroneous attributions of the ram-headed god of Mendes in Egypt that was incorrectly ascribed by the Greek historian, Herodotus, who visited Egypt in 450BC. Levi's symbolism represented the sum total of the universe and probably a close interpretation of Baphomet said to be worshipped by the **Knights Templar**. The **Church of Satan**, founded in San Francisco in 1966, adopted the goat-head inside an inverted pentagram as their emblem, while Aleister **Crowley** took the name of Baphomet upon joining the OTO (see **Goat**). SOURCE: *Dictionary of Demons*, Fred Gettings.

Bardo: An illusory dimension in which the soul finds itself after death according to Tibetan Buddhist belief, and similar to the astral plane of Western occultism.

Barley: In addition to being used for divination, barley may be scattered on the floor to keep away negative forces. It has been cultivated as a cereal crop since Neolithic times and ale made from malted barley was a staple drink in the medieval period. Ruling planet: **Saturn**.

Barren wort or **Epidemium:** A purple and yellow plant with heart-shaped leaves, given to 'robust' young women to drink as a contraceptive! No ruling planet is given by **Culpeper**.

Barrett, Francis: An occultist and popular demonologist, now best remembered for his work *The Magus, or Celestial Intelligencer – Being a Complete System of Occult Philosophy* published in 1801. Little or nothing is known of the author's life, although it is possible that he may have influenced the occult group (later led by the Victorian esoteric novelist, Bulwer-**Lytton**), with which Eliphas **Levi** was connected.

Barrows and **Earthworks:** The English landscape is littered with barrows and earthworks dating from Neolitic times. Often used by witches and magicians as a place to make contact with the Ancestors. SOURCE: *The Pagan Religions of the Ancient British Isles*, Ronald Hutton; *Historical Atlas of Britain*, ed Nigel Saul for the National Trust; *Britain BC*, Francis Pryor; *A Phenomenology of Landscape*, Christopher Tilley; *The Secret Country*, Janet and Colin Bord.

Basajaun: A Basque 'Lord of the forest', who lives in woods or caves high up in the hills and acts as a protector of livestock. In local tradition he is the cultural initiator, who instructs in the art of agriculture and metal work.

Basil: A common herb that draws poison from a sting and is drunk as a tea to bring on menstruation. The oil is used in medicine, perfumes and incense. Also used for strewing on floors to cover offensive smells. Ruling planet: **Mars** in **Scorpio**.

Basilisk: A crown-headed serpent that represents the evil eye. A notion derived from the ancient belief that the creature could kill with a glance, having sprung from the egg of a rooster, which had been guarded by a toad (see **Cockatrice**).

Basque Witchcraft: The Basques are a people of mysterious origin and during the 16th century they were accused of being Satan-worshippers. Behind the Papal propaganda there was an older type of witchcraft, the belief in which has persisted to the present day. The earliest texts relating to Basque witchcraft are, of course, Inquisitional sources but today in rural communities, there is still a wealth of traditions and practices identifiable as Craft. SOURCE: *A Dictionary of Devils & Demons*, J. Tondriau and R. Villeneuve; *The World of Witches*, J C Baroja.

Bast: Along with **Hathor**, Bast is one of the most popular of Egyptian deities, who was thought of as a woman's deity. Her sacred image is the domestic **Cat**.

Bat: Creatures of the shadows that have often been included in the ingredients of so-called witches' spells, according to Shakespeare (*Macbeth*) and Ben Jonson (*Masque of Queens*). Because of their magical association, the bat is also looked upon as a protective charm or amulet against the powers of evil, and as a luck bringer. In the Isle of Man and parts of Wales it was believed that witches could enter a house in the form of a bat (see **Shape-shifting**); while in Scotland if the animal was seen to fly straight up and plummet back down, it was a warning that the hour had come when witches had power over those without protective charms.

Bateman, Mary: Questionably referred to as the 'Witch of Leeds' this confidence trickster made her living by illusion, the most famous being the hen that laid a magic egg inscribed with the words: 'Christ is coming'. In 1809, she was found guilty of poisoning Rebecca Perigo, one of her gullible clients; was hanged at York and gibbeted afterwards in Leeds. It is said that souvenir hunters stripped the flesh off her bones for luck. Her skeleton was preserved and is now in Leeds Medical School.

Bath Spa: The legendary Prince Bladud was said to have discovered the healing properties of Bath's mineral springs when he cured his leprosy by bathing in the swamps of the district. From the Iron Age to the Romans, people were attracted to Bath to take the waters and by the time of Agricola (78–84AD) the town was a thriving spa. The Romans dedicated the baths to the healing and evil-averting powers of Sulis-Minerva. Bath was destroyed by the Saxons, and many of its earlier glories lay buried for more than 1000 years.

Bavarian Witchcraft: During the forty years from 1590 to 1630, under the guidance of Jesuit fanatics, the Dukes of Bavaria introduced a program of 'exterminating' witches in the country. SOURCE: *The Encyclopedia of Witchcraft & Demonology*, Rossell Hope Robbins.

Bay: A magical tree and used as an amulet since the Roman emperors adopted the wearing of a wreath of bay as a symbol of victory. The withering of a bay tree is supposed to be an omen of death. Large leaves are often used for amulets, so that magic words could be written on them. Dedicated to **Apollo** and **Æsculapius**, god of medicine, it has many medicinal and Craft uses.

Ruling planet: **Sun** in **Leo**.

Bean, Broad: A powerful ingredient in sexual and fertility spells; also used in charms and amulets to counteract witchcraft and the **Evil Eye**. Grown in Britain since the Iron Age, the beans were used in poultices to reduce inflammation and swelling as well as being a basic vegetable in medieval England. Ruling planet: **Venus**.

Bear: (1) Probably held sacred by Neanderthal man, and even up until the early 20th century, bear festivals were celebrated in Europe. Like other animals, bears figure frequently in folklore all over the world and were often thought to possess great supernatural powers. The fat of a bear in an ointment or potion induces fear in an enemy. Bear ghosts were not uncommon and Worcester cathedral was reputedly haunted by a bear in the 17th century. (2) The most easily recognizable constellation in the sky is **Ursa Major**, the Great Bear. (3) The bear and ragged staff was the heraldic emblem of Richard Neville, Earl of Warwick.

Beast, The: Name given to Aleister **Crowley** by his mother at an early age referring to the Beast **666** of Revelation, xvi.2; xix.23 and used by himself in later years. 'The mark of the beast', however, was a popular term of the period, given to an object or pursuit in order to denounce it or to condemn it as unorthodox. Some would even set the mark of the beast on theatres, others on dancing, gambling, the races, cards, dice, etc. Coming from a biblical background, his mother may have merely been using the jargon of her time. Crowley officially assumed the title when he attained one of the grades of Magus in the **A∴A∴** in 1915.

Bee: Frequently seen as a messenger of the gods and a symbol of ancient Egyptian royalty. In Europe it is always considered wise to tell the bees of a death in the family, or they would desert the hive. A bee coming into the house, forecasting that a message, or good news, will shortly arrive, is just one of the many superstitions surrounding the insect.

Beech: The 16th century herbalist Gerard wrote: *'the wood is hard and firm, which being brought into the house there follows hard travail of child and miserable deaths.'* This might explain why there is scant reference to it in folklore, despite it being an indigenous tree of the British Isles. Although it is classed as a native tree, pollen records show that it only arrived some 3,000 years ago compared with other indigenous species. Listed by **Aelfric**, the oil of the tree was used as an antiseptic and to treat skin diseases. Ruling planet: **Saturn**.

Beet or **Beetroot:** Cultivated in England since at least Anglo-Saxon times, **Culpeper** recommended white beet for internal cleansing, while red beet was said to cure 'the bloody flux and women's courses'. Ruling planet: **Jupiter** (white beet); **Saturn** (red beet).

Beggar's Buttons: see **Burdock**.

Bel-fires: *Caught between the bel-fires* – a dilemma. This refers to the two **Beltaine** fires kindled in every village, between which all men and beasts were compelled to pass.

Bell: Used for social, ritual and magical purposes from time immemorial. In the pagan temples of antiquity the bell's outer shell was regarded as female, and the clapper, a later substitution for the hammer with which the bell was originally struck, was male. The use of bells in the rites of religion probably stem from their early role in magic. SOURCE: *Man, Myth & Magic; Bells in England*, T. Ingrams.

Belladonna: [Italian] The name given to deadly nightshade from the practice of ladies of the nobility (*beautiful lady*) touching their eyes with it to make the pupils larger and lustrous. The berries of the plant are deadly and the leaves are used in fumes for evoking spirits.

Bell, Book & Candle: A phrase taken from the Roman Catholic ritual for excommunication and is, in fact, a Christian curse. The rite involves reading from the holy book, which the priest closes, rings the bell as a symbolic toll for death and then extinguishes the candle, representing the removal of the victim's soul from the sight of God. Excommunication represents the casting out into spiritual darkness with its attendant social repercussions. The rite was associated with witchcraft and heresy because the church believed all witches and occultists to be devil-worshippers who should be cast out. SOURCE: *Dictionary of Demons*, Fred Gettings.

Belomancy: Divination using arrows, which were thrown into the air, and the answers taken from the direction the arrows pointed.

Beltaine or **May Eve:** Before the coming of Christianity, the Celts in Northern Europe held two great fire festivals each year – Beltaine and **Samhain** – to mark the beginning of summer and winter, although there was no formal calendar in ancient times. Several spring festivals have been combined and modern Beltaine is now celebrated on 31st April (see **May Day**).

Bembine Tablet: A bronze and silver tablet, supposedly bought by Cardinal Bembo after the sack of Rome in 1527. Engraved with Egyptian hieroglyphics, it was interpreted as holding the key to many sacred alphabets.

Benben: The most scared object within an Egyptian temple – a conical stone symbolizing the primeval **Mound** that emerged from the primordial waters at the creation of the universe.

Bennett, Alan: Probably best remembered as the tutor of Aleister **Crowley** when he first joined the **Golden Dawn**. Bennett was an exponent of ceremonial magic and compiled part of the exhaustive magical reference system *777*, which was later published by Crowley as *777 & Other Qabalistic Writings* (see **Liber 777**). Alan Bennett left England in 1900 for Ceylon where he studied Eastern forms of mysticism, finally joining a Buddhist monastery in Burma. SOURCE: *The Confessions of Aleister Crowley*, Aleister Crowley.

Bennu Bird: The Egyptian symbol of rebirth and renewal, thought to be the blue heron. This mythical 'bird of return' is now used to describe the various cycles of time that vary according to specific astronomical references. Also referred to as the **Phoenix**.

Beowulf: Beowulf is the hero of the only long, complete poem left in the Anglo-Saxon language that is not primarily Christian in content, with a great deal of oral and native tradition left intact.

Bermoothes: A hypothetical island of Shakespeare's creation (*The Tempest*), said to be enchanted and inhabited by witches and devils.

Beryl: An opaque or transparent green stone that is said to hinder lust when worn as an amulet and drunk as a potion.

Bes: A rather demonic and un-Egyptian looking god, who was identified with childbirth, children, marriage and the 'toilet of women'. In carvings and paintings he is frequently shown full-face, which is also contrary to the familiar profile-style in Egyptian art. He was originally a local deity of the ordinary people, but during the New Kingdom he was adopted by the middle classes as a household god.

Besant, Annie: (1847-1933) Although her interest in the occult was a devouring passion, she 'gave unstintingly of her restless gifts in her successive devotions to Anglo-Catholicism, atheism, woman's emancipation, **Theosophy** and Indian nationalism'. A self-styled servant of the great Brotherhood and the most famous of British Theosophists, she believed 'that the great Sages exist... that they wield powers and possess knowledge before which our control of Nature and knowledge of her ways is but child's play.' On the death of Madame **Blavatsky**, a struggle for the leadership of the **Theosophical Society** developed between the British, American and Indian factions. Annie Besant eventually emerged as leader of all but a section of the American Theosophists, who went their own way. SOURCE: *The First Five Lives of Annie Besant* and *The Last Four Lives of Annie Besant*, A.H. Nethercot; *Man: Whence, How & Wither*, Annie Besant.

Besom: The English name for the witches' broom, traditionally made from birch, hazel and yew. The actual brush part of the besom is the female principle, with the handle representing the male. The besom's place within ritual is that of the bridge between the worlds in traditional Craft, and for the ritual 'cleansing' of the sacred space in Old Craft. SOURCE: *Witchcraft – A Tradition Renewed*, Evan John Jones.

Bestiary: A collection of moral tales about real or fabulous animals, which was very popular in medieval Europe.

Bethel: Literally means 'the house of God'.

Betony or **Woundwort:** A herb of the mint family that is worn as an amulet to strengthen the body and counteract witchcraft and nightmares. Medieval herbalists highly valued the healing properties of the plant, considering it a cure-all. Ruling planet: **Jupiter**. Wood Betony – ruling planet **Jupiter** in **Aries**. Water Betony – ruling planet **Jupiter** in **Cancer**.

Bewitch: To create in body or mind some form of trouble through a magic spell.

Bezoar: A stone from the stomach, liver or intestines of a goat or deer that was powdered and drunk as a cure for poisoning. It could also be worn as an amulet and touched to the body. In powdered form it gave strength and longevity (see **Animal Concretion**.

Bhavana: What has become known as Buddhist meditation, *bhavana*, meaning literally 'bringing into being'.

Bible Test: A test to determine the guilt of a person accused of witchcraft was to weight him or her against a Bible, the idea being that the holy book would outweigh the evil inherent in a witch.

Bible Witchcraft: One of history's ironies since the justification for persecuting witches on the basis of biblical texts hinged on material written originally for a belief that had no devil. SOURCE: *The Encyclopedia of Witchcraft & Demonology*, Rossell Hope Robbins.

Bibliomancy: (1) Divining by words or citations taken at random from the Bible. (2) Also refers to a method of finding guilt in those suspected of sorcery. They were placed on one side of a weighing scale with a Bible on the other; the suspects were burned if the weight of the Bible was the heavier (see **Bible Test**). SOURCE: *A Dictionary of Devils & Demons*, J. Tondriau and R. Villeneuve.

Bidding: To send a familiar spirit to accomplish a task set by the magician or witch.

Bifrost: In Scandinavian mythology, the bridge between heaven and earth, often seen as a rainbow. From the Icelandic, *bifa*, tremble; and *rost*, path

Binah: The third sephirah of the Tree of Life, which means 'understanding'. If this Understanding fails to illuminate the mind then no matter how academically brilliant a seeker may be, s/he remains nothing compared to those who have crossed the **Abyss**.

The **Names of Power** are those of the mother goddesses and the Saturnian gods (see **Saturn**).

Binding: A spell to prevent a person from doing harm (to themselves or others) by magical means. Unlike **Bottling**, a binding can be of short duration and can easily be undone once the danger is passed.

Birch: Known as the 'lady of the woods', there is a great deal of positive folklore and magic associated with the tree. The besom is traditionally part-made of birch and the common deformities (or galls) in the tips of the branches are known as 'a witch's broom'. **Culpeper** recommended that the sap or juice from the leaves be used as a mouthwash and to 'break the stone in kidney and bladder'. Ruling planet: **Venus**.

Bird: One of the earliest human works of art apparently shows a man masquerading as a bird. It is a scene painted during the Old Stone Age in the cave of Lascaux in France. To early man, the birds' ability to fly brought them into contact with the sky gods, while their coloring and behavior patterns earned them a place in universal superstition. Widely used in divination. SOURCE: *Birds in Legend, Fable & Folklore*, E. Ingersoll; *The Folklore of Birds*, E.A. Armstrong.

Birthstones: The origin of the beliefs that each month of the year has a special gemstone assigned to it, and that the stone of the month is endowed with particular virtues for those born during that month can be traced back to the 1st and 5th century. The writings of Josephus and St. Jerome give the connection between the twelve stones of the high priest's breastplate and the 12 months of the year, as well as the 12 zodiacal signs. Wearing birthstones as a natal talisman does not appear until the 18th century. SOURCE: *The Curious Lore of Precious Stones*, George Frederick Kunz.

Bitch-craft: An 'in-term' for the back-biting prevalent among many of the pagan factions. SOURCE: *Coven of the Scales*, A.R. Clay-Egerton.

Black: (1) The color of darkness and night, and by association, with death. It is linked with **Saturn**, the planet of time, death and sorrow; the symbol of mourning and gloom. (2) By contrast the ancient name for Egypt is Khem, which means 'black' in reference to the fertilizing soil that is left behind following the annual **Inundation** of the Nile. SOURCE: *Liber 777*, Aleister Crowley.

Black Art: A relatively contemporary euphemism for 'magic' that was mistakenly taken from the practice of **Alchemy**.

Blackberry: see **Bramble**

Black Book: (1) Traditionally a journal or **Grimoire** containing esoteric writing of a mystical, magical or mythological nature. (2) The most famous surviving example being the *Black Book of Carmarthen*, a collection of early Welsh literature from c1250. Much of the book is given over to poems about **Merlin** (see **Carmarthen**) but there are also religious poems full of the Celtic love of the land and creation.

Black Dog: Large black, spectral dogs which haunt lonely places such as crossroads and churchyards. These legends are common all over Britain, with each county calling the apparition by a different name, although the phenomena appear to be more widespread in East Anglia.

Black Egg: There is an old magical adage that says 'one should never haggle over a black egg'. This urges paying the full price for anything rare or unexpected that is required for magical usage and looking upon it as a 'gift' rather than a commercial transaction (see **Akasha**).

Black Hen or **Black Pullet:** (1) The name of a medieval magic book or **Grimoire**, sometimes added to the 1521 edition of the *Red Dragon*. (2) The feathers of a black hen are deadly when incorporated into a magical image or **Witch's Ladder.** SOURCE: *A Dictionary of Devils & Demons*, J. Tondriau & R. Villeneuve; *The Complete Book of Magic & Witchcraft*, Kathryn Paulsen.

Black Hole: In astronomy, a place where matter has collapsed in upon itself and punched a hole in spacetime, out of which no light can escape. **Time** in a black hole dies or comes to an end. SOURCE: *First Light*, Richard Preston.

Black Madonna: The feminine principle associated with the purifying of the Earth in alchemical terms and linked with the Egyptian goddess Isis in the form known to the Greeks and Romans. There are still around a dozen Black Madonnas in Europe, having survived by being linked to Mary, Mother of God. SOURCE: *Moon Magic*, Dion Fortune.

Black Magic: Most authors writing on the subject of 'black magic' such as A.E. Waite and Montague Summers: were Christians and so tended to present a jaundiced view of magic *per se*. In reality, there is no such thing as black magic because magic itself is morally neutral. Therefore, any so-called magical expert immediately calls his or her own 'expertise' into question by bandying the term about. SOURCE: *Applied Magic*, Dion Fortune; *The Black Art*, Rollo Ahmed; *The Book of Black Magic & of Pacts*, A.E. Waite; *Guide to the Supernatural*, Raymond Buckland; *The Magical Arts*, Richard Cavendish; *Magic – White & Black*, Franz Hartmann; *What You Call Time*, Suzanne Ruthven; *Witchcraft & Black Magic*, Montague Summers. [SEE PANEL]

Black Mass: A parody of the Roman

Black Magic, White Magic

Magic is, in itself, neutral. It is the art of employing invisible agencies to obtain certain visible results, and one of the most proliferate magical myths is that of black and white magic. Black magic is *supposed* to be evil and white magic, good. Black magic is *supposed* to be the 'black art' – but what is the original black art? It is alchemy! Its very name proclaims it - the ancient name for Egypt was Khem, meaning 'black' – from the annual flooding of the Nile that left behind huge quantities of *black*, fertile mud. Khem means 'the black land'.

Egypt was one of the homes of magic and known as '*Al Khem*' from which derives 'alchemy' – the art of the black land. When magic was condemned by the Inquisition, it was easy to ascribe to the theory that magical knowledge was black and evil; the opposite of miracles, which were white and good.

I have heard 'black' magic defined as that done for personal gain, while white magic is done for the good of others. Why do good for others? I am told that by doing so, you grow spiritually – and apart from that, you feel better for having done so. If *you* grow spiritually as a result of these actions (or even feel better because of them), *you* are gaining from your actions and so by qualification they must be black.

For once and for all, there is no such thing as black and white magic, or black and white witchcraft. The actions, good or bad, are solely the province of the individual. What matters is the sincerity of intention, not the act itself and I would even go so far as to say that what may seem good to one generation may appear evil to another.

The experienced occultist is driven to using this double talk as a result of a mistake made by an eminent occultist and published in sincerity. I refer, of course, to the ridiculous misusage of the 'left and right-hand paths'. Before the mistake was compounded by Madame Blavatsky, the ancients knew that the harsh light of the Sun, (i.e. the day), under which the right arm fought and toiled was considered to be male. The softer light of the Moon, and the night, when one could rest and sleep, was attributed to the female and, being opposite to the male, was the left-hand.

Madame Blavatsky, an Eastern European lady, of good family, with at least the upper middle-class social mores of the day, was a true product of her time and upbringing. She visited India and, being accepted as a genuine occultist, was permitted to attend a ceremony of one of the cults of the *Varma Marg*—from the Sanskrit meaning 'left-hand path'.

There she witnessed a young woman among many men, apparently being 'used' by an old man for the purpose of his oral sexual gratification. Apparently not having a clue what was going on (and incidentally there is no *actual* physical contact between the priest and priestess, though this would not be apparent to an onlooker), Madame Blavatsky's European morals were offended. Henceforth she wrote and spoke extensively of the horrific 'evil' of the left-hand path, referring to what she saw as 'black magic'. So, today, we have witches venerating a goddess of the moon, calling themselves followers of the (masculine, solar), right-hand path, and decrying the left-hand path (which they don't realize they follow) as evil.

As a result, even the experienced occultist now has the compounded problem – purely for the sake of communication, you understand – to use double talk and perpetuate the inaccuracies.

EXTRACT FROM COVEN OF THE SCALES
THE COLLECTED WRITINGS OF A.R. CLAY-EGERTON

Catholic Mass, that can only be performed by a disenfranchised Christian or defrocked priest. Every witches' sabbat was *supposed* to include this 'diabolical service', but the black mass is not found in any contemporary accounts and the term only became familiar at the end of the 19th century in connection with Satanism (a term first used in England in 1896) and the publication of books such as *Là-Bas* by J.K. Huysmans; . The academic verdict is that no matter how titillating, all accounts of black masses (with one exception) must be dismissed as unfounded speculation (see the **Chambre Ardente Affair**). Also known as the Mortuary Mass if celebrated to bring about the death of a living person. SOURCE: *The Black Art*, Rollo Ahmed; *A Dictionary of Devils & Demons*, J. Tondriau and R. Villeneuve; *The Encyclopedia of Witchcraft & Demonology*, Rossell Hope Robbins; *The Magical Arts*, Richard Cavendish; *The Satanic Mass*, H.T.F. Rhodes.

Black Shuck: The name given to the large black hound that appears frequently in English folklore, particularly in East Anglia. There are various different legends attached to the sighting of the hound, whose howls can be heard over the fiercest storms. Some say that he is an omen of death; others that he is harmless as long as he's left alone; or he may be seen as part of the pack following the **Wild Hunt**. SOURCE: *Folklore, Myths & Legends of Britain*; *Aubrey's Dog: Canine Magical Lore*, Mélusine Draco.

Blacksmith: Often considered to have magical or supernatural powers and features prominently in folklore and traditional witchcraft. Many of the items associated with the blacksmith's forge have very strong magical properties especially **Horseshoes**.

Blackthorn: A native shrub most strongly identified with traditional British Old Craft through its long associations with magic and the **Faere Folk**. Mentioned in Celtic Brehon law, it is even supposed to have its own special guardians who will take revenge on anyone cutting a branch at either the opening or closing of the year. Blackthorn used as a magical tool has long been associated with cursing. Ruling planet: **Saturn**.

Blake, William: (1757–1827) English poet, artist and mystic who introduced numerous esoteric notions into his literature and art. Blake's genius was perhaps as a creator of myths and a 'living world of gods and demons in the continuous activity of their uninhibited energy'. A lifelong Christian, his theology was based upon the Swedenborgian belief that a new church (which began in the inner world) was to be the religion of 'God as man'. SOURCE: *The Complete Writings of William Blake*, ed Geoffrey Keynes; *Dictionary of Demons*, Fred Gettings; *The Theology of William Blake*, J.G. Davies.

Blasting: see **Cursing**.

Blasting Rod: In traditional witchcraft this refers to the blackthorn staff used for cursing, while in ritual magic it can be something more elaborate. Alan **Bennett** was said to have used a crystal 'wand' that he used as a blasting rod.

Blavatsky, Helena Petrovna: (1831-1891) A Russian mystic who founded the **Theosophical Society** in 1875.

After a interesting life of world travel and adventure, she wrote several books merging Eastern and Western philosophy and religion, including *Isis Unveiled* and *The Secret Doctrine,* although her distortions in the translation of rituals of foreign cultures has meant that she did not always give a fair or accurate account.

'Blessed Be' or **'Bright Blessings':** In contemporary witchcraft and paganism this is used as both a greeting and parting in conversation and in correspondence. Originally the former was intended as a blessing bestowed by one initiate on another in traditional **Wicca** but is now used by anyone. It is rarely used in traditional Craft where **'Merry Meet'** is a more usual salutation.

Bletonomancy: Divination using the patterns of moving water.

Blinked: A dialect word found in Scotland and Ireland, meaning 'bewitched' or 'overlooked'.

Blood: (1) Has its uses in occultism whether to add to or charge magical charms and spells, or as a personal oath as in 'draining every drop of one's blood into the cup'. In ritual magic, and especially **Thelema,** the latter is a symbolic statement and not meant to be taken literally, although it does mean total and utter commitment to the Path one has sworn to follow. (2) Menstrual blood can be used as a powerful ingredient in love potions – or for impotency – although in some pagan circles menstruating women are barred from taking part in magical workings because it is believed this interferes with the raising of psychic energy. This is the opposite in ritual magic, where menstruating women are considered to be at their most potent, depending on the type of magic to be worked. (3) 'Drawing blood above breath', i.e. cutting or scratching the forehead, above the nose, was one method of negating a witch's power and is recorded by Shakespeare in *Henry VI, Part I,* when Talbot first meets Jeanne d'Arc: *'Devil or devil's dam, I'll conjure thee: Blood will I draw from thee, thou art a witch, And straightway give thou soul to him thou serv'st.'* (4) In magical or alchemical terms, blood is associated with the primordial sea and is the universal liquid, represented by gold and the planetary association of the **Sun.**

Bloodstone or **Heliotrope:** A greenish chalcedony with spots of red jasper that resembles blood. Worn as an amulet, it brings fame and long life.

Boar: (1) The ferocity of the wild boar made it a universal symbol of death and destruction, and an enemy of the gods – but it was also a symbol of fertility and the boar's head on a warrior's helmet or shield was believed to protect him by giving him the animal's courage and strength. (2) The ancient words of the *Boar's Head Carol* recall the traditional festivities of Christmas and its pagan predecessor, the winter feast of Yule. (3) The 'white boar' was the insignia of Richard III.

Boaz: The black Pillar of the Temple, representing Severity (see **Jachin).**

Bodhisattva: One who is on the way to becoming a Buddha, as a result of the merit he has gained in past lives. When he has mastered the 'six perfections', and escaped from the cycle of birth, death and rebirth, he can now choose where to be reborn so as to do the most good. He eventually becomes a Buddha unless, like the Dalai Lama and the Panchen Lama of Tibet, he has vowed to remain on earth until all living beings have reached enlightenment.

Bodleian Library: In 1556 an Act against Superstitious Books and Images was passed, including books on demonology, magic, alchemy, witchcraft and heresy – and as a result, Duke Humphrey's library at Oxford remained a 'great desolate room' for over 40 years after the Act. Sir Thomas Bodley, scholar and philanthropist, used his influence to refurbish the room in 1602 and lined its walls with books from all disciplines: philosophy, religion, science, the classics, mathematics, music and alchemy.

Boggart: An unusually malicious and destructive hobgoblin of the folklore of Northern England, which frequently attaches itself to a specific household.

Bogomils: A religious sect founded in Bulgaria in the 10th century, who believed that the visible world had been created by the Devil, and that all matter was therefore inherently evil. Because of their rejection of orthodox Christian principles, they were accused of sexual immorality, magic and witchcraft.

Boleyn, Queen Anne: Accused of witchcraft by Henry VIII and executed on the grounds of treason. Anne had a sixth finger on her left hand, which was said to be a mark of the Devil and endorsed the accusation.

Boline: A classic-shaped dagger with a curved blade. SOURCE: *Coven of the Scales*, A.R. Clay-Egerton; *Mastering Witchcraft*, Paul Huson.

Bolingbrook, Roger: An Oxford prelate who was also an astrologer and magician. He was hanged in 1441 for trying to murder Henry VI by demoniac means.

Bon: (1) The indigenous pre-Buddhist religion of Tibet, similar in relationship to shamanism. The term was probably derives from the ritual recitation (*bon*) of its practitioners. (2) In Japan, the 500 year old Bon festival honors the departed spirits of the ancestors. This custom has evolved into a family reunion during which people return to ancestral family places and clean their ancestor's graves; also when spirits of the ancestors revisit the household altars.

Bona Dea: In the Roman religion, a goddess of unknown name, probably an earth-spirit protective of women. Rites in her honor were celebrated annually in December and only attended by women.

Bones: Have always been looked upon as the root of life and in some primitive societies, **Shamans** and **Medicine** men undergo the mystical experience of 'death' in which the flesh is stripped from their astral bodies. Bones, both animal and human, are often found in medicine pouches.

Boneset: see **Comfrey.**

Bonfires: see **Fire Festivals.**

Book of Changes: See **I-Ching.**

Book of the Dead: Or *Chapters for Coming forth by Day* - the name given to the papyrus scrolls placed in Egyptian tombs from around the New Kingdom onwards. The texts were designed to help the deceased to find their way in the Otherworld, complete with spells and incantations. SOURCE: *The Book of the Dead*, R.O. Faulkner; *The Book of the*

Dead, E.A. Wallis Budge.

Book of the Dead or *Bardo Thödol*: A Tibetan Buddhist treatise on what happens at death, and in the interval between death and rebirth. It gives instructions in the art of dying and reincarnation. SOURCE: *The Tibetan Book of the Dead*, Robert A.F. Thurman.

Book of Kells: An Irish illuminated manuscript in Trinity College Library, Dublin, sometimes known as the *Book of Columba*. It was transcribed by Celtic monks around 800AD. The text includes several passages drawn from the earlier versions of the Bible known as the *Vetus Latina*. It is a masterwork of Western calligraphy and is widely regarded as Ireland's finest national treasure.

Book of the Law, The: A visionary work received by Aleister **Crowley** as direct-voice dictation from a preterhuman, possibly discarnate intelligence in Cairo in 1904. SOURCE: *The Eye in the Triangle*, Israel Regardie; *Gems from The Equinox*, ed by Israel Regardie; *The Law is for All*, ed by Louis Wilkinson; *The Thelemic Handbook*, Mélusine Draco.

Book of Revelation: The last book of the New Testament and a cryptic document that has been interpreted in many ways. Most of the interpretations fall into one or more of the following categories: the *Historicist*, which sees a broad overview of history; the *Preterist*, which mostly refers to the events of the apostolic era (first century); the *Futurist*, which is believed to describes future events; and the *Idealist*, or *Symbolic*, which holds that Revelation is purely symbolic, an allegory of the spiritual path and the ongoing struggle between good and evil.

Book of Shadows: A modern concept, which serves as a guideline for those working in the coven system. (Magical Journal is a more appropriate term for a common-place book for solitary practitioners.) There is no definitive 'book' for witchcraft in general, although there are dozens of claims for these texts having been passed on from hereditary sources. According to **Wiccan** coven tradition, there should only be one copy for an entire group that is given to a newly initiated witch to make their own Book to which they can add their own material. When Wicca was exported to other countries, particularly the USA, the *Book of Shadows* became firmly entrenched as the rulebook for witches. SOURCE: *Rites of Shadow* (formerly published as *The Devil's Prayerbook* in 1972), E.A. St. George.

Borage or **Star Flower**: Used to treat fevers, skin conditions and bronchial infections. It was believed to instill courage and included in the stirrup cup offered to Crusaders upon their departure. The young leaves were cooked like spinach or added raw to salads and wine. Ruling planet: **Jupiter** in **Leo**.

Borley Rectory: By the time it burned down in 1939, the rectory had acquired the reputation of being the most haunted house in Britain. Manifestations of one sort or another were witnessed by more than 200 people over the years, including the most famous of psychical researchers, Harry Price.

Botanical: Drug or medicine made from vegetable matter.

Botanomancy: Divination using plants, mostly from burning and foretelling the future from the ashes or smoke.

Bo-Tree: A sacred fig tree under which Gautama Buddha sat in meditation for 49 days and received spiritual illumination.

Bottling: see **Witch Bottles**.

Bow Hill, Sussex: The site of ancient yew plantations, tumuli and prehistoric flint mines; the terracing reveals a pattern of prehistoric cultivation.

Box: A native British tree that was listed by **Aelfric** in his herbal. Although all parts of the tree are poisonous, taken in small doses it was used as a substitute for quinine; **Pliny** recommended the berries for diarrhoea. Both wood and leaves produced an auburn hair dye, while the bark was used to make perfume. Ruling planet: **Mars** in **Scorpio**.

Bracken or **Brake: Culpeper** lists many uses for the plant but its magical use was the collecting of the minute fern-seeds at midnight on Midsummer's Eve in order to confer invisibility on the possessor. Ruling planet: **Mercury**.

Brahma: In **Hinduism**, the personification of the creator of the universe. In classical Indian thought, Brahma forms the **Trinity** with **Vishnu** and **Shiva**. Whereas Vishnu and Shiva represent opposite forces – existence and annihilation, light and darkness, preservation and destruction – Brahma is the balance between them, 'the possibility of existence resulting from the union of opposites' (see **Equilibrium** and **Catalyst**).

Brahman: In the Hindu religion *bráhman* is the eternal, unchanging, infinite, immanent, and transcendent reality, which is the Divine Ground of all matter, energy, time, space, being and everything beyond in this Universe.

Bramble: Blackberries have been eaten since Neolithic times, while the leaves were later prescribed in many medieval remedies. **Culpeper** recommended them to be used in a lotion for sores 'in secret parts'. Ruling planet: **Venus** in **Aries**.

Branding: Used instead of tattooing by some **Old Craft** covens.

Bran the Blessed: Plays a major role in the collection of medieval Welsh tales known as the **Mabinogion**, probably dating from the second part of the 11th century but containing material that is much older. He was a pre-Celtic deity who became part of the later Celtic Tradition. His emblem is the raven and the **Alder** tree; he was also the possessor of a magic **Cauldron** of healing, which could restore the dead to life. Bran is an archetypal British-Celtic hero, and it has been surmised that he is the root of the character known as the **Fisher King** from Arthurian romance (see **London**).

Brass: Popular folk superstition holds that brass repels the evil eye, hence its use in the making of harness bells and horse brasses. Brass carried as an amulet, or placed in, or incorporated into a house keeps away evil spirits and witches' spells.

Bratton Castle: An Iron Age hill fort on the north-west edge of Salisbury Plain. The internal area is about 24 acres, with two banks and ditches for most of its defenses, though one bank is omitted on the east side. A Neolithic long barrow with quarry ditch lies within the enclosure. There is also a horse carved into the chalk of the hillside to the west of the fort, called the **Westbury**

White Horse. The figure is more horse-like than the one at Uffington and was only recarved in 1778. Tradition has it that under favorable conditions from the air, that the outline of the original horse resembled that of the **Uffington** White Horse.

Braunston: A 2000-year old stone carving of a Celtic figure stands outside Braunston church, close to the north wall. It is thought to represent a goddess who was worshipped in primitive fertility rites that took place on the site of the church in pre-Christian times.

Bray, Chris: A highly respected magician and owner of the famous occult shop in Leeds, the **Sorcerer's Apprentice**. His personal stand during the 1990s **Anti-Occult Campaign** played an important role in debunking the **Satanic Child Ritual Abuse Myth** instigated by evangelical fundamentalists and social workers. He was also the organizer of the original *Occult Census* in 1989. SOURCE: *Malleus Satani – The Hammer of Satan,* Suzanne Ruthven.

Bread: One of the oldest foods of mankind, it has at various times and places been used as a witch detector, a love charm, and even as a means of locating the body of a drowned person. It was once thought to be a cure for indigestion, and it is traditionally considered unlucky to take the last slice of bread from a plate. The sealing of friendship and taking an oath involved the ritual sharing of bread and salt. SOURCE: *The Penguin Guide to the Superstitions of Britain & Ireland,* Steve Roud.

Breath: (1) The element of life and soul, and has been identified with a person's spiritual essence in many religions. (2) In magical terms, Eliphas **Levi** said that is a man breathes in a certain way upon the back of a woman's neck she will automatically surrender to his will.

Brehon Law: Early Irish law referring to the statutes that governed everyday life and politics in Ireland during the Gaelic period. Thought to be the oldest form of law in Northern Europe, the laws were civil and concerned with the payment of compensation for harm done and the regulation of property, inheritance and contracts. For example, under Brehon Law trees were divided into four categories with a scale of fines for their unlawful felling. Some modern **Celtic Tradition** groups have adopted Brehon Law as their 'coven code'.

Brennus: A Latin form of the Cymric word *brenhin* (a war chief). In times of danger the Druids appointed a *brenn* to lead the tribes into battle.

Bress: Irish god of fertility who was adopted by the **Tuatha De Danann**.

Briah: [Qabalah] The World of Creation.

Briar or **Dog Rose:** Fossilized wild roses have been discovered throughout Europe, including Britain. The plant has numerous uses, both medicinal and culinary – see **Eglantine** and **Rose**. Ruling planet: **Jupiter**.

Bride Stones: Although most of the mound has disappeared, the megalithic structure (though damaged) is still visible. There are traces of the semicircular forecourt at the east end and nearly 20ft of the long gallery still intact. Originally, the Cheshire barrow must have been huge and believed to have been over 300 ft in length.

Brigantia: The goddess of the Celtic

tribe of the Brigantes, who occupied what are now roughly the six northern counties of England. Her name, meaning 'the High One', links her with Brigit, daughter of the powerful tribal god, Dagda, according to early Irish literary tales. SOURCE: *Pagan Celtic Britain*, A. Ross; *The Tribes of Britain*, David Miles.

'Bright Blessings': see 'Blessed Be'.

Brigit: [Irish *brig* = power, authority] Daughter of the god Dagda and patron of smiths, poets and doctors. She is associated with the ritual fires of purification and the feast of **Imbolc (Candlemas)** on 1st February. Like **Brigantia** in northern Britain, she was associated with flocks and herds, springs and rivers. She was later incorporated into Irish Christianity as St. Brigid.

Brine: (1)Very salty water used for preserving. (2) Magically it refers to the consecrated water used for ritual cleansing.

Britford: The Church of St. Peta in Wiltshire is a cruciform church of Saxon origin, which contains some important 8-9th century carvings. It was restored in 1875 but its original form is still visible.

British Library: The national library that houses important manuscripts, especially those relating to British witchcraft trials.

British Museum: A treasure trove of artifacts linked to the magical past, including John Dee's Shewstone, the Sutton Hoo burial and Iron Age exhibits, in addition to antiquities from Egypt, Greece and Rome.

Britomartis: A snake goddess of Crete, who later merged with the figure of Artemis.

Brixworth: A Northamptonshire church of All Saints, which dates from the 7th century, and incorporates many Roman tiles. It was monastic until 870 and the belfry and spire were added to the Saxon tower in the 14th century. There is an effigy of a cross-legged knight of c1300.

Brocken, The: The highest mountain peak in Saxony and has long been famous as the place where German witches held their revels on the eve of **Walpurgis Night** (31st April) and featured in Goethe's *Faust*. The Brocken Spectre refers to the natural phenomenon of a giant shadow cast on cloud or fog below by a person standing on the hilltop.

Broom: Although the shrub had many medicinal uses, it is probably better known as being the badge of the **Plantagenet** kings, its Latin name being *planta genista*. Ruling planet: **Mars**.

Broom, Butcher's: Widely used in medieval medicine but traditionally by butchers to clean chopping blocks, and decorate meat on festive occasions when the broom bears red berries. Ruling planet: **Mars**.

Broomend of Crichie: A circular enclosure near Aberdeen, with an external bank and contained ditch about 110ft in diameter. The two standing stones near the ditch are contemporary with the monument, but that at the center is a later addition. Pictish symbols are carved on the center stone.

Broomstick: One of the ways recommended in superstition to identify a witch was to lay a broom across a doorway, because a witch couldn't pass without picking it up (see **Besom**).

Brownie: A Scottish house spirit; in England he is called Robin Goodfellow.

Browne's Hill, Carlow: One of the largest dolmens in Europe, with a capstone estimated to weigh over 100 tons.

Brugh na Boinne, Meath: The most famous prehistoric cemetery in Ireland. Many of the stones are carved with intricate Bronze Age spiral and geometric patterns, as are many of the massive curbstones that surround and retain the structure. There are also outlying megaliths and secondary burials (see **Newgrange**).

Bruisewort: see **Daisy**.

Bryn Celli Ddu, Anglesey: This cairn is a passage-grave of a type limited to the Atlantic area of Britain and commoner in Scotland and Ireland. The original mound, some 160 ft in diameter, was held within a circle of substantial uprights, and on the north-east side, a long entrance passage let to a 10 ft chamber near the center. Only one of the original capstones now remains, but in the chamber there still stands a carefully rounded upright stone set there, possibly for some religious purpose. SOURCE: *Facing the Ocean*, Barry Cunliffe.

Bryn Yr Hen Bobl, Anglesey: A burial chamber containing a kidney-shaped Mound. It is unusual in having a 320 ft long narrow terrace leading off to the south.

Bryony: The leaves applied to the skin keeps a person sober, brings pleasure and reveals secrets. Although poisonous, the plant has been valued medicinally since ancient times. The roots were often sold by the unscrupulous as 'English **Mandrake**', because the genuine root was rare and costly. Ruling planet: **Mars**.

Brythonic: Collective description of the group to which Welsh, Cornish and Bretons belong. [Welsh *Brython*, Briton – introduced in philological use by Sir John Rhys (1840-1915).]

Buckland, Raymond: The man responsible for introducing contemporary witchcraft, or **Wicca**, into America and for founding a new tradition, Seax-Wicca, based on the Saxon heritage of openness and democracy. Originally inspired by the writings of Margaret **Murray** and *Witchcraft Today* by Gerald **Gardner**, Buckland struck up a correspondence with Gardner and became his spokesman in the USA. Around 1973, Buckland moved away from the **Gardnerian** Tradition as it no longer fed his spiritual needs, and he could not cope with the power-trips prevalent among the Gardnerian priesthood. TITLES: *Buckland's Complete Book of Witchcraft; The Complete Book of Saxon Witchcraft* and *Guide to the Supernatural*.

Buddha: The word 'buddha' is not a name; it denotes a state of being.

Buddhism: Follows the tradition of thought and practice associated with Gautama, the Buddha, who lived in the 6th–5th century BCE. The word Buddha is not a proper name but denotes a state of being. In classical Indian texts it means 'the enlightened' or 'the awakened'. When half a million Indian untouchables converted to Buddhism immediately after Indian independence in 1948, the world was made aware that there was much more to it than mere personal salvation. Hidden deep within Buddhism are the ancient Mysteries of Tibet (see **Tibetan Buddhism**) from which much modern occultism has found its way into the West. SOURCE: *Ancient Wisdom, Modern World*, HH Dalai Lama; *The Art of Happiness*, HH Dalai Lama and Howard C. Cutler; *Eastern Religions*, ed Michael D Coogan; *The World's Religions*, Ninian Smart; *Penguin Dictionary of Religions*, ed John R. Hinnells.

Budge, Sir E.A. Wallis: Former Keeper of Egyptian and Assyrian Antiquities at the British Museum, best remembered for his translations of the Egyptian *Book of the Dead* and several other works on Egyptian language and magical practice. Although still used by magical practitioners, Budge's accuracy has been questioned by modern Egyptologists.

Bugloss: Used in medieval medicine and also as a pot-herb to flavor meat. **Culpeper** placed it under the same entry as **Borage** and according to **Gerard**, wild bugloss was also known as **Alkanet**. Ruling planet: Jupiter in **Leo**.

Bull: A symbol of strength and sacrifice for almost all of man's recorded history. In Britain, the remains found at Bryn Celli Dhu in the form of a foundation offering at a Neolithic passage grave suggests the existence of a bull-cult, which flourished right through to the Bronze Age. In Cretan and Mycenaean religions the bull was looked upon as being sacred to the sky god, and was sacrificed and buried in his name, while in Egypt the Apis and Mnevis bulls were embalmed and buried like kings after death. The bull was also an important symbol of Mithraism. SOURCE: *The Goddess of the Stones*, George Terence Meaden; *The Mysteries of Mithra*, Franz Cumont; *The Power of the Bull*, Michael Rice; *The BM Dictionary of Ancient Egypt*, Shaw and Nicholson.

Bulrush: see **Rush**.

Bulwer-Lytton, Edward: see Lytton.

Butler, W.E.: Recognized leading light of English occultism, having been a member of Dion **Fortune's** Fraternity of Inner Light. He has written extensively on the Western magical tradition and acquired an enviable reputation as a highly competent lecturer and teacher. He established a magical school, the Servants of the Light. TITLES: *Magic – Its Ritual, Purpose & Power; The Magician, His Training & Work; Magic and the Kaballah.*

Butterfly: Symbols of the soul and light, although there are ominous connotations. In the Middle Ages, the Carmelite monk, Riccordio, offered the Devil a butterfly every time he enjoyed a woman. In more recent times it was considered lucky to kill the first one encountered in the year.

Burdock or **Beggar's Buttons:** During the Middle Ages the plant was used for skin complaints, while **Culpeper** recommended it for treating sciatica; it was also used in 'dandelion and burdock' cordials and beers. The burrs catch onto clothes or animal fur in order to disperse the seeds. Ruling planet: **Venus.**

Burial: The disposal of the dead in contemporary society is rapidly becoming a brisk, professional and impersonal event. In ancient times, the burial rites were viewed as providing a gateway into the afterlife and, as such, the correct observances had to be made. In Greek and Roman times both burial and cremation were practiced, while the Egyptians made elaborate preparation for mummification. SOURCE: *The Ancient Egyptians*, J. Gardner Wilkinson; *Dying for the Gods*, Miranda Green.

Burin: A sharp, pointed instrument for engraving sigils on wood, metal, candles, etc.

Burning Times, The: A term used by witches and occultists for the mass murder of heretics that were carried out in Europe during the 15th to mid-18th centuries. Since fire is the element of purification, this was the punishment metered out to anyone found guilty of heresy. SOURCE: *Sex, Dissidence & Damnation*, Jeffrey Richards; *The Encyclopedia of Witchcraft & Demonology*, Rossell Hope Robbins; *Malleus Maleficarum*, Sprenger and Kramer.

Bury St. Edmunds Witchcraft: The trial of 1662 was not only one of the most thoroughly documented (the descriptive pamphlet consists of 60 pages), but it was widely known throughout New England and influenced the conduct of the **Salem** trials in America.

"The rhythm of Nature in the seasonal sequence has arrested the attention of mankind throughout the ages, and has has a profound and permanent influence on human behavior."

Seasonal Feasts & Festivals

Professor E O James

C

Caapi: An hallucinatory drug used by the native shaman in parts of South America, before resolving problems or casting spells. Because of it mind-expanding power it was held to be of great magical value.

Cabbage: A popular remedy today for treating skin inflammations and sores, the plant was used in medieval times for its culinary and medicinal properties. Ruling planet: **Moon**.

Cabiri: (*Kabeiroi*) Gods of fertility, worshipped in Asia Minor and parts of Greece and Boeotia. They were also regarded as protectors from dangers, especially those of the sea.

Cabochon: [French] An uncut but polished precious stone.

Cacodaemon: (1) An evil spirit. (2) Astrologers give this name to the Twelfth House of Heaven, from which only evil prognostics proceed. [Greek: *kakos daimon*.]

Cadbury Castle, Somerset: The reputed site of Camelot, the traditional seat of King **Arthur's** court, the fort crowns an isolated hill and is defended by no less than four ramparts, each with its external ditch. Ongoing attempts are being made by excavation to confirm the Camelot tradition.

Cader Idris: [Welsh] The name of a rock formation near Dolgelley that is known as the 'chair of Idris' … a mythical giant. There is a tradition that anyone who spends the night in the chair will be either raving mad or an inspired poet by morning.

Caduceus: The symbol of **Mercury**, represented by two serpents entwined around a central rod. The image has been traced back as far as 2600BCE, although the familiar wings at the top of the rod are a later Greek addition.

Caerleon: A town on the river Usk in Wales said to be the habitual residence of King **Arthur**, where he lived in splendid state, surrounded by knights. Also an important Roman stronghold (Isca) from 75AD, with parts of the permanent fortress of the 2nd Augustan Legion and the amphitheatre still remaining.

Caerwent: The Roman city of Venta Silurum, some nine miles east of Caerleon, was built to house and 'civilize' the conquered native **Silures**. Originally defended by double earthen banks and ditches, a 30 ft high stone wall was added later in the Roman period as a defense against the raids of Irish pirates

Cagliostro, Count Giuseppe Balsamo: (1743–1795) Showman, philanthropist and genuine seeker after esoteric knowledge, was a pupil of the Grand Master of the Order of The Knights of Malta, who was himself skilled in alchemy and a **Rosicrucian**. In attempting to combine Catholicism, **Freemasonry** and magic, he 'aroused exasperated opposition and met his death at the hands of the **Inquisition**'. SOURCE: *Man, Myth & Magic*, ed Richard Cavendish.

Caistor St. Edmund, Norfolk: Venta Icenorum, the cantonal town of the **Iceni**. The land is now cultivated but whenever a really dry summer occurs, the whole street plan is visible in the crop-cover from the high point on the main road, nearly a mile away across the valley.

Cakes & Ale: see **Feast**.

Calendar: Usually follows a 'religiously sanctioned system of dating', which is demonstrated by many different faiths and traditions from the modern pagan Wheel of the Year and the ancient Egyptian *Cairo Calendar*. In 1582, Pope Gregory XIII annulled the Imperial Roman or Julian calendar and 'lost' the ten days that had accumulated since its introduction; Britain did not adopt the change until 1752, by which time it was 11 days behind the rest of Europe. These 'lost days' explain why some seemingly inappropriate traditions are still attached to certain dates. SOURCE: *The Calendar*, David Ewing Duncan; *Calendars & Constellations of the Ancient World*, Emmeline Plunket; *The Eight Gates*, Prudence Jones; *The Egyptian Book of Days*, Mélusine Draco; *Lid Off the Cauldron*, Patricia Crowther; *The Oxford Companion to Classical Literature*, ed Sir Paul Harvey; *The Roman Book of Days*, Paulina Erina; *Temple Festival Calendars of Ancient Egypt*, Sherif El-Sabban; *Witchcraft – A Tradition Renewed*, Evan John Jones; *A Witch's Treasury of the Countryside*, Mélusine Draco; *Chambers Book of Days*.

Calendar Stone: One of the finest examples of **Meso-American** religious sculpture, weighing 24 metric tons, and with carved images of **Aztec** cosmogony depicting the five ages or 'suns' of the universe.

Calumet: The sacred peace pipe traditionally used by plains and western **Amerindians**. The clay of the stone bowl represents the earth; the wooden stem represents vegetation and the stem carvings symbolize the animals. The act of smoking is an affirmation of the cosmic nature of relationships.

Camēnae: From the word meaning 'foretellers' in the old Italian religion, they were water-nymphs who had the power of prophesy. In the later Roman religion,

Carmentis was originally a water-nymph possessing the power of prophesy, who later became a deity presiding over childbirth. Her festival was celebrated on the 11th and 15th January.

Campion Pendant, The: A segment of **Narwhal's** horn (believed to be that of a unicorn) mounted in gold and enameled in black in an arabesque design. The surface at the back shows signs of having been scraped away, probably for medicinal use. The pendant, c.1600, was long in the possession of the family of Campion of Denny and is now in the Victoria & Albert Museum.

Cancer: (1) The fourth sign of the zodiac, the Crab – 21 June–22 July – placed in the heavens by **Hera** after it was crushed by Hercules during his battle with the Hydra. (2) Millennia ago, the Sun reached its summer solstice (its northernmost position in the sky) when it was in front of this constellation. It was then overhead at a northern latitude known as the Tropic of Cancer. As a result of precession, the Sun's most northerly position has now moved westward to the border of **Gemini** and **Taurus**.

Candle: There are long standing beliefs that candles used in religious ceremonies, or in connection with rites for the dead, have special curative powers and to protect against ill-wishers. *Malleus Maleficarum* (1486) states that blessed candles were effective against witches... the same passage was repeated by Scot a century later in his *Discovery of Witchcraft* (1584). A popular superstition also says that if the candle burns with a blue flame ghosts or spirits are near.

Candle Magic: Spellcasting or divination by the use of different colored candles. Although early Christian writers scorned the pagan use of candles in ritual, they nevertheless quickly adopted the practice of using them in funerary rites or when appealing to the saints for help. SOURCE: *Practical Candle Magic*, Michael Howard; *Coven of the Scales*, A.R. Clay-Egerton; *Magic: An Occult Primer*, David Conway.

Candlemas: The early spring ritual of traditional witchcraft that falls on 2nd February and coincides with **Imbolc**, the start of the Celtic lambing season. Traditional witches use the church calendar name for the festival.

Canedon: According to tradition, as long as the church tower stands there will always be seven witches in the village. It has long been the center for many stories about witches, including those concerning George **Pickingill**.

Canicular Period: A cycle of 1461 years (or 1460 Julian years), also known as a Sothic Period, when it was supposed that any given day had passed through all the seasons of the year. Canicular Days refer to the Dog Days, corresponding with the overflow of the Nile from the middle of July to the beginning of the second week in September. An Egyptian Canicular Year is calculated from one heliacal rising of the Dog Star (**Sirius**) to the next.

Canon Episcopi: Upheld the official and accepted position of church that the acts of witches were all illusions and fantasies, and that belief in the actuality of witchcraft was pagan and therefore heretical. The Abbot of Treves, who published the text in 906AD, attributed authorship of the Canon to the Council of Ancyra (314AD) and it was for many centuries accepted as the highest authority on the subject. SOURCE: *The Encyclopedia of Witchcraft & Demonology*, Rossell Hope Robbins.

Caper: A man who has been given a magical potion that makes him impotent can cure himself by eating capers.

Capnomancy: Divination by the pattern of smoke rising from a specific object.

Capricornus: (1) The tenth sign of the zodiac in the form of a goat with the tail of a fish – 21 December–20 January. (2) Several thousand years ago, the Sun reached its southernmost position in the sky – its winter solstice) when it was in front of Capricornus. During this time it was overhead at a southerly latitude now called the Tropic of Capricorn. It still carries this name although the Sun, as a result of precession, is now in **Sagittarius** at the time of the winter solstice.

Carbuncle: A red gemstone, usually a garnet, of round shape, that prevents poisoning when worn as an amulet. The carbuncle also hinders lust, sadness and bad dreams. It keeps the bearer healthy, but if the person does become ill, the color of the stone will fade.

Carmarthen: *'When Merlin's Oak shall*

tumble down, Then shall fall Carmarthen Town.' The prophecy relates to an ancient tree bound with iron bands that stood in Priory Street. The town's Welsh name is Caerfyrddn, meaning Merlin's City, as it was the legendary birthplace of the wizard. SOURCE: *The Black Book of Carmarthen.*

Carmeltalia: The feast days of the goddess of prophesy and childbirth, Carmenta (11th and 15th January). She is attended by Porrina (Future) and Postuorta (Past), and is credited with inventing the 15-letter Latin alphabet.

Carminative: A medical charm from the Latin *carmen* – a charm. Magic and charms were an intrinsic part of early medicine and, in more modern times, carminatives were given to relieve flatulence.

Carmina Burana: A medieval anthology of mainly secular and often bawdy Latin songs from the 12th century with wine and women, love and nature as the recurring themes. The translation by David Parlett, *Selections from the Carmina Burana,* also contains an English concert arrangement for Carl Orff's cantata for soloists, choir and orchestra. A popular song for coven working is 'O Fortuna' from the suite.

Carnelian: A red stone worn against skin disorders.

Carole: A circle of dancers holding hands or opening into a linked chain. According to the entry in *Man, Myth & Magic,* the word comes from the Greek *choros,* although the concept springs from ritual practices that can be traced back to before 3400BC.

Carolina Code: The criminal code for the Holy Roman Empire, which derived from the famous *Bambergische*

Halsgerichtsordnung (1508), and under these laws most of the prosecutions for witchcraft were conducted. By the end of the 16th century, judges often ignored the Code and tried the accused according to their own whims.

Carnac: Pre-dating Christianity by some 2,000 years, this is the most impressive collection of megaliths anywhere in the world – line upon line of menhirs stretching across the Breton countryside for miles.

Carrot: Although eaten by the Greeks and Romans, carrots were not cultivated in Britain until medieval times, when they were used culinarily and medicinally. Ruling planet: **Mercury.**

Cartomancy: Refers to the art of telling fortunes by **Tarot** cards, or by ordinary playing cards: from Italian *carta,* 'card', and Greek *manteia,* 'divination'. SOURCE: *Book of Divining the Future,* Eva Shaw.

Cassiopeia: The striking W-shaped constellation is on the other side of **Polaris** from **Ursa Major.** Most prominent in the northern hemisphere's winter sky, Cassiopeia is visible all year from mid-northern latitudes. In Greek mythology she was the queen of Ethiopia and mother of Andromeda.

Castaly: A fountain on Mount Parnassus, sacred to the **Muses.** Its waters inspired the gift of poetry on anyone who drank from them.

Castlerigg Stone Circle: Surrounded by a rim of mountains two miles east of Keswick is the great prehistoric stone circle known as Castlerigg or Keswick Carles. The Circle has 38 stones standing or lying to make an oval that is approx 100 ft in diameter; a further ten stones beside the Circle are arranged to form a rectangle.

Castor: The stone of the beaver, hinders conception when powdered and drunk in a potion with the earwax of a mule! Used in an ointment, it cures diseases of the nerves (see **Animal Concretion**). The brownish secretion from the glands in the groin of the beaver is also called castor, and is also used in perfume, love and fertility charms. SOURCE: *The Complete Book of Magic & Witchcraft*, Kathryn Paulsen.

Cat: Worshipped as a goddess and feared as an agent of the Devil, sacrificed to banish evil spirits or cherished as a family pet. There is little mention of cats either in Greek or Latin literature, and it is doubtful to what extent the cat was domesticated in classical times. The animal appears frequently in folklore and nursery rhymes, in addition to its familiar role as a witch's familiar and provider of numerous ingredients for charms and potions. By contrast, in Egypt the position of the cat ranged from a beloved domestic pet to a symbol of deity and, as such, the whole household went into mourning when it died.

Catacombs: Large underground burial sites, the most famous being those in Rome. These consist of an extensive network of narrow passages with shelves cut in the walls on which the bodies were placed.

Catalyst: (1) The chemical influence of a substance on another, which is not itself permanently changed. (2) In magical terms, an element that causes or promotes change by its presence in a working, or its input into a spell or charm.

Cathars: Also known as the Albigenses, were a powerful religious sect that flourished during the 12–13th centuries in the south of France. The attempt to suppress these so-called heretics, who believed in chastity, poverty and simple piety, led to the founding of the **Inquisition** and the first crusade ever to take place inside Europe. The last open resistance to the Cathars led to their massacre at Montségur in 1244. SOURCE: *Medieval Heresy*, Malcolm Lambert; *The Treasure of Montségur*, Walter Birks & R.A. Gilbert.

Catoptromancy: Divination from the images or patterns produced by a light source reflected in a shiny surface or mirror.

Caul: A thin membrane that covers the head of some newly born babies that is seen as an omen of good luck, and as having powerful magical properties. The most common belief it that it will protect a sailor from drowning and if sold will transfer the 'luck' to the new owner.

Cauldron: (1) An object of sacred and ritual significance in both Celtic and earlier societies, which is echoed in medieval Irish and Welsh tales of magic cauldrons and archeological discoveries. (2) In modern magical terms, it represents the female principle and on a practical level, is used to cook the Coven supper. SOURCE: *Witchcraft – A Tradition Renewed*, Evan John Jones.

Cauldron, The: A British-based, non-profit-making pagan magazine, founded in 1976 and edited by occult author, **Michael Howard**. Devoted to traditional witchcraft, paganism and folklore.

Cauldside: At the head of the Cauldside Burn in Scotland stand the remains of two cairns, two stone circles and a large stone block carved with cup marks and spirals.

Cave: Caves have always played an important part in magico-religious observances, since these were often viewed as entrances to Otherworld. Prehistoric man often buried his dead in caves, while the Graeco-Roman Mystery traditions used caves for initiatory purposes. Traditional witchcraft often had a cave as its meeting place rather than an open air gathering. SOURCE: *The Gods of Prehistoric Man*, Johannes Maringer; *Coven of the Scales*, A.R. Clay-Egerton.

Cave Art: Refers to the prehistoric cave paintings that are connected with early tribal ritual magic to ensure fertility and success in hunting. The shamanic impressions drawn from the way the animals and humans are depicted can tell a great deal about the way primitive man viewed the world around him. The unusual nature of the images, and the fact that they are often deep in the most inaccessible parts of the caves, also suggests that these were connected to ritual. SOURCE: *Palaeolithic Cave Art*, P.J. Ucko; *The Art of Prehistoric Man in Western Europe*, A Leroi-Gourham; *The Origin of Humankind*, Richard Leakey.

Cave of Achadh Aldai: A cairn in Ireland named for Aldai, the ancestor of the **Tuatha de Danaan**.

Cavendish, Richard: Educated at Oxford and a leading author on magic and witchcraft, on which he has written and lectured extensively. He is the author of *The Magical Arts, The History of Magic, The Tarot, The Powers of Evil* and editor of the invaluable encyclopedia, *Man, Myth & Magic*.

Cayce, Edgar: American born psychic who died in 1945, and had remarkable diagnostic and curative powers. Often his conclusions contradicted orthodox medical opinion, but time and again he would be proved right and doctors wrong.

Celandine: A yellow-flowered spring plant under the influence of the **Sun** and used in solar charms.

Celestial Agriculture: The name given to the pursuit of alchemy during the Renaissance, while its adepts were referred to as 'laborers'. *Laborare et orare* (work and pray) was a famous alchemical motto.

Celonitis: A stone of the tortoise (see **Animal Concretion**). On the first day of the new moon, place it under the tongue in order to see into the future for half a day for the next 15 days: from sunrise to sunset if the moon is waxing, from sunset to sunrise when it is waning. SOURCE: *The Complete Book of Magic and Witchcraft*, Kathryn Paulsen.

Celts: The Celts were established in central Europe by 500BC as nomadic warrior tribes. They moved eastwards into Asia Minor and westwards into Gaul, Spain and Britain. Early Welsh and Irish literature preserves Celtic myths, while the religious practices are described by Posidonius and other classical writers.

Celtic Tradition: In magical terms, this is a revivalist system based on the culture and deities of the ancient Celts. Although the early Celts were composed of a number of different racial elements, there is an 'impressive uniformity of religious idiom' throughout the known Celtic world (see

Brythonic). SOURCE: *The Celtic Druids' Year,* John King; *Celtic Gods & Goddesses* and *Celtic Myths, Celtic Legends,* R.J. Stewart; *Celtic Myth & Legend,* Mike Dixon-Kennedy; *The Celtic Tradition,* Caitlin Matthews; *Pagan Celtic Britain,* Dr. Anne Ross; *The Pagan Religions of the Ancient British Isles,* Ronald Hutton.

Centaur: In Greek mythology, wild and half animal, they had a human torso and the body of a horse. They lived in the forests and mountains, with the most famous being Cheiron.

Centaury or **Feverwort:** The wound-healing properties of the plant were known to the ancient Greeks and **Culpeper** used it as a panacea for almost every kind of ailment. In *The Booke of Secretes of* **Albertus Magnus** *of the Vertues oh Herbes, Stones and Certain Beastes,* printed in 1560, it was claimed that the fumes caused people to believe they were witches. Ruling planet: **Sun.**

Centipede: One of the 'five venomous animals' or 'five poisons' in Chinese folk magic, which are used together in amulets against evil. In Scotland the centipede was used for working evil.

Cephalomancy: Divination by studying the shape of a person's skull to determine character and personality traits. Commonly known as **Phrenology.**

Ceraunium: The ancient name for an opal because of the notion it was a thunder-stone. [Latin, *ceraunium*; Greek, *keraúnios*]

Ceraunoscopy: Predictions for future events were made by deciphering the patterns of lightning during a thunderstorm.

Cerberus: The three-headed dog in Roman mythology that guards the entrance to the Underworld.

Ceremonial Magic: Usually refers to the more flamboyant ritualized magic practiced by a large group who prefer strict adherence to set forms of ritual, often taking several hours to perform a single rite, i.e. **The Hermetic Order of the Golden Dawn.** It is often a name (not always correctly) given to a form of magic involving the conjuration of spirits and/or demons. SOURCE: *Ceremonial Magic,* A.E. Waite; *The Complete Rituals of the Golden Dawn,* Israel Regardie; *Dictionary of Demons,* Fred Gettings; *Magick,* Aleister Crowley;

Ceres: An old Italian goddess of agriculture and, like her Greek counterpart, **Demeter,** she was also goddess of fertility and marriage. Her temple on the Aventine Hill was a central point for the common people. Her feast, the *Cerealia,* was celebrated on 19th April. SOURCE: *Gods and Goddesses, Devils and Demons,* Manfred Lurker; *The Roman Book of Days,* Paulina Erina.

Cerne Abbas: Carved in outline on a hillside is the huge 180 ft high, figure of the Giant – a naked man bearing a club. Perpetuating the myth that it is a fertility symbol, local superstition maintains that anyone wanting to conceive should sit on the phallic part of the monument.

Cernunnos: A Celtic god who sits cross-legged with a set of antlers on his head, and portrayed in this way on the Gundestrup cauldron (see **Horned God**).

Cerridwen: Celtic goddess of wisdom whose symbol is the cauldron. Many of the myths surrounding her have been absorbed into contemporary pagan belief. SOURCE: *The Book of Taliesin*.

Cerrig y Gof: A burial chamber of unique design among the many fine monuments (mainly of Bronze Age), dotted along the north Pembrokeshire coast. In the outer edge of a circular mound are set five megalithic chambers, rectangular in plan, which face outwards – a departure from the characteristic chamber of uprights supporting a capstone.

Chakra (plural **Chakram**): A system of natural energy points that exist within the body, and which form an integral part of **Tantric** doctrine. There are seven points used to focus and generate this energy, concentrating occult energies that work through the glands of the endocrine system. SOURCE: *The Chakras*, Naomi Ozaniec; *Hindu World*, Benjamin Walker; *The Magical Revival*, Kenneth Grant.

Chalcedony: A precious stone of half-transparent quartz. The chief varieties are agate, carnelian, cat's eye, chrysoprase, flint, hornstone, onyx and sard. According to Albertus Magnus: *'It dispels illusions and all vain imaginations. If hung about the neck as a charm, it is a defense against enemies and keeps the body healthful and vigorous'*

Chaldean Tradition: The most neglected classical influence in Western ritual magic and yet it represents the basis for some of the most important contemporary occult practice. The Chaldeans were alleged to be the first to develop **Astrology** and a system similar to the **Tree of Life; Mithraism** came from the Chaldean civilization as perhaps did the worship of **Hecate**. The concept that magicians/mystics could invoke the gods in ritual for specific illumination was also a Chaldean import and a number of early Mithraic passages are evident in Qabalistic writings.

Chalice or **Cup:** A special drinking vessel used for ritual purposes, signifying the female principle. SOURCE: *Coven of the Scales*, A.R. Clay-Egerton; *Techniques of High Magic*, Francis King and Stephen Skinner; *Witchcraft – A Tradition Renewed*, Evan John Jones.

Chambre Ardente Affair: A scandal that came to light when Louis XIV set up the Star Chamber to investigate widespread poisoning among the French nobility. The investigations lasting from January 1679 to July 1682 are probably the only witch-trials based on some element of truth, rather than the *'wild imaginings of young neurotics or the morbid logic of perverse witch judges and inquisitors'*. The Affair involved some of the highest in the land, including the King's former mistress and the main problem was how to suppress the biggest scandal of the century. SOURCE: *The Encyclopedia of Witchcraft & Demonology*, Rossell Hope Robbins; *The Satanic Mass*, H.T.F. Rhodes.

Chamomile: Highly valued as a soothing and mildly sedative tonic for nervous complaints and restlessness. One of the **Nine Sacred Herbs** of the Anglo-Saxons. Ruling planet: **Sun**.

Chanctonbury Ring, Sussex: A ring of beech trees planted in 1760 around the area enclosed by an Iron Age hill fort. The remains of a Roman temple, together with other contemporary buildings stand at the center of the site.

Changeling: The excuse that a deformed

or ugly child was one substituted by the **Faere** Folk and often gave rise to acts of unspeakable cruelty, even as late as the early 20th century when a suspected changeling was burned to death on a hot shovel.

Channel Islands Witchcraft: This small area suffered possibly more than any other part of Britain from witch persecutions. The Islands were politically English but culturally French, and so the apprehension and trial of witches followed the rougher custom of France. During the reigns of Elizabeth I, James I and Charles I, 58 women and 20 men, mostly natives of Guernsey, were tried for sorcery, and all except eight were convicted.

Channeling: Bringing instructions or information from beings from another plane or dimension via trance-work or meditation.

Chanticleer: A poetic name for a cockerel, from the French *chanter-clair*, to sing *clairment*, i.e. distinctly.

Chanting: One of the oldest vocal techniques for changing levels of consciousness.

Chaos: (1) Refers to the primal substance out of which all manifestation emerges. In mythology, it is the confusion that existed before the Universe was set in order, and also the forces of confusion and disorder that still exist. (2) In magical terms, all things are unpredictable but can be influenced. SOURCE: *Aleister Crowley & The Hidden God*, Kenneth Grant; *Condensed Chaos*, Phil Hine; *The Magical Revival*, Kenneth Grant.

Chaos Magic: A fairly new development in occultism, having grown out of the Chaos Theory in quantum physics.

Chaos magicians construct their working methods to suit themselves, although there must be some form of basic structure if results are to be achieved. In Chaos Magic magical change is effected in a sometimes apparently random fashion. SOURCE: *The New Believers*, David V. Barrett.

Chapbook: Small paper-covered booklets, cheaply printed and often crudely illustrated, poured in their millions from backstreet presses in Britain and Ireland during the 17th to 19th centuries. They were sold by traveling rural 'chapmen' on stalls at markets and fairs, the most popular being dream books and fortune-telling guides. A regular feature was some form of impressive chart – such as a magic circle with numbers that could translate into a personal reading.

Charge of the Goddess: Primarily a **Wiccan** concept that was popularized by Gerald **Gardner** and Doreen **Valiente** in the 1950s as part of rite of the '**Drawing Down The Moon**'. Allegedly, Gardner's first version was adapted from *Aradia: the Gospel of the Witches* with added extracts from Aleister **Crowley**. Valiente rewrote Gardner's version in verse and eliminated most (but not all) of Crowley's input, and over the years, various other versions have been written by other Wiccan practitioners. SOURCES: *Eight Sabbats for Witches, A Witches' Bible Complete*, Janet and Stewart Farrar; *Aradia: the Gospel of the Witches*, Charles G. Leland.

Charlemagne: (c742–814) King of the Franks and Emperor of the Romans, who actively encouraged the spread of Mediterranean herbs and spices throughout Europe and decreed that each city within his empire should have a garden planted with 'all herbs'.

Chariot: The seventh card in the **Major Arcana** of the **Tarot**, and archetypal martial symbol of Victory in the face of overwhelming odds.

Charm: A spell in the form of words, or an object believed to contain magic power, hence its broader meaning of attractiveness, fascination, allure or, as a verb, to enchant or bewitch; derived from the Latin *carmen*, 'a song'. [SEE PANEL]

Charm of Taciturnity: When witches and heretics were silent in the presence of their judges, they were said to have the 'Charm of Taciturnity' because the Devil had destroyed their vocal chords or paralyzed their tongues. The cause was probably aphasia or fear spasms in the face of imminent torture (see *Discours des Sorciers*). SOURCE: *A Dictionary of Devils & Demons*, J. Tondriau and R. Villeneuve;

Charon: In Greek mythology, the aged and irascible boatman who ferried the souls of the dead across the Styx. A coin was placed in the mouth of the deceased to pay the fare. The Roman poet Virgil draws a grim picture of Charon in the *Aeneid*.

Charybdis: A whirlpool off the coast of Sicily, twinned with **Scylla** (a rock) to signify two equal dangers.

Chela: A pupil.

Chelidonius: A stone from a swallow (see **Animal Concretion**). Red or black, it should be wrapped in linen and bound under the left armpit to protect from madness and disease, and to improve the memory.

Chelmsford Witchcraft: The first notable trial for witchcraft in England (1566) resulting from the bill of 1563 passed under Elizabeth I. The sole surviving copy of the pamphlet is now in Lambeth Palace Library. There is a copy of the second trial in a contemporary tract (1579), housed in the **British Museum**. The unique copy of the pamphlet for the third trial (1589) with its famous illustration of the three witches and their familiars, is also in Lambeth Palace Library. SOURCE: *The Encyclopedia of Witchcraft & Demonology*, Rossell Hope Robbins

Chemical Wedding: The allegorical term for the joining of Philosophic Mercury and Sulfur (purified silver and gold). The most famous event in alchemical literature is *The Chymical Wedding of Christian Rosencreutz* by J.V. Andreae, the **Rosicrucian**.

Cherry: The wild cherry tree is indigenous to Britain and listed by **Aelfric** in his herbal as producing a remedy for coughs, with which **Culpeper** agreed. Ruling planet: **Venus**.

Chesed: Known as the sphere or path of Cohesive or Receptive Intelligence on the magical Tree of Life because it contains all the holy powers, and from it emanate all spiritual values. The **Names of Power** are those of benevolent ruler gods (see **Jupiter**).

Chervil: A herb introduced by the Romans and listed by **Aelfric** as a cleansing tonic. It was also valued for its culinary uses. One of the **Nine Sacred Herbs** of the Anglo-Saxons. Ruling planet: **Jupiter**.

Chestnut or **Sweet Chestnut:** The tree was introduced by the Romans; by medieval times the nuts and leaves were used medicinally and in the kitchen. Ruling planet: **Jupiter.**

Ch'i: In Chinese medical and esoteric disciplines, this is a universal energy generated naturally and stored within the human body.

Chickweed or **Wintergreen:** Used during the Middle Ages to heal wounds and cure blood poisoning; **Culpeper** also used it for kidney and bladder problems. Ruling planet: **Moon.**

Chieftain Trees: The seven named trees in old Irish Law, the unlawful felling of which was regarded as a serious crime. These were the oak, hazel, apple, yew, holly, ash and pine. SOURCE: *Root & Branch*, Mélusine Draco; *The White Goddess*, Robert Graves.

Chimaera: (1) The off-spring of Typhon, a dreaded being associated with storm and tempest, and Echidna, who was part-woman and part-serpent. The famous bronze in the Archaeological Museum in Florence shows the Chimaera as a beast compounded of a lion, a goat and a serpent and it is referred to in Homer's *Iliad* (Books 6 and 16). The term has come to be used for any hybrid plant or animal, or in a metaphysical sense for any imaginary fear. (2) *The Flaming Chimaera* is the name of a site in the Lycian forest where an underground fire (presumed to be natural gas) breaks up from vents in the earth. In ancient times this was probably the site of a temple to the Spirit of Fire. SOURCE: *Accidents of an Antiquary's Life*, D.G. Hogarth.

Chinese Astrology: Still widely practiced in the East and increasingly popular in the West, this system is based on a 12-year cycle. With its triple view of the Emblematic Animal, the Companion in Life and the Element, the system provides 'a greater diversity of references and a totality of perspectives both more rich and more precise than those found in Western astrology,' according to *Chinese Zodiac Signs.*

Chinese Religion: The fall of the Ch'ing dynasty in 1912 meant the end of the great Sacrificial Rites (*Chi Li*) of imperial religion in China. The traditions of **Taoism** and Chinese Buddhism, together with many features of popular or diffused religion, continued to survive. SOURCE: *Chinese Gods*, Keith Stevens.

Chiromancy: Divination through the study of a person's nails, lines and fingers of a hand. See **Palmistry.**

Chokmah: The second sephirah of the Tree of Life, meaning 'wisdom' and represents the Sphere of Stars. The **Names of Power** are those of the father gods and goddesses of Wisdom, while the planetary attribution is that of the **Zodiac.**

Choronzon: The demon of dispersion and confusion, magical impotence and lack of control. John **Dee** described this 'demon' as 'quintessentializing the metaphysical antithesis of all that is implied by magic.'

Chresmomancy: Interpretation of a chance encounter with a series of magical sounds. SOURCE: *Book of Divining the Future*, Eva Shaw **Chresmonancy:** Divination through a *voice* from the ethereal world, transmitted through a psychic, providing knowledge or hidden wisdom.

Christmas: A Christian winter celebration that has its origin in three ancient pagan festivals: the great **Yule**-feast of the Norsemen, the birthday of **Mithra,** and the Roman **Saturnalia**, but it was only

Charms & Spells

Pick up any modern book on witchcraft and they're crammed full with charms and spells to find love, money or a job. Okay... you've done the business and met some divine bloke/bird down at the wine bar; Great-Aunt Bessie's died and left you a tidy sum, and an unexpected career move has you working six months of the year in the Bahamas... so now what?

Should we have to resort to magic to continually sort out our love life, finances and career prospects? And if the magic works for us, who's to say that it might be robbing someone else of their partner, inheritance or promotion. Magic is, and always has been, a double-edged sword, so we must be doubly careful how we wield it.

Let's start with that old magical chestnut – the luv spell! If it goes against someone's natural inclinations or instincts, or if the victim belongs to someone else, then it's black magic, however you want to glitz it up in your own mind. If you're looking for Prince(ss) Charming and expect magical impulses to deliver them to your door gift wrapped and eager, I'd have to say get off your backside and get out more! And if you're spellcasting to make yourself more attractive to the opposite sex, try checking yourself out in the mirror before going any further.

If, on the other hand, you're sending out a call on the astral and you're convinced that you're doing everything in your power to be in the right place at the right time, do be careful what you ask for – or you might just get it! In magical working the wording must be precise or there could be some nasty shocks along the way, so take your time in drawing up a list of attributes you'd like to find in a new partner. An acquaintance generated some pretty heavy artillery in attracting her new mate, who on the surface was everything she'd asked for. Except that three months after the wedding she discovered the hard way that he'd got a violent side to his nature... she'd forgotten to add kindness to her list!

In the current 'consumer credit crisis' everyone is feeling the pinch, so you might be a long time waiting for a windfall, even with a bit of magical assistance thrown in. Rather than a "Gissus the money" type of spellcasting, go for a divinatory or meditational result. Another acquaintance used this method and within days spotted a feature in a national newspaper that gave her all the information she needed to sort out her financial problems. With advice and support from an outside agency she was able to clear her debts within six months, but if she'd relied solely on a 'money spell' and waited for the cash to miraculously appear in her bank account, the problem would have escalated totally out of control.

Charms and Spells are influenced by the amount of effort put into them, but if you're content to just fool about with a colored candle and 'money drawing' anointing oil on a Thursday evening, the desired results might be a long time in the coming. Use magical knowledge to open the right channels in your mind, and be receptive to any information, ideas or advice that comes to your attention. Magic works in mysterious ways. Likewise in the career stakes, do be careful what you ask for and how you ask for it. Like the witchlet who went into a spellcasting saying she wanted to work with dogs or horses ... and found herself working for the local bookmaker!

Spellcasting is a very exact science and should not be undertaken in a spirit of levity, despite what the books offering 'spells and rituals to attract all the good things in life' may tell you. It ain't that easy.

EXTRACT FROM MEAN STREETS WITCHCRAFT
MÉLUSINE DRACO

in the 4th century that 25th December was officially decreed to be the birth date of Jesus. It was another 500 years before the term 'Midwinter Feast' was abandoned in favor of the word Christmas. Extending from Advent, which begins on the Sunday nearest to 30th November to **Candlemas** on 2nd February, the festival was also close enough to the **Winter Solstice** and the birthday of **Mithra** to acquire many of the associations still recognized today.

Chrysolite: Yellow or greenish transparent variety of magnesium iron silicate that prevents insanity when worn as an amulet. If a hole is bored in the stone, filled with hairs from the mane of an ass and worn on the left arm, it will protect from melancholy, foolishness and fear. Or it may be worn set in gold. It also prevents asthma and lung disease when powdered and taken internally.

Chrysoprase: A green chalcedony that is worn as an amulet for happiness and to strengthen the eyes.

Chthonian Belief: The devotion to the gods of the **Earth** (from the ancient Greek *chthon*) as against those of the sky or heaven. The term is often used with specific reference to **Otherworld**, although myths and rites relating to the earth and its fertility may also be referred to as 'chthonian'.

Church of Satan: Established in San Francisco on **Walpurgisnacht** in 1966 by **Anton LaVey** to promote **Satanism**. The Church of Satan's principles are based on LaVey's **The Satanic Bible**. SOURCE: *The Satanic Bible*, Anton Szandor LaVey; *Malleus Satani: The Hammer of Satan*, Suzanne Ruthven.

Chysauster, Cornwall: A remarkable Iron Age village, with four pairs of houses each fronting a village street. Each house is oval in plan, but the rooms are roughly circular, set in thick walls and all opening to a central courtyard. Now open to the sky, the rooms were apparently roofed with corbelled stone or with thatch, though the courtyards were open. When excavated, querns, pottery and other domestic debris, together with hearths, were found lying on the paved floors. Each house also had a stone-fenced back garden.

Cicuta: From the Latin *cicūta* and refers to the length of reed up to the 'knot', such as the internodes made into panpipes. It is also called cow-bane, one of the most poisonous of plants.

Cimitiere, Baron: [Voodoo] Lord of the Dead. The cemetery typifies the Place of the Cross, or crossing over to the realm of the dead; the crossroads (see **Samedhi**).

Cimmerians (*Kimmeroi*): A fabulous people, whose land according to Homer was on the limits of the world, in the stream Oceanus. It was shrouded in cloud and mist and the sun never shone on it; it was there that Odysseus had access to the spirits of the dead. Possibly the Homeric origins of Plato's reference to the fabulous civilization of **Atlantis**.

Cingulum: The witch's girdle or cord from the Latin for 'belt'. May signify rank or tradition by the use of different colors.

Cinquefoil: A plant with five-lobed silver leaves and ruled by Jupiter. It is a common ingredient for love potions and, when worn as an amulet, it brings eloquence in seeking political favors. It protects a house from witchcraft when hung in the entry.

Circe: The fair-haired sorceress described in Homer's *Odyssey*, daughter of Helios the Greek sun god and sister of Aeetes, the divine wizard and King of Colchis. Another celebrated sorceress, **Medea**, was her niece. It has been suggested that Circe could be identified with the powerful 'Lady of the Beasts', whose image has been found engraved on Minoan artifacts dating from a millennium before Homer's day.

Circle: From ancient times a circle often marked the boundary of a sacred area, and protected it against evil influences. The circle is a symbol of all things and an emblem of 'All is One', meaning that all the various phenomena of the **Universe** are linked together in unity.

Circle, The: Cast by both witches and magicians for protection, and to concentrate magical energies within a confined, sacred area. The use of a circle to mark a boundary of an area that is sacred, set apart from everyday life and to be protected against worldly influences is very ancient. Traditionally, a magic circle should be nine feet in diameter, drawn on the floor or the ground with a sword or knife. SOURCE: *The Goddess of the Stones*, George Terence Meaden; *The Magical Arts*, Richard Cavendish; *Magic: An Occult Primer*, David Conway; *Psychic Self-Defense*, Dion Fortune; *Witchcraft – A Tradition Renewed*, Evan John Jones.

Civet: Most well-known for the pungent secretion used in fumigations, ointments and love potions. Touch the doorposts with blood from the animal to prevent sorceries and enchantments, or wear its skin for protection.

Clan: (1) The Gaelic *Clann*, origin of the modern word, simply signifies the children of the family, the kith and kin. (2) A term used by some Celtic-based groups instead of 'coven'.

Clairaudience: Refers to hearing instead of seeing but distinguished from telepathy, which is the ability to sense other people's thoughts and mental states, or to convey your own to other people without the use of speech, gesture or the other normal methods of communication. An example of clairaudience were the voices heard by **Jeanne d'Arc**.

Clairsentience: An awareness of psychical manifestations akin to intuition, or the sensing of atmosphere.

Clairvoyance: The ability to see what is not present to ordinary sight, including objects or happenings at a great distance, and things in the future.

***Clavicles of Solomon*:** A collection of magical formulae that were supposedly proven according to the *Veritable Grimoire* and *Secrets des Secrets*.

Clay-Egerton, Alastair Robert and **Mériém:** 'Bob' Clay-Egerton was initiated into an Old Craft coven in 1941 and into a ritual magic order in 1943. His magical working partner and wife, Mériém, was a Doctor of Geology with a working interest in archeology and anthropology. In later years, they became well-known teachers in Warwickshire and Northern England of these magical Traditions but with a very strong scientific or academic bias rather than working by rote. SOURCE: *Coven of the Scales*, A R Clay-Egerton; ; *What You Call Time*, Suzanne Ruthven.

Cleansing: Another name for purification by the use of incense and holy water.

Cleavers: see **Goose Grass**

Cleidomancy: Divination using the swinging of a **Pendulum** to foretell the future.

Cleromancy: Casting objects onto a cloth marked out with divination sections to foretell the future. The Chinese have a similar system called *chiao-pai*, which is used throughout Asia.

Clidomancy: A system of proving guilt or innocence by the use of a key, a holy book and the index finger of a virgin. This ritual was performed during the Middle Ages… but only when the **Sun** or **Moon** was in **Virgo**, according to *The Book of Divining the Future* by Eva Shaw.

Clootie: The Scottish term for a cloven-hoof is 'cloot' – *Auld Clootie* refers to the Devil as 'old cloven-hoof'.

Closed Orders: Magical Orders that operate under a restrictive acceptance of new members, and often with a very strict system of learning. SOURCE: *Esoteric Orders & Their Work* and *Training & Work of an Initiate*, Dion Fortune.

Clove: A protection against witchcraft when carried; and a common witches' ingredient in love potions.

Clove Pink or **Gilly-flower:** The Latin name *Dianthus* derives from the Greek for 'divine flower' and **Culpeper** recommended a tincture of the 'July flower' as the best medicine for fainting, headaches and other nervous disorders. Ruling planet: **Jupiter**.

Clover: Grown as a forage crop for animals as well as having medicinal and culinary uses; **Culpeper** said that made into an ointment it helped relieve stings and bites. Ruling planet: **Mercury** (white clover) and **Venus** (red clover).

Cluricanne: In Irish folklore an elf of evil disposition, usually appearing as a wrinkled old man, who has knowledge of hidden treasure.

Clutterbuck, Old Dorothy: The priestess of the coven of hereditary witches in the New Forest, who initiated Gerald **Gardner** into Craft in 1939.

Coal: It is lucky to find a piece of coal in the street, and was thought to bring good luck if carried in the pocket as a good luck charm.

Cobalt: From the German *kobold* – a gnome. This metal was thought to be useless and troublesome and attributed to a mine-demon.

Cochrane, Robert (aka **Roy Bowers**): Claimed to be a genuine hereditary witch, drawing his teachings from a long and secret tradition. His ambition was to gather together as many strands of the Old Faith as he could, and then represent them as a cohesive whole. Unfortunately, he died in 1966 but what little he left behind still has a tremendous impact upon those who would follow where he once led. Most of his rituals were spontaneous and shamanic, and although Evan John Jones, author of *Witchcraft – a Tradition Renewed*, was a member of Cochrane's coven, much of what appears in print is only a shadowy outline of this tradition. SOURCE: *The Roebuck in the Thicket*, Michael Howard; *The Old Sod: The Autobiography of W.G. Gray*, Alan Richardson.

Cockatrice: A fabulous heraldic monster with a cock's head and wings, and a serpent's tail. Sometimes identified with the **Basilisk**.

Cockerel: According to *Man, Myth & Magic*, '*the proud strutting, aggressiveness* *and sexual ardour of the cockerel, together with its striking appearance and loud crowing, are the reasons for this bird's particularly widespread involvement in folk customs and traditions.'* The crowing of a cockerel dissolving enchantment is a tradition of extreme antiquity. According to **Iamblichus's** *Protreptics*, symbol xviii, the cock was also sacred to the goddess of wisdom, and to **Asclepius**, the god of health; therefore it represented time, wisdom and health, none of which are ever to be sacrificed (see **Sacred Animals**).

Cocytus: [Greek] One of the five rivers of Hell known as the 'river of lamentation'. The unburied were doomed to wander about on its banks for 100 years.

Codex Vindobonensis: see *De Materia Medica.*

Coffin Texts: Hieroglyphic inscriptions painted on the sides of the coffins of the nobility of ancient Egypt. They contain spells and instructions for the afterlife. SOURCE: *The Ancient Egyptian Coffin Texts*, R.O. Faulkner.

Cohoba: A hallucinogenic drug found in the West Indies, Northern and Central America. During rituals, the powdered form was inhaled, subjecting the user to bouts of wild excitement, followed by periods of tranquility and visions of prophecy.

Coincidence: The occurrence of events simultaneously or consecutively, in a striking manner but without any causal connection between them. SOURCE: *Coincidences*, Tony Crisp.

Colchester: There is the suggestion of a settlement dating back to the 5th century BC and in the 1st century AD Cunobelin (Shakespeare's *Cymbeline*) was king at Camulodunum. Roman invaders occupied the town in 43AD and five years later established a major colony there. In 60AD the Britons under Queen **Boudicca's** command rose up against Roman rule, massacred the Roman occupants, and destroyed the temple. During the Dark Ages, the Danes frequently raided the town.

Cold Water Ordeal: An ancient method of testing the guilt or innocence of the common people. The accused, being bound, was thrown into a river or pool. If they sank, they were held to be innocent; if they floated they were guilty. Later used as a test for discovering witchcraft.

Colewort or **Kale:** An important medieval pot-herb and medical preparation. According to **Culpeper** the twice-boiled leaves drunk with broth help relieve the pain of kidney and bladder infections. Ruling planet: **Moon**.

Collective Unconscious: According to **Carl Jung's** theory, this is the subconscious repository of the many universal mythic elements and **Archetypes**. SOURCE: *Man and his Symbols*, Carl G. Jung.

Cologne Witchcraft: With the exception of two witch hunts in 1625-26 and 1630-36, the city of Cologne had fewer persecutions than other parts of Germany; charges made from hearsay and common gossip about sabbats and neighbors' denunciations were generally ignored.

Colors: see **Correspondences**.

Coltsfoot: An ancient treatment for coughs and colds. **Gerard** said that the fumes of the dried leaves burned upon coals help to relieve those suffering from a shortage of breath. In France, a coltsfoot painted on a doorpost indicated an apothecary's shop. Ruling planet: **Venus**.

Columbine: [Latin *aquilegia*] Although poisonous (especially the seeds) the plant was used as an antiseptic and astringent lotion for sore mouths and throats. During medieval times it was one of a few herbs prescribed to treat the plague. Ruling planet: **Venus**.

Comet: (1) The appearance of a comet was long believed to mean that some cataclysmic disaster was likely to occur – war, famine, plague, the downfall or death of kings, or even the end of the world. The Bayeux Tapestry shows a comet appeared before the Norman Conquest of England, and comets marked both the birth and death of Julius Caesar. (2) Small body of ice or icy rock in orbit around the **Sun**. Near the Sun, the comet's ice evaporates, creating a tail of gases streaming away from the nucleus of the comet.

Comfrey (**Knitbone** or **Boneset**): Valued for its powers of healing bruises, wounds and sprains as a poultice; the pulped root applied around a broken limb sets like plaster. Comfrey tea alleviated the symptoms of colds, bronchitis and stomach ulcers, while a concoction sprinkled around the house wards off evil spirits. **Gerard** noted that the slimy substance from the root, added to a posset of ale, helped pain in the back, '*gotten by any violent motion, as wrestling, or over much use of women.*'. Ruling planet: **Saturn** in **Capricorn**.

Comparative Religion: The systematic study of all religions and to trace the history and relationship to the society in which they exist and not a commentary on the ethics, dogma or to evaluate the 'truth' of the belief.

Compass: The four cardinal points of the compass are an integral part of all magical working, representing as it does the four elemental quarters of the **Circle**. Sometimes the term 'compass' is used instead of Circle by traditional witches.

Compitalia: The Roman festivals of the **Lares** of the crossroads (*compita*), where offerings were made in the hope that the spirits would spare the living and be content with the 'gifts'.

Conclamatum est: It is believed that the sense of hearing is the last to fail in the hour of death. It was a Roman custom to call on the dead three times and if there was no response, death was considered certain. *Conclamatum est* – 'he has been called and shows no sign'.

Concordia: The Roman goddess of concord = harmony. She is portrayed as bearing a cornucopia and a sacrificial bowl.

Cone of Power: The term made popular by Gerald **Gardner** to refer to the raising and directing of a spiral of psychic energy, although he probably took the idea from ritual magic sources. According to Gardner, witches raise a cone of power by dancing in a circle around a fire or candle, then joining hands and rushing towards the fire calling out the object of the ritual, until the group collapses from exhaustion as the spell is directed on its way. SOURCE: *An ABC of Witchcraft Past & Present*, Doreen Valiente; *Wicca: The Old Religion in the New Millennium*, Vivienne Crowley; *Mastering Witchcraft*, Paul Huson.

Confabulation: A term used in psychiatry to describe the invention of experiences, either consciously or unconsciously, to replace gaps in the memory.

Confession: The **Inquisition** recognized two forms of confession: (a) the direct confession obtained by repeated torture, and (b) the denouncement, made without the knowledge of the accused. The Confession was an indispensable part of the proceedings and was sought by asking some 30 questions of the accused, whose answers were not important. In his *Cautio Criminalis* (Cologne 1632) the Jesuit Friedrich von Spee declared: *'The result is the same whether the sorceress confesses or not. If she does confess, her guilt is clear and she is executed... If she refuses to confess, torture is repeated up to four times... Since she has been arrested, she must be guilty...'* A complete collection of court records from Alsace from 1607 to 1675, occupying some 550 folios, is in Cornell University Library. SOURCE: *The Encyclopedia of Witchcraft & Demonology*, Rossell Hope Robbins.

Confucianism: Confucius (550–480BCE), or Kung Fu-tze, was a sage whose teaching underlies much of the traditional Chinese view of the **Universe**, the gods and human morality. After his death, a cult developed with shrines dedicated to him in a large number of temples, notably those in the administrative centers. SOURCE: *Analects*, Confucius; *Eastern Religions*, ed Michael D. Coogan; *The World's Religions*, Ninian Smart.

Conjunctio: An alchemical marriage; a joining or conjunction or fusion on different levels.

Conjuration: The method of raising demons or spirits in ritual or ceremonial magic. SOURCE: *Dictionary of Demons*, Fred Gettings.

Connecticut Witchcraft: Trials for witchcraft in America were generally spasmodic and fuelled by the Puritans, who had brought the belief in witches over with the early settlers. In total there were only nine executions for witchcraft between 1647 and 1662.

Consanguine: (1) Related by blood; of the same family descent. (2) Witches from the same family or clan (see **Hereditary**).

Consecration: The act of sanctifying an item required for magical use after it has been psychically cleansed. SOURCE: *Witchcraft – A Tradition Renewed*, Evan John Jones; *Mean Streets Witchcraft*, Mélusine Draco.

Constellations: see **Astronomy**.

Consus: In the Roman religion, an ancient god of agriculture and the underworld. His feast day was celebrated on 21st August in a harvest ceremony that took place underground. Consus was also associated with horses; there were chariot races at the *Consuālia*, and horses had a holiday on that day and were crowned with flowers. There was another festival of Consus on 15th December.

Consuālia: The day sacred to **Consus** and a day for special religious observance.

Contact: To get on one's contact(s) is to tune in to an altered state of consciousness prior to proceeding with a magic working. Some people can achieve this automatically, while others require a period of ritual preparation.

Contemplation: Holding an idea in the mind and fixing mental attention on it. In ancient times it referred to the Roman **Augur** who marked out with his wand the space (*templum*) in the heavens he intended to consult. The watching of the *templum* was called contemplating.

Copernicanism: The doctrine that the earth moves round the sun, in opposition to the doctrine that the sun moves round the earth. So called after the Prussian astronomer Nicholas Copernicus (1473–1543).

Coral: Believed by the Roman soothsayers to be a charm against lightning, whirlwind, shipwreck and fire. **Paracelsus** wrote that it should be worn around the neck of children as a preservative against 'fits, sorcery, charms and poison.' It was also believed to be effective in counteracting witchcraft and the **Evil Eye**, as Reginald Scot (1584) observed: '*The coral preserveth such as bear it from fascination or bewitching…*'

Cord or **Cingulum:** Part of the personal regalia of the witch or magician, and often used to mark the rank or degree of the wearer. Colors used for degrees within any group are only effective within that group or Order, and will bear no weight or authority within any other. SOURCE: *Witchcraft – A Tradition Renewed*, Evan John Jones; *Mastering Witchcraft*, Paul Huson.

Cord Magic: Spellcasting by the use of different colored or knotted cords.

Coriander: Grind the seeds and add them to love potions; fume them for working charms. Not listed or assigned a ruling planet by **Culpeper**.

Cormorant: A black seabird that has frequently been identified with Satan and, even if not exactly satanic, they have been considered bad news when sighted inland. On the plus side, there are numerous medicinal uses attributed to the 'sea-raven'.

Corn: Wheat was grown in the Middle East some 7,000 years ago and was known in Northern Europe as early as 1000BC. With its cultivation grew up the concept of a spirit or goddess living within the corn plant who must be kept alive from harvest time until next year's sowing to guarantee the renewal of the crop. An important ingredient of autumnal witchcraft rituals. SOURCE: *Ask the Fellows Who Cut the Hay*, George Ewart Evans; *A Witch's Treasury of the Countryside*, Mélusine Draco. .

Corn Dolly: An image made from the last corn to be cut at harvest time. This is kept in the house or barn over winter and ceremonially burnt and buried in the field at sowing time. In this manner the 'corn spirit' survived from one harvest to another and ensured the fertility of the soil in the spring.

Cornflower or **Hurt-sickle:** An infusion of the flowers was used for digestive and gastric disorders and to produce a lotion for tired eyes. **Culpeper** said that the juice put into fresh or 'green' wounds sealed the edges and was effective in healing sores and ulcers in the mouth. Ruling planet: **Saturn**.

Cornell University Library: The Witchcraft Collection contains over 3000 titles documenting the history of the **Inquisition** and the persecution of witchcraft in Europe. Although some of the books in the Witchcraft Collection can be found online in the Library Catalogue, most of the records have not yet been converted to electronic form.

Cornish Museum: Housed in one of the few remaining old fish-storage cellars in Looe, the museum illustrates the life and culture of Cornwall. The collection includes Cornish arts and crafts, local history and folklore, mining and fishing, games and pastimes, and literature. There is also a collection of charms and relics of Cornish witchcraft and superstitions.

Cornucopia: Taken from the Latin 'horn of plenty'. This is generally shown as a twisted horn overflowing with fruit and flowers, a symbol of abundance and prosperity.

Coronation Stone: (1) Seven Saxon kings were crowned at Kingston upon Thames during the 10th century, and the traditional coronation stone (King's Stone) now stands in front of the guildhall. (2) The Scottish coronation stone or Stone of Scone was seized by Edward I in 1297 and since the reign of Edward II all but two English sovereigns have been crowned on the coronation chair in Westminster Abbey. The chair is made of English oak and designed specifically to hold the Stone.

Corpse: Almost any object that has had contact with a corpse can be used in charms. Especially efficient are the garments of a corpse, or a candle that burned before it; parts of the body are even more effective.

Corpse Candle: (1) The *ignis fatuus*, so called by the Welsh because it was supposed to foretell death, and to show the road that the corpse would take. (2) Also refers to a large candle used at lich wakes – watching over a corpse prior to interment.

Correspondences: The ritual magic system of co-relating perfumes, colors, incenses, gemstones, images, symbols, etc, with deities representing the qualities, or magical energies of which the magician wishes to make use. SOURCE: *Liber 777*, Aleister Crowley; *The Magical Arts*, Richard Cavendish; *Magic: A Occult Primer*, David Conway; *What You Call Time*, Suzanne Ruthven.

Corvinus: All members of the crow family – rooks, ravens, crows, choughs, jays, magpies and jackdaws – have been regarded as magical probably due to their intelligence and cunning. In folklore most of the birds carry a sinister reputation and possibly second only to the **Raven**, the **Magpie** has attracted pagan or devilish significance.

Coscinomancy: This method was chronicled in the Old Testament for proving guilt or innocence using a sieve and a pair of scissors or shears.

Cosmic Axis: see **Axis Mundi.**

Cosmic Consciousness: A term coined by psychologist R.M. Bucke in 1901 to describe the ecstatic experience of illumination, giving an insight into the meaning of the universe.

Cosmic Egg: In Hermopolitan mythology the eight original beings deposited an egg on an island in the primordial waters, from which sprung the sun god, who began the work of creation. Around 600BC the Greek writer Epimenides mentioned the belief and the concept spread to Greece. SOURCE: *The Inner Guide to Egypt*, Billie Walker-John and Alan Richardson.

Cosmic Law: The ancient Greeks and Egyptians believed that the universe was ordered and that cosmic order identified with justice was a fundamental concept. SOURCE: *Supernature*, Lyall Watson.

Cosmogony: The theory of how the **Universe** was created; 'cosmos' meaning the Universe as an ordered whole. The great variety of **Creation Myths** can be divided into two groups – myths which were speculative accounts of how things came to be, and ritual creation-myths where essential elements of the ceremonies were meant to ensure the prosperity and stability of the people.

Cosmology: The study of the universe as an orderly whole, in which the magician looks upon the gods and deities as *symbols* of both the personality and aspiration with both positive and negative qualities. SOURCE: *The Ancient Gods*, E.O. James; *Starchild*, Mélusine Draco; *The Penguin Dictionary of Religions*, ed John R. Hinnells.

Cosmos: Order; universe. Cosmogonic myths later developed into **Theogonies**.

Country Lore: Relates to the superstitions, folklore, weather lore, farming customs, animal behavior and natural-history of the countryside. This knowledge is also an important element of witch-lore and the natural witch is as much part of the fields and hedgerows as the gamekeeper and the farmer. A considerable amount of esoteric information can be discovered in books written by genuine countrymen and women who are not necessarily connected to Craft. SOURCE: *The Making of the English Landscape*, W.G. Hoskins; *A Natural History of Man in Britain*, H.J. Fleure and M. Davies; *The Pattern Under the Plough*, George Ewart Evans; *Root & Branch*, Mélusine Draco. ; *Superstitions of the Countryside*, E & M A Radford; *A Witch's Treasury of the Countryside*, Mélusine Draco; *A Witch's Treasury of Hearth & Garden*, Gabrielle Sidonie.

Country Remedies: see **Folk Medicine**.

Coven, Covine: The name for a formal grouping of witches. Traditionally the coven is said to number 13, but many groups work with many more, or even as few as three or four. SOURCE: *What You Call Time*, Suzanne Ruthven; *Witchcraft – a Tradition Renewed*, Evan John Jones; *Coven Working*, Philip Wright & Carrie West; *Mastering Witchcraft*, Paul Huson.

Covenstead: The place where coven meetings are held.

Cowan: The term given to a non-initiate in traditional witchcraft; one who is not permitted to participate or observe any magical workings or inner circle activities. Cowans may be invited to join in seasonal or families celebrations but they are not recognized as members of the group or coven.

Cowslip: Listed by **Aelfric**, the plant has numerous medicinal and culinary uses. Commenting on the herb's reputation as a wrinkle-removing cream, **Culpeper** said that '*our city dames know well enough the ointment or distilled water of it adds to beauty, or at least restores it when it is lost*'. Ruling planet: **Venus** in **Aries**.

Crab: (1) The claws of a crab are used as a fertility charm, or to ward off the Evil Eye. Broken crab shell mixed in the food or drink of a former lover will harm their marriage. (2) The crab is the sign of **Cancer** in the zodiac.

Crab-apple: A native of Britain, the fermented juice (or **Verjuice**) was recommended for scalds and sprains. The wood was highly valued for fine carving and wood-engraving. One of the **Nine Sacred Herbs** of the Anglo-

Saxons. Ruling planet: **Venus**.

Cramp Rings: A circlet of stones, bones or beads worn to ward off cramp or epilepsy during the Middle Ages. Sometimes made from the handles, screws or nails from a coffin. The custom survived from the time of Edward the Confessor (1003–66) well into the 16th century, whereby the monarch was credited with the power to charge them with healing properties.

Craft: The generic term for witchcraft *per se*. A Crafter is one who practices witchcraft.

Creation Myths: One of the most enduring themes in primitive belief that have extended down to the present day. The early Egyptians believed that in the beginning the universe was filled with a primordial ocean called Nun, that had no surface and completely filled the universe. In North American Indian mythology it is one of the major themes. SOURCE: *Creation Myth*, R.J. Stewart; *Starchild*, Mélusine Draco *The Penguin Dictionary of Religions*, ed John R. Hinnells.

Creed: A summary of the articles or set of principles of religious belief.

Cremation: (1) In antiquity this method of disposing of the dead ranks only second to earth burial. (2) Burning an animal was a way of offering it to a god, the rising smell and smoke being thought to carry the essence of the sacrifice up to the god.

Crescent: The shape of the waxing moon and by association a symbol of increasing power, it is often used as the emblem of deities connected with the **Moon**. A 'horned' moon, i.e. when the new moon appears to be lying on its back with the horns pointing upwards, is a symbol of growth and fertility.

Cressing Temple, Essex: The manor was given to the Knights Templar in 1135, and was their earliest English possession.

Critomancy: Divination by studying grain or flour to predict the future.

Crone: (1) The 'wise' aspect of the goddess, but more appropriately, (2) in modern Craft, a female **Elder** of a Coven who is passed child-bearing age, i.e. post-menopausal.

Crook: The hooked staff of a shepherd, and a symbol of divine kingship in ancient Egypt, where it was specifically part of the ritual regalia of Osiris [i.e. crook and flail].

Crop Circles: A meteorological phenomena 'distinguished by the forced descent of a spinning volume of air, which leads to a spiral-centered circular mark on the ground or in a standing crop' and which are to be found in certain circle-prone areas. SOURCE: *The Goddess of the Stones*, George Terence Meaden.

Cross: An esoteric symbol that is much older than Christianity and found all over the world in different faiths and cultures, from ancient times to the present day. In metaphysical terms the equal-arm cross represents the world, the sun, fire and life. There are twelve types of cross in heraldry.

Crossroads: There appears to be a universal belief that the place where roads meet is a magnet for ghosts and evil powers, and the bodies of criminals were often hung at crossroad gibbets. In folklore and witch-trials this connection apparently made the crossroads a suitable place of witches' meetings, for making pacts with the

Devil and for purposes of **Black Magic**. SOURCE: *The Masque of Queens*, Ben Jonson.

Crow: The distinctive crow family (which includes the **Raven**) have featured in myths and legends from across the world, possibly because of their close association with death. The raven's habit of picking out the eyes from a corpse before pecking at the flesh was commented on by the Athenian poet, Aristophanes (448–380BCE), in *The Birds*. In Welsh folklore, however, it is believed that blind people showing kindness to ravens will regain their sight (see **Corvinus**). SOURCE: *The Folklore of Birds*, E.A. Armstrong.

Crowland: An abbey founded in Lincolnshire in 716 by King Ethelbald; it has been destroyed and rebuilt on numerous occasions. Hereward the Wake, the 'Last of the English' is said to be buried there.

Crowley, Aleister: Probably the most famous occultist of the 20th century and considered by those who understand his work as a magical genius. A prolific writer, most of Crowley's writing is based on the belief and philosophy of Thelema, a startling new vision of personal spiritual development. SOURCE: *Bibliography of the Works of Aleister Crowley*, G.J. Yorke; *The Confessions of Aleister Crowley*, *Moonchild* (a novel), *Magick Without Tears*, Aleister Crowley; *Aleister Crowley, The Black Magician*, C.R. Cammell; *Eye in the Triangle*, Israel Regardie; *The Legend of Aleister Crowley*, Regardie and Stephensen; *Selected Poems*, edited by Martin Booth; *The Thelemic Handbook* and *Starchild*, Mélusine Draco.

Crowley, Vivienne: A prominent Wiccan author whose work has helped further understanding between paganism and mainstream religions. She was initiated into Alex **Sander's** coven and when the group underwent drastic changes following the Sanders' separation, she left and joined a **Gardnerian** coven. She and her husband established their own coven in 1979, which they have maintained to the present day. In 2002 Dr. Crowley was appointed as a visiting tutor at the leading Jesuit university faculty, Heythrop College. Her books include *Wicca: The Old Religion in the New Millennium*; *Principles of Wicca*; *Principles of Paganism*, *A Woman's Guide to the Earth Traditions*, *A Woman's Kabbalah*, *Your Dark Side* (with Christopher Crowley).

Crowther, Patricia: Recognized as the Grand Dame of British **Wicca**, having been initiated into the Craft in 1960 by Gerald **Gardner**, to whom she was introduced by her husband, Arnold. The Crowthers were sought after by the media and became frequent guests on radio and television, writing articles for numerous periodicals such as *Prediction* and *The Lamp of Thoth*. Arnold Crowther died in 1974 at Beltaine. Her writings include *Lid Off the Cauldron*, *Witch Blood!*, *One Witch's World*, *High Priestess*. SOURCE: *The Old Sod*, Alan Richardson.

Crystal: Most crystals form when heat deep inside the Earth melts minerals in rocks. The minerals cool and harden into crystals, which are evenly shaped because they are made of tiny atoms that arrange themselves in the same regular way as the crystal grows (see **Lapidary**).

Crystal Gazing: Skrying by looking

into a ball of rock crystal; also used to communicate with spirits, as by Dr John **Dee** in the 16th century.

Crystallomancy: Casting lots using small stones or crystals. Not to be confused with **Crystalomancy**, which refers to the images received by gazing into a crystal ball.

Crystalomancy: see **Crystal Gazing**

Curandero: A Mexican medicine man, who is best known for his cures and beneficial spells, although he is capable of cursing. Among the tribes who use hallucinogenic agents, the *curandero* presides at initiation ceremonies.

Cú Chulainn: The central character in a collection of early Irish stories, known as the Ulster Cycle. The Celts venerated god and hero, with the latter possessing many of the qualities of the former. Cú Chulainn is the supreme example of the ideal Celtic hero.

Cuckoo: The loud call of the cuckoo heralding the arrival of spring is of great importance in folklore and **Augury**. There are many tales of cuckoos being linked to country fairs and nearly every country has its sayings and beliefs related to the hearing of the first cuckoo of the year.

Culpeper, Nicholas: (1616–1654) Studied at Cambridge and became an apothecary, physician and astrologer in London. His *Complete Herbal & English Physician* offers remedies for all ills known to 17th century society and is still in print today. He used astrology as part of his remedies and assigned each plant a ruling planet. SOURCE: *Culpeper's Medicine*, Graeme Tobyn; *Culpeper's Colour Herbal*, ed David Potterton.

Cult: An unorthodox religion usually linked to excessive admiration for a person or idea. SOURCE: *The New Believers*, David V. Barrett.

Cult of the Dead: The impulse to forge a link between the living and the dead by means of rites and offerings (see **Ancestor Worship**).

Culture Hero: A figure that provides a link between the primordial time of beginning (e.g. the golden age of the past) and the present human condition.

Cunning Man or **Woman:** The name given to the solitary witch or charmer, who possesses natural psychic and healing powers. They provide cures, remedies, charms, spells and divination for people in their locality, usually in exchange for a small 'gift'. This practice is as old as English folklore and the name comes from the Old English term *kenning* or *cunnan*, meaning 'to know', and under any name they were a regular feature of village and small town life for centuries. SOURCE: *Witches & Neighbours*, Robin Briggs.

Cunningham, Scott: Remembered as a prolific Wiccan author with a vast knowledge of **'Earth Mysteries'** – including herbalism, earth power, crystals, gems and metals. He claimed to have been initiated into several covens of various traditions but eventually opted to remain a solitary. He viewed **Wicca** as a modern religion, created in the 20th century and although it incorporated elements of European folklore, it was not a continuation of the ancient beliefs. His books include *Magical Herbalism, Earth Power: Techniques of Natural Magic, Cunningham's Encyclopedia of Crystal, Gem and Metal Magic.*

Cup Marks: The archeological term for the cup-like impressions made in prehistoric times in the huge blocks of Neolithic monuments. Because of the uniformity of the rings, it is believed that they had ritual or symbolic use.

Curlew: The 'call of the curlew' has been labeled the most wonderful wild sound in Britain and best heard on the high summer moorlands where the sound drifts across the heather. Like the barnacle geese, the curlew is sometimes identified with the **Gabriel** or Wish Hounds, and the **Wild Hunt**. Country people believe them to be weird and uncanny birds, linked with the supernatural.

Curse: In magical terms, a curse is a spell or hex placed on someone for revenge, retribution or sometimes merely for spite. Some believe that a curse can be placed and removed once it has achieved its purpose; while others will say that once 'fixed' a curse is permanent. Curses are the result of a *deliberate* ritual preparation or a public gesture; or they can be made silently with no word spoken or sign given. Ill-wishing, on the other hand, can be equally as harmful and sent by those with no magical ability whatsoever and the Christian rite of 'bell, book and candle' is a curse placed by the clergy. The Romans called a curse a *devotion* i.e. given up to someone of the gods. SOURCE: *Magic: An Occult Primer*, David Conway; *Religion and the Decline of Magic*, Keith Thomas; *Structural Anthropology*, Claude Lévi-Strauss; *Witchcraft – A Tradition Renewed*, Evan John Jones; *Phases in the Religion of Ancient Rome*, Cyril Bailey.

Cursing Well: The famous well at Llaneilian-yn-Rhos in Denbigh. To bring misfortune on an enemy, it was necessary to write his or her name on a piece of paper and give it to the custodian, who, for a small consideration, wrapped the paper around a stone and dropped it in to the water. It was believed the curse would only be effective as long as the paper survived in the well. In 1929 the well was covered over.

Cwn Annwn: Ghostly Welsh hounds that were portents of death. The curious thing about them was that as they came closer, their cries grew fainter, while at a distance their full-bloodied baying was charged with grief. They are described as being white with red ears, identical to the English **Gabriel Hounds**.

Cybele: Originally the 'Great Goddess of Nature' in Anatolia (modern Turkey) with her son/consort/lover, Attis – although as figures of classical mythology they are best known from the literature of Roman times. The cult and myth of Cybele originated with the Phrygians who entered Anatolia from Thrace in the 13th century BC. Although there was a temple dedicated to Cybele on the Capitol in Rome, and she was honored as a protective deity with the festival the *Megalensia*, '*in spite of its magical efficacy the cult with its rites was found scandalous in Rome, so that it was insulated with special rules. No Roman was permitted to join directly in its rites, still less serve as a priest* (Man, Myth & Magic).' SOURCE: *The Golden Bough*, Sir James Frazer; *Julian*, Gore Vidal.

Cycle: A period or series of events or numbers that recur everlastingly in precisely the same order.

Cyclomancy: Divination using a wheel

or revolving circle to foretell the future
(see **Wheel of Fortune**).

Cylicomancy: Divination using a small
bowl of water with a few drops of oil
poured into it.

"Learn about a pine tree from a pine tree, and about a bamboo plant from a bamboo."

Basho

[Japanese poet – 1644-94]

D

Daäth: The 'hidden' sephirah of the Tree of Life and represents conceptual knowledge, as opposed to Absolute Knowledge. It is the invisible sphere between the Supernal and Ethical Triangles in what is commonly referred to as the **Abyss**. The **Names of Power** are the primordial or otherworld deities and the planetary attribution is sometimes attributed to **Uranus**.

Dactyl: Mythical beings credited with the discovery of iron. There were originally three – the Smelter, the Hammer and the Anvil; this was later increased to five males and five females – i.e. dactyls or fingers. An important concept in traditional Old Craft.

Dactylomancy: Using a small tripod that moves around a board on which the alphabet is inscribed in order to answer questions. **Ouija Boards** are a modern version.

Dactyomancy: Divination using a finger ring suspended on a hair or thread over a circle of letters from the alphabet. This method of foretelling the future was first recorded as being used by **Pythagoras** around 540BC.

Daemon or **Daimon:** Powers or spirits which, in an early stage of Greek religion, were thought to people the world, occupying trees, rivers, springs, mountains, giving rise to everything that affects man. In Homer, *daemōn* is divine power generalized, not individualized in a particular deity. Later it became a beneficent personal spirit or guardian, or another term for a **Holy Guardian Angel**, which can act as an intermediary between gods and man. It was also the name by which Socrates called his genius, or the spirit within him. The word only took on a disparaging connotation in later **Demonology**. SOURCE: *The Oxford Companion to Classical Literature*, ed Sir Paul Harvey.

***Daemonologie*:** see **James I.**

Daffodil: Herrick's poem 'Divination by a Daffodil' (*Hesperides* 1648) belies the cheerful image of the flower as a welcome sign of spring, since it appears that the drooping head of the flower is a death omen.

Dagda or **Dagde:** (1) An Old Irish deity whose name means 'the good god'. He occupies a predominant position in the **Tuatha De Danann**. He is the god of contracts, and equipped with three attributes: a mighty club that slays and restores life; a magic harp and a cooking pot from which no one is turned away hungry. (2) Effigy used for spellcasting. SOURCE: *Dictionary of Devils and Demons*, Tondriau and Villeneuve; *The Dictionary of Gods and Goddesses, Devils and Demons*, Manfred Lurker.

Dagger: see **Knife.**

Dagyde: A witch's image-needle or pin.

Daimonia: Popular belief held them to be personal guardian spirits but became the name given in the 11th century to pagan idols and supposedly evil or sinister animals. Originally it was a Jewish translation from Greek chronicles; Catholic theologians later claimed that it meant all the gods of the Gentiles (*omnes dei gentium*) were demons. In Greek philosophy, *daimonion* came to mean the divine spark in man.

Daisy or **Bruisewort:** 'Daisy' is thought to derive from the Old English words for days and eve, or day's eye because it closes its petals at night. The plant was used in ointments to heal wounds and bruises, and all sorts of aches and pains. **Gerard** said that the juice of the leaves and roots, *'given to little dogs with milk, keepeth them from growing great.'* Ruling planet: **Venus** in **Cancer**.

Dakini: (1) The chief female hierophants among Tantrics who were often old crones of revolting ugliness. (2) On a mystical level this refers to the *shaktis*, or subconscious powers that manifest to the **Adept** in the course of his rites in the form of terrifying female demons.

Dakshina Marg: [Sanskrit] *Dakshina* – 'right'; *Marg* – 'path' is the Path of the Sun, as *Vama Marg*, the Left-Hand Path, is that of the Moon.

Daktyloi: [Greek *daktylos* = finger] In Greek tradition, demonic beings who discovered the art of metal working, who were indigenous to Asia Minor and Crete. A distinction is often made between right-hand *daktyloi*, who worked as smiths, and left-hand daktyloi, who were active as sorcerers and magicians (see **Dactyl**).

Dame: The archaic term for the female leader of a coven, still extant in Old Craft.

Damned: Those people condemned to damnation. A list of the famous damned can be found in the *Aeneid* of Virgil and also in Dante's *Inferno*.

Damnum Minatum: The threat of harm to a person made by a witch or sorceress. Any resulting injury to the person (*malum secutum*) was attributed to it.

Damson: In England the tree was commonly found growing wild in woods, thickets and hedges. An infusion of the flowers was prescribed as a mild purgative; the roots to check bleeding and lower fevers; while the gin from the fruit, because of its astringency, was recommended for diarrhea. Ruling planet: **Venus**.

Dana: see **Ana**.

Dance: Ritual dancing has been a significant form of religious expression in hunting and fertility rites from ancient times. While Westerners generally regard dancing as a pastime, many other people still use this as a form of prayer or magical energy building since behind many ritual dances is the belief that it is through the dance that man speaks directly to his gods. Among the Egyptians, Greeks and Romans, dancing was largely ceremonial and associated with religion, and they had a low opinion of dancing for other purposes. Perhaps one of the most effective pieces of music to evoke primitive senses is Stravinsky's *Rite of Spring*. SOURCE: *The Ancient Egyptians*, J. Gardner Wilkinson; *Dance in Society*, F. Ruse; *England's Dances*, D. Kennedy; *World History of the Dance*, C. Sachs.

Dancing the Mill: The ritual **Circle** dance within traditional witchcraft to raise power for magical working.

Dance of Death or **Danse Macabre:** An allegorical representation of **Death** leading all men and women inevitably to the grave and was a popular theme in late medieval art, following the plague years. This is reflected in the death-cult architecture of the medieval and Victorian periods of history. SOURCE: *The Dance of Death in the Middle Ages &*

the Renaissance, J.M. Clark.

Dance of St. Vitus: An illness characterized by convulsive and frequent movements. As with epilepsy (convulsions with loss of consciousness) and such illnesses as those known as 'sacred sickness', 'divine sickness', 'comitial sickness' (the latter known in ancient Rome). These complaints were often associated with divine or magical interference although St. Vitus' Dance is now known to be poisoning caused by ergot poisoning from eating bread made of diseased rye.

Dandelion: Recommended as a cure for numerous ailments and to cleanse the kidneys and bladder. The latter giving rise to the belief that picking the plant caused bed-wetting and subsequently known as 'pissabed'. Ruling planet: **Jupiter.**

Dante (Dante Alighieri): The Italian poet who gave us *The Divine Comedy* and the concept of the 'Ten Circles of Hell' and the earthly stations of those consigned to them.

Daoine sidhe: In Irish folklore, the remains of the divine fairy race, the **Tuatha de Danaan**, who were forced to take refuge in the hills after the country was conquered by the Celts.

Daphnomancy: Divination using the smoke from burning laurel branches. This is known today to have a hallucinogenic effect on those inhaling the smoke.

Dark Matter: The main constituent of the universe. No one knows what it is! SOURCE: *First Light,* Richard Preston.

Dark Night of the Soul: A stage on the road to spiritual enlightenment, characterized by depression, disbelief, uncertainty and a feeling of personal worthlessness. The experience usually precedes relevation and understanding.

Dark Orders, The: A shadowy brotherhood of magical practitioners, or the complete antithesis of the 'White Brotherhood'.

Dark Time: The moonless time of the month.

Darshana: One of the six salvation-philosophies of classical Hinduism, literally meaning 'insight'.

Dashwood, Sir Francis: see Hell-Fire Club.

Davy Jones' Locker: A sailor's term for the evil spirit of the sea, first recorded in the 18th century; his Locker is the bottom of the sea, and to go there is to be drowned or buried at sea.

Days: The belief that particular days are unlucky or lucky is universal. In antiquity, the Egyptian, Jews, Greeks and Romans all had complex systems that identified specific days, or mapped out an entire year, assigning each day as being lucky or unlucky. This notion was certainly known in Saxon times, and medieval calendars also identified days as good or bad. SOURCE: *The Egyptian Book of Days,* Mélusine Draco; *The Roman Book of Days,* Paulina Erina; *Chambers Book of Days.*

Dead Man's Hill: In March 1963 and on **Midsummer Eve** 1969 local people found what appeared to be evidence of a **Black Mass** in the gaunt and eerie ruins of St. Mary's church on Dead Man's Hill, near Clophill in Bedfordshire. An 18th century tomb had been desecrated and the bones arranged in a circle in the gutted nave of the church. On the second occasion, other tombs were smashed and graves desecrated. The national press had a field day and added fuel to the 1960s **Anti-occult Campaign**.

Dead Man's Hand: A widespread belief held that a certain cure for skin complaints was to stroke the affected place with a corpse's hand. In most cases, the hand of an executed criminal or suicide was preferred! SOURCE: *The Penguin Guide to the Superstitions of Britain and Ireland*, Steve Roud.

Dead Man's Teeth: Used to negate evil spells and particularly to untie the **Aglet**, or make oneself invisible.

Deadnettle: see **Archangel, White.**

Death: (1) There are numerous superstitions and omens connected to a person dying. (2) The thirteen card in the **Major Arcana** of the **Tarot** and the archetypal symbol of Passing from one stage to another; the universal link between material and spiritual.

Death Cults: As *Man, Myth & Magic* points out, the appeasing of ancestors by human sacrifice is a far cry from Poet's Corner in Westminster Abbey, or the Lenin mausoleum in Moscow but the basis for all these is the same – the impulse to forge a link between the living and the dead. There is also an identifiable link between the Osirian cult of the ancient Egyptians and the obsessive Victorian funerary practices of the late 1800s. SOURCE: *The Ancient Gods*, E.O. James; *The Egyptian Revival*, James Stevens Curl; *The Secret Lore of Egypt; Its Impact on the West*, Erik Hornung.

Decan: A segment of ten degrees in a circle divided into 36 segments, according to the cosmic system of the Babylonians and the Egyptians. The original 36 decans were an Egyptian concept of deities who ruled over the different sections of the zodiac: three decans per star sign.

Dedication: A ritual carried out either by an individual, or as part of a group rite, in which a person dedicates themselves to a particular deity, **Path** or **Tradition**. Usually undertaken prior to **Initiation** but this can differ from group to group.

Dee, Dr. John: One of the most remarkable scholars of his time. An authority on mathematics, navigation, astronomy and optics, he was also Astrologer Royal to Elizabeth I. Employed in the Queen's secret service, it is impossible to say how far his magical activities were a cover for espionage but it was the dividing line between science and the occult that Dee found fascinating. During his travels across Europe he collected an assortment of manuscripts, and many of his own personal writings are preserved in The **British Museum**. With his medium and skryer, Edward **Kelley**, he 'discovered' a new angelic language (see **Enochian**), which earned him a reputation of trafficking with demons. SOURCE: *Alchemy: An Illustrated A-Z*, Diana Fernando; *Elizabethan Magic*, Robert Turner; *The Enochian Magic of Dr John Dee*, Geoffrey James; *The Life of John Dee*, trans W.A. Ayton; *The Occult Philosophy in the Elizabethan Age*, Frances A. Yates; *The Queen's Conjuror*, Benjamin Woolley; *The Secrets of John Dee*, Gordon James.

Deer: Parts of a deer are frequently called for in magical potions and as a powerful protection against danger and bad luck; brings good luck in sport, games and war. Carry a piece of antler as a good luck charm.

Degree: Stages of **Initiation** in some ritual magic and witchcraft traditions, mostly based on Masonic rites.

Deism: A natural religion without revelation, or the belief that the study of **Nature** and the exercise of reason are better guides to the existence of God than the study of sacred scriptures. Deists dislike formal religious observance, ritual and hierarchy, and believe that all the major religions contain the same message. Believes there is a God, but does not believe in any superintendence and government, and thinks the Creator implanted in all things certain immutable laws, called the Laws of Nature, which act without the supervision of its maker. Like the **Theist**, does not believe in the doctrine of the **Trinity**, or in divine revelation. Many elements of witchcraft could fall under this banner.

Deities: Powerful supernatural beings (gods and goddesses) who are, or who have been worshipped or honored throughout the ages in the religions and belief systems of nearly every culture.

Déjà vu: The sensation of having previously experienced a present situation.

Delphi: The site of the most influential oracle of the ancient world. At the Temple of **Apollo** on Mount Parnassus, the Delphic Oracle was delivered by the priestess (the Pythia), who was seated on a tripod over a fissure in the rock. SOURCE: *The Oxford Companion to Classical Literature*, ed Sir Paul Harvey.

de Lubicz, R.A. Schwaller: Philosopher and mathematician who spent 30 years studying hermetic wisdom, followed by 15 years studying the Temple of Luxor before developing the theory that the ancient Egyptians had a very sophisticated understanding of metaphysics and universal laws.

Deluge, The: A universal myth of a great flood that destroyed mankind that can be found in numerous cultures – ancient and modern – from all around the world.

Dema deities: The label for a category coined by A.E. Jensen for the mythical, primeval beings who are revered in primitive cultures as occupying a midway position between gods and men. SOURCE: *The Dictionary of Gods and Goddesses, Devils and Demons*, Manfred Lurker; *The Dictionary of Religions*, ed John R. Hinnells.

De Materia Medica: Written about 64AD by Pedanius Dioscorides (a doctor in the Roman army) and listing over 500 plants, it became the principal and most influential source of Western herbal knowledge for over 1500 years. The earliest surviving copy, usually called the *Codex Vindobonensis*, was written and illustrated in about 512AD at Constantinople. In addition to being a milestone in botanical art, it is the earliest surviving illustrated herbal in the Western world.

Demeter: Greek goddess of the fertile soil and agriculture whose influences can be strongly detected in contemporary **Wicca**. The most important festivals held in her name were those ceremonies of initiation known as '**Mysteries**' – the most influential being the Mysteries of **Eleusis**.

Demiurge: The Creator of the Universe in Plato's *Timaeus*, and in Gnosticism the subordinate supernatural power but not the same as the supreme God.

Demonology: The study of demons is more often than not treated as a complement of witchcraft or ritual magic, and it is evident from the early texts that the theologians believed in such creatures that had to be dealt with by exorcism. SOURCE: *The Book of Black Magic & of Pacts*, A.E. Waite; *Dictionary of Demons*, Fred Gettings; *Dictionary of Gods & Goddesses, Devils & Demons*, Manfred Lurker; *The Encyclopedia of Witchcraft & Demonology*, Rossell Hope Robbins.

Demons: Often equated with evil spirits, although more often than not they are the personal guardians of humans and do not have the malevolence or negative aspects made popular by 'demonologists'. Many 'occult' names have derived from the literary sources of John Milton and Dante. SOURCE: *The Book of Black Magic & of Pacts*, A.E. Waite; *Commedia*, Dante Alighieri; *Dictionnaire Infernal*, Collin de Plancy; *A Dictionary of Devils & Demons*, J. Tondriau and R. Villeneuve; *Dictionary of Demons*, Fred Gettings; *Dictionary of Gods & Goddesses, Devils & Demons*, Manfred Lurker; *The Goetia*, Aleister Crowley; *Magic: An Occult Primer*, David Conway; *Paradise Lost* and *Paradise Regained*, John Milton.

Deosil: Moving sun-wise or clockwise around the witches' **Circle**.

De Parma, Anselm: A powerful Italian sorcerer and gifted astrologer c1440; he was the author of *Astrological Institutions*, a classic work in the field of astrology.

Descent of the Goddess: The act of channeling goddess-energy through the **High Priestess** or **Maiden** in Wiccan rites.

Destiny: Also known as **Fate,** it has long been debated by occultists whether destiny may be altered by the will of the individual. Those who believe this to be impossible are called fatalists.

Destroying Angel: The name for a beautiful fungus, *amanita phalloides*, which can cause hallucinations and death if eaten.

Deucalion: After the **Deluge**, he was ordered to cast behind him *the bones of his mother* (i.e. the stones of Mother Earth). Those thrown by Deucaluion became men, and those thrown by his wife Pyrrha became women.

Deva: (1) The general Vedic appellation for what is divine. (2) In **Zoroastrian** belief these are malevolent spirits ruled by the god of darkness. (3) By contrast, in **Theosophy** the term refers to the hierarchy of spirits that help to rule the Universe.

Devel or **Del:** The name given by the gipsies to their highest being – not to be confused with the Christian **Devil** or **Satan.**

Devil: (1) Has come to mean the personification of supreme evil, the foe of the Christian god (see **Lucifer**). The word 'devil' derives from the Greek *diabolos*, originally meaning an accuser. In translating the Old Testament into Greek, the Egyptian Jews of the 3rd century BC used the word *diabolos* for the Hebrew *satan*, an angelic entity whose function was to test men's fidelity to God. By the time the translators got to the New Testament, the Greek word *satanas* was used to mean an adversary against God, not an adversary against man, hence the Devil has no part to play in traditional witchcraft. (2) The fifteenth card in the **Major Arcana** of the **Tarot** and the archetypal symbol of **Pan**, and the force of unbridled **Nature**. SOURCE: *Dictionary of Demons*, Fred Gettings; *A Dictionary of Devils & Demons*, J. Tondriau and R. Villeneuve; *The Encyclopedia of Witchcraft & Demonology*, Rossell Hope Robbins; *Malleus Satani: The Hammer of Satan*, Suzanne Ruthven.

Devil's Arrows: Three great standing stones in a straight line, spaced 200ft and 370ft apart at Boroughbridge in Yorkshire. They stand between 18 and 22 ft high and were brought, as the stone shows, from a quarry at Knaresborough 6½ miles away. They were erected in the Bronze Age and the irregular surfaces are due to weathering.

Devil's Coach Horse: A large black beetle that turns up its tail in an almost scorpion-like attitude of aggression. It is often regarded as a symbol of corruption, and if anyone had dealings with and took money from the Devil, it was said that the beetle would appear in the hand.

Devil's Dictionary, The: Ambrose Bierce introduced satirical definitions into his weekly newspaper columns in 1875, under the heading *The Demon's Dictionary*. One of the most influential of American journalists, he ventured into revolution-torn Mexico and was never heard from again. The collection was reprinted by Dover in 1993.

Devil's Door: The north door in a church that was not used by the congregation, but which was opened at baptisms and communions to let the devil out.

Devil's Dyke: A remarkable 7th century bank and ditch that runs across country for some 7½ miles, straddling the

Icknield Way, a prehistoric trackway that had served East Anglia for more than 2000 years. One end of the Dyke rests on the Fen-edge and the other would originally have reached virgin forest in the Stour basin.

Devil's Mark: A scar or blemish that was said to be the sign of a witch during the late-medieval burning times and called the *stigmata diaboli* or *sigillum diaboli*. In *Laws against Witches and Conjurations*, published in 1645, it stated that witches had an extra teat for suckling a **Familiar**.

Devil Worship: Accusations of devil worship have been leveled at most victims of an opposing religious belief, such as those made against the **Knights Templar, Cathars,** etc, and witches by the Church of Rome.

De virtutibus herbarum: A Latin poem compiled in France in the first half of the 11th century and widely copied by hand throughout Europe. It became the first herbal to be printed in the Western world at Naples in 1477.

Dew Pond: A natural, or sometimes man-made hollow supplied with water by mist. Believed to be places of natural energy. SOURCE: *Mirrors of Magic*, Philip Heselton.

Dharana: [Sanskrit] Concentration of mental energy on one point.

Dharma: Virtue or righteousness arising from observance of social and moral law; truth as laid down in Buddhist scriptures.

Diamond: A brilliant gem that may be used as an amulet to procure fame and fortune, and prevent witchcraft. Because of its hardness it also endows the wearer with strength and invulnerability, and brings victory when worn on the left arm.

Diana: Roman goddess identified with **Artemis**. Her most famous cult, as *Diana Nemorensis* (meaning 'of the grove'), was at Aricia, and although she was especially worshipped by women, she was also associated with the plebian classes and slaves (see **Aradia**).

Dianic: Contemporary all-female covens or groups, devoted solely to worshipping the Roman goddess, Diana as the Great Goddess.

Dian Cecht: In ancient Ireland, the god of healing who could perform miraculous cures. When the god Nuadu lost his hand in battle, Dian Cecht providing him with a silver one.

Di Consentēs: In Roman religion, the twelve great gods, six male and six female, according to two lines taken from Ennius: *Juno, Vesta, Minerva, Ceres, Diana, Venus, Mars, Mercurius, Jovi, Neptunus, Volcanus, Apollo.*

Di Deaeque: Refers to the gods of ancient Rome. These varied widely from the highest (**Jupiter**, chief of the state gods and **Mars**, god of war) down to the protectors of *'specific processes, such as one stage in the growth cycle of corn'*. The correct naming of the Roman deities was important to the successful outcome of supplication, but there were many different formulae to allow for 'extra unknown powers'. SOURCE: *Phases in the Religion of Ancient Rome*, Cyril Bailey.

Dii Penatēs: Roman household gods, and used to describe those household items particularly prized by the lady of the house.

Dill: Its name deriving from the Norse *dilla*, or the Anglo-Saxon *dylle*, both meaning to lull or sooth. Apart from its medicinal and culinary uses, the herb was added to love potions and witch spells; mixed with salt it offers protection against evil spirits when carried, hung or scattered. Ruling planet: **Mercury.**

Dinedor Hill: Site of an Iron Age camp, occupied by the Roman general Ostorius Scalpula, in his campaign against the British chief Caractacus.

Dionysia, The Great: A week-long spring festival in honor of **Dionysus**, which later became the principal occasion for staging new tragedies and comedies. Although Greek drama began largely as an act of worship of Dionysus, the actual plays that developed out of the Dionysian contests had little or nothing to do with, or say, about the god.

Dionysus: Greek god of fertility, wine and drunkenness (see **Bacchus**).

Discarnate entity: An entity with mental attributes that exists independently of a physical body. [SEE PANEL]

Discours des Sorciers: Equally as infamous as the *Malleus Maleficarum*, this text was written by Henri Boquet and published in 1602 in Lyon and in 1605 in Paris; it ran into twelve editions in twenty years. The appendix of this work codifies in seventy articles the statutes and procedures of the witchcraft tribunals. Boquet was the Grand Judge of St. Claude (Jura) who analyzed the powers and marks of witches and the punishments to be afflicted. His influence in France was enormous and his cruelty made him infamous; he is credited to have had more than 600 witches burned in the Burgundy region alone.

Discoverie of Witchcraft, The: A book

written by Reginald Scot (1538–99) in which he claimed that witches were victims of superstitious absurdities. His claims earned him the antipathy of **James I** who was so incensed by Scot's work that he ordered the public executioner to consign every book to the flames. The king wrote his *Daemonologie* 'chiefly against [Scot's] damnable opinions'. *Discoverie* is now comparatively rare as the second edition did not appear until 1651; there is a copy in Cornell University Library.

Disir: [Old Norse; Old High German *idisi*] The collective appellation for deities of fertility and destiny in Germanic mythology. The disir sacrifice (*disablot*) celebrated in the autumn also suggests the cult of the harvest.

Disquisitionum Magicarum: An encyclopedia of witchcraft by the Jesuit scholar Martin Del Rio, and the most complete of all the writing on the subject as the infamous *Malleus Maleficarum*. The *Disquisitionum Magicarum Libri Sex* was written about 1596 and first published in 1599; it was constantly reprinted, and translated into French in 1611. By 1747, when it was last printed, there had been about 20 editions.

Dittany: The famous 'Dittany of Crete' (*origanum dictamnus*) was an ancient wound herb, and in medieval England the names dittany and dittander often referred to the same plant. Dittany is a member of the *Rutaceae* family; Dittander, the *Cruciferae* family and Dittany of Crete, the *labiatae* family. As well as numerous medicinal and culinary uses, the herb often features in magical spells. Ruling planet: **Venus.**

Dius Fidius: Refers to the old Italian religious concept of the 'god of faith', called upon to preserve the sanctity of contracts and human relations.

Divalia: A day sacred to Dia, a goddess venerated in the old Roman calendar on the day called *Brumalia*, the shortest day of the year and a special day for religious observance.

Divination: A method of telling the future by reading the present and encompasses such techniques from **Aeromancy** to **Zoomancy**. Divination has existed in all societies and cultures, often under the auspices of religion, such as the **Delphic Oracle** or the Tibetan state oracles. Some methods are more effective than others, although each person seems to have their own particular approach that brings about satisfactory results. SOURCE: *The Ancient Gods*, E.O. James; *Book of Divining the Future*, Eva Shaw; *The Dictionary of Omens & Superstitions*, Philippa Waring; *The Penguin Dictionary of Religions*, ed John R. Hinnell.

Divining rod: A forked branch of hazel used to locate the presence of underground springs, metal, etc.

Djinn: Supernatural being of Arabic folklore and Islamic tradition; spirits of fire whose favorite abode is the desert.

Dock, Common: The plant was listed by **Aelfric** and has numerous medicinal and culinary uses. **Culpeper** said that all docks 'being boiled with meat, make it boil the sooner'. Ruling planet: **Jupiter**

Doctrine of Signatures: According to this theory, **Nature** labels every plant with a mark to show what it is good for. For example: turmeric, being yellow, was supposed to cure jaundice, while red plants were good for fever and white

Discarnate Entities & Extra-terrestrial Intelligences

What a witch or ritual magician calls upon for magical purposes – deities or gods, demons or angels – they are what we summon to the quarters to protect us, invoke into ourselves to channel magical energy, or act as a Guardian.

The magical practitioner needs to learn to differentiate between the various forms encountered on the astral, but what we should never lose sight of is the fact that these energies can be helpful or harmful; and must be treated with the greatest respect and caution. They are cosmic energies on a very lowly level but are far more powerful than we can ever imagine, and can destroy us if treated in a cavalier manner.

Larvae: An unformed life force, or raw energy that has not yet grown into a tangible spiritual form. Attracted to bursts of psychic energy, particularly from individuals who radiate psychic power without being able to contain it adequately. There is nothing 'evil' about larvae, they behave by instinct, like a psychic leech.

Elementals: There are two basic varieties of elemental. The first is the naturally occurring kind, usually linked to specific natural features e.g. cliffs, lakes, and can sometimes be thought of as guardians of such places. The second is deliberately created by a witch for use as a familiar spirit.

Nature Spirits: Encountered as the guardian of a plant, pool or tree. There are places where it is easier to encounter them, usually where man has not intruded too much into the landscape, or where the land has been left to look after itself.

The Ancestors: Spirits who are part of our universal magical and cultural heritage: these are the 'spirits' the witch or magician will summon as a source of both magical knowledge and additional magical potency; they can be called upon to link the human world to that of the 'gods'.

Qliphoth: Psychic husks of those who were once living. Neither good nor evil; any 'identity' they adopt is a product of the summoner's imagination – often the product of worst nightmares. Although normally associated with ritual magic, a witch will encounter qliphoth and should learn to recognize them.

Psychic Vampires: Can be manifestations from the astral realms but, more often than not, psychic vampires are living humans – crafty, cunning individuals that siphon off energy from unwitting neophytes. Most Adepts will have come across at least one during their years of studying the occult. They can cause extreme fatigue and sickness if the attack is prolonged.

Whatever we wish to call these 'powers' they *do* have the necessary link to the attributes that the magical practitioner strives for in the hopes of finding all s/he seeks. If the invocation (or evocation) is gone about in the right manner, there is no reason why this cannot be achieved – but remember that they are not interested in your development, only their own. Not all will work well for you, and some not at all, so try to understand the different attributes in preparation for your next ritual. It's a case of trial and error at first but whatever happens do not be blasé in your manner of dealing with them, as you may get more than you bargained for. Once summoned, the entity requires *your* energy on which to feed and if you do not keep it under firm control, or forget to close down properly, it may continue to gorge until it manifests into something unpleasant and difficult to banish.

Only by encountering them can the witch or magician learn to differentiate between the positive/negative, active/passive beings that exist out on the other planes. Be careful with your preparations and protections, because for every one that will help, guide and give advice, there are the same number who will hinder, deceive and even harm you, if given the opportunity.

EXTRACT FROM THE ARCANUM FOUNDATION COURSE

ones for rigor.

Dodona: Site of the famous oracle of **Zeus** where the priests interpreted the rustling of the leaves of a sacred **Oak** as the words of the god; they may have also drawn oracles from the sound of the sacred spring in the grove.

Dog: Almost all parts of a dog, particularly the teeth and claws, have magical virtue to counteract witchcraft and keep evil spirits at bay (see **Hounds**).

Dog Hair: Used in a number of folk cures, especially for whooping cough and dog bites. *'Hair of the dog'* now means to take another drink of the same to cure a hangover.

Dog Rose: see **Briar.**

Dog Saliva: Believed to have a curative effect on human wounds and a standard part of British folk medicine for centuries (see **Aralez**).

Dogma: In theology, a tenet or principle of belief stated to be true by the controlling religious body. It is derived from the Greek word for 'an opinion'.

Dogon: A primitive farming people who inhabit the caves in the Hombori Mountains of southern Mali, whose religion is based on accurate scientific information about the dual star system Sirius, impossible to observe without advanced astronomical equipment – and only fully confirmed by professional astronomers in 1970.

Doll: A doll found buried in Hereford in 1960 was the effigy of someone on whom a curse had been placed, for tucked into its skirt was a spell that read: *'I act this spell upon you from my whole heart, wishing you to never rest nor eat nor sleep the restern part of your life. I hope your flesh will waste away and I hope*

you will never spend another penny I ought to have.' The doll is now in the Hereford Museum labeled 'A Witch's Curse', although there is little about the spell that suggests genuine witchcraft.

Dolmen: Megalithic altars resting on two or three pillars, believed to form a vault with special resonating properties.

Domestic Plant Medicine: see **Folk Medicine.**

Domidūca: In Roman religion, the spirit (*numen*) that conducted the bride to the bridegroom's house.

Doppelgänger: A term that comes from Germanic folklore and refers to an apparitional double of a still living person.

Dorset Cursus: An enormous cursus (Neolithic processional way) by far the longest in the country, which stretches for some six miles across country. Flanked by a bank and ditches, there are also long barrows marking its course.

Dove: One of the most important birds in mythology and folklore, with a curiously mixed symbolism. It is the bird of love, and also the bird of death and mourning.

'Do What You Will': [French, *Fay ce que vouldras.*] An occult maxim with a long history. It is usually attributed to Rabelais but he had adapted it from an older saying of St Augustine, and used it as the only 'rule' of his imagined Utopian Abbey of Thélème in *Gargantua*. It later appeared in French over the doorway of the infamous **Hell-Fire Club**, and was subsequently incorporated into Aleister **Crowley's** Thelemic teaching – the word **'Thelema'** being Greek for 'Will'.

Dowsing: The method used to search for

hidden objects, underground springs, sacred sites, etc, using dowsing sticks or rods. Recognized as one of the most widely accepted of the esoteric arts, with local councils and water authorities employing dowsers to locate underground pipes and water sources.

Draco: The largest constellation in the heavens but it is difficult to trace as it winds between several others. It has been identified with a number of dragon myths and is best seen during the warmer months. **Thuban**, the brightest star in the constellation was the pole star in ancient times, but the Earth's precession has since moved the pole star to **Polaris**. SOURCE: *Sky Dragons & Celestial Serpents*, Alastair McBeath.

Draconian Tradition: The Cult of Set, whose symbol is the Dog-Star Sothis, and who was the first named male deity ever to be worshipped. Kenneth **Grant** describes it as the full flowering of the primal African Mysteries as they occurred in ancient Egypt in pre-monumental times. *'It is the cult of the Fire Snake represented celestially by the stellar complex Draco, the Dragon or Fire-breathing Beast of the Great Deep (of Space).'* SOURCE: *Cults of the Shadows*, Kenneth Grant.

Dracs or **Dracae:** In his *Otia Imperialis*, Gervais de Tilbury first introduced dracs as feminine, aquatic spirits who tried to lure women and children into their lair by scattering jewels of pieces of gold in the water.

Dragonfly: The insect has a long and distinguished history, and was certainly well developed over 200 million years ago. Enormous species with a 24-inch wingspan flew among the plants of the coal swamps. They may have been the largest insects that have ever existed. And then there is the incredible speed at which they fly... *'a dragonfly/Shot by me like a flash of purple fire,'* wrote Tennyson, in **Lover's Tale**.

Dragon Lore: *'Here be dragons'* claimed the early map-makers and wherever myths are encountered in the world there is usually a dragon of some sort, although legends differ as to whether they are looked upon as benevolent or malevolent. After the Norman Conquest the heraldic dragon became an important royal badge, the most famous being the red dragon of Wales. SOURCE: *Dancing With Dragons*, D.J. Conway; *Dictionary of Demons*, Fred Gettings; *A Dictionary of Devils & Demons*, J. Tondriau and R. Villeneuve; *Sky Dragons & Celestial Serpents* and *Tiamat's Brood*, Alastair McBeath.

Dragon's Blood: A red resin used in magical charms.

Drama: Early Christians condemned drama, because of its pagan or immoral associations – until the medieval Mystery or Miracle plays were developed.

Drawing Down The Moon: A Wiccan ritual to channel goddess-energy, which has its roots in ancient Thessali. It is the transformation of the high-priestess of a coven into the goddess.

Dream or **Vision Quest:** A spiritual trial undertaken by the Plains Indians of North America, involving fasting, praying and seeking guidance.

Dream Books: Cheaply produced publications aimed at those who believed dreams to be prophetic (see **Chapbooks**).

Dreams: Regarded by occultists as gateways for astral journeying, divination and for tapping into the 'collective unconscious'. This belief may stem from Greek classical literature where, according to Homer, there were two *Gates of Dreams*, one of ivory, the other of horn, through which passed false and true dreams. Some magical practitioners accept the archetypal gods of mythology can be revealed in dreams or visions, although for **Jung**, dreams were a 'kind of impartial photography of unconscious life'. SOURCE: *The Dream Book*, Betty Bethards; *Dreamwork*, Strephon Kaplan-Williams; *The Meaning of Dreams*, R De Becker; *Memories, Dreams & Reflections*, C.G. Jung.

Dreamtime: The mythic age of the **Australian Aborigine** to explain the beginnings of their race, and also refers to the 'land' to which the spirits of their dead must travel.

Druidism: (1) One of the largest growing areas within modern paganism with currently around 35 different organizations in the UK alone. (2) Originally, the Druids were the teachers/priesthood of the Celtic tribes but the revivalist groups are more closely aligned to modern Wicca with many of the practitioners being both Druid and Wiccan. The classic source for scholars of Druidry is the *Commentarii de Bello Gallico* written by Julius Caesar. SOURCE: *The Book of Druidry*, Ross Nichols; *The Druid Renaissance*, Philip Carr-Gomm; *The Druid Source Book*, John Matthews; *The New Believers*, David V. Barrett; *Druid Priestess, Principles of Druidry, Ritual and Spirits of the Sacred Grove*, Emma Restall Orr.

Druid's Stone: An ancient stone in St. Mary's Priory churchyard at Bungay, Suffolk. Known locally as the Druid's Stone, it was probably placed there long before the Druids came to Britain, and is believed to hold some strange powers left over from pagan times.

Drumming: The throbbing beat of the drum in many cultures forms a bridge to Otherworld, or different levels of consciousness. It is an integral part of magico-religious rites and rituals, particularly those of a shamanic nature. Drake's Drum in Buckland Abbey near Plymouth is supposed to sound of its own accord whenever war threatens the British Isles.

Drumtrodden, Wigan: A site of three rock faces, each one carved with cups, cup and ring markings, radial grooves and other channels from pre-historic times.

Dryads: In Greek mythology, these were female nature spirits who inhabited oak trees, although later they were identified with sacred groves and woods in general. The hamadryad was the life-spirit of each individual tree and when the tree died, so did the spirit. They are also found in Celtic folklore and known as *sidhe Draoi*.

Dualism: The belief that there are two ultimate controlling powers, which means that 'God' may be ambivalent – both benevolent *and* malevolent.

Duat: One of the names of the Egyptian afterlife. The Duat was written in hieroglyphics with a five-pointed star: meaning the **Nut** Star, or Nut as the stars in the night sky. The Nut Star within a circle meant the Duat of Afterlife World. Another name for the

Otherworld was **Amenti**, which means 'hidden land'.

Dublin: A prehistoric burial site in Phoenix Park, at some 4000 years old, is Dublin's earliest monument. The site must have been important in Celtic times, since it had a ford and the natural harbor provided by the river mouth. Norse sea-rovers really founded the town, establishing a settlement in 841.

Duloe Circle: Eight standing stones in a small circle some 37 ft in diameter. It is unique in Cornwall as a megalithic structure, because the builders used **Quartz** instead of Cornish granite.

Dun Aengus: The most spectacular of the Aran Islands' many prehistoric monuments, this is a huge drystone semicircular fort standing on the edge of a 300 ft cliff dropping sheer into the sea.

Duncan, Helen: (1897–1956) Billed in the media as 'the last witch in Britain', she was a spiritualist medium who was the last person to be charged under the **Witchcraft Act** of 1736. She was brought into the spotlight in 1944, found guilty and sentenced to nine months in prison.

Durga: The mother-goddess of Hindu tradition. Her name literally means 'she who is difficult of approach; the inaccessible' and is often portrayed riding on a tiger.

Dust or **Land Devils:** Naturally occurring mini whirlwinds. These atmospheric vortices were the objects of fear and reverence in historic times since they are invisible until something 'moveable' is drawn into them. SOURCE: *The Goddess of the Stones*, George Terence Meaden.

Dwarves: The small, dark people of Norse mythology, renowned as workers in metal and magic, who live underground.

Dying God: The traditional theme of the killing of the 'god' has taken a firm hold on the European imagination and is the predominate focus of the Christian faith, despite its ancient origins. The myth of the sacrificial god of Nature who dies and is reborn occurs in many religions, reveals a *'complex web of myths, the meaning of which differs profoundly according to the social and cultural setting'* (see **Sacrificial King**). SOURCE: *The Ancient Gods*, E.O. James; *The Golden Bough*, Sir James Frazer.

Dynasty: (1) The division of the Pharaonic period into dynasties was a chronological system introduced by the priest Manetho in the early third century BC, when he composed his history of Egypt (the *Aegyptiaca*). (2) A succession of kings of the same family, or of members of any powerful family or connected group.

"Every man and every woman is a star ..."
Aleister Crowley
[Liber AL Vel Legis pt 1 v.3]

E

Ea, or **Enki:** God of the waters and one of the supreme deities of the Babylonian pantheon; the other two being Enlil, god of storms and Anu, god of the sky.

Eagle: Because of its size and strength, its aristocratic bearing and the ability to outsoar all other birds, the eagle became the recurring symbol of divinity and kingship, particularly in ancient Rome. Almost all parts of the eagle's body have magical virtue.

Eagle-stones: (*Aetītes*) Yellow clay ironstones said to have magical properties if taken from an eagle's nest. According to *Brewer's Dictionary of Phrase & Fable*, the stones clung to the dead flesh of lambs and when the eagle carried the carcass away to its nest, it carried the stones with them.

Earth: (1) Magically and spiritually significant for representing fertility and the divine Mother of all things, as well as the home of the dead in nearly all cultures, ancient and modern. In medieval times it was seen as the fundamental component of all things. Earth or dirt is a common ingredient in many sorts of spells. (2) Earth is the center of the astrological universe and a horoscope is cast taking into account where on Earth a person was born, in relation to the positions of the known planets at the time. (3) Among all the planets, the Earth is a unique in several respects but the most remarkable is the fact that over 70 per cent of its surface is covered by water in either liquid or solid form. Liquid water is not seen on the surface of any other planet in the Sun's domain. (4) In alchemy it is associated with lead (**Saturn**) and salt. (5) Earth corresponds to the **Empress** in the **Tarot** and Malkuth in the **Qabalah** (see **Elemental Earth**).

Earth, Air, Fire, Water: An anthology of British songs, rhymes and ballads with pre-Christian and pagan elements, compiled by Robin Skelton and Margaret Blackwood. The authors have gathered together over 250 poems and compositions.

Earth Force: Refers to the natural electromagnetic energy contained within the landscape. SOURCE: *Ancient Energies of the Earth*, David R. Cowan and Anne Silk; *The Pattern of the Past*, Guy Underwood.

Earth Mother: The consort of the **Sky father** in the earliest folk-religions of the ancient world (see **Gaia**).

Earth Mysteries: Refers to the harnessing and utilizing of the earth's natural energy forces and channeling them through magical working. SOURCE: *Ancient Energies of the Earth*, David R. Cowan and Anne Silk; *Earth Mysteries*, Philip Heselton; *Neolithic Britain*, Joshua Pollard; *What You Call Time*, Suzanne Ruthven. [SEE PANEL]

Earthworks: Man-made monuments of earth from **Silbury Hill** (Bronze Age), the largest artificial mound in Europe and Neolithic cairns and long barrows, to the pre-historic hill forts. SOURCE: *The Goddess of the Stones*, George Terence Meaden; *Discovering Prehistoric England*, James Dryer; *Historical Atlas of Britain*, ed Nigel Saul; *A Phenomenology of Landscape*, Christopher Tilley; *The Secret Country*, Janet and Colin Bord

Eassie, Scotland: A fine Pictish symbol stone stands in the ruins of Eassie church. It is carved on one side with a cross and figures; the other has an 'elephant' symbol, disc and Z-rod symbols, together with men and animals.

Ebony: A black wood that is believed to have strong magical properties and was used by magicians to make magical apparatus.

Eclipse: The masking of a heavenly body by another passing between it and the observer. Astrologers have been able to predict the phenomena for thousands of years, but usually interpreted them as omens of disaster.

Eco-paganism: An area of modern pagan belief that combines pagan spirituality and environmental activism.

Ecstasy: A rapture of the soul that draws it away from the realities of this world. **Shamanism** is an excellent example whereby the soul or spirit is released from the body. A variety of ecstatic phenomena can be experienced by individuals while in the state of spiritual ecstasy or trance.

Ectoplasm: A whitish, slightly luminous substance exuding from the body of a medium during a trance, which gradually takes on the shape of a face or body.

Edda: The title given to two Icelandic books providing the bulk of information about Norse mythology. The *Elder* or *Poetic Edda* and the *Younger* or *Prose Edda* were probably composed in Iceland in the early 13th century AD, and contain the myths and legends associated with the Norse gods and heroes.

Eel: It has been suggested that the eel's remarkable journey across the ocean originated at the time in evolutionary history when the European and American continents were closer together. Eels live in fresh water for an average of 10–20 years before they migrate downstream to the sea; with all European eels finally finding their way to the Sargasso Sea between the Bahamas and Bermuda. Apart from their culinary uses, eels have a wide range of medical and magical uses.

Effigy: A model, likeness or image of a human used in different types of magic.

Egg: The concept of a 'world egg' from which the first Creator sprung is another of those universal myths (see **Cosmic Egg**) that permeate all human memory and from the earliest times the egg became the symbol of life. Eggs play an important part in folklore and there are all sorts of superstitions and customs governing the giving and receiving of ordinary chicken eggs. Eggs are used extensively in fertility charms and potions. SOURCE: *The Dictionary of Omens & Superstitions,* Philippa Waring; *The Penguin Guide to the Superstitions of Britain & Ireland,* Steve Roud.

Eggshells: A belief that eggshells should be destroyed or burned to prevent witches or fairies using them to do mischief to whoever had eaten the egg. First recorded in the 1560s in Scot's *Discoverie of Witchcraft.*

Eglantine: A native of Britain, the seed oil was applied to help regenerate skin and scar tissue, and to heal burns and scalds. **Culpeper** recommended that the hips be made into a conserve that had many medicinal uses. Ruling planet: **Jupiter.**

Egyptian Rite Freemasonry: A form of Freemasonry founded in the late 18th century by Alessandro di **Cagliostro** and based on the ancient Egyptian Mysteries.

Egyptian Tradition: A modern revivalist adaptation of the ancient magical/ mystical system based on the religion and magic of Egypt. It acknowledges that the daily life, religion and magic (*heka*) of the ancient Egyptians were inseparable. SOURCE: *The Ancient Egyptians,* J. Gardner Wilkinson; *The British Museum Dictionary of Ancient Egypt,* Ian Shaw and Paul Nicholson; *Egyptian Magic,* Christian Jacq; *The History of Magic,* Kurt Seligmann; *The Inner Guide to Egypt,* Alan Richardson and Billie Walker-John; *Liber Ægyptius,* Mélusine Draco; *Magic in Ancient Egypt,* Geraldine Pinch; *Origin of Egyptian Symbolism,* Iamblichus; *The Setian,* Billie Walker-John; *Temple Festival Calendars of Ancient Egypt,* Sherif el-Sabban; *Karnak: The Temple of the Sun,* Justine Norbury.

Eichstätt Witch Trial: Held in 1637, this trial was recorded by the official scribe during the actual courtroom hearing and in the torture chamber. It was first published in 1811, but the actual names of those concerned were omitted from the text. The original manuscript has since been lost. SOURCE: *The Encyclopedia of Witchcraft and Demonology,* Rossell Hope Robbins

Eidolon: A **Wraith** or **Fetch**. Witch power formulated into semi-tangible human shape. SOURCE: *Mastering Witchcraft,* Paul Huson.

Eight: The number of knowledge, wisdom and understanding. It is a strange, mysterious number underlying determination and willpower but also the higher consciousness. Number VIII equals **Adjustment** (or **Justice**) in the **Tarot** (or four Eights of the Minor Arcana), **Hod** in the **Qabalah** and is ruled by **Mercury**.

Eightfold Path: The way to Buddhist enlightenment and consists of (1) right understanding; (2) right aspiration or purpose; (3) right speech; (4) right bodily action; (5) right means of livelihood; (6) right endeavor; (7) right mindfulness; (8) right concentration.

Eisteddfod: From the Welsh meaning a 'session' and traditionally an assembly of bards and musicians. The modern annual festival owes its popularity to a revivalist interest in Celts and Druids in the 19th century (see **Druids**).

Ekhi: A **Basque** personification of the Sun. Sorcerers and evil spirits lose their power when a ray of sunshine falls on them.

El: The supreme deity of the Canaanites and Phoenicians, who's wife, Asherah, was called **Astarte** by the Greeks.

Elder: Known in rural areas as 'the poor man's medicine chest' because every part of the tree can be used medicinally. Despite being one of the sacred trees, it is unlucky to put 'ellen' wood on a hearth or domestic fire; and to cut down an elder tree will bring ill-luck on the household. It is also a tree with strong connections to the **Faere Folk**, which may account for its avoidance by country people, although many magical cures are performed using elder. SOURCE: *Root & Branch* and *A Witch's Treasury of the Countryside,* Mélusine Draco; *Superstitions of the Countryside,* E. & M.A. Radford.

Elder: A senior member of a **Coven**, with at least twenty years experience at

Earth Mysteries

What exactly do we mean by Earth Mysteries? Is it an overwhelming love of the planet which has spawned charities, political parties, numerous magazines and countless green-eco groups? Is it part of the 1990s mega-myth that the Earth cannot fend for herself and that if world governments do not take heed of pollution and global warming, then Gaia is heading for destruction? Is it really taking part in an 'Earth Healing Day' by sitting in a meditative trance to channel combined energies into closing the wounds made through greed and commercial exploitation? Or is it a pilgrimage to a sacred site to plug into the power emanating from the Ancestors?

In 'The Pathway of Nuit' published in *Phoenix* Magazine, Dr. Mériém Clay-Egerton took a far more brutal and far-reaching view of humanity and its puny efforts to survive. 'The planet is shaking itself free, initially to try and eradicate the parasites which are disturbing it... All that *homo sapiens* could have produced now bucks, wavers and breaks down, and will finally disappear. It is no longer a bright and proud future, but dark and sullen. The Earth realizes that to free herself she must destroy herself and start again with new building bricks. But she can't tell the guilty from the innocent, all will go as they must into infinity..."

But to return to the popular concept of Earth Mysteries. Before conjuring up the inevitable picture of some weird figure doing something 'strange in the woods', perhaps it is easier to refer to Shinto, the indigenous religion of Japan for a universally accepted and comparable example of a 'living' nature belief. Essentially a compound of ancestor and nature worship, Shinto's silent contemplation of a flower, stream, rock formation or sunset is, in itself, a normal, everyday act of private worship. As part of a national ritual, each year at the blossoming of the cherry trees, thousands of Japanese leave the city to enjoy the beauty of the short-lived flowering. Neither is it uncommon for a Japanese to spend a whole evening gazing at the moon; or sit for hours 'listening to the stones grow'. Inconsiderately, some might think, Shinto shrines are usually to be found in locations of breathtaking natural beauty – with little thought for the convenience of the worshipper.

For the traditional Japanese there is no dividing line between the divine and human, since the forces that move in Nature, move in man according to Zen teaching:

"When one looks at it, one cannot see it:
When one listens for it, one cannot hear it:
However, when one uses it, it is inexhaustible."

Even rocks are possessed of the divine spark and often form part of the intricate designs used to create those familiar Zen temple gardens for contemplation – reflecting the belief that the Buddha nature is immanent not only in man, but in everything that exists, animate or inanimate.

Recognizing this instinctive feel for the divine spark of spirituality inherent in Nature is one of the fundamental abilities of a witch. A solitary walk by a rushing spring river; a stroll through the woods in autumn; the awesome thrill of an approaching thunderstorm in late summer; or the first snow fall of winter are times for the working of natural magic.

When referring to Earth Mysteries, it is also necessary to understand the difference between a 'place of power', and a sacred or historical site. For example, a large number of modern pagans treat any ancient earthworks as either power places or sacred sites, without any evidence of its religious antecedents. As a Gardnerian priestess, pointed out, such activities are on a par with worshipping at a castle moat or Neolithic flint quarry! Simply because something is old does not mean it has, or had, a religious or ritual significance.

Nevertheless, all these natural phenomena can make even the most ordinary person hanker for more of these feelings of elation that can grow from the experience of coming into contact with Earth Mysteries.

EXTRACT FROM WHAT YOU CALL TIME
SUZANNE RUTHVEN

Initiatory level, who acts as an advisor or mentor to individuals within the group.

Elect: In magical terms, the belief that an individual has been 'chosen' to carry out some particular spiritual role, and which often goes against the will of the recipient.

Electromagnetism: Strange effects associated with the earth's magnetic field (see **Earth Mysteries**) and believed by some to be the energy that fuels many magical applications.

Electrum Magicum: An alloy of the seven sacred metals. Aleister **Crowley** described its composition in *Magick: 'First the gold is melted up with the silver during a favourable aspect of the sun and moon; these are then fused with tin when Jupiter is well dignified. Lead is added under an auspicious Saturn; and so for the quicksilver, copper and iron, when Mercury, Venus and Mars are of good augury.'*

Elegba or **Legba**: The African equivalent of **Priapus** and Pan.

Elegy: (*Elegeia*) Originally a Greek song of mourning.

Elementals: The four group-souls that have dominion over the four elements of **Earth, Air, Fire** and **Water.** The element of fire is usually associated with energy, purification, transformation, passion and aspiration. Air is connected with breath, soul, speech, flight and freedom. Earth is associated with the solid and practical, with gloom and death but also with riches and material success. Water is the 'fount and origin of everything', the primal waters, the unconscious depths of the mind, and unfathomable mystery. Elementals are the creatures composed entirely of a single element – Earth/Gnomes; Air/Sylphs; Water/Undines; Fire/Salamanders – but the term is now loosely applied to any nature spirit.

Elements: (1) The classical components of the magical universe - **Earth** (north), **Air** (east), **Fire** (south) and **Water** (west) ascribed to the four cardinal points of the compass for the purpose of magical working. (2) From the scientific perspective, in 1789, Antoine Lavoisier, a French aristocrat compiled a new listing of 23 elements that included sulfur, mercury, iron, zinc, silver and gold. Another 32 were later added to the list. SOURCE: *The Magic Furnace*, Marcus Chown; *Techniques of High Magic*, Francis King and Stephen Skinner.

Elephant: Ivory is a protection against the **Evil Eye**, jealousy and nightmares. The animal's tail, made into amulets using gold, serves the same purpose.

Eleusinian Festivals, The: The most important and influential Greek agricultural festivals were those held annually in Attica in honor of **Demeter** and **Kore**, the Lesser and Greater **Eleusinian** Mysteries. It is thought that the original Lesser Mysteries were held in the open air for the benefit of the newly sown seed-corn, before they became the first stage in the initiation of the *mystae*.

Eleusinian Mysteries: Ceremonies of initiation and held in honor of **Demeter** and **Persephone (Kore)**. The nature of the rites was a closely guarded secret, any breach of which was punishable by death. Unlike other types of initiation, the **Mysteries** were not restricted by age or sex since the agricultural emphasis would demand the input of both male and female energies. The Lesser Mysteries, which took place in the month of *anthesterion* (February–March), were rites of purification and preparation. The Greater Mysteries took place six months later in the month of *boedromion* (September–October); there were two grades of **Initiation** and a year had to elapse before the final grade of *epopteia*, meaning 'spectacle' or 'vision'. SOURCE: *Eleusis & the Eleusinian Mysteries*, G.E. Mylonas.

Elf: In northern European mythology elves were originally small, semi-supernatural beings of two kinds, the fair folk of Alfheim and the dark folk of Swartheim; they later became known collectively as the **Faere Folk**. Elves feature in the folk-tales of the Celtic people where Faere-lore plays an important part; according to the lore, Old Craft witches learn their Craft from the Faere or Elven Folk.

Elf-fire: Needfire or Wildfire. Flame to light the coven balefire produced without the use of metals.

Elf-marked: Those born with a natural defect, according to Scottish superstition, are marked by the elves for mischief. Shakespeare wrote that Richard III was 'elfish-marked'.

Elf-shot: (1) The name given to the small, flint arrowheads from the Stone Age that are found all over Europe. (2) In some parts, elf-shot refers to the tiny fragments of meteorites that reach the Earth's surface and are made of meteoric iron.

Eliade, Mircea: Appointed Professor of the History of Religions at the University of Chicago in 1958, he was an accepted authority on classical mysticism, symbolism and initiatory patterns. His titles include *Rites & Symbols of Initiation, The Sacred & the Profrane, Cosmos & History, The Forge & the Crucible*, etc.

Elixir: Usually refers to a 'potion for long life' or a panacea for all ills. European alchemists referred to the **Philosopher's Stone** (which was believed to have universal curative powers) as the Elixir of Life.

Elixir Rubeus: Aleister **Crowley** used this expression to refer to the 'moon-juice' or lunar current manifesting periodically through the **Scarlet Woman**.

Elizabeth I, Statute of: Between 1547 and 1563 no laws against witchcraft were on the statute books in England. The chief provisions of the Act were the death penalty for murder by sorcery, and a year's imprisonment and the pillory for witchcraft 'undeadly'. On the surface, the statute only enforced the death penalty for murder, but this Act started the whole witch-mania in England; it was replaced by a more stringent Act under **James I.**

Elizabethan Magic: While the Elizabethan age saw unsympathetic changes in social attitudes towards witchcraft, occult philosophy under the aegis of magicians like John **Dee** and Robert **Fludd** blossomed and developed. Although they were not without their share of persecutions, occultists were treated less severely in England than in the rest of Europe. SOURCE: *Elizabethan Magic*, Robert Turner; *The Occult Philosophy in the Elizabethan Age*, Frances A. Yates; *Religion & the Decline of Magic*, Keith Thomas.

Ellyllon: In Welsh mythology, the souls of the ancient **Druids** which, being too good for hell, and not good enough for heaven, are permitted to wander upon the earth until judgement day, when they will be elevated to a higher state of being.

Elm: In English folklore the tree was also known as 'elven' because of its association with the elves. Its bark is used in magical recipes against diseases; its leaves for ointments for burns and wounds; sap for curing baldness – while the inner bark of Slippery or Red Elm was used as a laxative and abortions. Ruling planet: **Saturn**.

Elohim: One of the names of God in the Old Testament. Magicians inscribed the name on their magic circles to infuse divine power and ward off evil influences.

El Shaddai: [Hebrew] The primal star god of the Chaldeans whom the Jews replaced with Jehovah when the Solar cult superseded that of the Moon and Stars.

Elven-race or **Elven-folk:** Traditionally the hybrid descendants of the **Watchers** who mated with human women to produce a race of magically-mystically gifted offspring. Said also to be the ancestors of true witches.

Elysium: Also known as the **Islands of the Blessed**. In Greek mythology a land of perfect happiness where those favored by the gods lived without dying; later classical writers referred to it as part of **Hades** to which the heroes went after death. According to Homer, the Elysian Fields were to be found at the end of the earth, on the banks of the river Oceanus.

Emanation: In magical terms it refers to the outflowing of the supreme principle or divine essence into a series of secondary forms, demonstrated by the *sefiroth* or spheres on the Qabalistic **Tree of Life**.

Embarrer: A magical application whereby a woman can be made incapable of sexual relations. This is known as 'embarrer' and is accomplished by the tying of **Aglet** knots.

Emerald: A green beryl worn as an amulet brings the wearer wealth, good fortune, and the ability to foretell the future. It banishes evil spirits.

Emerald Tablet: One of the oldest alchemical texts, which is usually ascribed to **Hermes Trismegistus** or the Egyptian god, Thoth. Legend has it that it contained the 13 precepts of **Hermes** and that it was found by Alexander the Great in the tomb of Hermes but in reality it is a 9th century Arabian text from the *Book of Causes*. SOURCE: *Secret of the Emerald Tablet*, Dr Gottlieb Latz, trans by D.W.Hauck.

Emergence: Proyet season of the ancient Egyptian calendar when crops could be planted following the receding floodwaters of the **Inundation**. This meant that popular festivals were kept to a minimum as those employed on the land would be working from dawn to dusk. SOURCE: *The Egyptian Book of Days* and *Liber Ægyptius*, Mélusine Draco.

Empress: The third card in the Major Arcana of the standard **Tarot** deck; the archetypal symbol of the beneficent Queen and the epitome of charity and kindness.

Emperor: The fourth card in the Major Arcana of the standard **Tarot** deck;

the archetypal symbol of a great King, a wise and powerful ruler – all that is positive in the masculine persona.

Empiricism: The doctrine that there is no knowledge of the world except what is derived from sense experience.

Emptiness or **Voidness:** It can be used in reference to meditations to demonstrate their tranquil nature, quite empty of noisy distraction or subtle disturbance.

Empyromancy: An ancient divination technique by interpreting the smoke generated by burning laurel leaves. Laurel can produce hallucinogenic effects, which is probably why **Pythagoras**, the Greek prophet, mystic and philosopher, used it as early as 550BC. See **Daphnomancy.**

Enchanter(ess): One who sings incantations from the Latin *in-canto*, meaning 'to sing over' or 'against someone'.

Encyclopedia of Witchcraft and Demonology, The: Rossell Hope Robbins took his doctorate at Cambridge University in 1937 and became an acknowledged authority on historical witchcraft. The *Encyclopedia* was first published in 1959, and in 1979 he wrote the definitive introduction to the huge catalogue of the Witchcraft Collection at **Cornell University Library**.

Endor, Witch of: In the Bible [*Book of Samuel*] Saul, fearing an attack by the Philistines, consulted this witch. Although necromancy was considered a crime, the witch made the ghost of his predecessor, the prophet Samuel, appear to act as his advisor.

Energy: An invisible force which is believed to permeate all things in the universe, and which can be raised and focused for magical use.

English Folklore: The surviving customs and superstitions of English folklore provide a unique insight into the forgotten religions and social systems that have long been abandoned but still serve as a memory bank that reveals the hopes and fears of the numberless generations of our ancestors. Although it has been greatly diluted by Victorian folklorists, there are still many traceable elements of the pre-Christian peoples that lived in the British Isles (see **Folklore Society**).

English Witchcraft: The concept of witchcraft in Anglo-Saxon and medieval England meant that it was what witches *did* that counted, not what they or their neighbors *thought* they did. Up to 1550, punishment was light unless the crime involved murder or arson (see **Elizabeth I, Statute of**). In most of the English trials, the reason for a person being accused was some simple accident or annoyance, and these relatively minor irritations took up more attention than any serious charges. SOURCE: *The Encyclopedia of Witchcraft and Demonology*, Rossell Hope Robbins; *Witches and Neighbours*, Robin Briggs.

Enochian Communications: 'Calls' from the angels of the Thirds Aethhyrs, and were later tested under ceremonial conditions by Aleister **Crowley** and Victor Neuberg with surprising results. A dictionary of Enochian calls was later published by Israel Regardie and the system is often seen as an alternative to the **Qabalah**. SOURCE: *Advanced Guide to Enochian Magick*, Gerald Schueler; *The Complete Golden Dawn System of Magic*, Israel Regardie; *The*

Complete Enochian Dictionary, Donald C. Laycock; *Dictionary of Demons*, Fred Gettings; *Elizabethan Magic*, Robert Turner; *The Enochian Magic of Dr. John Dee*, Geoffrey James; *Gems from the Equinox*, Aleister Crowley.

Enoptromancy: A divinatory method of placing a shiny surface or mirror in water to foretell from the reflections whether a sick person will live or die.

Entity: In magical terms, a disembodied spirit, or energy.

Enya: A popular Irish composer and singer whose work has provided the musical accompaniment to countless coven meetings, especially her early albums, *Watermark* and *Shepherd Moons*.

Epagomenal Gods: The Egyptian deities **Osiris, Isis, Nephthys, Horus** and **Set**, who presided over the five unlucky days that divided the old year from the new. They fell at the point of high summer when widespread disease, illness and pestilence was rife. SOURCE: *The Cairo Calendar*.

Epatoscomancy or **Extispiciomancy:** The ancient practice of examining the entrails of animals for the purpose of divination.

Epidemium: see **Barren wort.**

Ephesus: The famous temple of **Artemis,** which was of great antiquity even in classical Greek times.

Epona: [Celtic = big mare] Originally a Gaulish goddess usually shown riding a horse. Her attributes are the **Cornucopia** and a dog; her worship came to Britain with the Roman legions.

Epping Forest: The great Forest of Essex once stretched from Bow in London almost to Cambridge and Colchester. Its dark glades and isolated villages have sheltered those with uncanny abilities for centuries. Gipsies were numerous, many belonging to the Lee family who told fortunes at the forest fairs; the most famous inhabitants were Old Dido, a hermit who prescribed remedies based on forest herbs, and Old Mother Jenkins the Goose Charmer.

Equilibrium: The state of attaining perfect balance to empower a magical working. SOURCE: *Magick*, Aleister Crowley;

Equinox, The: An encyclopedia of **Magick** in ten volumes written by Aleister **Crowley** for his own magical Order the **A.A**; it was followed the 'Blue' *Equinox* Vol III number 1. *The Gems From the Equinox* is a single volume compilation by Israel Regardie.

Equinox of the Gods: A magical term denoting a change of **Aeon**, when a new influence radiates through the stellar girdle (zodiac) of the Cosmos, effecting radical changes in human and other forms of consciousness. SOURCE: *The Equinox of the Gods*, Aleister Crowley.

Equiria: These festivals (27th February and 14th March) had both religious and military significance and involved the purification of the army.

Erebus: The names given by the ancient Greeks to the region stretching under the world but above **Hades**. According to Hesiod, it was primeval Darkness sprung from Chaos and the father (by his sister Night) of Day.

Ergon: In spiritual alchemy, the *'right eye of the soul, by which it looks to the eternal. The left eye looks towards time and this is the Parergon'*.

Eriu: [*Eire*] The personification of the goddess of Ireland.

Erótes: Boy-like love deities in late classical art; known in Latin as *amoretti*. They were taken over in the Renaissance, and remained popular through the Baroque and Rococo periods in the guise of *putti* or genii.

Erzulie: *Erzulie Freda Dahomey* is the gracious goddess of the **Voodoo** Rahda rites, equivalent to Venus and Mary. *Erzulie Ge-Rouge* is the demonic form of Erzulie Freda and the **Scarlet Woman** of the Voodoo Petro rites.

Esbat: The monthly meeting of a coven to discuss business, or conduct magical workings.

Esclepius: see **Asclepius**.

Esoteric: Refers to that 'which is secret or mysterious' and taught only to a select few. The opposite of exoteric – intelligible to the uninitiated.

Etheric Body: The second body, or mirror image of the physical appearance, which can be projected some distance. See **Doppelgänger**.

Ethike: Morality in the Greek classical religion. Mortals should, above all, worship the gods, respect their parents, honor their oaths, and behave well to guests, suppliants, heralds and the dead.

Etruscan: The belief of the pre-Roman Italians was a somber religion with emphasis on divination, sacrifice and death. Many of the old Etruscan deities were later incorporated into the religion of Rome.

Euhemerism: The theory that mythology has its origins in history, which was advanced by the Greek scholar Euhemerus (3BC), that the gods were ancient kings who had been deified.

Euphorbia: Poisonous plants used by witches for ointments and potions; any member of the spurge genus of plants.

Eurythmy: The art of movement or spiritual dance, developed by Rudolf **Steiner**.

Evil: According to the encyclopedia *Man, Myth & Magic*, evil and its attendant woes came into the world because of 'the caprice of the gods', human sin, or error. The belief that an 'Evil One' and his hellish host, all bent on the destruction of mankind, has persisted up to the present day across Europe, the Middle East and Asia.

Evil Eye: A magical power that is said to be possessed by certain humans of an evil disposition and which is bestowed on another by means of a glance. SOURCE: *Dictionary of Demons*, Fred Gettings; *A Dictionary of Devils & Demons*, J. Tondriau and R. Villeneuve; *Gestures*, Desmond Morris.

Evocation: To call or summon forth, i.e. command, as opposed to **Invocation**, which is couched in the form of a prayer or request. SOURCE: *Coven of the Scales*, A.R. Clay-Egerton; *Techniques of High Magic*, Francis King and Stephen Skinner.

Exaltation: An old astrological term: a planet was said to be in its 'exaltation' when it was in that sign of the zodiac in which it was supposed to exercise its strongest influence.

Excalibur: The enchanted sword of King **Arthur**, which was probably connected with the magical sword, *Caladbolg*, that belonged to the Irish hero Fergus.

Execution: In Europe (except England) both the ecclesiastical and secular courts burned a convicted witch. In Italy and Spain the heretic was burned alive. In Scotland, Germany and France, it was customary to first strangle the victim (by garroting or hanging) and then immediately light the pyre; if a confession was revoked they were left alive on the stake.

Existentialism: A term covering a number of related philosophical doctrines denying objective universal values and holding that people, as moral free agents, must create values for themselves through actions and must accept the ultimate responsibility for those actions. SOURCE: *Existentialism & Humanism*, Jean-Paul Sartre.

Excommunication: The ultimate penalty inflicted by the Catholic Church where the offended is cast out of the Christian community and solemnly cursed with 'Bell, Book and Candle'.

Exegesis: The interpretation of sacred texts to find the deeper meaning that is believed to underlie the plain words.

Exorcism: Not a term used generally used by genuine occult practitioners, who prefer to conduct a '**Banishing**'. Exorcism is usually the province of the Christian clergy, or more commonly the evangelical sects, who still firmly believe in demonic possession. SOURCE: *The Devil Within*, Marc Cramer; *The Devils of Loudun*, Aldous Huxley; *Dictionary of Demons*, Fred Gettings; *The Encyclopedia of Witchcraft & Demonology*, Rossell Hope Robbins.

Extrasensory perception or **ESP:** The ability to transmit and receive information by other means other than the recognized senses. It is normally divided into three areas: clairvoyance, telepathy and precognition and is being taken more seriously in academic circles as parapsychology. Since research indicates that ESP, working independently of known physical laws, may be common to all mankind – and not the prerogative of a gifted few. SOURCE: *ESP – Your Sixth Sense*, Brad Steiger; *Experimental Psychical Research*, R.H. Thouless; *The Paranormal*, Brian Inglis.

Extra-terrestrial Intelligence: The question of whether mankind is alone in the universe is one of the oldest problems of philosophy, science and occultism. Many occultists belief that some entities contacted during magical working belong to this category (see **Discarnate Entities**). SOURCE: *Are We Alone?* Paul Davies; *Coven of the Scales*, A.R. Clay-Egerton; *Starchild*, Mélusine Draco.

Eye: Going back to the Stone Age, the eye has been full of religious symbolism; the symbol representing intelligence and spirituality, but also as an image of terror. For example, the **Third Eye** of Eastern religions may stand for spiritual insight and vision, while the **Evil Eye** is destructive. Mediterranean fishermen often paint eyes on the prows of their boats to avert the dangers of the evil eye and to ensure a good catch. In the Egyptian religion the Eye of Horus refers to the left and right eye of the god, representing the sun and moon; the Eye of Re is the destructive power of Sekhmet.

Eye-biting: Cursing with a glance (see **Evil Eye**).

F

Fable: A short story with a moral purpose and one of the earliest forms of folktale. The most famous examples are those of the Ionian slave, Æsop, dating from 600BC.

Faere Folk or **Fairy:** Seen as being both good and evil and have, at various times in history, been blended and confused with witches – although prior to the 13th century, having fairy-blood was something to be admired. The original Faere Folk are thought to be the small-statured races that populated parts of Europe in the Neolithic and Bronze Ages, *before* the spread of the Celts. In Ireland they were known as the **Tuatha de Danaan** and in Wales as the **Tylwyth Teg** ('The Fair People') but in England the earliest mention of them is the Anglo-Saxon charm against **Elf-shot**. The world of Faere, is said to run parallel to the physical world (see **Elf**). SOURCE: *Fairy Mythology*, Thomas Keightly; *The Fairies in Tradition & Literature*, K.M. Briggs; *Lord of the Rings*, Tolkien; *Fairy & Folk Tales of the Irish Peasantry*, W.B. Yeats; *Religion & the Decline of Magic*, Keith Thomas.

Fairy Led: One who walks around in a dream, or is light-headed.

Fairy Rade or **Ride:** A magnificent procession of the Faere Folk on horseback.

Fairy Rings: (1) Circles of grass of different color or texture from that of the rest of the field, where fairies are said to hold their dances. Anyone brave enough to run nine times round a fairy ring at full moon was thought to be able to hear them talking and feasting – but it was dangerous to sit in a ring on May Eve or All Hallows Eve as the victim might be spirited away. (2) The rings are caused by a fungus below the surface that attacks the roots of the grass.

Fairy Sparks: Believed to be the lights prepared for fairies at their revels, caused by a natural phosphoric light from decaying wood.

Faith: A wholehearted belief in the spiritual without commitment to an established religion.

Faith Healing: More often than not the term used to describe 'the laying on of hands' which is a traditionally Christian method, used by a variety of churches in conjunction with prayer. Often described as 'a great source of hope to the otherwise hopeless'.

Fakir: An Arabic or Asian holy man who has renounced the material world and put his trust in God.

Falcon: Hawk (*falconidae*) used for falconry: kestrel, merlin, hobby and peregrine. The name is very old, originally Norman French and first occurs as *faucon* in c1250. Feathers from these raptors are often used in magical spells.

Fama: Roman personification of rumor. She plays no part in religion, and is purely a product of Latin literary allegory. Virgil pictures her as a horrible creature with several tongues and babbling mouths, while the Greek author, Hesiod, makes her a goddess under the name of Pheme.

Familiar: The word comes from the Latin *famulus*, or 'servant' and in Old Craft terms denotes a slave-spirit. During the **Burning Times**, all manner of small creatures were said to be proof of a witch's pact with the Devil, although in terms of historical witchcraft, the 'small animal kept as a crony appears fairly late'. In Continental witchcraft, accusations concerning familiars appear to have played little part; the 'pet imp' in the form of an animal was 'typically, if not exclusively, a British phenomenon'. SOURCE: *The Encyclopedia of Witchcraft & Demonology*, Rossell Hope Robbins; *Man, Myth & Magic*, Richard Cavendish.

Fanatic: Those transported with religious or temple madness. From the Latin *fa'num*, meaning a temple.

Farr, Florence: Introduced by W.B. **Yeats** to magical practice in the **Golden Dawn's** Isis-Urania Temple, she quickly tired of the autocratic posturing of the MacGregor **Mathers**. She left to form her own group called The Sphere and subsequently published a volume called *Egyptian Magic*, which contains several key Egyptian texts and invocations relating to the modern tradition.

Farrar, Janet and **Stewart:** Probably the most famous Wiccan authors in the public eye. Although both were initiated by Alex **Sanders**, upon breaking away they formed their own covens in England and Ireland, preferring to call themselves 'Wiccans who are working on the Pagan path'. Over the years they continued to dispel the misconceptions surrounding contemporary **Wicca** and make it more accessible to the public. Stewart Farrar died in 2000. TITLES: *What Witches Do*, Stewart Farrar; *Spells & How They Work*, *A Witches Bible Complete*, Janet and Steward Farrar; *The Pagan Path* and *The Complete Dictionary of European Gods & Goddesses*, with Gavin Bone.

Fascination: (1) Literally means 'slain or overcome by the eyes' and is an allusion to the notion of bewitching by the power of the eyes; another name for the **Evil Eye**. (2) Process of casting a spell upon someone using only the projection of witch-power in close personal proximity (see **Glamouring**).

Fascinum: Originally a Roman phallic amulet, which was worn by women and children against bewitchment. They were also used in France for several centuries.

Fasting: The disciplined control of the body's natural appetites as a means of spiritual progress is widely practiced in most religions, both ancient and modern.

Fata: Women in medieval romance not dissimilar to witches, taken from the Italian for 'fairy' as in Fata Morgana (Morgan le Fay), the half-sister of King **Arthur**.

Faticaria: A name in some Latin countries meaning witchcraft. A witch is known as *faticeira*, possibly from the Latin root for 'announcing fate' or prophesying.

Fate: The word derives from the Latin *fatum*, meaning a spoken decree presumed to come from the gods. It has come to mean a pre-ordained destiny or inevitable lot. The Greek triple goddesses of fate were Tisiphone, Alecto and Megaera, although we are more familiar with the names recorded by Hesiod as Clotho (the spinner of man's destiny); Lachesis (who weaves the web of life); and Atropos (who cuts the thread when death comes). Also linked with fate are **Nemesis** – the divine anger – and the **Furies**, who hounded and punished the guilty. All represent the triple aspects of the goddess and echo Robert **Graves'** researches for his epic poem (see **Karma**). SOURCE: *The Oxford Companion to Classical Literature*, ed Sir Paul Harvey; *The White Goddess*, Robert Graves.

Fate Line: One of the lines in the palm of the hand said to reveal specific characteristics of a person.

Father of Wicca: see **Gerald Gardner**.

Fauna: (1) An Old Italian goddess of fields and woods with the attributes of **Faunus**. Her festival was held on 3rd December with secret rites held in her honor, attended only by women. (2) The collective scientific term for living creatures, i.e. 'flora and fauna'.

Faunalia: Sacred to Faunus (see **Fauna**), this festival was more popularly celebrated in rural areas, being a celebration of nature and animals.

Faunus: In the Roman religion, a woodland deity, endowed with prophetic power, and guardian of crops and herds, developed from an earlier concept of a number of Fauni, who were spirits of the countryside.

Faust: The story of Dr. Faustus, believed to be based on a real 15th century character, who sold his soul to the Devil in exchange for greater knowledge and power, has inspired countless books and plays over the centuries. Under Christian influence the magus was transformed into a seedy charlatan who must suffer in life ands face eternal damnation after death. Faust, with his pact and mythical deeds, became the archetypal magician. SOURCE: *Malleus Satani: The Hammer of Satan*, Suzanne Ruthven.

Faustae Felicitati: A day set aside (9th October) to pay homage to Felicitas, the Roman goddess of good luck and joy.

Fay or **Fey**: An older word for **Fairy** and was originally used to describe the people themselves; now refers to someone who has 'second-sight'.

Feast, The: An integral part of any witch's ritual, although it is by some referred to as 'Cakes and Ale'. This is the offering and libation made to the gods in thanks for their power and blessings; the officiant samples the food and then shares it among the participating group, as well as leaving some for the wild life as the Divine's share. Food and drink taken in friendship at the end of a ritual also acts as replenishment after psychic working and helps to ground any superfluous energy. SOURCE: *Witchcraft – A Tradition Renewed*, Evan John Jones.

Feathers: A common ingredient used in spellcasting, particularly in **Voodoo**.

Februa: A great Roman feast of expiation and purification.

Felidomancy: Divination through the behavior of **Cats**, domestic or wild. A black cat crossing a person's path can mean good luck (in Britain) or bad luck (in America).

Fell: Baneful.

Fellowship of Isis: A goddess-based organization that mingles neo-paganism, Druidry, Egyptian and Celtic influences in its rites. Because they venerate all goddesses (and gods), members include people from a variety of religions, including Hindus, Buddhists, Christians and Spiritualists. SOURCE: *The New Believers*, David V.

Barrett.

Fennel: A yellow-flowered plant with seeds that are used in charms and recipes to keep away evil spirits. It was one of the **Nine Herbs** held sacred by the Anglo-Saxons. It had numerous medicinal and culinary uses and was strewn on the floor to sweeten the air. Ruling planet: **Mercury**.

Feng Shui: An ancient Chinese practice of locating earth energies, literally translated as 'wind and water'. According to the principles of feng shui, living in harmony with the earth's field of energy will promote prosperity, peace and happiness. SOURCE: *Feng Shui*, Kwok Man-Ho and Joanne O'Brien; *The Living Earth*, Stephen Skinner; *Principles of Feng Shui*, S Brown.

Fenrir or **Fenris:** The wolf; son and the brother of Hel in Nordic myth.

Feralia: A religious holiday (21st February) sacred to **Jupiter**; and the last day of the *Parentalia*, when the temples would be reopened at noon.

Fern Seed: The seed from certain species of fern is so small that it cannot be seen with the naked eye and was believed to confer invisibility on those who carried it. *'We have the receipt of fern seed, we walk invisible,' Henry IV*, act iv.4.

Festivals: Annual celebrations usually dedicated to a particular deity or social custom. The Egyptians, Greeks and Romans followed a set calendar of pre-prescribed events throughout the year, with many of the festivals linked to seasonal observances. The great majority of Roman festivals were held on odd days of the month, as these were believed to be luckier than even days. One of the oldest in Britain is the

Abbots Bromley Horn Dance that takes place each year. SOURCE: *The Oxford Companion to Classical Literature*, ed Sir Paul Harvey; *Folklore, Myths & Customs of Britain*, Marc Alexander; *Seasonal Feasts & Festivals*, E.O. James.

Fertility: An exceedingly common word in religious history and the most famous fertility symbol in the British Isles is undoubtedly the **Cerne Abbas** Giant, cut into a Dorset hillside. This is a subject where religion, magic, folklore and superstition overlap. Primitive man believed that fertility, the principle at the root of all life, was entirely subject to the control of the gods. This ancient belief is still reflected in the spring and autumn celebrations of contemporary paganism (see **Beltaine**). SOURCE: *Man, Myth & Magic*, ed Richard Cavendish.

Fetch: A word that has developed a dual-meaning in contemporary witchcraft. (1) In modern Wicca the term is used to mean a messenger or summoner, and is a title given to a *human* member of a group. (2) In traditional Craft, a fetch is the projected spirit or thought-form sent to do a witch's bidding; a wraith or disembodied ghost of a living person.

Fetish: An object believed to procure for its owner the services of a spirit lodged within it. A fetish can be used to ward off evil, or to carry it to a specific person who will immediately recognize the symbolism. Any object can be used as a fetish as long as the person receiving it believes it to be endowed with magical properties.

Feverwort: see **Centaury**.

Fey: see **Fay**.

Field of Reeds: The ancient Egyptian metaphor for death.

Fig: Used in love potions and cures. It was said that a woman could charm any man she desires by giving him figs. Ruling planet: **Jupiter.**

Figwort: The name refers to the herb's ancient use in treating hemorrhoids and as a mild laxative. Medieval herbalists used it to treat the 'king's evil' or scrofula. Ruling planet: **Moon.**

Filbert: Nut of the cultivated hazel. The wood may be used to make a magic wand.

Finland, Witchcraft in: Pagan belief in natural and magical powers continued for longer in Finland than elsewhere in Europe and consequently fuelled the new doctrines of Christian demonology. There were victims but generally Finland 'met the delusion with far greater composure, common sense and integrity' than most of its neighbors.

Finn: Warrior-magician and poet, conqueror of giants and monsters, Finn is the central figure in a cycle of Irish heroic tales. His exploits are commemorated even today in the folksongs of Gaelic-speaking Ireland and Scotland. He may have been a pagan Irish deity in keeping with the Celtic predilection for gods in triple form. The meaning of the Gaelic name for Tara, early Ireland's main royal center is 'Tara of the three Fionns'.

Fir: Usually a symbol of fertility and longevity, the fir or **Pine** tree was also associated with ancient funeral customs. In northern Europe and Russia it was the tree of the shaman or medicine man.

Fire: The concept that fire embodies some form of creative divinity is an underlying theme in nearly all of the world's religions, both ancient and modern. (See **Elemental Fire** and **Need Fire.**) Fire has also played an important part in social events such as the annual fire-festivals that were ignited to symbolize the passing of the seasons; to act as a beacon in times of danger; part of a purification rite for cattle and livestock; or as a focus for celebration. The symbol of fire, the **Salamander** was a mythical lizard-like creature that could live within the fire without injury to itself.

Fire Festivals: Many of these ancestral relics still survive from the pagan fire festivals held in honor of the Sun. These include the bonfires that burn all over England every Guy Fawkes' Day, which hold memories of the rites associated with the Celtic **Samhain** (October 31st) when fires were lit to strengthen the winter sun; the fire ceremony of Up Helly Aa, held in Shetland on the last Tuesday in January; and the chain of bonfires which blaze every midsummer across Cornwall. SOURCE: *Folklore, Myths & Legends,* Reader's Digest; *A Companion to the Folklore, Myths & Customs of Britain,* Marc Alexander.

Fire Poker: It was a common belief that placing the iron poker to form a cross against the horizontal bars of the grate would ward off witches or other evil powers.

Fire Snake: see **Kundalini.**

Firmament: The solid sphere of the sky in which the starts were thought to be fixed.

First Footing: Although now considered a Scottish custom, it was common in England and parts of Wales and based on the first person entering the house in the New Year bringing either good or bad luck for the next 12 months. SOURCE: *The Penguin Guide to Superstitions of Britain and Ireland*, Steve Roud.

First Light: (1) Seeing something for the first time. (2) In astronomy, the earliest light emitted from objects when the Universe was young.

Firth, Violet Mary: see **Dion Fortune**.

Fish: Since ancient times fish have been associated with the sacred and the supernatural. For example, in the West there is the salmon of Wisdom, while in Japan, Kwannon, the goddess of Mercy, is often shown standing on the back of a black carp – a symbol of strength and virility. The heart and liver burned upon hot coals will banish evil spirits.

Fisher King: A well-known example of a legend that combines early pagan themes with later Christian elements is the story of the Fisher King whose infirmity is bound up with the desolation of his land and people. He is the crippled Lord of the Grail Castle and Keeper of the Grail, and can only be cured by the right question asked by the hero of the Grail-quest.

Five: The great mystic number being the sum of 2 + 3, the first even and first odd compound since Unity is Deity alone, i.e. without creation and representing all the powers of Nature, the masculine aspects. The number V equals the **Hierophant** in the **Tarot** (or four Fives of the Minor Arcana), **Geburah** in the **Qabalah**, and is governed by **Mars**.

Five-Fold Kiss, The: In traditional **Wicca** this refers to the ritual kissing of five parts of the body, carrying out in certain rites and ceremonies. SOURCE: *The Magical Arts*, Richard Cavendish.

Flagellum Daemonum: A book of the occult by one 'Mengus', which contains cures for people suffering from possession, together with recipes for counter-magic against spells and sorcery.

'Flag, Flax, Fodder & Frigg': Usually abbreviated to FFF or FFFF, and used as a blessing when ending a letter between traditional witches. Flag (sometimes Fire) represent the hearth/home/warmth; flax is clothing; fodder is food (both animal and human) and frigg is sex – the blessing hopes the person to whom the letter is sent has all these things in abundance.

Flamen: A sacrificial priest of ancient Rome of which there were 15 in number, each serving a particular god.

Flax or Linseed: Fibers from the stems of flax, one of the world's oldest crop plants, were woven into linen by many ancient civilizations. In Britain the plant has been cultivated since prehistoric times. It also has culinary and medicinal uses, and **Charlemagne** demanded that his subjects ate flax seeds to maintain good health. Ruling planet: **Mercury** (see **Flag, Flax** ...).

Flint: An extremely hard stone used in striking fire. Worn as an amulet it keeps away the **Incubus** and other evil spirits. A flint amulet with a hole in it (see **Hagstone**) keeps away nightmares.

Flitter Mouse: see **Bat**.

Flood: It is estimated that there are hundreds of different flood-legends around the world; the preservation of an elect group of men and women, while the rest of mankind perishes having given offense to the gods. More localized folk-beliefs often refer to drowned cities or kingdoms, where bells from underwater churches can be heard to toll.

Floralia: A Roman festival honoring **Flora**, goddess of flowers, which was celebrated from 28th April to the beginning of May

Flowers or **Flora:** (1) There are lots of legends and superstitions surrounding flowers, and in the countryside many were used for their healing powers. (2) Roman goddess of growing corn and blossoming flowers. (3) The collective scientific name for plants, i.e. 'flora and fauna'.

Fludd, Robert: An English physician and mystical philosopher, who apparently discovered the **Qabalah** while writing his *History of the Macrocosm*, in which he makes the now-famous observation that man is a miniature version (or microcosm), physically and spiritually of the **Universe** (the macrocosm). SOURCE: *The Complete Golden Dawn System of Magic*, Israel Regardie; *Elizabethan Magic*, Robert Turner; *The Occult Philosophy in the Elizabethan Age*, Frances A. Yates; *Robert Fludd & Freemasonry*, A.E. Waite.

Flying Ointment: It is known how some of these ointments were made because a number of 16–17th century writers described the various methods and recipes: all the recipes, or *sabbati unguenti*, contained extracts from strongly poisonous plants. **Cornell University Library** possesses a copy of Jean de Nynauld's book on metamorphosis, *De la Lycanthropie Transformation et Extrase des Sorciers*, which includes recipes of magic ointments for flying through the air, and for turning into animals. SOURCE: *The Encyclopedia of Witchcraft & Demonology*, Rossell Hope Robbins; *The Witch-Cult in Western Europe*, Dr. Margaret Murray.

Fogou or **Souterrain:** Underground chambers of Cornwall and Ireland, primarily associated with Iron Age settlements. Formed by cutting a passage in the soil and concealing it with a covering of stones and earth; lined and paved with stone slabs, they were used for storage purposes, or as escape routes from the village when it was under attack. The passage of Carn Euny near Brane, Cornwall is over 60ft long and has a small circular room near the entrance, which was once underground but is now open to the sky. SOURCE: *The Secret Country*, Janet and Colin Bord.

Folk hero: A historical personage whose exploits have turned into legend, and who is seen to embody the national characteristics of the people who honor them. Llewellyn, Finn, Arthur, Boudicca, Hereward the Wake, Owain Glyndwr, Robin Hood, Robert the Bruce and Sir Francis Drake, etc., fall into this category.

Folklore: The name given to ancient cultural, magical and religious practices of the 'folk' or common people. There are similar themes found in the folk tales and beliefs of different ages and different parts of the world and many are linked to very old religions and superstitions. SOURCE: *Dictionary of British Folktales*, K. Briggs; *Folklore, Myths & Legends of Britain*, Marc Alexander; *The Golden Bough*, Sir James Frazer; *The Secret Country*, Janet & Colin Bord.

Folklore Society, The: Founded in England in 1878 to study traditional vernacular culture, including traditional music, song, dance and drama, narrative, arts and crafts, customs and belief. The foundation was prompted by a suggestion made by Eliza Gutch in the pages of *Notes and Queries*. The Society publishes a quarterly journal *Folklore*, and since 1986 a newsletter, *FLS News*. It has library facilities at the Warburg Institute and the DMS Watson Library at University College, London.

Folk Medicine: Unlike **Wort-lore**, folk medicine is the everyday usage of plants by ordinary people to cure minor wounds and ailments without the use of magic. By definition, it has no distinct 'practitioners' and was simply a family collection of first aid remedies that had been passed down through generations of country folk. SOURCE: *Memory, Wisdom & Healing*, Gabrielle Hatfield. [SEE PANEL]

Folk-mote: Anglo-Saxon for a 'folk meeting'

Fomore: In Irish tradition, the demons who are the adversaries of the gods, the **Tuatha De Danann** and who were defeated at the battle of Mag Tured.

Fontinalia: A festival (13th October) in honor of Fontus, Roman god of springs, fountains and wells, which would be decorated with garlands of flowers.

Fool, The: (1) An enigmatic character that appears in all manner of history, folklore and customs, including **Morris** dancers. The fool or jester held a privileged position and was allowed a wide latitude for satirical comment on establishment and sacred institutions. (2) The Fool is also the first card of the Major Arcana in the **Tarot**: a symbol of holy madness, he stands for the Nothing, which contains the potential existence of all things.

Fordicidia: A Roman festival to promote the fertility of cattle and fields, held on 15th April.

Foretelling: The ability to prophesy an event before it happens.

Forgotten Ones, The: The Elder Gods or the **Old Ones**.

Forneus: Appears in late medieval literature of magic and necromancy as a demonic being.

Fornicalia: A Roman spring corn festival celebrated in honor of Fornax, goddess of ovens on 4th February.

Forrabury Common, Cornwall: A unique survival of the Celtic (pre-Saxon) system of land-tenure – stitchmeal. There are 42 'stitches' or small fields grouped at the edge of the common, each field containing a portion of better soil and not so good soil.

Fortalicium Fidei: The first book ever printed (in 1467) on the subject of witchcraft by Alphonsus de Spina: the title meaning 'Fortress of Faith'. There is a copy in **Cornell** University Library, that originally belonged to the Benedictine Monastery of St. Maximin at Treves and *'nowhere in all Europe did the persecution of these unfortunates rage with greater violence than within the jurisdiction of this old abbey during the last decades of the 16th century.'* SOURCE: *The Encyclopedia of Witchcraft & Demonology*, Rossell Hope Robbins.

Fortean Times: A British monthly magazine of news, reviews and research into strange phenomena and published continuously since 1973.

Fortuna: (1) An Old Roman goddess of women, whose cult was, in part, oracular. She later turned into the goddess of good fortune and was popular with the poorer people. (2)

In art, Fortune was portrayed with a cornucopia and a globe; by the Renaissance she had been given a wheel = **Wheel of Fortune**. (3) The popular musical representation is Carl Orff's 'O Fortuna' from the *Carmina Burana* is popular with magical groups for creating atmosphere.

Fors Fortuna: One of several festivals to honor the goddess Fortuna

Fortune, Dion: (1891–1946) Born Violet Mary Firth, she became a member of the Golden Dawn in 1919 and began to write occult fiction based on her understanding of magic and the astral world. Her fiction is considered by many to be the best introduction to the world of magic and should be on the reading list of anyone who wishes to know more about the subject before making any major commitment. Like many occultists, she used fiction as a teaching device, well aware that she could disseminate truths otherwise incommunicable to uninitiated minds. In 1924 she established the Society of the Inner Light. TITLES: *The Demon Lover, The Goat-Foot God, The Winged Bull, Sea Priestess, Moon Magic, Applied Magic, Sane Occultism, The Mystical Qabalah* and *An Introduction to Ritual Magic*, with Gareth Knight. SOURCE: *Priestess*, Alan Richardson; *The Story of Dion Fortune*, Charles Fielding and Carr Collins.

Fortune Telling: see **Divination.**

Fossil: The remains of fauna and flora that were trapped inside rocks and turned to stone. The most common are in the shape of shells, bones, teeth, leaves and tree bark. Perfect for amulets and magical work involving 'time'.

Foundation Sacrifice: The killing and burial of a sacrificial victim in the foundations of a building in order that its spirit will keep away evil or negative influences. In ancient times, the victim may have been human but, up until comparatively recently, animal remains have been discovered beneath the threshold of old buildings, or under the floorboards. SOURCE: *The Realm of Ghosts*, Eric Maple; *White Horse: Equine Magical Lore*, Rupert Percy.

Four: A sacred number representing completeness, since it encompassed the four elements, and thought to be the luckiest of the even numbers – hence, the four-leaf clover. It represents earth orientation and balance. The number IV equals the **Emperor** in the **Tarot** (or four Fours of the Minor Arcana), **Chesed** in the **Qabalah** and governed by **Jupiter.**

Four Ways: The crossroads. **Hecate** was the Greek goddess of the 'parting ways' whose three heads were that of a maned horse (left), a snake (middle) and a frenzied bitch (right).

Fowlis Wester, Perthshire: A fine Pictish symbol stone, 10 ft high, that stands inside railings in the village. The carvings are elaborate examples of Pictish work.

Fox: Features surprisingly little in the superstition of the British Isles except among the hunting fraternity, and yet its image is widespread on British inn signs, especially in hunting country. The animal's fur and teeth have valuable magical properties.

Fox Stones: see **Orchis.**

Frankincense: A gum resin used in incense and perfume. It is ruled by the **Sun** and **Saturn** and is used in their fumes; it keeps away witches when

Folk Medicine: Nature's Medicine Chest

Unlike the wort-lore of traditional witchcraft, folk or domestic plant medicine is the everyday use of plants by ordinary people to cure minor wounds and ailments. Although there is a wealth of material from the classic herbals and herbalists recorded by the Benedictine monk Aelfric, the Physicians of Myddfai and the 17th century apothecary, physician and astrologer, Nicholas Culpeper, very little has been preserved of the common plant remedies used by our forebears.

Effective home remedies did not require any accompanying ritual to make them work and a countrywoman would merely pick the necessary plants from the garden or hedgerow to make a preparation for the family's fever, or to treat a wound. A hot infusion made from diaphoretic and febrifugal herbs, such as yarrow, comfrey and cayenne, will increase perspiration and help to reduce a high fever. While towards the end of WWI, the British government used tons of sphagnum moss as surgical dressing, placed directly on to wounds when the demand for cotton bandages could not be met. Fortunately this folk remedy had not faded from memory and is still used in some rural areas.

Similarly, feverfew has been used since the Middle Ages for its analgesic properties. Culpeper recommended the herb for 'all pains in the head' and current research has proven the efficacy of feverfew in the relieving of migraines and headaches when taken as a tea.

The common 'weed' plantain has long been recognized as an excellent restorative and tonic for all forms of respiratory congestions – nasal catarrh, bronchitis, sinusitis and middle ear infections. The plant's demulcent qualities make it useful in an infusion for painful urination. As a lotion, plantain calms the irritation and itching of insect bites, stings and skin irritations; and as a disinfectant and styptic for wounds and how many of us automatically search for a dock leaf after a close encounter with a stinging nettle?

With all its magical connotations and fairy connections, the elder has long been known as the 'poor man's medicine chest' because its flowers and berries have so many uses in treating respiratory infections and fevers. The leaves make a useful ointment for bruises, sprains and wounds, while an ointment made from the flowers is excellent for chilblains. The inner bark has a history of use as a purgative dating back to the time of Hippocrates, and we must not forget the 'tonic' of elderflower champagne and elderberry wine!

Through the daily life of ordinary country people, the use of folk medicine had been preserved with remarkable accuracy from one generation to another up to the early 20th century. As a result of two world wars and with the large-scale dispersal of country people to the towns, the need for folk medicine diminished. The old people who remained no longer had anyone left to whom they could pass this age-old wisdom and so it died out for lack of interest.

Today there is a renewed interest in natural medicine and the old remedies are being researched by a joint project called Ethnomedica. Involving medical herbalists and botanists, their aim is to gather information about country remedies throughout Britain.

EXTRACT FROM FIELDCRAFT
A WITCH'S GUIDE TO FIELDS AND HEDGEROWS
MÉLUSINE DRACO

hung in the entry of a house.

Fraudulent Mediums Act: The Act of 1951 finally took the concept of witchcraft off the statute book by repealing the **Witchcraft Act** of 1736.

Freemasonry: An international all-male organization, devoted to charitable and social activities, and the practice of certain esoteric rites. It is not a religion, although in most countries masons must acknowledge a 'Supreme Being', venerated as the 'Great Architect of the Universe'. Members of a Masonic lodge begin by taking three degrees, which are conferred with impressive rituals dramatizing the soul's progress from darkness to spiritual light and rebirth. Freemasonry began in the Middle Ages, but nearly all Freemasonry in existence today can ultimately be traced to the Grand Lodge of England constituted in 1717. SOURCE: *Bibliotheca Masonica*, F.L. Gardner; *Born In Blood*, John J. Robinson; *Freemason's Guide & Compendium*, B.E. Jones; *Man, Myth & Magic*, Richard Cavendish; *The Mason Apron*, Frank Higgins; *The Tau*, J. Cooper Malcolm; *Speculative Freemasonry*, John Yarker; *The Templar Orders in Freemasonry*, A.E. Waite.

French Witchcraft: The European witchcraft heresy started in France as a result of theological and legal discussions that created a detailed concept of a pact with the Devil on which the justification of trials for witchcraft were built. Following the formula, suggested by the University of Paris in 1398, sorcery passed from magic to religion, and witchcraft became an anti-Catholic heresy, and subject to the Inquisition. *The Encyclopedia of Witchcraft and Demonology* by Dr Rossell Hope Robbins provides a short but detailed history of witchcraft in France under 40 separate entries.

Frensham Cauldron: In a cave near Waverley Abbey lived a witch known as Mother Ludlam who would lend anything to her neighbors, providing it was returned within two days. Someone failed to return a **Cauldron** within the stipulated time and the witch never lent anything again. When the cauldron was finally returned, she ignored it and tradition says it was taken to the Abbey, and then to Frensham church where it remains to this day.

Freud, Sigmund: The mystic and the occultist are in touch intuitively with the hidden recesses of the mind: Freud developed a method of exploring the unconscious that has influenced nearly every aspect of contemporary life.

Freyja and **Freyr:** The principal deities of the **Vanir**.

Friday the 13th: Supposed to be an unlucky day whenever this falls in the calendar. One theory is that it refers to the day – Friday 13th October 1307 – when the **Knights Templar** were arrested and eventually executed, on the order of Philip IV of France.

Frog: Widely used in cures for human ailments but to kill a frog was believed to be unlucky. Various parts of the creature were given as frequent ingredients in many fictional magic potions and recipes, such as those in *Macbeth* and *Masque of Queens*.

Frost Giants: Germanic mythology differs from Celtic in its greater emphasis on the adversaries of the gods. The **Aesir** were under continual threat from the frost giants, representing cold, chaos and sterility.

Fudo Myoo: Japanese folk god who wields the sword of knowledge in his fight against hate and greed, which are characteristics of ignorance.

Fukurokuju: [Japanese = luck, riches, long life] Japanese god portrayed with an exaggeratedly high cranium, and accompanied by a crane and a tortoise as symbols of longevity.

Fulmar: A gull-like bird, white with a grey back, that has acquired almost legendary status in Britain – and naturalist James Fisher's huge monograph, *The Fulmar*, now fetches a small fortune in second-hand bookshops. It was once essential to the economy of small islands and was hunted for its oil and flesh; the bird's vomit was collected and shipped to England and Edinburgh was used medicinally.

Fumarole: [Latin *fumus*, smoke] A hole emitting gases in a volcano or volcanic region.

Fume: Smoke or vapor. The traditional term for burning herbs and incense within a magical operation.

Fumitory: A plant of the genus *Fumaria*. Old French *fume-terre*, literally earth-smoke, so called because its rapid growth was thought to resemble the dispersal of smoke. Used in magical workings to create **Illusion**.

Funerary Rites: The word 'funeral' comes from the Latin *funis*, a torch, and refers to a torchlight procession because funerals among the Romans took place at night. The custom of giving a feast at funerals also came from the Romans, who not only feasted the friends of the dead, but also distributed meat to their employees. SOURCE: *Death & the Pagan*, Philip Wright & Carrie West.

Fungi: The collective botanical term for mushrooms and toadstools. Britain has more poisonous fungi than any other country in Europe and knowledge of these would have been part of traditional witchcraft. SOURCE: *Mushrooms & Toadstools of Britain and Europe*, Edmund Garnweidner.

Furrinalia: In Roman religion, the goddess Furrina's nature and function became obscure although her festival (25th July) continued to be observed right up until Cicero's time.

Furry Dance: A public festival that takes place on the nearest Saturday to the Feast of St. Michael (8th May) at Helston in Cornwall. The name is derived either from the Middle English word *ferrie*, implying a festival, or the Celtic *feur*, meaning a holiday or fair; its seasonal setting suggests the dance may once have been a pagan spring festival.

Futhark, Elder: The oldest form of runic alphabet of 24 runes used by the Germanic tribes from the 2nd to 8th centuries for inscriptions on artifacts such as jewelry, amulets, tools, weapons and runestones. Unlike the Younger Futhark, which remained in use until modern times, the knowledge of how to read the Elder Futhark was forgotten, and it was not until 1865 that the Norwegian scholar Sophus Bugge managed to decipher it.

Futhark, Younger: Also known as Scandinavian runes is a reduced form of the Elder Futhark, consisting of only 16 characters that was in use from c800AD.

Futhore: A runic alphabet used by the Anglo-Saxons from around the 5th century onwards. It was developed from the Elder **Futhark** of 24 runes, and contained between 26 and 33 characters.

Furze: see **Gorse**.

Fylgir: In Germanic belief they were protective spirits or guardians attached to individuals. If they chose to appear, it was in the form of a woman or an animal. They were not the object of any sort of worship.

G

Gaia: (1) A popular term to refer to the **Earth** as an idealistic form of the Great Mother; taken, from the 'Gaia Hypothesis' presented by Dr. James Lovelock and Dr. Sidney Epton (1975) in the *New Scientist*. (2) In classical Greek mythology, Gaia or Ge is the personification of the Earth, having sprung from Chaos, according to the writings of Hesiod.

Galactite: A stone, probably a nitrate of lime when powdered and mixed with water appears milky. Taken in a potion it was believed to increase the flow of a woman's milk, and also enhance her breasts.

Galaxy, The: The 'Milky Way', the long white luminous track of stars that seems to encompass the night sky. According to classic fable it is the path to the palace of Zeus. From the Greek, *gala*, milk, genitive, *galaktos*.

Galen: (129–199AD) A Greek physician and philosopher, he continued to exert an important influence over the theory and practice of medicine until the mid-17th century in Europe and the Middle East. Along with **Hippocrates**, Galen formed a vital landmark of 600 years of Greek medicine and Galenism became the means by which Greek medicine was known to the world and handed down to subsequent generations. SOURCE: *Lithotomy to Music*, Dr. Harold Selcon.

Gallicenae: The nine virgin priestesses of the Gallic oracle. By their charms they could raise the wind and waves, turn themselves into any animal they chose, cure wounds and diseases, and predict future events.

Gamaheu: A natural cameo (chiefly agate) containing an image of plants, landscapes or animals. Pliny writes that the Agate of Pyrrhus contained a representation of the nine Muses with Apollo in their midst. **Paracelsus** called them natural talismans. **Albertus Magnus** mentioned them as having magical powers.

Gardner, Gerald Brousseau: (1884–1964) Known as the 'father of modern **Wicca**', having brought about the witchcraft revival following the repeal of the Witchcraft Act in 1951. Gardner was always interested in magic and occultism and spent a lot of time expanding his contacts when he returned to England from the Far East. He was initiated into the coven of the New Forest witches in 1939 into what he claimed was a hereditary group. In 1946 he met Cecil Williamson, the founder of the Museum of Witchcraft on the Isle of Man; in 1947, he was introduced to Aleister **Crowley**, shortly before the latter's death. By 1952 he had bought the museum building and display cases from Cecil Williamson and operated his own museum. TITLES: His first book, *High Magicks' Aid* was a novel, which was followed by two non-fictional works, *Witchcraft Today* and *The Meaning of Witchcraft*. SOURCE: *Wiccan Roots: Gerald Gardner & the Witchcraft Revival* and *Gerald Gardner & the Cauldron of Inspiration*, Philip Heselton; *Lid Off the Cauldron*, Patricia Crowther; *The Pickingill Papers: The Origin of Gardnerian Witchcraft*, W.E.

Liddell, ed by Michael Howard.

Gardnerian Tradition: The name given to a branch of modern **Wicca** named after its founder Gerald **Gardner**. It is generally accepted that Gardner 'invented' the tradition to satisfy his own sense of the esoteric, drawing upon the magical texts of Aleister **Crowley**, basic **Freemasonry**, Margaret **Murray**'s theories, together with a smattering of witch-lore, folklore and assorted mythology.

Garlic: Used for thousands of years as a protection against vampires, the evil eye and other supernatural forces. It has also been used more commonly in the treatment of a wide range of ailments. Ruling planet: **Mars**

Garnet: see **Carbuncle**.

Garrett, Eileen: Born in Ireland in 1893 and one of the most remarkable mediums of the 20th century, who was unusual in that she was never prepared to take her psychic abilities at face value, and always attempted to give them a strictly scientific validation. She died in 1970.

Garter: (1) Worn in rituals and as badges of rank, with snakeskin garters being the emblem of high rank within Craft. Some were also made of the strips of a young hare's skin saturated with motherwort, to give the witch speed to escape her pursuers. There are many styles of witch garters in existence but they are only worn on specific occasions. (2) Garters play a large part in folklore and are worn by Morris dancers, with *Green Garters* being the name of an old tune used for the Morris. (3) Part of the insignia worn by members of The Most Noble Order of the Garter. Founded by Edward III c1348, it is the highest

order of knighthood, comprising the sovereign and 25 knights. According to legend it was established after the Countess of Salisbury accidentally dropped her garter while dancing with the King; having retrieved it he made the remark *Honi soit qui mal y pense* (evil to him who thinks evil of it). It is believed that the garter was a sign that the Countess was a witch. SOURCE: *Malleus Satani, The Hammer of Satan,* Suzanne Ruthven; *Mastering Witchcraft,* Paul Huson.

Gastromancy: Divination during which a psychic transmits a baritone voice that is unlike the usual voice of the psychic.

Gaueko: In **Basque** tradition, the lord of darkness, or spirit of the night. He may on occasion prove friendly and helpful, but he can also appear as a devil. He manifests as a cow or a gust of wind.

Geb: The Egyptian earth god and brother-consort of the sky goddess Nut, on whom he fathered the deities of the Osirian mythos. Geb features widely in the Pyramid era where he is frequently depicted with green skin (a characteristic he shares with his son, **Osiris**).

Geburah: Known as Might and the fifth Path on the **Tree of Life**, known as 'radical intelligence' it is also called *pachad* (terror), which refers to the misuse of strength. The **Names of Power** are of war, protector and avenger deities (see **Mars**).

Gehenna: The Biblical term for Hell because it carries the connotations of torture and unhappiness. The word comes from *Ge Hinnom*, which was a small valley on the outskirts of Jerusalem, where the ancient god

Moloch was worshipped. This gave the place its sinister reputation and it later became the city's dumping area for waste materials. The bodies of dead animals and criminals were burned there and acrid smoke continually rose from the valley where the flies of Beelzebub were said to live.

Geller, Uri: Born in 1946, he became an international celebrity with the ability to bend a variety of metal objects, and who has undergone numerous laboratory tests to prove that his powers are genuine.

Gelomancy: Derived from the Greek *geleo* = to laugh, this method of divination interpreted sounds other than those used in speech, particularly laughter.

Gematria: The fact that the letters of the Hebrew and Greek alphabets also stood for numbers is the basis of gematria, a method of finding hidden meanings, underlying the surface of a written text by turning the word into a number and then finding another word that has the same total.

Gemini: (1) The third sign of the zodiac (20 May–21 June), which various cultures have seen as twins – either as gods, men, plants or animals – the Greeks naming them Castor and Pollux. (2) The constellation of Gemini is located above Canis Minor.

Gemstones: see **Lepidary**. [SEE PANEL]

Genii or **Genius:** (1) In the Roman religion, the indwelling spirit (*numen*) of man, which gave him the power of generation and later came to mean the fully developed power of man. The corresponding spirit in woman was known as 'Juno'. (2) Any locality, such as an open space, might have its own *genius loci*, or protecting spirit.

Gentian: All gentians were once regarded as a panacea. The species most used in medieval European medicine was the great yellow gentian (*gentiana lutea*). Ruling planet: **Mars.**

Geomancy: A form of divination by interpreting the patterns and shapes of objects or events found in nature; inspecting the configurations made by scattered pebbles, the blowing of dust upon a smooth surface; the casting of twigs, grain or seeds; watching ashes on the hearth or dead leaves floating on a pool. The word is derived from the Greek words, *gaie*, the earth and *manteia*, divination. SOURCE: *The Complete Golden Dawn System of Magic*, Israel Regardie; *Earth Divination, Earth Magic*, John Michael Greer; *Techniques of High Magic*, Francis King and Stephen Skinner.

Gerard, John: Herbalist and superintendent of Lord Burghley's gardens, published *The Herball* or *Generall Historie of Plantes* in 1597.

German Witchcraft: *Schrecken* = horror, is the German for witchcraft. According to Dr. Rossell Hope Robbins in his *Encyclopedia of Witchcraft and Demonology*, at least 100,000 people were executed as witches in Germany and the torturous methods used to extract confessions knew no bounds. One executioner constructed an oven in which, over a nine year period, he roasted to death over 1,000 persons, including children of two to four years of age.

Gesture: To convey meaning without words. Most cultures have ritual gestures as part of their culture or belief; ceremonial magic employs a large number of ritual gestures.

Gemstones, Rocks & Crystals

Although shop-bought rocks and crystals are beautiful things to own, those with the greatest magical properties are the ones we find for ourselves. Our world is built of rocks and crystals, made from hundreds of minerals, in differing amounts to make up hundreds of different kinds of rock.

The traditional witch was more likely to use a local piece of rock (or pebble) as a power object or amulet, and most people can visit a shingle beach — here we will find a wide variety of colorful and beautiful semi-precious stones which are ours for the taking. Having said that, good pebbles are to be found anywhere in the shallow stream bed, on the sandy banks of an inland river, turned over in a plowed field, even dug up our own garden.

It isn't necessary to acquire a degree in geology to collect 'magical' pebbles because our choice is reliant on a small stone that catches our eye because of its unusual color or shape. We may discover it under unusual circumstances, or it may be something that we feel the need to pick up and possess. Having come straight from the Earth, how much more potent this will be than a polished crystal that has been mined and commercially prepared for the High Street 'Crystal Cave'.

Quartz is one of the most popular of 'crystals' and pebbles having quartz as their dominant constituent are to be found on almost every beach in Britain. The differences in color and appearance are due to varying amounts of other minerals in each one, and also to the way in which the quartz has formed. Did you know that quartz is solid silica and if it did not crystallize when it solidified it is known as flint? Everyone knows that two flints struck together will produce a spark, but it is not generally known that *all* quartz pebbles will do the same and often produce bigger and better sparks. This can be viewed as magical fire from the very Earth itself — but would you want to risk smashing expensive, shop-bought quartz together to produce the same result? Clear quartz will produce an orange spark if two pieces are struck together in a darkened room, together with the smell of burning.

These crystals cost £££s in occult shops, but how much more satisfying to discover our own raw variety. It may not have been subjected to the lapidary's polishing techniques but it will be all the more magical for that. Even a crude flint hagstone straight from the field will have more earth-energy than a glittering lump of amethyst that has been sitting on a shelf in a shop and having everyone pawing over it.

EXTRACT FROM *MEAN STREETS WITCHCRAFT*
MÉLUSINE DRACO

SOURCE: *Gestures*, Desmond Morris.

Ghost: see **Hauntings.**

Ghost Dance: Following the disappearance of the buffalo and the increasing intrusion of the white man, Native American medicine men introduced the Ghost Dance in the late 1880s to call upon the imminent resurrection of the dead **Ancestors** and the restoration of the past. Although essentially peaceful, it instilled fear in the 'white man' and prompted a violent reaction from the government. The movement came to an end with the massacre at Wounded Knee in 1890. SOURCE: *500 Nations*, Alvin M. Josephy.

Ghoul: An entity supposed to feed on the dead and the most dangerous species of demon, from the Arabic *ghul*.

Giants: A belief in the former existence of a race of giants is worldwide. They feature in mythology and folklore, in local legends and fairy tales – their immense strength and size often made them objects of terror. Geoffrey of Monmouth in his *History of the Kings of Britain* (1135) tells the story of **Gog** and **Magog**, the only survivors of a race of giants in Britain.

Gilgamesh, Epic of: The story of the Babylonian hero Gilgamesh's (c1760BC) search for eternal life and of the origin of kingship. The epic also gives the earliest-known account of a universal flood, which is thought to have influenced the flood narrative in the Bible.

Gilles de Rais: A soldier and companion of **Jeanne d' Arc**, he was accused of performing ritual sacrifice and black magic to replenish his dwindling wealth, although modern examination of the trial records suggests an element of family conspiracy against him. He was executed in 1440. SOURCE: *Gilles de Rais*, A.L. Vincent and Clare Binns.

Gilly-flower: see **Clove Pink**. The name 'gilly-flower' was used in medieval times to also describe stocks or wallflowers.

Ginger: Brought by the Romans to Britain, as a hot, dry herb, the root of ginger was prescribed to warm the stomach, promote perspiration and treat colds. In powdered form it was used as a spice and added to cakes, confectionary, gingerbread and ginger beer. Ruling planet: **Mars**.

Glamouring: A spell frequently used by witches to cast **Illusion** and **Fascination**.

Glastonbury: Believed to have been a pagan holy place in the middle of a vast area of water and marshland. Geological studies reveal that before being drained during the Middle Ages, Glastonbury Tor was virtually an island for most of the year. Welsh legend says it is the entrance to Otherworld and the home of Gwyn-ap-Nudd, Lord of the **Faere Folk** and leader of the **Wild Hunt**. It is also said to be the last resting place of King **Arthur**. SOURCE: *Folklore, Myths & Customs*, Marc Alexander.

Glastonbury Zodiac: In 1927 an English artist, Katherine Maltwood, claimed to have discovered that a system of landmarks and prehistoric earthworks around Glastonbury could be interpreted as a gigantic zodiacal chart imprinted on the landscape. Skeptics question whether the ancient culture that is supposed to have created the layout would have had the same interpretation of a zodiac that had come originally via the Greeks and Romans.

Glossolalia: The technical term for 'speaking in tongues'; the ability to use an unknown and mysterious language when in a state of trance or intense religious excitement.

Gnosis: The general term for seeking knowledge without the use of the five traditional senses.

Gnome: A creature of Elemental Earth. Spirits made from the atoms of earth in which they live.

Gnosticism: The pursuit of knowledge of the 'Real as opposed to the unreal'. The basic doctrine is that knowledge is the way to salvation; those who are worthy receive the saving knowledge from a redeemer-revealer. Originally the Gnostics were of a semi-Christian faith originating in Egypt, who refused to accept that God had made the wicked world. They held the dualistic belief that the visible world was created by the **Demiurge**, a type of being somewhere between God and created beings. SOURCE: *The Elements of Gnosticism*, Stuart Holroyd; *The Gnostic Religion*, H. Jonas; *The History of Magic*, Kurt Seligmann.

Gnostic Mass, The: The essence of *The Book of the Law* transmuted into ritual for performance as a group working. SOURCE: *Gems From the Equinox*, edited by Israel Regardie

Goat: A much-maligned creature known for its proverbial lechery, its stench and its links with the Devil, all of which were connected in reports of the witch-trials in Europe. The goat was also connected with **Azazel**, the leader of the **Watchers** in Jewish tradition, whereby an animal was selected each year and formally loaded with the sins of the people before being driven out into the wilderness – hence the term 'scapegoat'. Herodotus recorded the libidinous activities surrounding the goat-worshipping cult of the people of Mendes (which was, in fact, a ram and sacred to Amun), which he also equated with the Greek god, **Pan**. Much later, the goat was identified in esoteric literature by Eliphas **Levi** as the Goat of **Mendes**, or **Baphomet**, which he believed to have been the Devil of the witches' sabbats.

Goat's Hole Cave: see **Paviland**.

Goblin: A general term for a small, dark, ugly and mischievous or evil fairy.

Goddess, The: In contemporary **Wicca** and paganism she is the embodiment of the Great Mother, 'whose limitless fertility brings forth life'. Most modern traditions emphasize the Goddess aspect of the Divine Force, some almost to the total exclusion of the male principle, the **Horned** God. The latter is the major cause for the schism that exists between modern Wicca and Old Craft, since older forms of witchcraft are generally god-oriented. SOURCE: *The White Goddess*, Robert Graves.

Gods and **Goddesses:** Supernatural beings, worshipped in various cultures and religions throughout history as creators of the universe, personifications of natural forces and controllers of human existence. SOURCE: *Dictionary of Gods & Goddesses, Devils & Demons*, Manfred Lurker.

Goeteia, Mageia: A classic term for witchcraft. Although the Greeks disapproved of it, they made great use of its properties. '*Mageia* boomed in Hellenistic times, enriched as it was by new, oriental material. Clients of all classes sought to win somebody's love, or to harm their enemies, etc. The means used included spells (*epodai*) and curses (*katadeseis/katadesmoi*), which were inscribed on tablets and buried, preferably in graves.' In addition, wax figurines were melted or stuck with pins, or bound lead figurines were placed in graves. SOURCE: *The Penguin Dictionary of Religions*, ed by John R. Hinnells.

Goetia: A form of magic involving the 'penetration of subconscious strata', i.e. the abode of spirits and demons disassociated from the human life-wave. SOURCE: *The Book of Black Magic & of Pacts*, A.E. Waite; *The Goetia*, Aleister Crowley.

Gogmagog: A legendary giant whose story is told in Geoffrey of Monmouth's *Historia Regum Britanniae*, and the hill figure on the Gogmagog Hills located by T.C. Lethridge in the 1950s. The figure is obscured by grass but there is a full account of them in his book *Gog Magog: The Buried Gods*. The original statue of Gogmagog was destroyed in the Great Fire of London in 1666; it was replaced by *two* new statues in 1708 and the legend arose that these were Gog *and* Magog, the last of the British giants. The present statues replaced the 18th century ones that were destroyed when the Guildhall was bombed in 1940 (see **Giants**).

Goibniu: In ancient Ireland the god of the **Blacksmith's** craft, whose magical powers enabled him to turn out weapons that could not fail. He also possessed the mead that gave eternal life. In the Welsh tradition he was called Govannon, and farmers need his help to clean the ploughshare.

Gold: From the earliest of civilizations, gold has been treasured and valued in its physical substance, and also as a symbol of something equivalent in value and rarity in the mental and spiritual life of man. Identified with the **Sun**.

Golden Bough, The: The classic collection of folklore, religion, magic and superstition by Sir James Frazer. The primary aim of the book was to explain the remarkable rule that regulated the succession of the **Dianic** priesthood and the influence of superstition and magic on different cultures. The 'golden bough' of the title refers to the **Mistletoe**, which was sacred to the **Druids**.

Golden Age, The: Nearly all cultures have in their mythology a time of innocent happiness, when men lived without strife or labor, or injustice; the earth yielding its fruits in abundance. For the Greeks, this was a time when **Saturn** and Cronus ruled the world; for the Egyptians it was *zep tepi*, the 'First Time'. This was followed by the Silver Age when mankind was impious and almost destroyed by the gods; then came the Bronze Age when men destroyed one another. This was followed by the Heroic Age, a time of heroic exploits, only to be succeeded by the present Iron Age, which is seen as the worst of all.

Golden Dawn: see **Hermetic Order of the Golden Dawn**.

Golem: A Hebrew word for an artificially created being, a homunculus. Now more commonly associated with a character from J.R.R. Tolkien's *The Hobbit* and *The Lord of the Rings*. SOURCE: *Alchemy: An*

Illustrated A-Z, Diana Fernando.

Good Woman or **Good Wife:** An early medieval term for a village witch.

Goofer Dust: A **Voodoo** term for **Graveyard Dust**.

Goose: The impressive flight of flocks of geese flying overhead gave rise to countless myths and legends. The noise made by migrating barnacle geese at night became associated with the Gabriel **Hounds**. The farmyard goose is derived from the Greylag goose and has been domesticated for at least 4000 years, although the Celts have a long taboo against eating geese, which were kept for ritual sacrifice. SOURCE: *Fauna Britannica*, Stefan Buczacki.

Goose Grass or **Cleavers:** A native plant of Britain, medieval herbalists used it to make a general cleansing tonic, and for treating glandular and urinary problems. **Culpeper** said that is was a good remedy for strengthening the blood. Ruling planet: **Moon**.

Gooseberry: Although native to Britain, the gooseberry was rarely grown in medieval English gardens. **Culpeper** said that the fruit *was 'cooling and astringent, creating an appetite and quenching a thirst.'* **Gerard** recorded that the fruit *'is much used in dinners, sauces for meats and used in broth instead of verjuice.'* Ruling planet: **Venus**.

Gorse (Furze or **Whin):** A native to Britain, the shrub was listed by **Aelfric**. In folklore it was considered unlucky to take gorse into the house, although it was used for fuel, as hedging to protect livestock from predators and for hanging washing. A decoction made from the flowers was prescribed for jaundice and kidney problems; the flowers were used to make gorse wine.

Ruling planet: **Mars**.

***Gospel of the Witches*:** see ***Aradia*.**

***Gospels of the Devil*:** Under this title, Claude Seignolle gathered together many popular French superstitions, describing the traditional infernal underworld.

Gothic Society, The: (1990–1998) Described as England's purplest literary society, the organization encouraged serious scholarship alongside outrageous costume parties – and is fondly remembered for the famous Summer Party held in the Reptile House at London Zoo.

Gough's Cave, Cheddar: A cave occupied during the last phase of the Ice Age, where excavation has revealed large quantities of flint and bone implements and ornaments, as well as food debris. A burial of this period has also been found and has been preserved on site. The uppermost layers of the cave floor contained evidence of the cave's occupation in Iron Age and Romano-British times.

Gowdie, Isobel: In four separate confessions, made apparently without torture between 13th April and 27th May 1662, Isobel Gowdie gave what amounted to a resume of popular beliefs about witchcraft. It was the longest and most detailed witch trial in Britain. The court records do not give details of her fate but she was finally hanged at Elgin. SOURCE: *The Encyclopedia of Witchcraft & Demonology*, Rossell Hope Robbins; *Man, Myth & Magic*, ed Richard Cavendish; *Folklore, Myths & Customs*, Marc Alexander.

Goya, Francisco: The paintings of witches by this famous Spanish artist are among the most spectacular in esoteric art. Witches are shown in all manner of guises, *Caprichos* being an excellent example of his interest in this field.

Graces: In Greek mythology, the Three Graces, or *Charites*: Aglaia (the radiant), Thalia (the flowering) and Euphrosyne (joy) were personifications of grace and charm (see **Fate** and **Triple Goddess**).

Grail, The: Has as its secret *'those things that the heart of mortal man cannot conceive nor tongue relate'*. In classical terms, although the Grail is more often than not a product of **Arthurian** romance, the roots of the legends relating to it are much older (see **Cauldron**), although most of this has now been submerged under Christian myths referring to the 'blood' of Christ. SOURCE: *The Mabinogion; Man, Myth & Magic*, Richard Cavendish; *The Quest of the Holy Grail*, P.M. Matarasso.

Grain: As a protection against witchcraft, scatter grain around the sleeping place. It was believed that a witch would not be able to count the grain before sunrise and therefore could do no harm.

Grant, Kenneth: A devotee of Aleister Crowley's Law of **Thelema**. In 1955 he set up his own Isis Lodge in England to further the study and application of *The Book of the Law*, following the form of magick pursued by Crowley after the latter's Egyptian initiation in 1904. He is head of several organizations, which serve as channels for the Typhonian Tradition, about which he has written extensively and in depth in a series of trilogies including *The Magical Revival, Aleister Crowley & the Hidden God, Cults of the Shadows, Nightside of Eden, Outside the Circles of Time* and *Hecate's Fountain*.

Graphology: Interpretation of personal characteristics through the study of handwriting. Now used as a forensic science in crime detection.

Grave Goods: The archeological description given to any items that are buried as part of a ceremonial interment. SOURCE: *The Goddess of the Stones*, George Terence Meaden; *Britain BC*, Francis Pryor.

Graveyard Dust: A deadly ingredient of spells and charms to kill or harm enemies. Needs to be taken from an actual grave site.

Gray, William (Bill) G: A modern ritual magician and author, whose works included *The Ladder of Lights, Magical Ritual Methods, An Outlook on Our Inner Western Way, Sangreal Sacrament, Inner Traditions of Magic* and *Seasonal Occult Rituals*. He was considered by Israel Regardie to be the best modern author on occult matters. Born to an astrologer mother in 1913, according to his obituary, he represented a direct link with traditional 19th century magical groups as well as being a direct influence on the emerging **Wiccan** movement. SOURCE: *The Old Sod*, Alan Richardson.

Great Beast, The: The name by which Aleister Crowley was known for most of his life. Taken from the *Book of Revelation*, this refers to the beast of the Apocalypse, whose number is 666 (see **Beast**).

Great Rite, The: Represents the inner marriage of the soul and spirit and, depending on the tradition, is performed within the Circle at initiations (such as third degree initiations in the **Gardnerian** and **Alexandrian** traditions) and handfastings. As part of the initiation ceremony the Rite is performed either 'in token', that is symbolically, or 'in true' between intimate partners.

Great Work, The: An alchemical or magical term denoting the bringing of substance or energy to the fullest possible degree of perfection. Also designates the nature of the next stage in the evolution of humanity/consciousness = the union of the microcosm and the macrocosm.

Greek Tradition: In the religion of classical Greece, elements from Minoan Crete blended with elements from the Greek mainland: *'the most dramatic form of the lengthy process was a struggle, never quite to be resolved between the concept of a mother goddess (**Hera**) and the newer concept of a dominating male god,* **Zeus**.*' According to the entry in *Man, Myth & Magic*, the history of Greek religion reflects an uneven, halting but recognizable development from magic to officially sponsored religion; from an epoch when men had not clearly separated themselves from **Nature** and natural forces to a time when gods and goddesses were worshipped in human shape. SOURCE: *Arcana Mundi: Magic & the Occult in the Greek & Roman Worlds*, Georg Luck; *Epilegemena: Brief Summary of the Origins of the Greek Religion*, J.E. Harrison; *The Greeks & Their Gods*, W.K.C. Guthrie; *The History of Magic*, Kurt Seligmann; *The Iliad* and *The Odyssey*, Homer; *The Oxford Companion to Classical Literature*, ed by Sir Paul Harvey.

Green: The only color to be consistently regarded as unlucky, possibly because of its connection with the **Faere Folk**, who were said to resent mortals wearing it.

Green Man, The: Representative of the spirit of the woodlands, often appearing in medieval art, including the carved stonework in churches; a good example can be found in the cloisters of Worcester Cathedral, just opposite the Chapter House. He is also called Jack-in-the-Green or Green Jack, and a large number of these representations can be found on medieval ecclesiastical buildings, while more modern interpretations can be found on British pub signs

Gregorian Calendar: The reformed calendar of the Church of Rome, introduced by Pope Gregory XIII in 1582, which corrected the error of the civil year, according to the **Julian** Calendar.

Gremlin: A mischievous air spirit believed to play havoc with airplanes. The name is said to have been coined by a British bomber squadron prior to WWII. Now used to explain glitches with anything mechanical.

Griffin or **Gryphon:** A fabulous creature with the forequarters of a dragon, the hindquarters of a lion, an eagle's head with prominent pointed ears, and small bat wings. They were known to the Greeks and Romans as their coins and sculpture testify, and said to be one of the fiercest, most active and quickest of animals. SOURCE: *The Concise Encyclopedia of Heraldry*, Guy Cadogan Rothery.

Grimalkin: Shakespeare has one of his witches in *Macbeth* say: *'I come Graymalkin...'* meaning her diabolical master. The cat, supposed to be the companion of witches, is often called by the same name.

Grimes Graves: The Neolithic flint mines in Norfolk from which the flint extraction was at its peak around 2100–1800BC. In 1939 a small votive group, consisting of a roughly fashioned female figure, fertility symbols and antler picks, was discovered in one of the abandoned tunnels. The 'altar' to a little chalk goddess may still be seen in one of the open pits.

Grimm Brothers: Generations of children have been entranced by the fairy tales of the Grimm brothers, who were not only distinguished German linguistic scholars, but also the founders of scientific folklore.

Grimoire: Old books of magical rituals that include directions for the making and use of magical equipment. Although the material in the grimoires are drawn from Hermetic, Hebrew and Latin sources, most came into popular circulation during the Middle Ages and the Renaissance when they were not just the property of sorcerers and magicians, but also the clergy, physicians and nobles. They usually contain long and laborious instructions for evoking demons and spirits, who would be directed to do the magician's bidding. SOURCES: *The Book of Black Magic & of Pacts*, A.E. Waite; *Goetia*, Aleister Crowley; *The Book of the Sacred Magic of Abra-Melin the Mage*, S.L. MacGregor Mathers; *Dictionary of Demons*, Fred Gettings;

Grim Reaper: (1) The personification of death as a cowled or skeletal figure, carrying a scythe and an hourglass. (2) The image is used for **Death** in the Major Arcana of the **Tarot**.

Gris-Gris: The **Voodoo** term for charms or talismans kept for good luck or to ward off evil; they are usually small cloth bags filled with herbs, oils, stones, and personal items.

Groundsel: Although a common weed, groundsel has been valued as a healing herb since at least Roman times and listed by **Aelfric**. Ruling planet: **Venus**.

Grove: Sacred groves of trees have played an important part in the religious rites of many different societies, including those of the Semitic peoples of the Near and Middle East, the Greeks and Romans, and the early Celtic and Germanic tribes. In Britain, the most well-known sacred groves refer to those of the **Druids** and the **Iceni**. SOURCE: *Root and Branch*, Mélusine Draco.

Guardian: The belief that each person has a personal guardian daemon, spirit or angel is very widespread among different cultures.

Guide: The source of energy used by mediums, although the term 'control' is used for a spirit that is channeled from the spiritual plane through to a psychic's mind.

Guide Star: A bright star used as a reference point for meditation or magical working.

Gules of August, The: 1st of August from the Latin *gula*, the throat; the entrance into or the first day of that month. 1st August is **Lammas** Day.

Gull: The archetypal sea-bird, whose cry was said to be that of drowned sailors. They have been called 'gulls' since the 15th century – a word meaning 'wailer' in medieval Cornish – and spread widely during the Tudor period when Cornishmen provided much of the manpower of the English navy. The bird has various superstitions and medicinal uses attributed to it.

Gullveig: A sorceress belonging to the **Vanir** race of gods in Old Norse mythology.

Gurdjieff, G.I.: (1877–1949) A modern mystic who believed that man could develop spirituality only through consciously laboring and suffering. His teachings were said to bring not so much peace as 'a special kind of inner warfare'.

Gurney, Edmund: (1847–1888) A founder of the **Society for Psychical Research** and one of the most important pioneers in the scientific investigation of paranormal phenomena.

Guru: In Hindu terms, means a 'preceptor' or teacher, and has come to refer to a religious teacher of any kind who has undertaken to give personal instruction to a pupil or disciple.

Gwydyon: An ancient Welsh divinity who has affinities with the gods of Germany and Gaul. He is a poet and magician, prophet and astronomer; and embodies the virtues and skills that the Celts revered in both their gods and their heroes. In later folklore the Milky Way – seen as the path taken by the dead – was called *Caer Gwydyon*

Gypsies: see **Romany**.

Gyromancy: Divination by moving in a circle until dizziness or exhaustion overcomes the psychic.

"There is another world or dimension that mirrors our own: it is located underground ... The inhabitants of this world are real beings in their own right, and have certain substantial supernatural powers."

R J Stewart

[*Earth Light*]

H

Hachiman: Originally a *kami*, or spirit protector of fishermen and cultivators in Japanese Shinto. Today Hachiman is popularly known as the god of war and about one third of all **Shinto** shrines are dedicated to him.

Hades: The Greek name of the god of the **Underworld**, and also for the Underworld itself, the word meaning 'the unseen'. The concept of the return from Hades figures largely in the **Mysteries**, particularly those of **Demeter** and **Orpheus**. This realm of the dead is separated from that of the living by the rivers Styx or Acheron, across which the dead were ferried by Charon. Besides the Styx and Acheron, three other rives intersect Hades – Phlegethon ('the fiery'), Cocytus and Lethe (forgetfulness).

Hadit: The Chaldean form of **Set** used in *The Book of the Law*.

Hadrian's Wall: It runs for 73 miles from Wallsend on Tyne to Bowness on the Solway Firth, taking advantage of every natural point of strength and, at its highest, is 1230 ft above sea level. The wall was garrisoned by infantry and cavalry, usually auxiliaries from all over the Roman Empire, hence the varied collection of religious objects found along the way. Among these are votive stones and altars dedicated to many different deities – Jupiter, Fortune, Germanic gods, Mother goddesses and the soldiers' god, Mithra. On the wall at Carrowburgh a Mithraic temple has been excavated.

Hag: (1) The word *hag* is the Anglo-Saxon name for a hedge and a hawthorn hedge in particular that provides a protective boundary for the community – the tree was also known as the *hag*thorn. (2) A derogatory term for an old, ugly woman, who is usually a witch. Because of the witch-connection, both hag-tracking and hag-stones are used as terms in magical procedure.

Hag-knots: The tangled manes of wild ponies that witches were supposed to use for stirrups.

Hag-ridden: (1) Horses found sweating and frightened in their stables in the morning were said to have been hag-ridden, although it may have been a symptom of colic. The most widespread method of protection was to hang up a **Hag stone**. (2) Modern usage now refers to a bullied or henpecked husband.

Hag's Taper: see **Mullein**.

Hag Stone: A small stone or pebble that has a natural hole bored through it. Kept about the person as an amulet, or hung in the stables to protect the horses.

Hagiography: The biography of a holy man. Aleister **Crowley** referred to his own autobiography, *Confessions*, by this description.

Hair: (1) It was once thought that a witch's power resided in her hair, and once shorn of her bodily hair even the most stubborn of witches would become helpless and make the confession required of her. (2) Hair is also an important ingredient used in spellcasting, along with nail parings and the saliva from the person for whom the spell is intended.

Hallows: All Hallows, **Samhain** – 31st

October Eve.

Hallowe'en: see **Samhain.**

Hallucinations: Although caused through incorrect sensory images to the brain, hallucinations have always been thought to have been transmitted to a human from a supernatural power or source. Often experienced during shamanic trance working via the application of hallucinogenic drugs.

Halomancy: Interpreting the formation of salt crystals poured onto a flat surface.

Hammurabi's Code: Hammurabi, king of the first dynasty of Babylon (1792–1750BC) is attributed with the compilation of the famous Code of Laws from the gods. Preserved on a black stone stele, the Code states that the gods instructed the king to create justice in the land.

Hand: In English country lore, each finger was referred to by a specific name: Towcher (index), Long-man (middle) Lech-man (ring), Little-man (little) and Thuma (thumb). Purification rights are often performed with the middle-finger, while the index finger is also known as the 'cursing finger' (see **Gesture**).

Handfasting: A general term for a contract, i.e. being bound at the hand, but now more commonly used to refer to a pagan marriage. SOURCE: *Witchcraft – A Tradition Renewed*, Evan John Jones.

Hand of Glory: The severed right hand of a hanged murderer, ideally severed while the corpse still hung from the gibbet and magically preserved. Once preserved, the hand was fitted with candles between the fingers and used to render people speechless.

The flames could only be dowsed with milk according to the *Ingoldsby Legends* and other folklore. '*De hand of glory is hand cut off from a deadman as have been hanged for murder, and dried very nice in de shmoke of juniper wood,*' Sir W. Scott: *The Antiquary*. One such relic is displayed in Whitby Museum. SOURCE: *Dictionary of Demons*, Fred Gettings; *A Dictionary of Devils & Demons*, J. Tondriau and R. Villeneuve; *The Encyclopedia of Witchcraft & Demonology*, Rossell Hope Robbins; *The Penguin Guide to Superstitions of Britain and Ireland*, Steve Roud.

Hanged Man, The: The twelfth card in the Major Arcana of the **Tarot** and the archetypal symbol of Redemption through sacrifice and submission to Divine Will – as in the universal myth of the **Sacrificial God**.

Harae: Purification by exorcism is the oldest of **Shinto** practices and first mentioned in 8th century Shinto literature.

Hara-kiri: The vulgar term for ceremonious suicide by disemboweling in Japan, meaning literally 'belly-cutting'. Long practiced by the samurai, the correct term is *seppuku*. The cut was made with a short sword, drawn across the abdomen and turned upwards; sometimes the final blow was delivered by a friend or relative who beheaded the victim. The act of *seppuku*, performed with due ritual solemnity, restored the personal honor of the suicide. SOURCE: *The Japanese Achievement*, Hugh Cortazzi; *Samurai Warlords*, Stephen Turnbull.

Hare: Long associated with traditional **Old Craft** in Britain, it was believed that witches could shape-shift into the animal's form at will. Before the coming of Christianity, the creature was associated with the moon and revered as a holy animal but later feared as a beast of ill omen. In country lore in some parts, it is still considered bad luck to kill a hare or eat its flesh, or even to have one's path crossed by a hare. The magical symbol of the hare is the triple image that shows the animals chasing each other in a circle, but with only three ears between them. SOURCE: *The Leaping Hare*, George Ewart Evans and David Thomson; *The Penguin Guide to Superstitions of Britain and Ireland*, Steve Roud; *Fauna Britannica*, Stefan Buczacki.

Harebell: In folklore the plant was best avoided because of its association with witches, the **Faere Folk** and other supernatural beings. In folk medicine, harebell roots were applied as a compress to heal wounds, staunch bleeding and reduce inflammation. Ruling planet: **Venus**.

Harlequin: A sprite supposed to be invisible to all but his faithful Columbine. It originally referred to a type of drama in two parts, the *introduction* and the *harlequinade*, acted in mime.

Harpies: [Greek *harpyiai* = snatchers] Female malevolent demons in Greek mythology. They are described as hideous hybrids, part woman, part bird.

Haruspex: **Augurs** who interpreted the will of the gods by inspecting the entrails of animals offered in sacrifice. Cato commented: *'I wonder how one haruspex can keep from laughing when he sees another.'*

Haruspicy: A divinatory method from the ancient world that interpreted the

cracks that appeared in the shoulder blade of a roasted animal, particularly a sheep or an ox.

Hathor: One of the most popular and fun-loving of all the Egyptian deities, she is the goddess of women and the family, who loves music and dancing. She is usually shown cow-headed and her emblem is the **Sistrum**.

Harvest: (1) This is the most important time in the country calendar and although it represents the end of the 'growing year', it is the time when rituals are carried out to ensure an abundance of crops in the coming year. On the evening of the day when the last load has been brought in, the farmer would traditionally provide a good meal for the reapers – known as Harvest Home. The church took over the celebrations and each year churchgoers sent vegetables, fruit and flowers for the Harvest Festival service, which is usually followed by a Harvest Supper. (2) In ancient Egypt, the harvest was called Shomu-Season with the crops ripening during March–April. The highlight of the season was the Festival of **Min**, and since the harvest was a central feature in the lives of the people, it was a very popular public event. (3) The Greek and Roman calendars had numerous festivals relating to the harvest. SOURCE: *The Golden Bough*, Sir James Frazer; *Seasonal Feasts & Festivals*, E.O. James; *A Witch's Treasury of the Countryside*, Mélusine Draco; *The Egyptian Book of Days*, Mélusine Draco; *The Roman Book of Days*, Paulina Erina.

Harvest Moon: The first full moon after the **Autumn Equinox**. Its peculiarity being that it rises for several days at sunset around the same time.

Hatha Yoga: The branch of yoga that specializes in methods of physical training and is a beneficial preliminary to the more difficult mental training of the Yoga Darshana.

Haunting: A belief that the dead still walk in the land of the living, some seeming to re-enact a crisis from their former lives. The best authenticated phenomenon of history is the recorded sightings of ghosts, and Britain has more ghosts to the square mile than any other country in the world. The term 'ghost' has been used for centuries but still defies a precise definition. Broadly speaking, it encompasses alleged manifestations believed to arise from a human or animal, once living but now deceased. SOURCE: *A Dictionary of Ghosts*, Peter Haining; *Haunted England*, Christina Hole; *Folklore, Myths & Legends of Britain*, Reader's Digest; *Ghost & Ghoul*, T.C. Lethbridge; *The Realm of Ghosts*, Eric Maple; *Religion & the Decline of Magic*, Keith Thomas; *Chamber's Dictionary of the Unexplained.*

Hawk: A hawk possesses the magical virtues of an eagle but with a lesser intensity. This huge family of raptors (*accipitridae*) embraces all birds of prey except owls, falcons and the osprey. The feathers and talons are valuable ingredients in magic spells.

Hawthorn: May Day was originally an agricultural festival, the beginning of summer, and the may blossom, or hawthorn (see **Hag**), was its emblem. It was also believed that witches and fairies were extremely active on this day. Spencer, Shakespeare and Herrick all mention the hawthorn's use as part of the pagan celebrations. It was

also known as 'fairy thorn' because it was believed that fairies lived under them, and therefore could be thought to be an unlucky tree. Nevertheless, the tree had many medicinal uses and its ruling planet is Mars. SOURCE: *Root and Branch*, Mélusine Draco and Paul Harriss; *A Witch's Treasury of the Countryside*, Mélusine Draco.. [SEE PANEL]

Hazel: A particularly powerful tree in magic, used to make magic wands and divining rods, while the mythology surrounding it is as old as mankind. The leaves, bark and fruit had both medicinal and culinary uses. Ruling planet: **Mercury.**

Hazelwort: see **Ginger.**

Head: Belief in the healing power of water drunk from an ancestor's skull still survived into the last century in Scotland: this is one example of the conviction that the human head contains powerful magic, which comes out particularly strongly in the headhunting of primitive peoples and in the role of the head in Celtic religion. SOURCE: *Man, Myth & Magic*, Richard Cavendish; *Pagan Celtic Britain*, Anne Ross.

Healing: Seen as one of the most important functions of modern 'mind, body & spirit' practice, and based on holistic principles in a form of medicine that considers the whole person, physically and psychologically, rather than just treating the stricken part of the body. In ancient Greece, many successful cures at the shrines of **Asclepios** (the most famous healing god of classical antiquity) were treated through dreams – an early example of what we now call psychosomatic medicine: the healing of the body through the mind. SOURCE: *The Healing Gods of Ancient Civilizations*, W.A. Jayne.

Healing Stones: Venerated for healing powers, standing stones with holes bored through them were regarded as the most potent. The most famous remaining holed stone is the Men-an-Tol in Cornwall.

Heart: Among the vital organs of the body, the heart 'that secret hidden center' has been seen as the seat of the soul, of the emotions and the intellect; in magic it dominates the rites of love and hate.

Hearth: The household hearth is the symbolic center of the home and the soul of the family: at one time its fire was never permitted to die. The **Yule**-log was lit each year among great festivity from a fragment of the previous year's log, to ensure continuity and good fortune. **Hestia** was the Greek goddess for the hearth, both of the family and the public altars; her Roman counterpart was **Vesta**, whose sacred flame was tended by the **Vestal Virgins**. SOURCE: *A Witch's Treasury for Hearth & Garden*, Gabrielle Sidonie; *Mean Street Witchcraft*, Mélusine Draco.

Heathen: Literally 'a dweller on the heath'. A re-creation of the Old Norse and Germanic religions, beliefs and practices. Also known as Odinism, **Asatru** and the **Northern Tradition**.

Heather or **Ling:** Thought to bring good luck, particularly the white variety. Burning the heather on the moors and hillsides was thought to bring rain; and in some parts, the witches' besom was traditionally made of heather or broom.

Preparations of heather were mainly prescribed for urinary and kidney problems. It was also used to relieve rheumatic and arthritic pains, and as a mild sedative. No ruling planet is given by **Culpeper**.

Hecate: A deity that appears to have originated in Caria, in the south-west corner of Asia Minor, where her name means 'remote' or 'distant'. It was only later that she became identified with the magical arts and the earliest full account of her is in Hesiod's *Theogony*. Homer does not mention her in the *Iliad* or the *Odyssey*. Her connection with the Underworld comes from the *Hymn to Demeter*, where she alone hears the cries of Persephone, after the girl had been carried off by **Hades**. By the end of the 5th century AD, literature presents her as the mistress of ghosts and spectres, and 'of everything dark and uncanny' and in the *Argonautica* of Apollonius, the sorceress **Medea** shows Jason how to win Hecate's aid by making a sacrifice. Statues or other representations of her with three heads are probably another contributing factor to the modern image of the **Triple Goddess**.

Hedgehog: The creature was often associated with witches and as late as the 19th century there was a case in Co Wexford of a hedgehog being thrown into a pond to see if it could swim, and because it swam to the bank was considered to be a witch and burnt. The most famous witches in literature, stirring their cauldron while incanting: *'Trice, and once the hedge-pig whined.'* *Macbeth*, Act 4, Scene 1.

Hedgewitch: A name coined by Rae Beth for her original book, *Hedge Witch:*

Tree Lore: Hawthorn

There are two indigenous types of hawthorn, the common (*crataegus monogyna*) and Midland (*crataegus laevigata*). The leaves of both trees have a nutty flavor and were eaten by children as 'bread and cheese'. The hawthorn blossoms in May (hence its familiar name), when the trees are smothered in clusters of white blossoms that give out a strangely disturbing but unmistakable perfume.

Common hawthorn has been used for about 2000 years as natural fencing because its tangle of thorny branches makes an ideal barrier for enclosing and protecting livestock. Its name derives from Anglo-Saxon *haegthorn*, which means hedge-tree and signs of defensive hawthorn hedges have been discovered round the edges of excavated Roman forts. The natural lifespan is around 100 years but some trees have reached the ripe old age of 300 years. Slow growth produces a very hard wood and although it burns well, hawthorn timber is little used today except for tool handles and walking sticks.

Medicinally, the hawthorn can rival the elder. Culpeper recommended it, while in modern herbalism the properties of some of the hawthorn's active constituents are now better understood. Some constituents strengthen the heart's action; others slow it slightly and improve the blood supply. For culinary use, hawthorn berries or flowers were used to make jellies, wines, liqueurs and sauces.

Hawthorn has perhaps more connections with ancient beliefs, folklore and traditions than almost any other native tree in the British Isles apart from the blackthorn. The appearance of the blossom at the beginning of May heralded the end of winter and the beginning of summer, when it was said to be unlucky to take May flowers into the house because of the associations with the Faere Folk.

For the Romans, however, the hawthorn was a symbol of hope and protection, and cuttings were brought into the home to ward off evil spirits; it also echoed the ancient British tradition that the tree was associated with marriage and fertility. An old country rhyme recommends the tree as protection for man and animals in thunderstorms:

Beware the oak—it courts the stroke.
Beware the ash—it courts the flash.
Creep under the thorn—it will save you from harm.

Like the elder, the hawthorn was a doorway to Otherworld and perhaps it is this association and its links with the old pagan festivals that give the tree its 'unlucky' reputation. Quite recently it was discovered that one of the chemicals that make up the flowers' distinctive scent is also produced during the decay of corpses! On the other hand, the fragrance of the blossom is also reputed to have a strong aphrodisiac effect, particularly on men.

Taking all things into account, it would appear that the pre-Christian view of the hawthorn was one of protection. It is appropriate to use hawthorn for the Beltaine bonfires, which the cattle were driven through and the villagers leapt over to ensure their fertility in the coming year. The tree can also be used to protect babies and young children. Hang a sprig above a child's bed as a protection, or keep a pouch of the leaves sewn into the pillow.

Hawthorn can be planted by the home to keep out negative influences and protect it from lightning strikes. Make a wash of flowers and leaves to sprinkle around the house to repel negative energies; the wood, berries and leaves can also be burnt in incense form to purify and attract beneficent energies.

Hawthorn is said to be sacred to the powers of Elemental Fire and any demon or malevolent spirits can be controlled with a wand or staff of hawthorn. This is one of the trees of the *White Goddess*, Cardia who casts her enchantments with a hawthorn wand. Make sure to leave a suitable offering if you take any wood from the tree —perhaps bread or cheese.

EXTRACT FROM *ROOT & BRANCH: BRITISH MAGICAL TREE LORE*
MÉLUSINE DRACO

A Guide to Solitary Witchcraft, which she uses to describe the contemporary 'parish pump' type of village witchcraft. Like her predecessor, the modern hedgewitch is a solitary who still observes the seasons, practices 'wort' charming and preserves the old tales – usually through the auspices of modern publishing rather than story-telling. There is now an Association of Hedgewitches. TITLES: *Hedge Witch, Hedge Witch's Way.*

Heimdall: A Germanic god who acts as the watchman of heaven.

Heiromancy: Divination through the use of sacred artifacts.

Heka: The ancient Egyptian word for magical power.

Hel: In Scandinavian mythology, the queen of the dead – the goddess of the ninth earth or netherworld. She dwelt beneath the roots of the sacred ash, **Yggdrasil**, and was the daughter of **Loki**.

Heliotrope: see **Bloodstone**.

Hell: Predominantly a monotheistic concept as a place of everlasting torment, presided over by a **Devil** or **Satan**. The most detailed description comes from Dante's *Commedia*, a fictional depiction of hell. SOURCE: *Commedia*, Dante Alighieri; *Dictionary of Demons*, Fred Gettings; *Man, Myth & Magic*, Richard Cavendish

Hellebore: A poisonous plant of the genus *Helleborus*; used in fumes, recipes and spells of Mars. Special precautions should be observed when gathering black hellebore. The gatherer should dress in white and pluck the plant with the right hand and, hiding the hand with the robe, transfer the plant to the right hand.

Hell-Fire Club, The: This was *not* an occult or satanic group, despite the sinister reputation that has persisted down the centuries. When one of its members, John Wilkes, was prosecuted for the 'obscene libel' of his *Essay on Women* in 1763, the repercussions produced one of the biggest political scandals of all time as a shocked public learned that senior government officials were part of the 'weird story of the amorous Knights of Saint Francis (Dashwood) of Wycombe.' In short, the Hell-Fire Club was a glorified sex-club where debauchery was the order of the day, not occultism. SOURCE: *Dashwood: The Man & the Myth*, Eric Towers; *The Hell-Fire Club*, Donald McCormick; *The Hell-Fire Club*, Daniel P Mannix; *The Hell Rakes*, Jack Loudan; *The Hell-Fire Clubs*, Geoffrey Ashe.

Hemlock: (see **Insane Root**) This plant is very poisonous and is said to be the drug used to poison **Socrates**. The distinguishing features are the purple blotches on the stem, its great height and attractive feathery leaves. Despite its poisonous reputation, it was valued for its medicinal qualities. Ruling planet: **Saturn**.

Hemp: Grown at least 5000 years ago as a fiber plant used to make rope, cordage, sacking and sailcloth. According to **Herodotus**, a Greek historian of the 5th century, its use as a mind-affecting drug was used by the Scythians, who got high by inhaling the fumes of the roasted seeds. In medieval England the stout cloth woven from the plant by cottagers in their homes was known as 'hempen home-spun'. The herb was widely cultivated in monastic gardens for its medicinal value. Ruling planet:

Saturn.

Henbane: A poisonous narcotic herb of the *Solanaceae* family used by witches in potions and flying ointment. It is fumed to evoke spirits. Traditionally the herb came under the ruling planet of **Jupiter** but **Culpeper** maintained that it came under the dominion of **Saturn**. SOURCE: *The Complete Herbal and English Physician,* Nicholas Culpeper

Henges: A prehistoric enclosed circular or oval area; the most famous being **Stonehenge, Avebury** and **Seahenge**.

Henotheism: Concentration of attention upon a single god where many other deities are included in the pantheon, while the existence of the other gods is admitted or not questioned. Also known as **Monolatry**.

Heortai and **Panegyreis:** Greek festivals in honor of one or more deities. *Panegyreis* were of inter-state importance, whereas *heortai* were festivals within the city-state. Many of the events were agrarian and cities sent embassies to each other's festivals.

Hepatomancy: Observance and interpretation of the surface and cavities of animal livers. The **Augurs** were known as 'liver gazers' by their detractors.

Hephaestus: The rough and ready, Anatolian god of **Blacksmiths** (who was himself a smith) was originally a god of fire, in the aspect of flaming gas rising from the earth in certain places. His name was used poetically as a synonym for fire from Homer down to poets who were familiar with **Nature** (or natural) philosophy. It was only much later that he came to be associated with the volcanoes in Sicily and Italy: the word volcano comes from **Vulcan,**

the Latin name of the god. SOURCE: *A Handbook of Greek Mythology,* H.J. Rose; *History of the Greek Religion,* M.P. Nilsson.

Hera: The principal Greek goddess and wife of **Zeus**. Her Roman counterpart was **Juno**.

Heraldry: A practice that can be traced back to the dawn of history, before writing, when pictorial representatives were used to identify individuals, families and tribes. Early on, heraldry took its place as an integral part of warfare and by the Middle Ages, it had blossomed into a complex system of fabulous colored images emblazoned upon the shields, helmets and surcoats of lords and knights. In the heat of amour-clad combat, it was a vital means of identifying friend from foe. SOURCE: *The Concise Encyclopedia of Heraldry,* Guy Cadogan Rothry.

Herbalism: One of the oldest of the occult 'sciences' to gain a firm foothold in the 21st century. Herbal medicine has been with us for a very long time and every age and culture was not without its cures and potions drawn from natural sources. The traditional, or witch's name for herbalism, is wortlore and one of the best places to start reading about the subject is *Potter's New Cyclopaedia of Botanical Drugs & Preparations,* R.C. Wren, which was first published in 1907. SOURCE: *An Ancient Egyptian Herbal,* Lise Manniche; *Book of Herbal Beauty,* Kitty Campion; Brockhampton's *Guide to Herbal Remedies; Brother Cadfael's Herb Garden,* Rob Talbot and Robin Whiteman; *The Complete Herbal,* Nicholas Culpeper; *Culpeper's Medicine,* Graeme Tobyn; *The RHS Encyclopedia of Herbs & Their*

Uses, Deni Brown; *Green Pharmacy: A History and Evolution of Herbal Medicine*, Barbara Griggs; *Herbal Medicine for Everyone*, Michael McIntyre; *HerbCraft*, Susan Lavender and Anna Franklin; *Perfume Power*, Joules Taylor; *Wonders in Weeds*, William Smith.

Herbarium of Apuleius: The oldest illustrated Anglo-Saxon herbal is a translation of the Latin version, originally compiled in the 5th century. The Anglo-Saxon translation (produced between 1000–1050) appears to have been copied from an Italian manuscript. One of the illustrations depicts a **Mandrake** being pulled out of the ground by a lead attached to a dog.

Herba Sacra: The 'divine weed', vervain, believed by the Romans to cure the bites of all rabid animals; to arrest the spread of poison, 'to cure the plague', to avert sorcery and witchcraft. So highly esteemed was it that feasts called *Verbenalia* were held annually in its honor. The **Druids** were said to hold the plant in similar veneration.

Herb of Grace: The name for rue because of its use in exorcism, during which the Roman Catholic church sprinkles holy water with a bunch of the plant.

Heresy: The actual charge brought against anyone accused of witchcraft, from the Greek meaning 'free choice'. According to Thomas Aquinas and Canon Law it was *'religious error held in wilful and persistent opposition to the truth after it had been defined and declared by the Church in an authoritative manner.'* The most common heresy most frequently linked to witchcraft was the alleged **Pact** with the Devil. The significance of heresy lay in the theory that it was not merely a sin, but a crime punishable by death. SOURCE: *The Encyclopedia of Witchcraft & Demonology*, Rossell Hope Robbins; *Medieval Heresy*, Malcolm Lambert; *Sex, Dissidence & Damnation*, Jeffrey Richards.

Hermaphrodite: A person combining both sexes in one body; a rare but naturally potent magical phenomenon. In Greek mythology, the son of **Hermes** and **Aphrodite**, who was loved by the nymph Salmacis; she prayed to the gods to make them as one.

Hermes: One of the most popular of Greek gods and the divine messenger, he is equipped with the herald's staff, winged sandals and helmet. Protector of tradesmen and travelers, his Roman counterpart is **Mercury**.

Hermes Trismegistus: see *Hermetica*.

Hermetica, The: Made up of 42 sacred books of mystical wisdom named after Hermes Trismegistus, 'Thrice-Greatest Hermes' – the Egyptian god, Thoth. The traditions deriving from the *Hermetica* were influential on most forms of European magic, alchemy and mysticism. It is basically a mingling of religious and philosophical literature dated from between the 1st century BCE and the 2nd century AD, an example being *The Seven Golden Chapters of Hermes Trismegistus*, dating from an 1815 edition. SOURCE: *Hermetica*, Walter Scott; *Hermetic Magic*, Stephen Edred Flowers.

Hermetic Art: The art or science of alchemy. Hermetic philosophy was a system that acknowledged only three chemical principles – salt, sulfur and mercury – from which it explained every phenomena of nature. Hermetic powder was a sympathetic powder, supposed to possess a healing influence from a distance.

Hermetic Order of the Golden Dawn, The: Founded in 1888 and much of what passes for occultism today owes much of its direction to the rituals derived from five Masonic grades discovered in the papers of a deceased English **Rosicrucian**. Dr. Wynn **Westcott**, a London Coroner and **Freemason**, encouraged Samuel (later 'MacGregor') **Mathers** and his wife to expand the material so that it formed the basis of instruction for a new occult society. SOURCE: *The Complete Golden Dawn and Golden Dawn*, Israel Regardie; *The Eye in the Triangle*, Israel Regardie; *The Golden Dawn Studies Series (10 vols)*, ed by Darcy Kuntz; *The Ladder of Lights*, W.G. Gray; *Ritual Magic in England*, Francis King.

Hermit: (1) A solitary religious ascetic. (2) The ninth card in the Major Arcana of the **Tarot** and the archetypal symbol of the Silence surrounding Inner Knowledge, and that which must be sought after.

Herne the Hunter: A spectral huntsman in English folklore and often mistakenly identified with the **Wild Hunt**. Tradition has it that he is the ghost of a 14th century keeper, associated with Windsor Forest, who hanged himself from a tree that was afterwards known as Herne's Oak until it blew down in a gale in 1863. Queen Victoria ordered that another oak be planted in its place to keep the tradition alive. Shakespeare knew the story and it is from him that we have the first written record in *The Merry Wives of Windsor*. SOURCE: *In Search of Herne the Hunter*, Eric Fitch.

Hero: Mortals who after death became 'semi-gods'. Most great mythological heroes were connected with cities or nations as founders, or were appropriated as Ancestors by the ruling families. Many had cult-status and the hero's power was centered on his grave.

Herodiades: A mythical 'sovereign of the night', who presided at sabbat assemblies towards the end of the 12th century, which may have been the origin of **Diana's** daughter from *Aradia: Gospel of the Witches*. Bishop of Chartres, Jean de Salisbury, spoke out against these beliefs in his work *Policraticus*: '*This evil mind has taken such license as to make certain people suffer through their overactive imagination. They believe totally. Thus they say that an entity called Nocticula or Herodiades covenes nocturnal assembles where they banquet and indulge in all kinds of exercises. Some are punished and others recompensed, according to their merits…*'

Herodotus: The Greek historian (480–425BC) who is known as the 'father of history' because of his extensive writings on Egypt, Greek and Persia. Much of what was known about these ancient civilizations before the dawn of archeology has its source in Herodotus. In comparatively modern times George Rawlinson published his *History of Herodotus* in 1860; a translation accompanied by valuable historical and ethnological notes. SOURCE: *Herodotus*, H.F. Cary; *The Oxford Companion to Classical Literature*, ed by Sir Paul Harvey.

Heroic Age: The time of a nation that comes between myth and history. Usually when the sons of the gods mated with the daughters of men, and the offspring are born with a dual character.

Heron: Like swans, herons were once royal birds and during the Middle Ages they were often to be found in the dining halls of the nobility. There are dozens of different names for the bird and it was a widespread belief that when herons fly low, or fly repeatedly up and down, rain is to be expected. There were also numerous medicinal uses. The blue heron is believed to be the **Bennu Bird** of the ancient Egyptians.

Herrick, Robert: (1591–1674) Described as 'one of Nature's poets', Herrick's verses have a distinct pagan element, despite the fact that he was a clergyman. Many of his verses taken from *Hesperides* can be used in magical workings. SOURCE: *Earth, Air, Fire, Water*, Robin Skelton and Margaret Blackwood; *Mean Streets Witchcraft*, Mélusine Draco.

Herring: The fish is fumed on hot coals to produce magical visions, according to the entry in *The Complete Book of Magic & Witchcraft*, published in 1970.

Hesperus: The evening star.

Hestia: The Greek goddess of the hearth, the symbol of the home and family. There was a hearth consecrated to her in every home and government building in every capital city where a sacred fire was kept burning. Her Roman counterpart is **Vesta**.

Hex: see **Cursing.**

Hexagram: Made of two triangles, one superimposed on the other. The triangles, one pointing up, the other pointing down, combine the esoteric symbolism of 'As above, so below' and the emblem for fire and water. Better

known as the 'Star of David' or the 'Seal of **Solomon**', this ancient symbol was believed to have been used by King Solomon to control the genii who helped him build the Temple.

Hidden Company: Discarnate entities that remain earthbound to act as spirit guides or mentors. A similar concept to the **Bodhisattva** in Buddhism.

Hidden Masters: Described by Madame H.P. **Blavatsky** as superhuman beings with mystical powers that remained hidden in the Tibetan Himalaya. Public interest in the Hidden Masters, which peaked with the growth of the **Theosophical Society**, has proved to be remarkably enduring. TITLES: *Isis Unveiled* and *The Secret Doctrine*.

Hieroglyphs: The word comes from the Greek meaning 'sacred carved [letters]'.

Hierophant: (1) One who reveals secret things: taken from the title of the chief priest of **Eleusis** who displayed the holy objects in the main ceremonies of the **Mysteries**. In some occult societies, the title is often used of the official who presides over initiation ceremonies. (2) The fifth card of the **Major Arcana** of the **Tarot**, sometimes called the Pope, and the archetypal symbol of the Teacher who imparts esoteric knowledge to the people, in a practical and oral way they can understand.

High Priesthood: Western ritual magic is overloaded with high-ranking titles, and High Priest/ess is usually a term used in modern **Wicca**. Traditional covens more often than not use 'Magister/Dame' or 'Lord/Lady' for those responsible for the group.

High Magic: see **Ritual Magic.**

Hilaria: Roman festivals of Joy held on

25th April and 3rd November.

Hill: Prayers were offered on the tops of high hills, and temples 'built in high places' from the notion that the gods could better hear the prayers.

Hill Figures: Giant figures created on hillsides by cutting away turf to reveal the chalk beneath. The **Uffington** White Horse dates back to the Bronze Age, while the **Cerne Abbas** Giant may only be a few hundred years old.

Hinduism: A Persian word, meaning simply 'Indian' and Hinduism refers to the national religion of India, which is 'eternal and ageless' having no known founder and is considered to have existed for all time. A considerable amount of Hindu belief has infiltrated into Western occult tradition, particularly in the form of **Tantrism** and **Karma**. SOURCE: *Eastern Religions*, ed Michael D. Coogan; *The World's Religions*, Ninian Smart.

Hinokagutsuchi: The Japanese fire god. When he was born from the goddess **Izanami**, she went up in flames. An analogy linked with the death of the old year and the birth of the new.

Hippocrates: c400BC Greek scientist, teacher and doctor and considered to be the 'Father of Medicine' who gave his name to the 'Hippocratic Oath' still taken by doctors.

Hippomancy: Interpreting the behavior and coat color of horses to foretell the future. The pattern of the hoof prints in the dust was also taken into account.

Hippomanes: A small piece of flesh (usually black) on the head of a newborn foal that has various magical uses.

Hive Off: The forming of an independent coven that maintains its links with the mother-coven with the blessing of the coven **Elders**.

Hocus Pocus: A term believed to have originated from the Latin *hoc est corpus*, which is said during the Catholic mass. Generally used to mean a skill in conjuring or deception.

Hod: The eighth Path of the **Tree of Life** is called the Absolute or Perfect Intelligence because it represents all the intellectual activities of the mind. The **Names of Power** are those of messengers and teachers, both male and female (see **Mercury**).

Holistic Medicine: A form of medical treatment that considers the whole body rather than just concentrating on the symptoms.

Holy Guardian Angel: see **Augoeides**.

Holy Well: Springs of fresh water flowing naturally from the earth, venerated from early times as places of healing.

Holly (Holm or **Hulver Bush):** An important part of traditional witchcraft custom in that the tree represents the crowned Holly-King of the winter woods. The ancient Romans exchanged sprigs of holly during **Saturnalia**, with wishes for health and well-being. Pliny wrote that the branches of the tree 'defended houses from lightening, and men from witchcraft'. Ruling planet: **Saturn**.

Homœopathy: An alternative therapy that has now become part of established medical practice. It works on the principle of 'like cures like', which has parallels in magical practice.

Homunculus: Refers to a living creature that some alchemists claim to have made from semen and various metals. In alchemical terms, the symbol of transformation from nonliving to living and the most detailed instructions for the manufacture of a homunculus are to be found in the writings of **Paracelsus.** SOURCE: *Moonchild*, Aleister Crowley.

Homer: The great Greek epic poet, who was regarded in antiquity as the author of the *Iliad* and the *Odyssey*. He was the object of deep reverence in ancient Greece and his writings also came to be regarded as a source of general wisdom and were constantly quoted.

Honey: For thousands of years, honey was the only sweetener known to man. It features widely in magic and witchcraft because of its healing properties.

Honeysuckle or Woodbine: Honeysuckle was found in the wild and grown in medieval gardens; it is the emblem of fidelity and affection. The berries are extremely poisonous but the plant was used for treating colds, asthma, constipation, skin infections and urinary complaints. Ruling planet: **Mars**.

Honorian Script: Another name for the **Theban** alphabet system.

Hopkins, Matthew: The **Witch Finder General** took just one year from 1645 to 1646 to acquire a reputation for evil that has been handed down to the present day undiminished. During the 14 months in which he searched for witches in East Anglia, Hopkins is believed to have been responsible for about 400 deaths. SOURCE: *A Dictionary of Devils & Demons*, J. Tondriau and R. Villeneuve; *The Encyclopedia of Witchcraft & Demonology*, Rossell Hope Robbins.

Horae: [Greek *horai*] The Greek goddess of the three seasons: Spring, Summer and Winter and originally represented the seasonal forces of growth. The Athenians called them Thallo (goddess of blossom), Auxo (goddess of growth) and Karpo (goddess of ripened fruit).

Horehound: A native to Britain, the herb was known to the Anglo-Saxons and listed by **Aelfric**. It has long been cultivated to treat various ailments, especially coughs, catarrh, asthma and respiratory complaints. Ruling planet: **Mercury**.

Hornbeam: Although there appears to be no references to the hornbeam in folklore, it is a native British tree, arriving around the same time as the **Beech**.

Horne, Janet: The last woman to be found guilty of witchcraft and officially executed in Britain at Dornock in Scotland in 1727.

Horned God, The: The traditional 'male energy' of witches. The outstanding courage and virility of the male horned animal led man to adopt the horn as the emblem of manhood and the gods themselves were frequently depicted as horned in ancient times. Most of the popular symbolism has been taken from **Cernunnos**, the horned male heads or figures that occur frequently in Celtic art, going back to the Bronze Age. On a Paris relief an antlered god sitting crossed-legged is inscribed 'Cernunnos' (Horned One), and the name has been adopted for this type of deity. He frequently has a neck-ornament and a purse or pouch, and is accompanied by a ram-headed serpent, a stag, and other animals. In the Celtic religion the role of horned animals was of special importance and in the old fertility dance that has survived into this century at **Abbots Bromley**, the dancers wear reindeer horns. In Ledsham Church there is a roughly carved slab thought to represent the horned god of the **Brigantes**, a tribe who lived in the North of England. SOURCE: *The God Year: Festival Days of the Sacred Male*, Nigel Pennick and Helen Field; *Man, Myth & Magic*, Richard Cavendish; *Masks of Misrule*; *The Horned God & His Cult in Europe*, Nigel Jackson.

Horn of Plenty: The **Cornucopia** is a ram's horn filled with fruits and flowers

Horoscope: A personal interpretation of an individual's fate and character based on the positions of the stars and planets at a particular moment, usually birth. The horoscope is based on the twelve signs of the **Zodiac** and derives from a system that has been in use for more than 2,000 years.

Horse: The horse has been highly esteemed since Homeric times; the animals were said to have been created by **Poseidon** (Hippios being one of his titles) and feature widely in folklore and superstition (see **Hippomancy**). SOURCE: *Horsemanship*, Xenophon; *The Horse in the Furrow* and *The Pattern Under the Plough*, George Ewart Evans: *The Life, History & Magic of the Horse*, Donald Braider; *White Horse: Practical Equine Magic*, Rupert Percy; *The Penguin Guide to Superstitions of Britain and Ireland*, Steve Roud.

Horse Brasses: Originally an amulet used to safeguard horses from evil. Emblems symbolizing good were fashioned from solid brass and a full set numbered around 20 different pieces. SOURCE: *Discovering Horse*

Brasses, John Vince.

Horse Hair: Incorporated into various magical spells for its strength, especially any to do with **Binding**.

Horseman's Word, The: A tradition of Scotland and East Anglia whereby the 'Word' was passed on during a highly secret initiation ceremony. SOURCE: *Folklore, Myths & Legends of Britain*, Reader's Digest; *The Horse in the Furrow* and *The Pattern Under the Plough*, George Ewart Evans; *The Quest for the Original Horse Whisperers*, Russell Lyon.

Horseshoe: The protective iron horseshoe has hung on stable doors for centuries to bring good luck and general prosperity in most countries where horses are an important part of the culture. The reason behind the belief may stem from the fact that blacksmiths were thought to possess supernatural powers. However, a shoe has to be *found* in order to possess any power. SOURCE: *The Horse in the Furrow*, George Ewart Evans; *White Horse: Equine Magical Lore*, Rupert Percy; *Old Horseshoes*, Ivan G. Sparkes; *The Penguin Guide to Superstitions of Britain and Ireland*, Steve Roud.

Horseshoe Nail: Powerful ingredient in 'fixing' a magical spell or curse.

Horse Whispering: The ability to control a horse by whispering what is known as 'the **Horseman's Word**'. The small number of men who have inherited the secret and who have preserved it to the present day jealously guard this knowledge. SOURCE: *The Horse in the Furrow* and *The Pattern Under the Plough*, George Ewart Evans; *The Quest for the Original Horse Whisperers*, Russell Lyon; *White Horse: Equine Magical Lore*,

Rupert Percy.

Horus the Elder or **Re-Harakhte:** The Egyptian sky god whose eyes symbolized the sun and the moon. Old Kingdom texts frequently describe him as the 'God of the East' and the sunrise. Harakhte means 'Horus of the Horizon' and merged with Re, he becomes Re-Harakhte – a name linked with the King in the **Pyramid Texts**, since he was the great solar god of Heliopolis, sovereign Lord of Egypt and Lord of the Universe. SOURCE: *The Setian,* Billie Walker-John; *The Egyptian Book of Days,* Mélusine Draco.

Horus Eye, The: A popular Egyptian image to be found in all shapes and sizes to decorate amulets, or in the settings of magnificent jewelry. It was also used to measure grain with each of the six parts being a fraction of the whole. The sum of the six fractions added up to 63/64 with the Egyptians believing that **Thoth's** magic would make up the remaining 1/64.

Horus the Younger: The son of **Isis** and **Osiris,** principally concerned with the struggle to avenge the murder of his father and to claim his rightful heritance, the throne of Egypt.

Hougue Bie, Jersey: A prehistoric burial ground containing a tomb dating from the New Stone Age. Great stones dragged from the nearby beach were arranged to form a central chamber reached by a passage with three side chambers. The whole was then covered by earth and rubble. The church on top of the hill was probably built to banish the pagan associations still clinging to the site.

Hound: From the bones of dogs discovered in caves, burial mounds and lake dwellings in Europe it is known that a breed of hunting dog existed there in the New Stone Age, and in the Bronze and Iron Ages. Individual dogs play an important part in human history and many ghostly forms haunt the British countryside such as the likes of **Black Shuck** and the **Gabriel** Hounds. SOURCE: *The Ancient Egyptians,* J. Gardner Wilkinson; *Aubry's Dog: Canine Magical Lore,* Mélusine Draco; *The Life, History & Magic of the Dog,* Fernand Mery.

Hound's Tongue: A herb widely valued for its soothing, healing and painkilling properties. **Culpeper** recommended it as a treatment for coughs and colds, as well as venereal disease. The bruised leaves were rubbed on insect bites. Ruling planet: **Mercury.**

House: In astrology the whole heaven is divided into 12 portions, called 'houses', through which the heavenly bodies pass every 24 hours.

Houseleek: Because the plant was thought to protect buildings against lightning and fire, it was planted on roofs, especially inflammable thatch. **Charlemagne** passed an edict that every one of his subjects should grow houseleeks on their roofs. The Anglo-Saxons knew it as *leac,* or leek and used it to treat burns, scalds and ulcers. Ruling planet: **Jupiter.**

House Spirits: Family guardians that resided within the property and were responsible for the good or bad fortune of the house. Often considered to be ancestral spirits as is the case in modern times, i.e. Japanese *kami.* The ancient Romans had their household gods, the *penates* and *lares.*

Howard, Michael: Editor of the long-standing journal, *The Cauldron* (founded in 1976), which is devoted to the Old Religion and related subjects. A genuine Initiate into the magical traditions, he is also the author of several occult books and a regular contributor to many esoteric magazines. He compiled and edited *The Pickingill Papers*, which deal with the **Pickingill** covens and their influence on the origins of modern **Wicca**, and has also edited *The Roebuck in the Thicket*, an anthology of the Robert **Cochrane** witchcraft Tradition. His most important work to date is *The Pillars of Tubal Cain* (with Nigel Jackson), which addresses for the first time in print the **Luciferian** Tradition, covering in detail the role of Fallen Angels and the **Watchers**. Other titles include *Faery Beasts & Animals of Legend, Practical Candle Magic, The Mysteries of the Runes, The Occult Conspiracy, The Sacred Earth Guide, The Sacred Ring: Pagan Origins of British Folk Festivals & Customs, The Mysteries of the Runes, Way of the Magus.*

Hru: In Thelemic teaching, the personification of the Guardian presiding over the Tarot. The latter comprising of the power-zones visualized in *The Book of Thoth*, with a marked preference for wheels and discs, which represent the power-zones of the **Tarot** as vortices of magical energy represented by the **Sephiroth**.

Hsun Tzu: (300–230BC) A Confucian philosopher who argued that human nature is basically evil, and that goodness must be produced by moral training and, if necessary, formal constraints.

Human Sacrifice: In primitive times, most of the emerging civilizations offered up human sacrifice to their gods. In time this was replaced by animal sacrifice but the image remains so powerful that the word 'sacrifice', even today, has sinister undertones for many people.

Hunter's Moon: The full moon following the **Harvest Moon**, as the hunting season does not begin until after the **Harvest**.

Hunting Magic: Whether we approve of it or not, hunting in all its forms runs parallel with the religion and magical development of our ancestors. Magical rites and beliefs surround every phase of both hunter's and victim's passage between human society and **Nature**. The hunter's weapons and auxiliary animals (usually hounds and horses) are also frequent objects of magical treatment. In fact the concept of the man-animal relationship underlying the practice of hunting magic is often extremely sophisticated and complex, and also varies widely from culture to culture. SOURCE; *The Ancient Egyptians,* J. Gardner Wilkinson; *The Forest of Symbols,* Victor Turner; *The Golden Bough,* Sir James Frazer; *A Witch's Treasury of the Countryside,* Mélusine Draco..

Hurlers, The, Cornwall: A group of three Bronze Age stone circles set in a straight line, with the uprights carefully shaped and of equal height. The central circle had a single stone at its center, while the north-east circle appears to have had the unusual refinement of a paved floor.

Hurtsickle: see **Cornflower**. **Culpeper** supposed the name came from the fact that the tough stems of the plant blunted the edges of the sickles that cut the corn.

Hyakinthia: A joint celebration in honor of **Apollo** and Hyakinthos, an ancient vegetation god who, according to the later mythology, was killed accidentally by Apollo with a discus.

Hydromancy: Divination by staring into water and interpreting what is seen there.

Hyena: The hair or whiskers may be used in image magic, or in spells of **Necromancy**.

Hyperborians: The most northern people who lived beyond Boreas (the seat of the north wind), placed by Virgil under the North Pole. They were said to be the oldest of the human race; the most virtuous, and the most happy; to live for a 1000 years under a cloudless sky, in fields yielding a double harvest, and perpetual spring. When sated with life they crowned their heads with flowers and plunged headlong from the mountain into the sea and entered paradise. Both **Herodotus** and Pliny wrote of them.

Hypnotism: The inducement of a sleep-like trance by repeated commands and mental concentration in which the subject acts only on the suggestion of the hypnotist.

Hyssop: Introduced into England by either the Romans or the Normans, and used to treat coughs, chest and lung complaints, urinary inflammations, and rheumatism. As an herb it had a wide use in the kitchen. Ruling planet: **Jupiter**.

Hysterical Possession: It is almost certain that those who were believed to be bewitched or possessed were in fact suffering from forms of mental illness and/or sexual repression; the attitude of society of the time creating a climate that fostered such hysterical manifestations. SOURCE: *The Devil Within*, Marc Cramer; *The Witches of Salem: a documentary narrative*, ed Roger Thompson; *The Devils of Loudun*, Aldous Huxley.

I

Iamblichus: (242–326CE) A Graeco-Syrian mystic and alchemist normally accredited with the authorship of *De Mysteriis Aegyptiorum*, the 'bible' for **Adepts** of ritual Egyptian magic. SOURCE: *The History of Magic*, Kurt, Seligmann.

Iao: The Gnostic designation of Supreme Deity.

Iatromancy: The ability to diagnose illness by psychic methods.

I Ching or *Book of Change:* One of the oldest books in the world, originating in China around circa 1000BC. Confucius and the Taoist sages held it in high regard, revering it as a sacred book and prizing its powers of divination. Aleister **Crowley** made great use of the I Ching, consulting the oracle regularly. It is said that this ancient source of wisdom, which has been used by the Chinese for divination for hundreds of years, yields astonishingly apt counsel to the serious inquirer but gives a random or even dismissive response to the frivolous. SOURCE: *The I Ching*, Stephen Karcher; *Techniques of High Magic*, Francis King and Stephen Skinner; *The Pocket I-Ching* (The Richard Wilhelm Translation), edW. S. Boardman; *Twelve Channels of the I Ching*, Myles Seabrook.

Icknield Way: A prehistoric road that runs across England from The Wash to Wiltshire. For much of its length it is still a green track, said to be haunted at twilight by Roman legionaries, **Black Dogs** and **Boudicca's** charioteers who galloped along it on their way to sack St. Albans in 61AD.

Icthyomancy: Observing fish both in and out of water, or by examining the internal organs for the purpose of divination.

Icon: A symbolic sacred image.

Iconography: The use of a symbolic sacred image, many of which are venerated and used in religious ceremonies. The oldest known image of a deity is the **Venus** of Laussel, but the most fascinating product of Paleolithic art is known as the Dancing Sorcerer. This strange figure is partly painted and partly engraved on the wall of one of the innermost recesses of a cave in south-west France. Source: *Man, Myth & Magic*, ed Richard Cavendish.

Ideology: A system of beliefs shared by a group of people that affects the kinds of behavior of which they approve or disapprove.

Idol: An image or object representing a divine being.

Ignis Fatuus: Meaning a 'fabulous fire' and another name for Jack-o'-Lantern and **Will-o'-the-Wisp.**

IHVH: The male-female potencies united in a single name with the relevant elemental correspondences: Fire (the Father), Water (the Mother), Air (the Son) and Earth (the Daughter) (see **Tetragrammaton**).

Iliad: The tale of the siege of Troy as an epic poem by **Homer** in 24 books.

Iliad of Ills: A number of ills (misfortunes) falling simultaneously. There is scarcely a calamity in the whole catalogue of human ills that isn't mentioned in the *Iliad*, hence the Homeric poem was the fountain of classic tragedy.

Ilkley Moor: On Rombald's Moor there are numerous rocks carved with the characteristic Bronze Age cup and ring ornamentation. Unfortunately, many of the best examples have been brought down and stand in the gardens facing the parish church. With them is the Swastika Stone, which may belong to the Iron Age. On the moor are several stone circles, three of which – the Twelve Apostles, the Grubstones Circle and the Horncliffe Circle are the most important. The others lie to the east of the Grubstones.

Ill-starred: Unlucky or fated to be unfortunate. The allusion is to the astrological belief that the stars influence the fortunes of the human race.

Illuminati, The: A secret society devoted to anti-priestly and democratic ideals, where Initiates were trained in material philosophy under the guidance of the *Aeropagus* (inner directorate). Founded in 1776, the society took its name from the Latin meaning 'the enlightened ones' – the aims being to combat ignorance, superstition, religious restraint and tyranny. Although it attracted men of progressive viewpoints, it never managed to develop the appeal of the **Freemasons** and the order collapsed following a decree banning its activities in March 1784. There have been several attempts to revive the Order but without success. SOURCE: *Illuminati Conspiracy*, D. Holmes and Robert A. Wilson; *The Occult Conspiracy*, Michael Howard; *Secret Societies*, Arkon Daraul.

Illusion: A deceptive appearance or apparition; a false sense or impression of 'something' actually being present.

Ill-wishing: see **Cursing**.

Imbolc: Candlemas in the church calendar and the start of the Celtic lambing season. Celebrated on 2nd February it is one of the four major festivals of the modern pagan calendar.

Imhotep: The Grand architect at the court of the Egyptian King Djoser. He became the patron of scribes and the protector of all those who were occupied with the sciences and occult arts. He also became the patron of doctors and when the ordinary people began to celebrate his miraculous cures, he was proclaimed 'the demi-god of medicine'.

Imitative Magic: Mimicry for magical purposes is deeply embedded in human nature and the use of a doll or image to kill, injure, draw or repel the person the image represents was known from ancient Egypt and Mesopotamia, from India, Greece and Rome, and from all over the world, both ancient and modern. SOURCE: *The Magical Arts*, Richard Cavendish; *Magical Ritual Methods*, W.G. Gray.

Immersion: The earliest source where immersion was used as proof against sorcery is in the old Babylonian law code of **Hammurabi** in 3BCE. It is also mentioned in the Anglo-Saxon laws of King Athelstan (925–939), and was used by English tribunals in the 18th century (see **Swimming**).

Imp: A small demonic creature, usually kept inside a bottle and used for healing, divination and charms in both magic and alchemy. During the witch-hunts, victims were accused of keeping imps in the form of toads and rodents. The most famous imp being the **Lincoln Imp**, which gained some notoriety because the image was used in A.E. Waite's *The Book of Ceremonial Magic*.

Inari: The **Shinto** god of food, represented as a bearded man carrying two bundles of rice. His messenger is the fox, and this is why there are always stone or wooden foxes sitting in front of Inari shrines. In popular belief, the god and the fox could merge together to form one being. In Japanese myth there was also a goddess of rice called Inara, who could also assume the shape of a fox.

Incantation: Words are weapons of power in magic; knowing the name, knowing and reciting the qualities of a thing gives a magician magical power over it. *'There is a difference between a magical incantation and a prayer, where the former uses language that is impressive in sound, deliberately evocative and atmospheric, and clear in meaning.'* The essence of incantation is command and the magician orders supernatural forces to do his bidding. SOURCE: *The Magical Arts*, Richard Cavendish; *Magick in Theory & Practice*, Aleister Crowley.

Incarnation: Literally 'to make flesh' and in religious terms, both ancient and modern, refers to a 're-birth' in a different physical form.

Incense: Burned by all Paths and Traditions, both to purify the air and drive away any negative energies from the working area. Traditionally loose, blended incense should be used in a special fireproof container (see **Thurible**), although many modern witches and magicians use joss sticks or incense cones which are less messy but not as magically pure. SOURCE: *Magic:*

An Occult Primer, David Conway.

Incubus: A male night demon intent on sexual gratification. Can be a natural phenomena, or deliberately manifested by a magician (see **Succubus**). SOURCE: *A Dictionary of Devils & Demons*, J. Tondriau and R. Villeneuve; *The Encyclopedia of Witchcraft & Demonology*, Rossell Hope Robbins; *Magic White & Black*, Franz Hartmann; *Sex & the Occult*, Gordon Wellesley; *What You Call Time*, Suzanne Ruthven.

Indra: Supreme god in the **Vedic** pantheon. He brings rain, and is the heavenly representative of warriors.

In Extremis: At the very point of death: *in artículo mortis*.

Infernal Court: According to Wier's *Pseudomonarchia daemonum*, and many other demonologists, the Infernal Court is presided over by the Princes, The Ministers, The Ambassadors, The Justice, The House of Princes and The Lesser Pleasures.

Infernal Tortures: Punishment reserved for the damned in Hell. Virgil (*Aeneid*) and Dante (*The Divine Comedy*) have given the two most important descriptions of these.

Infidel's Bible, The: In 1867, an antiquated wooden post mill in Huntingdonshire was alleged to have been 'becalmed by witchery'. The mill's owner had apparently found a book of black magic called *The Infidel's Bible* among his dead brother's belongings. He hid it in the mill, which immediately stopped working. Three years later, the book was allegedly found and burnt, whereupon the mill sails began to turn again!

Inaugurate: To be led by the **Augurs**. The Roman augurs met at their college doors the high officials about to be invested, and led them up to the altar – hence to install.

Initiation: In contemporary occultism and witchcraft a formal rite marks the passage from neophyte to acolyte and the *beginning* of the spiritual journey on a chosen Path. Unfortunately, many view initiation as a final result rather than as a beginning. SOURCE: *Coven of the Scales,* A.R. Clay-Egerton; *Knowledge of the Higher Worlds,* Rudolf Steiner; *Lid Off the Cauldron,* Patricia Crowther; *Rites & Symbols of Initiation,* Mircea Eliade; *Witchcraft – A Tradition Renewed,* Evan John Jones.

Ink: (1) Red and black inks are the most commonly used in magic. (2) There is also the practice of gazing into a bowl filled with ink for divinational purposes.

Inquisition, The: The Catholic tribunal charged with exposing and punishing religious unorthodoxy, emerged c.1200 because of the mounting insecurity, weakness and immorality of the Roman Church. When the Inquisition had crushed the religious deviations in southern France (i.e. Albigensians and Waldensians), it had little justification for continuing to exist. Its work was done but it set about introducing and developing the parallel heresy of witchcraft, thereby widening its scope with its fantastic and impossible allegations (see **French Witchcraft**). And were it not for the Inquisition not one person would have died for witchcraft; but as all records show (and as even the inquisitors admitted), once accused, the chances of escaping death were almost nil. Even the Roman Catholic De Cauzon's *Histoire*

de l'Inquisition (1909) stated that the Inquisition *'had invented the crime of witchcraft and… relied on torture as the meaning of proving it.'* SOURCE: *Ecclesia Militans: The Inquisition,* trans Janet Fraser; *The Encyclopedia of Witchcraft & Demonology,* Rossell Hope Robbins; *The Inquisition: The Hammer of Heresy,* Edward Burman.

Insane Root or **Hemlock:** It was believed that those who ate hemlock could see subjective things as objective. In *Macbeth,* Shakespeare has Banquo saying to Macbeth, on encountering the witches, who vanished as suddenly as they appeared: *'Were such thing [really] here… or have we eaten the insane root, that takes the reason prisoner [so that our eyes see things that are not].'*

Intuition: The power of the mind by which it immediately perceives the truth of things without reasoning or analysis; immediate, instinctive knowledge or belief.

Invisibility (or **Cloak of Invisibility**): A ritual magic technique that prevents other people from seeing the magician by an 'enchantment of blindness' being cast over those around him. There is a Jewish charm for the same result recommended in the 14th century work the *Sefer Gematriot.* SOURCE: *The Golden Dawn,* Israel Regardie.

Invocation: To call upon a deity in the form of prayer or supplication, i.e. by magical means, to solicit earnestly for assistance and / or protection. SOURCE: *Coven of the Scales,* A.R. Clay-Egerton; *Techniques of High Magic,* Francis King and Stephen Skinner.

Inundation: The annual flooding of the Nile marked the Egyptian New Year = Akhet season, when no work could

be carried out on the land; so many of the important festivals took place during the first four months of the year.
SOURCE: *The Egyptian Book of Days*, Mélusine Draco.

Ipsissimus: Generally accepted to be beyond the comprehension of the lower degrees or grades within the Western ritual magic traditions. An Ipsissimus is free from all earthly limitations and necessity, and lives in perfect balance with the manifest universe. It is the highest level of attainment and corresponds to **Kether** on the **Tree of Life.**

Iris or **Yellow Flag:** The iris root was used for unguents and medicine, although **Culpeper** noted that it could cause violent and dangerous reactions. According to **Pliny**, it 'was hot by nature, and when handled raises burn-like blisters,' which might explain the traditional Craft salutation of **'Flag, Flax…'** The flowers were hung about the doors of houses to ward off evil spirits and in medieval times the leaves were strewn on the floor. Ruling planet: **Moon**.

Irish Folklore: Unlike England, Irish folklore generally escaped the interest of the Victorian folklorists, and has persisted to the present day in a small number of recorded folk tales that, while not strictly mythological, feature personages from Ireland's heroic age. Tales about its fairy-folk are very similar to the Scottish versions but more light-hearted.

Irish Witchcraft: Witchcraft hysteria almost bypassed Ireland and, as a result, the first trial of Lady Alice Kyteler (charged with heretical sorcery) in 1324 is well-known. After a farcical series of events, Lady Alice decamped to England. The final witch-trial took place in 1710–11, when the accused were sentenced to one year's imprisonment.
SOURCE: *Irish Witchcraft*, St. John D. Seymour.

Iron: This metal plays a curious role in magic. The combination of fire and iron has an alchemical mystery of its own; and in theory the 'unnatural' iron was believed to neutralize the natural magic of a spell, which gave rise to the belief that witches and the **Faere Folk** would be repelled by it. However, in *Witchcraft – A Tradition Renewed,* Evan John Jones explains the reason why stangs should be shod with iron, when many covens refuse to have iron in the **Circle**. By having a stang shod with iron, the magical power was unable to 'earth' and remained within the body of the stang (or altar) thereby creating a magical generator that held power for future use. The Egyptians weren't afraid to use iron in their Holy of Holies and many of their sacred implements were made from meteoric iron.

Isiac Tablet: A questionable artifact of copper, engraved with most of the Egyptian deities associated with the mysteries of **Isis**. It is said to have been found at the siege of Rome in 1525, and later preserved at Turin. The word 'Isiac' is an adjective formed from Isis.

Isidis Navigium: The principal Roman festival (5th March) of the imported Egyptian cult of **Isis**, which reached its height during the 2–4th centuries.

Isis: Egyptian goddess and the sister/ wife of Osiris. Originally a modest deity associated with the Delta, very early she was identified with **Osiris** and **Horus** to form the Osirian Triad. She became so

Isles of the Blessed

In the Isles of the Blessed, heroes and other favored mortals in Greek and Celtic mythology were received by the gods into a blissful paradise. These islands were thought to lie in the Western Ocean near the encircling River Oceanus: Madeira, the Canary Islands, and Cape Verde have sometimes been cited as possible matches. It was the Greek poet Hesiod, who first wrote of those who 'untroubled in spirit dwell in islands of the blest by deep-eddying Ocean, happy heroes for whom the grain-giving fields bear rich honey-sweet fruit three times a year.'

It has been suggested that this was little more than a 'comforting metaphor' to help people come to terms with the inevitability of death, in much the same way as later religions created their own concepts of heaven or paradise. Nevertheless, it is easy to understand why the earliest beliefs placed the Islands beyond the ocean, in the direction of the setting sun, and why the image remained a powerful theme well into the Middle Ages, and up to the present day.

The first British concept appears in Geoffrey of Monmouth's 1136 pseudo-historical account *Historia Regum Britanniae* (*The History of the Kings of Britain*). He dealt with the subject in more detail in *Vita Merlini*, in which he describes, for the first time in Arthurian legend, the enchantress Morgan le Fay as the chief of nine sisters who live on the island of Avalon, and his description of the island indicates that a sea voyage was needed to get there.

His description also reveals the magical nature of the island:

The island of apples which men call 'The Fortunate Isle' gets its name from the fact that it produces all things of itself; the fields there have no need of the ploughs of the farmers and all cultivation is lacking except what nature provides. Of its own accord it produces grain and grapes, and apple trees grow in its woods from the close-clipped grass. The ground of it own accord produces everything instead of merely grass...

Referred to as 'Insula Avallonis' in the *Histori*, in the later *Vita Merlini* Geoffrey called it 'Insula Pomorum' – the isle of apples. It seems most likely that the word is of Celtic origin; the word for 'apple' in modern Welsh is *afal*, and *aval* being 'apple' in modern Cornish. As an 'Isle of the Blessed' Avalon also has parallels in many Indo-European mythologies, in particular the Irish Tír na nÓg, and the Greek Hesperides, also noted for its apples. J.R.R. Tolkien later used the concept of 'going into the West' in *The Lord of the Rings* as the final destination of the Elves when they leave the world of men.

It's an overused analogy to say that life is a journey, but it is an accurate description of how we are all swept along to an inevitable end. Our journey begins in the misty and mysterious fountain that wells up among the rocks on the distant mountain slopes of childhood. It passes through the changing scenery of swift flowing brooks and streams of adolescence, often becoming confused in murky backwaters, swamps and marshes before entering the calmer tributaries and rivulets of adulthood. The vast river moves through our mature years until we reach the estuary and shore of the great sea where this journey ends – and another begins.

The spectre of Death and the sea are never far removed from each other. For the sea witch there is an obligation to honor our departed ancestors (whether we believe them to be over the sea, or under it), which is not out of place with the observations traditionally carried out at Samhain. In all aspects of traditional Craft there are strong associations with Otherworld and a powerful element of ancestor-worship – for the sea witch there is no difference.

EXTRACT FROM *SEA CHANGE*
PRACTICAL CRAFT MAGIC FOR THE SEA WITCH
MÉLUSINE DRACO

popular that she eventually absorbed the qualities of all the other goddesses and in this guise her cult spread from Egypt throughout the Roman Empire. According to the **Hermetica** she is the goddess of women, and as such frequently appears in contemporary **Wicca**, just as her image was absorbed by the Virgin Mary in Christianity. She has now become the embodiment of all goddesses in one (see **Fellowship of Isis**).

Isle of Lewis: The island has a prehistoric stone circle, 37 ft in diameter, with avenues of monoliths radiating from it, and whose mystery and grandeur rivals Stonehenge. Inside the circle of thirteen great stones is a burial chamber. Legends link the stones to the **Druids** and the monoliths are called Fir Chreig in Gaelic, of 'False Men'. It was also the island where the famous 'Lewis Hoard' – 78 chessmen – was discovered. Carved from ivory, probably by 12th century Norsemen, they are now in the British Museum.

Isles of the Blessed: Usually located in the far West where the sun sets, and the place to which heroes depart in death, especially among people who lived on the coast, including the Greeks and Romans. The belief later passed into **Arthurian** legend. SOURCE: *Sea Change*, Mélusine Draco; *Facing the Ocean*, Barry Cunliffe. [SEE PANEL]

Ius Divinium: The sacred law of Rome, consisting essentially of traditional norms expounded by the priests in the light of their written records of past incidents and the comments of their predecessors. It remained a priestly preserve until the emperors usurped the power.

Ivy: A magically powerful plant connected with the Roman **Saturnalia** and the Greek god **Dionysus**. Also connected with inspiration and poetry, and believed to diminish drunkenness. In British folk medicine the leaves were used for a variety of cures and divination. Ruling planet: **Saturn**.

Izanagi and **Izanami:** The primeval pair of divinities in Japanese **Shinto**. Izangi is the embodiment of all that is bright and heavenly; while Izanami embodies everything that is earthly and the gloomy. Their children are **Amaterasu** (the sun goddess) and **Tsukuyomi** (the moon god). When giving birth to her youngest son, Izanami died, and went to rule over the underworld.

J

Jachin: The right-sided Pillar in the Temple, which is white, representing Mercy, as opposed to **Boaz**, which is black and represents Severity.

Jacinth: When worn as an amulet, it protects against disorders of the heart. Ground to a powder it was also given as a cure for internal disorders connected with bleeding. The stone changes color according to the weather and is ruled by the Sun.

Jack-in-the-Green: see **Green Man.**

Jack-o'- Lantern: The phosphorescent light seen in marshes and swamp areas, which in folklore is thought to be the manifestation of a lost soul or a death omen. A natural phenomena it is known by a variety of names: **Will-o'-the-wisp** and corpse-light (England) and fairy light, or fox fire (America).

Jade: Often used as an amulet to assist women in childbirth and to make men victorious in battle. In China it is used as a divination medium; while according to *The Dictionary of Devils & Demons*, in Mexico the Maya used it for their sacrificial knives. For a long life, eat from a jade bowl.

James I: King of England from 1603 to 1625, and the author of *Daemonologie*, which reveals his own views about witchcraft and reflects the popular views of the day. When he became King he brought out a new edition of his book and within a year of his accession to the English throne, he had coerced Parliament to pass a new **Witchcraft Act**, which changed the emphasis of the charge and no doubt heightened the attack against witches.

Although at the beginning of his reign in Scotland he was a firm believer in the evils of witchcraft, by the end of his reign in England he had become as firm a skeptic.

Janus: The word 'janitor' is derived from the name of the mysterious two-faced Roman god of gateways and passageways, who was also the protector and promoter of beginnings. His name was also given to January, as the first month of the New Year when the new civil calendar was introduced.

Jasmine: Sweet-smelling flowers that are an excellent ingredient for love potions. The earliest record of its cultivation in England dates from 16th century and is mentioned by **Culpeper**. Ruling planet: **Jupiter** in **Cancer.**

Jasper: A semi-precious stone used as an amulet, either in a polished form, or with inscriptions of charms. It was believed to strengthen the intellect and prevent epileptic seizures.

Jet: Sometimes called black amber, is a variety of lignite with a black glow. Real jet burns like carbon and in magic is used to chase away negative energy. It is said to have eight virtues: (1) Protection from storms. (2) Protection for the house from negative forces. (3) Protection from poison. (4) *'That which before was profoundly concealed, will soon be visible.'* (5) Cure from any disease. (6) Protection from Sorcery. (7) Encourages a smooth, unblemished skin. (8) Protection from snakebite.

Jewel: From the priceless diamond to the humblest of corals, jewels and semi-precious stones have been prized, not just for their rarity and beauty but for their healing properties and occult powers. SOURCE: *Magical Jewels*, Joan Evans; *The Curious Lore of Precious Stones*, George Frederick Kunz.

Jimson Weed: A narcotic plant of the genus *Datura*, the seeds and roots of which have been used by native Amerindians in medicine and ceremony. The Aztecs considered the plant sacred and a protection against evil spirits.

Jingan-ji: Japanese shrine-temples built to protect Shinto shrines where Buddhist priests could chant sutras to enlighten the **Kami**. All were destroyed or renamed in the Meiji period (1868–1912) because it was thought that they disgraced the concept of the original *kami* of Japan.

Jinn, also **Djinn:** [English *genie*] Arabic spirit-beings originally created from fire, which were believed to form an intermediate creation between mankind and the angels. In popular lore, they represent the untamed spirits of wild and desert places, normally invisible but capable of assuming the form of men or animals. They are also associated with the practice of magic and the service of talismanic formulae.

Jinx: A bringer of bad luck or an unlucky influence.

Joan of Arc or **Jeanne d'Arc:** Contrary to popular belief she was not burned at the stake by the English on charges of witchcraft, but for being a lapsed heretic who denied the authority of the Church. SOURCE: *The Trial of Joan of Arc –being the verbatim report of the proceedings from the Orleans Manuscript, translated with an Introduction and Notes by W.S. Scott.*

Joker: Also juggler or **Trickster.**

Jones, Evan John: The late Witch Master of the Clan of Tubal Cain. His main aim after Robert **Cochrane's** death was to keep the name and tradition of Tubal Cain going and to pass it on to others who would keep the tradition alive. He also wrote many articles concerning Traditional Witchcraft (mainly for *The Cauldron*) and also authored two books on the subject: *Witchcraft – A Tradition Renewed* (with Doreen Valiente) and *The Roebuck in the Thicket* (with Michael Howard).

Jonson, Ben: (1572–1637) His masques and courtly entertainments vary enormously in size and seriousness. For the great court masque, in which the richest ladies in the land vied to outdo one another, thousands of pounds might be invested in costumes, musicians and stage-machinery – we have the greatest of these, *The Masque of Queens,* together with a set of the dramatist's handwritten notes, *'which make it evident just how much scholarly substance lay hidden behind his use of a single name or theatrical prop.'* SOURCE: *Ben Jonson's Plays & Masques,* ed by Robert M Adams; *Earth, Air, Fire, Water,* Robin Skelton and Margaret Blackwood.

Jormungandar or **Midgardsormen:** The 'earth monster' of Scandinavian mythology. The great serpent, brother of **Hela** and **Fenrir,** and son of **Loki**. It used to lie at the root of the celestial ash **Yggdrasil** until it was cast into the ocean where it grew so large that in time it encircled the earth, and was forever biting its own tail (see **Uroboros**).

Joss Stick: A fragrant tinder mixed with clay and burnt as an offering in rituals because the aromatic smell is thought to be pleasing to the gods and odious to evil spirits.

Jotunheim: The home or region of the Scandinavian giants or *jotun*.

Journey: In esoteric terms, the journey is the symbol of the seeker's attempt to gain enlightenment or spiritual perfection; the method of attaining wisdom is often referred to as a path, road or way.

Jove: (1) Another name for the Roman **Jupiter** deriving from *Jovis-pater*. (2) Jovial means merry and sociable, like those born under the planet Jupiter, which astrologers considered the happiest of the natal stars. '*Our jovial star reigned at his birth.*' Shakespeare, *Cymbeline, v.4*.

Joyeuse: Charlemagne's sword, which bore the inscription *Deccm oraeceptorum custos Carolus*, which took Galas three years to make. According to legend, it was buried with the king.

Judgement: The twentieth card in the Major Arcana of the **Tarot**; although called **Aeon** in the **Thoth** pack, the interpretation is similar. The archetypal symbol of the final decision concerning the past and a new current for the future; life progressing a little further along the Path.

Judgement of the Dead: '*That the fate of the dead is decided at a post-mortem judgement is an idea which is very ancient and widespread,*' wrote S.G.F. Brandon. The earliest records occur in Egyptian texts dating from around 2400BCE, although the belief was already well established by that date. Virgil's account of the underworld recognized it as a place of retribution; in Orcagna's version, *Inferno*, the wicked were their

own tormentors, while in Dante's *Inferno* he describes ten divisions of hell in which the punishment is suited to the crime. Surprisingly, 'neither the Greek not the Roman religion offered hope of a significant afterlife, and therefore no ground existed for belief in a post-mortem judgement." SOURCE: *The Ancient Egyptian Book of the Dead*, R.O. Faulkner; *The Judgement of the Dead*, S.G.F. Brandon; *Man, Myth & Magic*, Richard Cavendish; *The Tibetan Book of the Dead*, W.Y. Evans-Wentz.

Judicium Dei: [Latin] The trial of guilt by direct appeal to God, under the notion that the innocence would be defended, even by a miracle. There were numerous methods of appeal, as by single combat, ordeal by fire or water, eating a crust of bread, standing with the arms extended, consulting the Bible, etc.

Julian: Known as the 'Apostate' by later Christian writers, he was the Emperor (361–363CE) who attempted to stem the tide of Christianity and restore pagan worship into the Roman Empire. He was killed in the third year of his reign in an expedition against the Persians but was hailed as the first pagan 'martyr' as there was some questions surrounding his death. SOURCE: *Julian*, Gore Vidal; *The Oxford Companion to Classical Literature*, ed by Sir Paul Harvey; *Religion of Julian the Apostate*, Dr J Stokes. [SEE PANEL]

Julian Calendar: The Imperial Roman, or Julian Calendar, was introduced in 45BC by Julius Caesar. Its use spread through the Empire until it was replaced by the **Gregorian** Calendar in 1582. Britain did not adopt the change until 1752, by which time it had fallen

Julian – The First Pagan Martyr

Flavius Claudius Julianus – or as he has come to be known by his Christian detractors, 'Julian, the Apostate' – was a Greek Stoic, who attempted to reintroduce paganism and force the newly powerful Christians to accept the traditional Roman policy of Universal Toleration once he became emperor of Rome.

He was born in Constantinople in 331AD, his father being half-brother to the emperor Constantine. On Constantine's death, his successor Constantius II conducted a purge of many of his relatives, particularly targeting the families of Constantine's half-brothers. Julian and his brother Gallus were spared, probably on account of their young age, and in the intervening years Julian was educated by some of the most famous names in grammar and rhetoric in the Greek world at the time.

In 351 Gallus was made Caesar by Constantius II but was executed for treason in 354; Julian was summoned to Italy and kept under house arrest for seven months before the emperor's wife, Eusebia, convinced her husband that the boy posed no threat. This allowed Julian to return to Greece and continue his life as a scholar, until he was again summoned to the Imperial Court and made Caesar.

Within a few days of being raised to the purple, he was married to Constantius' sister, Helena, and promptly dispatched to restore order along the Rhine. Surprisingly, the scholar showed himself to be a capable soldier and diplomat, and as a result of his vigorous campaigning was able to negotiate a peace with all but a handful of the Gaulish leaders. Jealous of Julian's success, in 360 Constantius stripped him of many of his troops and officers, ostensibly because the Emperor needed them for his planned campaign against the Persians, which lead to a mutiny among the soldiers — who promptly proclaimed Julian emperor. Julian wrote to Constantius to reaffirm his loyalty but events overtook them both, despite the uneasy peace that simmered between the two emperors.

Constantius died unexpectedly of natural causes just as the opposing factions were about to face each other on the battlefield and Julian became sole emperor of Rome. He took the occasion of his cousin's fortuitous death to openly declare his paganism and, having noted that the Christians had made life difficult for those upholding their pagan beliefs, began to chip away at the tight control the Christians had gained under the neo-Flavian emperors.

What later historians tend to overlook is the fact that Julian was initiated into the Mysteries at Ephesus, in the twentieth year of his age, at a time when the Old Ways still retained some vestiges of their primeval sanctity. According to Gibbon, as these ceremonies were performed in the depths of caverns and in the silence of the night, the inviolable secret of the Mysteries was preserved by the discretion of the Initiated, concerning the visions of comfort and knowledge breaking upon them in a blaze of celestial light:.

In the caverns of Ephesus and Eleusis the mind of Julian was penetrated with sincere, deep, and unalterable enthusiasm… From that moment he consecrated his life to the service of the gods; and while the occupations of war, of government, and of study seemed to claim the whole measure of his time, a stated portion of the hours of the night was invariably reserved for the exercise of private devotion… and it was in honour of Pan or Mercury, of Hecate or Isis, that Julian, on particular days, denied himself the use of some particular food, which might be offensive to his tutelar deities.

This truly genuine Initiate of the Mysteries set out on his ill-fated campaign against the Persians in March 363AD. He died of wounds sustained in a skirmish with the Persians and by rights should receive all due honour as the first pagan 'martyr' on the date of his death: 26th June.

EXTRACT FROM *THE ROMAN BOOK OF DAYS*
PAULINA ERINA

11 days behind the rest of Europe. Many traditional witches celebrate their festivals 11 days later than the present calendar in accordance with the Old Ways. SOURCE: *The Calendar*, David Ewing Duncan.

Julian Period: According to *Brewer's Dictionary of Phrase & Fable* the period is calculated by multiplying together the lunar cycle, the solar cycle, and the Roman indiction. *'The first year of the Christian era corresponded to the year 4713 of the Julian; to reduce our BC dates to the Julian, we must subtract them from 4713, but our AD dates we must add to that number.'* The system was named from Julius Scaliger, who devised it and not Julius Caesar.

Julium Sidus: The name of the comet that appeared at the death of Julius Caesar, and which was looked upon as the *apotheosis* (deification) of the murdered man.

Jumala: The supreme god of the ancient Finns and Laps, but it is more commonly used by Scandinavian poets for the Almighty.

Jump the Broomstick: To marry in an informal way. It has been suggested that the original word was *brom*, which refers to the bit of a bridle and that to 'jump to *brom*' was to avoid the restraints of marriage. The reference to the 'broomstick' is therefore a corruption. Nevertheless, in modern pagan wedding ceremonies the couple jump or step over a broomstick to confirm their union.

June Marriage: *Good to the man and happy to the maid'* is an old Roman superstition. The festival of *Juno monēta* was held on the calends of June, and **Juno** was the greatest guardian of women from birth

to the grave.

Jung, Carl G.: (1875–1964) He introduced the theory of the **Collective Unconsciousness** having made a careful and enlightening study of occultism and spirituality. He believed that racial traits and myths were passed on by instinct, and is also remembered for being one of the co-founders of the **Theosophical Society**, along with Madame **Blavatsky.**

Juniper: A native British tree, the juniper is famed for its medicinal uses, although its country name 'bastard killer' arose from the eating of the berries to procure an abortion. No ruling planet is given by **Culpeper.**

Junner: A giant in Scandinavian mythology, said in the *Edda* to represent the 'eternal principle'. Its skull formed the heavens; its eyes the sun and moon, its shoulders the mountains; its bones the rocks, etc.

Juno: As Juno Regina, she protected the whole Roman Empire, but as the protector of women and marriage her feast day was the *Matronalia*, held annually on 1st March. She equates with the Greek, **Hera.**

Jupiter: (1) The Latin form of **Zeus**. Verospi's statue of the god is in the Vatican but one of the **Seven Wonders** of the World was the statue of Olympian Jove by Phidias, destroyed by fire in Constantinople in 475AD. This gigantic statue was nearly sixty feet high and seated on a throne. The figure was made of ivory and the throne of cedar wood, adorned with ivory, ebony, gold and precious stones. (2) A particularly powerful sign that governs **Sagittarius** and **Pisces**, endowing those born under it with wisdom, optimism and personal magnetism. (3) With over 300 times the mass of the Earth, and about 2½ times the mass of all the other planets put together, Jupiter is the dominant planet in the Solar System. (4) The planetary association in alchemy was designated tin. (5) The planet is associated with (the four fours of the **Minor Arcana**) and the **Wheel of Fortune** in the **Major Arcana** of the **Tarot** and **Chesed** in the **Qabalah**.

Jupiter's Beard: see **House Leek.**

Jurōjin: Japanese god of longevity. He rides on the back of a deer, and is often accompanied by cranes and tortoises as symbols of long life and a happy old age.

Justice: The eight card in the **Major Arcana** of the **Tarot**; although in the **Thoth** deck it is called **Adjustment**, the meaning remains the same. The archetypal symbol of **Equilibrium**; the concept of Justice being tempered with Mercy, and Mercy tempered with Justice.

Jyotiska: Stellar gods in Jainism. Five classes are distinguished: suns, moons (both in the plural), planets, stations of the moon and fixed stars.

"It was inevitable that meteorites should inspire awe. They came from some remote region high up in the heavens and possessed a sacred quality enjoyed only by things celestial."

Mircea Eliade
[*The Forge & the Crucible*]

K

Ka: An almost untranslatable term used by the Egyptians to describe the creative force of each individual, whether human or divine. The *ka* was represented by a hieroglyph consisting of a pair of raised arms. SOURCE: *The BM Dictionary of Ancient Egypt*, Shaw and Nicholson.

Kabbalah: see **Qabalah.**

Kachinas: Symbolic representations, sometimes in human form, of the many powers and manifestations of nature and the ancestors in Pueblo Indian belief. They serve as intermediaries between men and the principal Pueblo deities.

Kahunas: Similar to a **Shaman**, Kahunas were practitioners of the indigenous Hawaiian religion and known as 'Keepers of the Secret'. They had powerful psychic skills and healing powers.

Kale: see **Colewort.**

Kale-month or **Sprout-Kale:** The Anglo-Saxon name for February, for the vegetable that began to sprout at this time.

Kali: [Lit. Black] The Hindu Goddess of Time and Cycles of Time. She has come to represent the powers of dissolution (cosmic and otherwise), and is equated with Night, Darkness and Death.

Kali Yuga: In Hindu and Buddhist mythology, the Dark Age that marks the ultimate degeneration of the human species.

Kami: Sacred objects, divine beings, natural phenomena or venerated symbols in Japanese **Shinto**. They are usually described as having an ancestor-descendant relationship, being omnipresent in nature with strong associations with specific mountains, rocks, waterfalls and other features. They are not all-powerful, nor are they always benign.

Kamikaze: The origin of this term comes from the 'divine winds' or storms that dispersed the Mongol invasion fleets in 1274 and 1281, and which were believed to have been sent by the gods of Japan. The myth inspired the *kamikaze* pilots of WWII, who believed death defending their homeland was preferable to the dishonor of surrender.

Kappa: Mischievous Japanese water spirits that are very knowing, and can sometimes be helpful.

Karma: Originally an Indian tradition that means primarily action, work or deed. In its secondary sense it signifies the 'effect' of an action, or the sum total of the 'effects' of past actions. Karma determines our condition both in the next world and in the next life on earth; in a very literal sense we fashion our own fate. SOURCE: *Karma & Reincarnation*, Dr. Hiroshi Motoyama; *Karma Manual*, Dr. John Mumford; *The Scales of Karma*, Owen Rutter; *The Penguin Dictionary of Religions*, ed John R. Hinnells. [SEE PANEL]

Karezza: Described by Kenneth **Grant** in *Aleister Crowley and the Hidden God* as an ancient mode of magic in which energy is built up by erotic stimulation and directed to occult ends without physical discharge of sexual fluid. It was introduced to the West by Thomas Lake Harris (1823–1906), who adapted

Karma & Reincarnation

Many Westerners and those following alternative religions have embraced the concept of reincarnation and *karma*, without having any real understanding of the true meaning. To begin with, *karma* is a Sanskrit word meaning 'action'. It denotes an active force, the inference being that the outcome of future events *can* be influenced by our actions. To suppose *karma* is some sort of independent energy that predestines the course of our whole life is simply incorrect.

Since it is important to avoid the popular pagan mix-and-match approach that debases genuine Buddhist teaching, the ideal person to explain this is HH The Dalai Lama: *'Who creates karma? We ourselves by what we think, say, do, desire, and omit, create karma... In everything we do, there is cause and effect. In our daily lives, the food we eat, the work we undertake, our relaxation, all these things are a function of action. We cannot therefore throw up our hands whenever we find ourselves confronted by unavoidable suffering. To say that every misfortune is simply the result of karma is tantamount to saying that we are totally powerless in life. If this were correct, there would be no cause for hope. We might well pray for the end of the world!'*

Possibly because of its seemingly liberal appearances, and despite its growing popularity, the Dalai Lama has no desire for the global population to become Buddhist. He would much rather people of other faiths developed a greater *understanding* of Buddhism, while remaining firmly within their own religion. And although there are marked similarities between all faiths, they nonetheless differ in terms of philosophy. Although on the surface, the philosophical contradictions may not appear important, we must accept that culture does not necessarily equate with religion.

At some point we are compelled to acknowledge those fundamental differences. For example, the concept of rebirth in Buddhism and various ancient Indian traditions is incompatible with the Christian idea of salvation. Even within Buddhism itself, in the realms of metaphysics, there are diametrically opposing views.

Hindus and Buddhists believe that the soul of the deceased,

after an interim period in Otherworld, is reborn in accordance with the merits (or de-merits) acquired during its previous lifetime. Although orthodox Christians, for example, find it hard to explain the death of a child, the reincarnationists view this as merely adjusting the balance sheet of their previous lives. Some are receiving their reward, some their punishment, for what they have done before. This, in effect, absolves 'God' from any accusation of injustice, favoritism, cruelty or caprice, since everyone is ultimately responsible for his or her own destiny.

When the insights or practices of other traditions offer useful advice, it is important to take notice – even to implement certain of those elements. If this is undertaken in a manner that does not detract from the spiritual value, then it can be achieved without compromising any religious integrity. Used correctly, and resisting the urge to impress our friends with our new-found knowledge, certain insights can significantly improve our universal harmony and well-being. It is important, however, to be realistic about what we are doing and understanding the point of the exercise without accrediting it with any mystical over/undertones.

There is a little gem of Buddhist philosophy that says: *'If you wish to know of your past life, consider your present circumstances; if you wish to know of your future life, consider your present actions.'* In other words, when it comes down to the question of *karma* and reincarnation, it is all about taking responsibility for our own actions at all times.

Our individual spiritual quests will take us into realms where we may either have to change our worldview and perspectives; or bring us up against barriers that we consider insurmountable. The more we fully understand about these other beliefs, the easier the transition from 'I don't know' to *'I know'*.

EXTRACT FROM *EXPLORING SPIRITUALITY*
SUZANNE RUTHVEN & AERON MEDBH-MARA

it from **Tantric** practice.

Kashrut: A general term for Jewish dietary requirements. The word *kosher* means 'fit to be eaten'.

Kebla: The point of adoration; the quarter-point of the compass towards which a person turns when they worship.

Kelidomancy: Another term for **Cleidomancy** or using a **Pendulum** – a favored method used by Uri Geller.

Kelley, Edward: See **Dee, Dr. John.**

Kelpie: A Scottish water spirit that usually takes the form of a horse. They graze on the banks of rivers and lakes and, having enticed travelers to mount them, they are tossed into the water to drown. To see a kelpie was said to be a sure portent of drowning.

Kent's Cavern, Devon: A Paleolithic cave dwelling first investigated in the early 19th century, when evidence of human occupation from the Middle Paleolithic Age onwards could not be accepted because it clashed with the prevailing views on the date of Creation (biblical calculations suggesting that Adam had lived only about 4000 years before).

Kepler's Fairy: The theory of Johann Keplar (1571–1630) that each of the known planets were guided in their elliptical orbit by a resident angel.

Kether: The first sephirah of the Tree of Life and forms the apex of the Supernal Triangle above the **Abyss**. Known as the 'admirable' or 'hidden intelligence' because it is the Light, giving the power of comprehension. The **Names of Power** are all creator/creatrix deities, while the planetary attributions are the 'first swirlings'. SOURCE: *The Hollow Tree*, Mélusine Draco.

Key: (1) An important symbol in magic, religion and folklore because it provides and prevents access to some sought after place or spiritual condition, such as the Mysteries or degrees of Initiation. (2) On a more mundane level, keys to stables or cow houses often have a stone with a hole in it and a piece of horn attached to the handle. This is the relic of a very old superstition that the **Hag stone** kept away the nightmares, while the horn was to ensure the protection of the god of cattle, **Pan.**

Key of Solomon: A **Grimoire** that was supposed to be the key to all wisdom and ranking next to the **Emerald Tablet** as the most celebrated of magical texts. A printed version had no value as the text had to be copied out by hand by each person who wished to use it, so that the mind of the magician would personalize it.

Khabs: A star – see *The Book of the Law.*

Khem: Literally 'black', was the ancient name for Egypt, and *alkhem* or **Alchemy** was originally the 'black art' that had its origins in that land (see **Temple of Khem**).

Khepri: The emblem of the creator-god as a scarab is one of the most familiar images in Egyptian art. The scarab is a dung beetle in which the people saw the symbol of the self-generating aspect of the sun god. Khepri was the god of transformations, which, like the scarab, emerges from its own substances and is reborn of itself.

Khnum: The ancient status of this ram-headed Egyptian god, who created the human race from clay fashioned on a potter's wheel, can be seen from his image as a flat-horned ram, which became extinct around 2000BC.

Khu: The magical power *par excellence* referred to in *The Book of the Law*.

Kia: A term coined by Austin Osman **Spare** to denote the Atmospheric 'I', symbolized by the Eye; pure or preconceptual energy. SOURCE: *Cults of the Shadow*, Kenneth Grant.

King, Francis: Looked upon as the literary successor to **A.E. Waite**, insofar as he documents the growth and development of the occult traditions in modern society. In the early years of the 20th century Waite dealt mostly with Qabalistic, Rosicrucian and Masonic influences leading up to the advent of the **Golden Dawn**; King has specialized in the more contemporary groups such as the **OTO** and the Stella Matutina. TITLES: *Ritual Magic in England, The Secret Rituals of the OTO* and *Techniques of High Magic* with Stephen Skinner.

King's Evil: A former name for scrofula, a disease that was believed could be cured by the touch of the monarch. English and French kings had the gift to cure and those who had been touched were often given small coins, or 'touchpiece'.

Kingfisher: The halcyon was the Greek kingfisher and the word in the sense of 'calm, peaceful, undisturbed' has been in use in the English langue since 1578. The Greeks believed the bird to possess the power to keep the sea calm while it built its nest on the surface. The 'halcyon days' were seven days before and seven days after the **Winter Solstice**.

Kirlian Photography: The art of photographing the auras of animate and inanimate objects. Discovered in the 1930s by a Russian electrician and photographer, Semyon Kirlian. The system has been used to detect serious ailments such as cancer and tumors.

Kiss of Shame: (*Osculum infame*) One of the accusations leveled against witches was the belief that at the Sabbat they had to kiss the Devil 'under his tail'.

Kit's Coty House: A Neolithic burial chamber near Aylesford in Kent, which legend tells us was erected by the powers of four witches. The remnants of a sacrificial rite seem to have clung on in the form of a local myth. Anyone wanting an object to disappear should place it on the capstone at full moon, and walk around the monument three times – and the object will have disappeared.

Knife: The symbol of the witch's individual Will and in most forms of Craft, everyone is expected to have one that has been cleansed and consecrated. SOURCE: *Coven of the Scales*, A.R. Clay-Egerton; *Magic: An Occult Primer*, David Conway; *Techniques of High Magic*, Francis King and Stephen Skinner; *Witchcraft – A Tradition Renewed*, Evan John Jones.

Knight, Gareth: The pseudonym of an English magician who was previously associated with W.E. **Butler**. Like Butler, he received his training in the **Fraternity** of the Inner Light founded by Dion **Fortune**. TITLES: *A Practical Guide to Qabalistic Symbolism, Occult Exercises & Practices, The Practice of Ritual Magic* and *An Introduction to Ritual Magic* combined with the writings of Dion Fortune.

Knights Templar: The Order of the Poor Knights of the Temple of Solomon was a religious-military Order, and the most formidable fighting machine of the time. Besides this military prowess, they also possessed immense wealth and political power, becoming bankers and brokers to medieval Europe and the allies of kings and popes – until their suppression in 1312 on charges of heresy and magical practices. The original aim of the Order had been to protect pilgrim routes to Jerusalem and other holy places. Later they became enormously rich and were destroyed for this reason by Philip IV of France who coveted their wealth. SOURCE: *Born In Blood*, John J. Robinson; *Dungeon, Fire & Sword*, John J. Robinson; *Europe's Inner Demons*, Norman Cohn; *The Murdered Magicians*, Peter Partner; *The Templars*, Edward Burman.

Knitbone: see Comfrey.

Knockers or Tommyknockers: Underground sprites that inhabited Cornish tin mines. The old miners considered them to be lucky and often left a scrap of their midday meal for them. A similar belief can be found in Wales where they are called *coblyns*.

Knot: A powerful magical weapon, because to tie a knot is to impede the person against whom the spell is directed; to untie the knot is to release the victim from the spell (see **Witches' Ladder**).

Knot Grass: Gathered when the Moon is waning, this weed with nodes on its stem is said to strengthen and protect the eyes.

Koan: A brief statement in the form of a question or puzzle in **Zen**, the answer to which can only be discovered by direct perception rather than common sense or logical deduction.

'Know Thyself': A saying of Solon, the Athenian lawgiver (638–558BC), which has become the principle instruction for any magical practitioner.

Knox Ompax: The words of dismissal in the **Eleusinian** Mysteries, which loosely interpreted means: *'So be it. The ceremonies are concluded.'*

Kore: see Persephone.

Korrigans or Corrigan: Nine entities of Breton mythology. They have the power to predict future events, **Shapeshift**, move as 'quick as thought' from place to place, and cure disease or wounds. In appearance they are no more than two feet high, with long flowing hair that they are fond of combing. They are veiled in white, are excellent singers and their favorite haunt is beside a fountain. Their breath is deadly and they flee at the sound of a bell or benediction.

Kotha!: *'Thou Hollow One'*. An invocation of the primal goddess that appears in an ancient Gnostic-Coptic **Grimoire**, which Aleister **Crowley** restored and re-presented as *Liber Samekh*. SOURCE: *Magick*, Aleister Crowley.

Kronotypes: A term used by Gerald Massey in *The Natural Genesis* to denote the celestial timekeepers, whether stars or planets.

Ku: The Chinese term for malevolent magic (see **Wu**).

Kundalini: The Fire Snake coiled at the base of the spine, which is dormant in the spiritually unawakened individual. According to Hindu mystics, this is a potential source of immense power but extremely dangerous if aroused without due care and preparation. Those who wish to further their knowledge of the *kundalini* by practical experience have to submit to a long period of preparation, for the ability to control the released energies takes many years of arduous training to acquire. SOURCE: *A Chakra & Kundalini Workbook*, Dr. John Mumford; *Hindu World*, Benjamin Walker; *Aleister Crowley and the Hidden God*, Kenneth Grant.

Kuthun: According to the entry in *A Dictionary of Devils & Demons* by J. Tondriau and R. Villeneuve, any object or document given by one witch to another at the time of her death. A witch's inheritance often passed to a neophyte for destroying, or as a legacy.

Kybele: see **Cybele.**

Kyphi: Latin version of the Greek transcription of the ancient Egyptian *kapet*, but of all the perfumes from the ancient world, kyphi is the one whose name is remembered by posterity.

Kyteler, Alice: The first recorded witch trial in Ireland in 1324. She was a woman of a wealthy, influential Anglo-Norman family and was charged with witchcraft, largely due to her three previous husbands dying and a fourth taken ill. She fled to England and was condemned in her absence as a witch and heretic, but nothing more is known about her. SOURCE: *Irish Witchcraft*, St. John D. Seymour.

"The hare is linked all over Britain with witches, and there are few people who have not come across this association either in stories written for children, or in the tales which are part of the rural tradition."
George Ewart Evans
[*The Leaping Hare*]

L

Labarum: The standard borne before the Roman emperors. It consisted of a gilded spear, with an eagle on the top, while from a cross-staff hung a splendid purple streamer with a gold fringe, adorned with precious stones. The eagle was later replaced with a crown during the reign of Constantine.

Labyrinth: A mass of passages or garden walks, so complicated as to puzzled strangers to extricate themselves (see **Maze**). SOURCE: *Chartres: The Making of a Miracle*, Colin Ward.

Lacnunga: An Anglo-Saxon manuscript from the 10th century containing an alliterative lay, or charm in praise of the nine sacred herbs of the Nordic god Woden [**Odin**]. These nine herbs, which *'have power against nine magic outcasts, against nine venoms, and against nine flying things, against the things that over land rove'* were mugwort, waybread (plantain), stime (watercress), maythen (chamomile), wergulu (nettle), chervil, fennel, crab apple, and the unidentified 'atterlothe'.

Ladybird: Apart from the bee, ladybirds have always been the most popular of insects, often believed to be fortune-tellers and bringers of good luck.

Lady Chapel: The small chapel east of the altar, or behind the screen of the high altar and dedicated to the Virgin Mary. Usually found in old churches and often used as a focus for surreptitious pagan worship in the Middle Ages.

Lady's Mantle: Traditionally known as 'a woman's best friend', the plant was used for treating female ailments; **Culpeper** also considered it to be one

of the 'most singular wound-herbs'. The petals collect large 'pearls' of dew overnight, which was used by medieval alchemists in their experiments to turn base metals into gold and silver – its botanical name being *Alchemilla* ('the little magic one') is thought to derive from the Arabic for alchemy. Ruling planet: **Venus**.

Lamia: Another word taken from classical literature to mean 'witch' and has numerous associations in folklore and legend. It later became identified as a vampiric being, part-serpent, part-woman.

Lammas: 1st August is Loaf-mass day. The day of the first fruit offerings when a loaf made from the first corn to be cut was used in thanksgiving. The Wiccan festival of **Lughnasadh**, still referred to as Lammas in traditional Craft. [SEE PANEL]

Lampadomancy: Divination by interpreting the movements of, and shapes formed by the flame of a candle or oil lamp.

Lamp, The: The altar lamp of ritualized magic and an important part of the regalia. SOURCE: *The Hollow Tree*, Mélusine Draco; *Magick*, Aleister Crowley.

Lamps of Art: The consecrated lamps or candlesticks used within a witch's circle. White consecrated candles should be used at all times during a ritual unless otherwise directed.

Lamps, Sepulchral: *Brewer's Dictionary of Phrase & Fable* cites the Romans as being said to preserve lamps in some of their sepulchers for centuries.

Lammas and the Harvest Home

During the autumn of 1621 the settlers at Plymouth Colony gathered to give thanks for the harvest after their first year in the New World. That was America's first Thanksgiving, but it has grown into probably *the* most important family occasion of the year, where everyone gathers to enjoy a meal of roast turkey, cranberry sauce and pumpkin pie.

Its roots, however, have their origin in the traditional Harvest Supper – or Harvest Home – of the English farming community. In truth, the practice of holding a Harvest Festival service was only established in the 19th century in an attempt to control the Harvest Home celebrations, which the Church of the time considered too raucously pagan!

Harvest celebrations were some of the holiest of the pagan year. Traditionally, the harvest continued for most of August from Lammas, when bread was made from the first corn to be cut; right through to the last fruits being gathered in early September. Any housewife worth her salt would be bottling fruit, making pickles and jams, drying herbs and preparing potions from the natural harvest in the hedgerows for the months ahead when the fresh ingredients would not be available.

There has always been a spiritual quality surrounding harvest time: a celebration of the good things that have happened during the year. A perfect time to gather friends and family together for a celebratory supper in a spirit of thanksgiving, whether we are urban or rural dwellers, market trader or stockmarket trader. And although the American celebration is held on the fourth Thursday in November, a Harvest Home should be around the Harvest Moon, or Autumn Equinox.

A typical 17th century Harvest Supper would have consisted of '... *puddings, bacon or boiled beef, flesh or apple pies, and then cream brought in platters... hot cakes and ale...*' *A Witch's Treasury for Hearth & Garden* brought the menu up to date with home-made soup, honey-glazed ham, apple pie with cream and a selection of cheeses, served with celery, accompanied by good beer, cider or robust red wine.

To set the atmosphere, display any freshly prepared produce for decoration as this will be your own harvest festival. If you've made jams or pickles, give each guest a jar as a gesture of sharing. Should your talents lean more towards the arty, give each guest a corn dolly to take home. Corn has long been regarded as the embodiment of productivity and fruitfulness; a simple plait of corn straw tied with ribbon can be hung in the kitchen to insure a productive year to come.

It would also be nice to think that the modern 'wheel of the year' isn't always driven by the need to use the festivals for spellcasting. Before the end of the meal, make sure everyone has a full glass and propose a toast to your own equivalent of the 'bounty of the harvest', and ask your guests to join you in pouring a libation on the ground outside. Even in financially-troubled times, we still have something to be grateful for and if we can reintroduce the spirit of thanksgiving at the turning of the year, we will be reconnecting with the simple faith of our forebears.

'Thanksgiving' isn't about preserving *ye olde* pagan ways with copious amounts of cider swilling, accompanied by endless verses of *John Barleycorn*, it's about bringing together family and close friends for the purpose of celebration. An annual pilgrimage back to our pagan roots, or to wherever our pagan roots have been transplanted. We can gather around the simple kitchen table, or set the dining room glistening with starched linen, crystal and silver. There is no preset formula of observance... just the willingness to enjoy each other's company, count our blessings and reflect on our *good* fortune.

EXTRACT FROM *FIELDCRAFT*
A WITCH'S GUIDE TO FIELDS AND HEDGEROWS

During the papacy of Paul III one of these lamps was found in the tomb of Tullia (Cicero's daughter), which had been shut up for 1,550 years. At the dissolution of the monasteries a lamp was found that it was claimed had been burning for 1,200 years. Two such lamps are preserved in the Leyden museum.

Lancashire Witches: Possibly the most famous of all witch-trials that immortalized the names of the '**Pendle** Witches', and of all the many texts describing witch-trials in England, *The Wonderful Discoverie of Witches in the Countie of Lancaster* (1613) is also outstanding. The document records the mass trial of 20 alleged witches, of which ten of the accused were hanged.

Land of Youth: Tír na nÓg is one of the several Irish names for a realm of bright beauty and fair women, free from death or suffering, which in Irish literature lies across the sea, or within the *sid* (burial mound).

Langaj: A term used in **Voodoo** to denote a sacred tongue or language.

Lapidary: Refers to both 'object and agent' – i.e. a book classifying stones and those who work with them. There were dozens of such books on the subject in the Middle Ages and the most popular were the Arabian versions that concentrated on the efficacy of stones as talismans (see **Jewels**). Some of the earliest were *The Book of Stones*, long attributed to Aristotle, with translations in Hebrew and Latin, examined the magical power of stones; *The Flowers of Knowledge of Stones*, Shihab al-Din al-Tifashi (1154) and *Lapidario*, Alfonso X of Castile (c1300); SOURCE: *Crystal Power, Crystal Healing*, Michael Gienger;

Liber 777, Aleister Crowley; *Magical Jewels*, Joan Evans; *The Curious Lore of Precious Stones* and *The Magic of Jewels & Charms*, George Frederick Kunz.

Lapis Lazuli: Metamorphosed form of limestone, rich in the mineral lazurite that is dark blue in color and often flecked with impurities of calcite, iron pyrites or gold. The Egyptians considered it to be superior to all materials other than gold or silver.

Larentalia: The festival of **Acca Laurenta**, an early Italian earth goddess and a day (23rd December) for special religious observance.

Lares: Minor deities that were found in every Roman household, in field shrines, at busy crossroads and in the state temples. The oldest manifestation was the *Lar Familiaris* (Household Lar), which received regular monthly offerings of garlands on the hearth as well as daily observance at mealtimes. There were also the *Lares Compitāles;* these were dangerous spirits of the crossroads who had to be propitiated; and the Lares Praestitēs (Guardians) of the State. SOURCE: *Fasti*, Ovid, trans Sir James Frazer; *The Oxford Companion to Classical Literature*, ed by Sir Paul Harvey.

Larvae: A malignant ghost of the ancient Romans who had died tragically; in the Middle Ages they became terrifying spirits who brought great sadness. For **Paracelsus** and some other Qabalists, the Larvae were 'the children of Adam's solitude, born in filth and squalor during the night' and obviously refer to nocturnal emissions. Also known as **Lemures**.

Laurel: The ancients believed that laurel communicated the spirit of prophecy and poetry, hence the custom of crowning the pythoness and poets, and of putting laurel leaves under they pillow to acquire inspiration. Bay laurel was also supposed to avert lightening. In modern times it is the symbol of victory and peace.

La Vecchia – the Old Religion – is the title given to witchcraft in Italy and Sicily, because the tradition has its foundation in the Greek, Etruscan and Egyptian rites that were incorporated into the official Roman religion. SOURCE: *Apologia*, Apuleius; *Aradia: or the Gospel of the Witches*, Charles Leland.

Lavender: Introduced into Britain by the Romans it was not only valued for its medicinal properties, but for its fragrance and as a strewing herb, insect repellent, and a mask for unpleasant smells. Ruling planet: **Mercury**.

Laverna: Old Italian goddess of the underworld. Libations to her were poured out with the left hand as was customary in funerary observations.

LaVey, Anton Szandor: Founder and leader of the Church of Satan in the USA, which in the 1970s had some 9,000 members worldwide. SOURCE: *The Satanic Bible*, Anton LaVey; *Secret Life of a Satanist*, Blanche Barton; *Malleus Satani, The Hammer of Satan*, Suzanne Ruthven.

Lead: Thought to have magical properties and the oldest of the seven metals recognized in traditional alchemy. It is traditionally the metal of death and of **Saturn**, the planet of Time; holy relics were often encased in lead to keep their sacred force intact. Placed at the entrance of a house, it protects against witchcraft and evil spirits.

Le Champion des dames: The earliest known picture of witches flying on broomsticks comes from a manuscript (c1440) by Martin le Franc. The text states that not one, two or three, but three thousand witches go to see their familiar devils! SOURCE: *The Encyclopedia of Witchcraft & Demonology*, Rossell Hope Robbins.

Leconomancy: The sound or movement when a pebble is thrown into water covered with a film of oil. **Nostradamus** was said to have favored this method.

Lectisternium: A religious ceremony adopted at Rome after consultation of the **Sibylline** Books in 399BC, and repeated later in times of great emergency. Images of certain gods were placed on couches and a meal set before them.

Leech: A Saxon doctor or 'one skilled in leech craft' (see **Medicinal Leech**).

Leech Book of Bald: The earliest surviving Anglo-Saxon manuscript dealing with the virtue of herbs. Written in the vernacular in the early 10th century it embodies beliefs that date back to primitive times long before the Roman invasion.

Leek, Sybil: Claimed to be able to trace her witchcraft ancestry back to the twelfth century and to have been initiated into the Craft in France by her paternal aunt. Not only that, aged eight years old she became acquainted with Aleister **Crowley**, who was a frequent visitor to the house. She moved to America in 1960 where she tried to dispel the media-hype surrounding the Craft and died there in 1983. SOURCE: *The Complete Art of Witchcraft, Diary of a Witch* and *Cast Your Own Spell*, Sybil Leek; *The Truth About Witchcraft*, Hans Holzer.

Left: Believed to be unlucky by the Roman **Augurs**. Having marked out the 'field of observation' with the space divided from top to bottom. If birds appeared on the left side of the divination, the augury was unlucky; if the birds appeared on the right side, the augury was pronounced favorable. Greek augurs considered all signs seen by them over the left shoulder as being inauspicious.

Left-hand Path: The so-called lunar-female-goddess aspect of magical/mystical working (see **Varma Marg**). The Latin word *sinister*, meaning on the left side from the view of the bearer of the shield, not the beholder (in heraldry), has not helped to clarify the situation, and sinister in modern terms means evil. SOURCE: *Applied Magic*, Dion Fortune; *Coven of the Scales*, A.R. Clay-Egerton.

Legends: Traditional stories distinguished from myths and folk tales by the fact that they are attached to a historical event, person or place, and are often claimed to be true.

Legis Tor, Devon: A Bronze Age settlement covering more than four acres. There are four walled enclosures with accompanying huts, which probably belonged to a tribe of herdsmen, who built the enclosure walls to protect their livestock from wolves and bears.

Lemegeton: A 15th century version of the *Clavicula Salomonis* (Little Key of Soloman), the Qabalistic **Grimoire** that alchemists such as Dr. John Dee had studied.

Lemnian Earth: A type of soil of a yellowish-grey color, found on the island of Lemnos, and said to cure the bites of serpents and other wounds.

It was called *terra sigillata* because it was 'sealed' by the priest before being prescribed. Lemnos was the island where **Vulcan** fell when **Jupiter** flung him out of heaven, and may be an ancient volcano.

Lemon: A common ingredient in **Voodoo** spells and in North African magic; often used as the vessel (carrier) for other magical substances.

Lemuria: The concept of the lost continents of Lemuria and **Mu** have generated almost as much interest as **Atlantis**, especially once Madame **Blavatsky** incorporated the idea into her theory of the 'five vanished races'.

Lemuria: Roman observations held in honor of the spirits of the dead.

Lemures or **Larvae:** Souls of the dead who sometimes return to the world to reunite themselves with their bodies. Plato wrote of them in *Phaedra*. The Etruscans and Romans believed lemures to attach themselves to the living in order to torment them, and appeased them by conducting strange ceremonies known as the *Lemuria*, held every May and November.

Lenaia, The: An Athenian festival connected with **Dionysus**, held in the month of January, with processions, general merrymaking and joking to promote fertility of the autumn-sown seed, and of the soil in general during the winter recess.

Leo: (1) The fifth sign of the zodiac, the Lion – 22 July–22 August – reclines in the heavens like the Egyptian Sphinx. (2) The meteor shower Leonids peaks annually on 17th November, and in 1966 observers recorded up to 40 meteors per second at its peak.

Lepanthropy: The ability to transform

oneself into a hare, i.e. **Shape-shifting**. Witches were often accused of taking the form of a hare.

Lethbridge, T.C.: Archeologist, Cambridge don and Honorary Keeper of Anglo-Saxon Antiquities at the University Museum of Archaeology and Ethnology. He experimented extensively with pendulum dowsing and wrote a number of books on the subject. He also investigated ghostly phenomena and concluded that many of the apparitions were not spirits of the dead, but natural 'recordings' impressed upon their surroundings (particularly damp and dismal places) and 'replayed' when conditions were favorable.

Lethe: The Greek **River** of forgetfulness that departed souls drank from, to wipe away any memories of any past lives (see **Hades**).

Lettuce: The ancient Greeks, Romans and Egyptians credited the plant with magical properties, as well as many medicinal and culinary ones. The lettuce commonly used in salads today has had the medicinal virtues of its wild relative bred out of it. Ruling planet: **Moon** (garden lettuce) and **Mars** (wild lettuce).

Lévi, Eliphas: Born in Paris in 1810. He studied for the seminary but was obliged to leave because of his sexual permissiveness. He developed an interest in occultism around 1844 and some ten years later visited London where his reputation as a magus preceded him. He returned to Paris and attracted pupils who studied **Qabalah** under his tuition and published his best-known books, *Transcendental Magic*, *The History of Magic* and *The Key of the Mysteries*, which can still be obtained in English translation.

Leviathan: Comes from the Hebrew to mean 'that which gathers itself into folds' or 'that which is drawn out', and has come to be used to describe any huge water creature from a whale to a crocodile. SOURCE: *Dictionary of Demons*, Fred Gettings.

Levitation: Describes the rising and hovering in the air, or making a person or object rise and float in the air, by paranormal means. **Simon** the Magician and Apollonius of Tyana became famous because of their levitational abilities.

Lexdon Barrow: A burial mound near Colchester was opened in 1924 to reveal what may have been the remains of Cunobelinus, a 1st century British ruler. Many bronze items, now in the Colchester and Essex Museum, were found including statuettes and a table. It was claimed at the time that the barrow contained a king in golden armor but there is no record of this tradition before 1924.

Leyden Papyrus: A Late Kingdom, Egyptian magical papyrus.

Ley Lines: Direct lines of natural electromagnetic energy that criss-cross the landscape and were first noticed by Alfred Watkins. First published in 1925 and out of print for many years, *The Old Straight Track* remains the most popular source for the study of an ancient system that was old when the Romans came to Britain.

Lha-Dre: The *lha* (gods) and *dre* (demons) are the supernatural beings of indigenous Tibetan folk-religion.

Li: (Rites of Propriety) The two components of the Chinese character *Li* mean 'spirit' and 'sacrifice', and generally refers to formal rituals and the rules of correct behavior.

Libanomancy: Observing and interpreting the smoke rising from incense for the purpose of foretelling the future and first used by the Babylonians.

Libation: A drink offered to a deity, or the pouring out of a drink: the offering might be poured onto the ground or floor, on an altar, or onto the fire. The Greeks and Romans poured a libation to the household gods at mealtimes.

Liber: (1) An old Italian deity, probably a general spirit of creativity, whose characteristics were submerged by Greek overlay as the patron of vine-growers. (2) Practitioners of ritual magic will be familiar with the prefix 'Liber' on numerous magical texts, the most well-known being Aleister Crowley's *Liber 777*, the definitive collection of **Correspondences**.

Liberalia: The festival of **Liber** was celebrated on 17th March with the *Liberālia* when Roman youths first assumed the *toga virilis*.

Libra: (1) Seventh sign of the zodiac connected with Themis, the Greek goddess of justice, whose attribute was a pair of scales – 23-September–23 October. (2) Looking like a high-flying kite, Libra is easy to find by extending a line westwards from Antares and its two bright neighbors in **Scorpius**.

Lichen: Found growing on rocky outcrops and on the bark of trees. The abundance on trees indicates a clean atmosphere, while the absence of particular species is a measure of air and rain pollution. Many lichens were valued by old herbalists for their antibiotic properties. Ruling planet: Jupiter.

Ligature: Magical **Binding** of a person in order to prevent them accomplishing a specific thing, or course of action.

Light Bearers: see **Watchers**.

Lightning: The classic preventions against being struck by lightning were the eagle (chosen by **Jupiter**); a sea-calf (Augustus Caesar) and **Laurel** (Tiberius III). Bodies scathed or struck dead by lightning were believed to be incorruptible; anyone struck was held in great honor. For the Egyptians, lightning was a manifestation of the storm god, **Set**.

Like Cures Like: *Similia similibus curantur* covers the three linked concepts in folk medicine. That the thing which causes a malady is the best means of cure; the physical similarities between the illness and the item supposed to cure it; and the **Doctrine of Signatures**.

Lilith: In Talmudic lore, Lilith was the first wife of Adam. She represents in the **Mystery** Schools the sexual shadow, or succuba, formed of uncontrolled desire. Lilith is a vampire force, which if projected beyond the aura of the magician can obsess the object of its attentions. SOURCE: *Dictionary of Demons*, Fred Gettings; *Malleus Satani*, Suzanne Ruthven.

Lily: A favored plant of the Greeks and Romans, it was certainly known to the Anglo-Saxons; widely used for skin treatments and for spells to counter witchcraft. Lily of the Valley has been cultivated in Britain since at least medieval times and although potentially poisonous, used to treat various complaints. Ruling planet: **Moon** (lily) and **Mercury** (lily of the valley).

Lime or **Linden Tree:** Despite its impressive history as an indigenous tree and its multilayered medicinal use, it is surprising that the lime does not play any significant part in British folklore apart appearing in songs and poetry.

Lincoln: The ancient Briton's town of Lindon was renamed Lindum by the Romans, and after colonization was called Lindum Colonia as a root for the present name. In 48AD a Roman garrison was set up to control the meeting of two great highways, Ermine Street and Fosse Way.

Lincoln Imp, The: This one foot tall imp, high on a pillar in the cathedral's Angel Choir, it is said to have wrought havoc in the great building until an angel turned him into stone. Whatever the stonemason's reasoning behind placing the image in the cathedral, Christian fundamentalists were clamoring for the imp's removal during the 1980s Anti-occult Campaign – despite the fact that RAF pilots carried an image of the imp as a good luck charm during WWII.

Lineage: The ability to trace a particular Craft-line and its 'family tree' from which a witch takes her/his **Tradition**, but not necessarily **Hereditary**.

Ling: see **Heather**.

Lingam: A term used in sacred texts for the phallus as an emblem of male generative and creative power.

Linking: Process of mental identification of past adepts, or appropriate symbols within a magical operation.

Linseed: see **Flax**.

Lion: An emblem or great strength and courage; often used as a symbol of royalty.

Lir: Sea god in the Irish tradition and the bravest of the **Tuatha De Danann**. In Irish poetry, 'the plain of lir' refers to the waves of the sea. In Wales, the god was called Llyr.

Litha: The Summer Solstice.

Lithomancy: Divination by casting colored stones, particularly crystals or gems, to foretell the future or interpret omens. May also refer to skrying with jewels and crystals.

Little People, The: see **Faere Folk**.

Living Fire: see **Elf Fire**.

Llud or **Lud:** Originally regarded as a sky god by the indigenous native Britons.

Llyn y Fan Fach: A mountain lake that lies a few miles to the south of Myddfai in Dyfed and described as one of the most magical places in Wales. It is said that the magic comes from the lake, where the water fairies live. One of these water fairies was the mother of the long line of the legendary Physicians of Myddfai that only died out in the 19th century.

Loa: Term for god, spirit or guardian angel in **Voodoo**, the set of occult beliefs and practices found in Haiti. The antecedents of the Loa go back to roots in Africa, and have acquired many traits of the Catholic saints (see **Santeria**).

Loci Inferni: To the Romans these inferior places were thought to be the home of the dead.

Lodestar: The leading star by which mariners are guided – usually Polaris, the pole star.

Lodestone: A magnet or stone that guides or directs; a variety of magnetite that attracts iron and is used as a test for truth or faithfulness. The lodestone enables the bearer to foretell the future and will endow them with divine inspiration and secret knowledge. If a question is asked about the future, it will reveal a truthful answer.

Lodge: see **Temple.**

Logos: In Stoic philosophy, the active principle living in and determining the world; the Word of God incarnate from the Greek meaning 'reason'.

Loki: A Scandinavian god of fire, strife and a **Trickster**. He was intelligent and perverse and often compared to the Christian Devil. Loki was primarily responsible for the death of **Balder**.

London: Mortally wounded in the foot with a poisoned spear, the ancient British (Welsh) war god, **Bran** is said to have ordered his companions to take his severed head to the White Mount, where the Tower of London now stands. Bran means 'Raven' in Welsh and ravens have always been kept in the Tower; it is said that if they fly away then England will be lost. So the birds have their wings clipped to prevent this from happening. By Roman times there was a tremendous variety of worship and many cults in London, imported into the country by the legions and traders. Hundreds of artifacts have been found by archeologists, including a magnificent head of **Mithras** wearing the Phrygian cap, that was found during excavations if the Mithraic Temple and now in the Guildhall Museum. Among the wealth of historic buildings that still stand, the Temple Church dating from the 12th century is one of the finest monuments in England to the **Knights Templar.** SOURCE: *Discovering London*, Macdonald.

Long Compton: *'There are enough witches*

in Long Compton to draw a load of hay up Long Compton Hill' runs the saying. Local belief in witches was confirmed in the late 19th century, when a man accused of murdering a woman in the village claimed that he had killed her because she had bewitched him. Sixteen other witches in the district deserved the same fate, he added. Long Compton has a long history of witchcraft, from the witch of folklore who prevented a warlord from becoming master of all England (see **Rollright Stones**), and the strange stone image in the church porch, to the nearby murder of Charles Walton in 1945 at **Lower Quinton**.

Lookback Time: In astronomy the amount of time it takes for light from a distant star to reach the Earth. Looking farther outward into the sky is equivalent to looking backward in time, since the farther one sees outward, the more ancient the image.

Lord & Lady: Can refer to either the witch-god and goddess; to the **Coven** priest and priestess.

Lord of Misrule: Master of the revels, (or Feast of Fools), who presided over the festivities and buffoonery of the Midwinter season. In France he was call the Abbot of Misrule (*L'abbe de Liesse*) and in Scotland, the Master of Unreason. SOURCE: *A Witch's Treasury of the Countryside*, Mélusine Draco..

Lord's Prayer, The: (1) A widespread belief that witches were unable to recite the Lord's Prayer from start to finish. The test was considered infallible during formal witch-trials. (2) It was also claimed that saying the Prayer backwards was part of the devilish rites.

Lotus: A sacred symbol of rebirth for the

ancient Egyptians and the richest in symbolism of all flowers, the lotus has a vast range of meanings in religion, philosophy, mythology and art. In Homer, the poet refers to the 'lotus eaters' who have eaten of the plant and forgotten their family and homeland. In recent times an experiment was done to test whether the plant did indeed have any hallucinogenic properties but the tests were inconclusive. Used in or engraved on an amulet, the lotus averts the **Evil Eye** and brings success and good fortune.

Loudun: The scandal involving the nuns of an Ursuline convent at Loudun in France, and the scene of the most famous case of alleged demonic possession in European history. A priest named Urbain Grandier was accused of bewitching the Mother Superior and other nuns, was found guilty, and after appalling torture was burned alive in 1634. SOURCE: *The Encyclopedia of Witchcraft & Demonology*, Rossell Hope Robbins.

Lounge-craft: Often used as a derogatory description for those who never venture outside to practice magic through personal choice, preferring the warmth and comfort of their own sitting room. On the other hand, many would-be witches do not have access to the great outdoors because of ill-health, disability or urban restrictions. SOURCE: *A Witch's Treasury of Hearth & Garden*, Gabrielle Sidonie.

Loup Garou: A species of French werewolf that was transported to the North American bayou by French settlers.

Lovecraft, Howard Phillips: An American author who wrote a mixture of bizarre occult-mythology stories originally for the pulp fiction market. This writing has since earned him cult status, following his creation of the 'dread Cthulhu' and the '*Necronomicon*' – an imaginary book created by Lovecraft, but one which many people now believe to be real. Lovecraft's stories are now available in collections: *The Tomb, At the Mountains of Madness, The Case of Charles Dexter Ward, The Haunter of the Dark, The Lurker at the Threshold* and *The Shuttered Room*.

Love Magic or **Divination:** There are two types of love spell: first, the general charm that works on anyone, with its easily recognizable symbolism; and second, a specially adapted and individual charm that usually requires some personal object or ingredient. SOURCE: *The Penguin Guide to Superstitions of Britain and Ireland*, Steve Roud.

Lovers, The: The sixth card of the **Major Arcana** of the **Tarot** with the archetypal representation of the alchemical Union of man and woman (i.e. opposites) on all levels. (See **Yin** and **Yang**.)

Lower Quinton: On St. Valentine's Day 1945, the body of an elderly Warwickshire hedge-cutter, Charles Walton, was found pinned to the ground by a hayfork. Over the years, speculation and rumor has linked the alleged ritual killing to the **Long Compton** witches because of a similar case that had occurred in 1875, when a ploughboy stabbed to death a woman he claimed had bewitched him. SOURCE: *Murder by Witchcraft*, Donald McCormick.

Lucid dreaming: A form of daydreaming in order to produce psychic images.

SOURCE: *The Lucid Dreamer*, Malcolm Godwin.

Lucifer: The morning star. Originally translated from the Hebrew, *helel ben shahar*, which means 'day star, son of the dawn' and the Latin *lucifer* (meaning 'carrier of fire' and the Greek equivalent *phosphoros*, with much the same meaning) it was only in later Christian texts that it became equated with **Satan**. SOURCE: *Dictionary of Demons*, Fred Gettings; *A Dictionary of Devils & Demons*, J. Tondriau and R. Villeneuve.

Luciferian: A 13th century German cult who were persecuted for devil-worship. They claimed that Lucifer was the brother of the Christian God and believed that he had created the world; that he was the provider of all good things on earth. He had been wrongfully and treacherously ousted from heaven because he wanted to spread knowledge and enlightenment among mankind. The spirit who will free man from the servitude of the creator.

Luck: Is luck a gift of the gods, or the product of one's own temperament, the individual's response to events? Is it 'luck of the draw', or can we make our own luck? In magical law, the belief is that the future is not fixed and that various methods of divination show how things are now, or how they will be if they are not subject to magical change. How we attempt to implement those changes depends on the personality and character of the magician – the outcome being viewed by outsiders as good or bad luck.

Lug: The Irish Lug (the Shining One) is a god of many skills, including music,

poetry, wealth, magic and warfare. His festival is **Lughnasadh**.

Lughnasadh, or see **Lammas:** (1) Falls on the 1st August and is one of the four major festivals of the modern pagan calendar. (2) To celebrate the start of the harvest when the Lammas loaf was baked from the first corn in traditional Craft.

Lunar, or **Moon Magic:** *'There is a magical power in the moon, for it is supposed to draw to itself the hidden potencies of the stars and constellations.'* Almost a quarter of a million miles away from earth, the moon has an immense attractive power, which affects even the land masses of the planet. But the moon's influence on the sea is especially strong; the whole watery surface is moved by its magnetic pull, creating the tides of the sea. In folklore and mythology the moon is believed to have a profound influence on all living things: as the moon wanes, growing things similarly decrease in energy. *Moon Magic* is the title of an occult novel by Dion **Fortune**.

Lunar Month: About four weeks from new moon to new moon.

Lunar Year: There are thirteen lunar months in a year: 13 x 4 = 52 weeks.

Lunatics: The Romans held that the mind was affected by the moon, and that 'lunatics' were more and more frenzied as the moon approached full.

Lupercalia: A very ancient festival at Rome when worshippers gathered at the Lupercal, a cave on the Palatine, where Romulus and Remus were reared by a she-wolf. The festival is believed to be older than Rome itself, when the festivities were run by the Luperci, or 'Brotherhood of the Wolf'.

A day for special religious observance.

Lupins, Les: In many parts of France, but more especially Normandy there was a long-held belief in certain fantastic wolf-like beings known as *lupins*. Although they generally avoid man, in some districts they are fierce and of the werewolf race, since they are said to scratch up graves and gnaw on the bones of the dead.

Lur: **Basque** word meaning 'earth' and the name of the earth goddess.

Lurker: A form of elemental or sprite that lingers around furtively on the periphery of the vision during magic workings. Can be seen as filmy images in the smoke arising from incense. They are usually banished when the magical operation is closed down.

Lustrātio: Originally a Roman ceremony of purification and protection, which consisted of a procession round the place or object to be purified or protected, together with libation and prayer at various points surrounding it. **Lustration** – the act of carrying out the rite of purification.

Lustral Water: Used for aspersing worshippers is a custom found in almost all nations of antiquity. Those who entered or left the temple might dip their fingers into the water or be sprinkled by a priest. In Rome the priest used a small laurel or olive branch for sprinkling the people.

Lux or **LVX:** [Gnostic] The Light of Consciousness, or the **Holy Guardian Angel** that links man with Those beyond.

Lycanthropy: (1) From the Greek word for 'wolf' and 'man', it refers to the transformation of a human being into some other carnivorous animal, especially a wolf – but alternatively a bear, tiger, leopard or jaguar. (2) It also refers to a form of insanity in which the sufferer believes he is the animal and behaves accordingly. (3) In magical terms, a chain-dance 'assumption' of animal form. (4) The projection of a wraith in animal form. SOURCE: *The Encyclopedia of Witchcraft & Demonology*, Rossell Hope Robbins; *Mastering Witchcraft*, Paul Huson.

Lyceum: A grove and gymnasium near Athens where Aristotle taught.

Lynchomancy: Divination using the wick of a burning candle or lantern to interpret an omen or foretell the future.

Lyonnesse: A tract of land between Land's End and the Scilly Isles, now submerged under 'forty fathoms of water'. King **Arthur** was said to come from this mythical country.

Lytton, Edward Bulwer: (1803–1873) An English novelist and politician who is remembered for his novels dealing with the occult. He organized a club for the practice and investigation into ceremonial magic but was best known for his novel, *The Last Days of Pompeii* and considered his best books were those, like *Zanoni* and *A Strange Story*, which carried strong occult themes. On several occasions he entertained Eliphas **Lévi** at his family home at Knebworth, and was at one time the honorary Grand Patron of the *Societies Rosicruciana*, a predecessor of the **Golden Dawn**. He died in 1873 and was rumored to have been one of a long line of **Rosicrucian** initiates.

"The essence of the lie is to be found in its deception, not its words."
Book of Grammayre

M

Ma'at: Egyptian goddess of truth, justice and order, whose symbol was an ostrich feather. The heart of the deceased was weighed against the feather of Ma'at during the **Judgement of the Dead**.

Mab: The 'fairies' midwife' as a midwife of dreams and often referred to as Queen Mab, meaning elf-queen or woman in Anglo-Saxon.

Mabinogion: Much that belongs to the half-forgotten world of Celtic Britain and the pagan past is enshrined in the stories of the *Mabinogion*, especially some of the earliest surviving material of the **Arthurian** legends. A collection of medieval Welsh tales that have had a profound effect on European literature and esoteric belief and which show that the origin of many of the elements from which these tales were composed was not found in the glittering medieval courts but in pagan Britain. *'The various motifs must at one time have formed part of the cult legends and the folk tales that circulated orally in the Celtic world in pre-Christian times, to be welded together much later by the skill of Welsh writers.'* SOURCE: *Mabon & the Mysteries of Britain,* Caitlin Matthews; *Myths & Legends of Wales,* Tony Roberts.

Mabon: The Autumn Equinox.

Macaber or **Dance Macabre:** The dance over which Death presides, supposed to be executed by the dead of all ages and conditions. It is an allegory of the mortality of man, and was a favorite subject of artists and poets between the 13th–15th centuries *'What are these paintings of the wall around us? The dance macabre,'* Longfellow: *The Golden Legend.*

Macbeth: The three witches appearance in Shakespeare's play of the same name was one of the most influential in establishing the stereotypical witches as evil, ugly hags.

Macha(s): In the old Irish religion, a group of three goddesses who discharge various functions in the fields of motherliness, agriculture and war.

Machen, Arthur: (1863–1947) Regarded as one of the finest Welsh mystical writers of the 20th century. He gave up medical studies to work for George Redway, who was publishing some notable books on the occult tradition at that time. Machen was a friend of Oscar Wilde and W.B. **Yeats**, with whom he shared a love of Celtic lore and Grail legends. In 1900 he joined the **Golden Dawn** following the death of his first wife, but never became a prominent figure in the organization. His finest writings are *The Great God Pan, The Bowmen, The Shining Pyramid* and *The Three Imposters*, all of which have a sense of wistful mystery about them.

Macrocosm and **Microcosm:** The principle that there exists between man and the universe a correspondence in which the universe (*macrocosm*) is represented in miniature in the man (*microcosm*). Though discarded by modern science, the theory has retained its value for occultists and magicians, who believe that science's view of the universe only accounts for a small part.

Macroprosopus: The Qabalistic sign for one of the four basic elements: *macroprosopus* represents the magic of Earth.

Maculomancy: The study of the shape, placement and size of birthmarks on the skin in the belief that they reveal personal fortune or misfortune, as well as a guide to health.

Madder: Valued in both medicine and dyeing by the ancient Egyptians, as well as the Greeks and Romans, the plant was also listed by **Aelfric**. Ruling planet: **Mars**.

Maelström: Norwegian for 'whirling stream'.

Maes Howe, Orkney: Said to be the finest chambered cairn in north-western Europe and still in fairly good condition. The impressive stone chamber is entered via a 36 ft long passage. Several times parties of Vikings left runic inscriptions in Old Norse: one of these records that they found treasure.

Magen David: The six-pointed Star of David that has come to be identified as a typically Jewish symbol (see **Hexagram**). Its use as a uniquely Jewish symbol only dates back several centuries; prior to which it was frequently used as a decorative or magical motif by non-Jewish people. The occult symbol, referred to in medieval times as the Seal of **Solomon**, displays each triangle in a different color and is interpreted as representing the Higher Self intermingled with the mundane nature in the perfectly balanced and evolved individual.

Magi: (1) Originally a priestly tribe among the ancient Medes and the official priesthood of western Iran; learned priests who were revered as sages, magicians and diviners. In esoteric circles a **Magus** was an exalted title of the highest rank in magical Orders and meant a great Adept of the occult arts. (2) Now used to describe anyone who practices Western Ritual Magic. SOURCE: *Magic: A Occult Primer*, David Conway; *Techniques of High Magic*, Francis King and Stephen Skinner.

Magic: A ritual activity intended to produce results without using the recognized causal processes of the physical world. According to Aleister **Crowley**, *'The question of magick is a question of discovering and employing hitherto unknown forces in Nature...'* SOURCE: *Magic In The Middle Ages*, Richard Kieckhefer; *Magick in Theory & Practice*, Aleister Crowley; *Magic: A Occult Primer*, David Conway; *Magic: Its Ritual, Power & Purpose*, W.E. Butler; *Magic – White & Black*, Franz Hartmann; *Practical Magic & the Western Mystery Tradition*, W.E. Butler; *Techniques of High Magic*, Francis King and Stephen Skinner; *Ritual Magic in England*, Francis King; *What You Call Time*, Suzanne Ruthven. [SEE PANEL]

Magical Papyri: Magic and religion always walked hand-in-hand in ancient Egypt, and are often impossible to separate. The magical papyri are a rich source of material for illustrating beliefs and practices of the Egyptians. SOURCE: *The Leyden Papyrus*, ed by F.L. Griffiths and Herbert Thompson.

Magic, Ceremonial: A form of 'high' magic that involves highly elaborate rituals guided by a complex set of correspondences.

Magic, Chaos: A contemporary form of ritual magic that uses any method to attain an altered state of consciousness.

Magical Fiction: The subtle method of using the novel as a teaching device, which has been used extremely successfully by Dion **Fortune** and Aleister **Crowley**. Fortune's books – *The Winged Bull; Sea Priestess; Moon Magic; The Demon Lover* and *The Goat-Foot God* are still as magically potent today as when she first began to write in the 1930s. Crowley's *Moon Child* and his stories of Simon Iff are interlaced with Thelemic philosophy and magical references.

Magical Tools or **Weapons:** The magical regalia that is placed on the altar during a magical operation. SOURCE: *Book 4,* Aleister Crowley; *Coven of the Scales,* A.R. Clay-Egerton; *The Crafting & Use of Ritual Tools,* Eleanor and Philip Harris; *Magic: An Occult Primer,* David Conway; *Magical Ritual Methods,* W.G. Gray; *Magick,* Aleister Crowley; *Ritual Use of Magical Tools,* Chic and Sandra Cicero; *Techniques of High Magic,* Francis King and Stephen Skinner *Witchcraft – A Tradition Renewed,* Evan John Jones.

Magician or **Magus:** (1) Usually refers to a practitioner of ritual magic. (2) The second card in the **Major Arcana** of the standard **Tarot** deck, although sometimes called 'the Juggler' and in the Marseilles (and other French packs) it is called Le Bateleur. It is the archetypal image of the Magician of myth and legend, who is also our mentor and guide.

Magick: This distinctive spelling denotes anything written by or about Aleister **Crowley's** magical philosophy of **Thelema**. He used it to distinguish his magick of the New Aeon, which is of a directly electro-chemical nature, according to Kenneth **Grant** in *The Magical Revival,* and differs from the ceremonial techniques of the previous Aeon. This spelling used in any other context is pure affectation as there is a very good reason why he chose to use it! *Magick* is also the title of a book by Aleister Crowley.

Magistellus: An elemental servant or **Familiar**.

Magister: The title for the male leader of a coven as the representative of the **Horned God** and taken from the Latin 'master'. Sometimes he also takes the role of the **Man in Black**.

Magnetism: A force that was thought to pervade the universe and although not considered identical with electromagnetism, it does possess certain similarities. The theory offered by Franz A. Mesmer in 1766 was that it was especially concentrated in 'animal nervous systems and magnets'.

Magnum Opus: The chief or most important of a person's works.

Magpie: A bird that is generally regarded as being mysterious and sinister, partly because of its black and white plumage, and in many areas it is still thought to be unlucky. Nevertheless the magpie was held in high esteem by the Iceni, and had been a bird of divination, certainly from when it was first recorded in 1159 up to the 16th century when folklore deemed the bird to be unlucky. SOURCE: *The Penguin Guide to Superstitions of Britain & Ireland,* Steve Roud; *Fauna Britannica,*

Stefan Buczacki.

Magus: (1) A male magical practitioner, usually referring to a ritual magician. The word comes from archaic Persian *magi*. (2) A specific grade of magical attainment within the **A∴A∴**.

Magus, The: (1) A compendium of magic and occultism compiled by Francis Barrett and published in London in 1801. Little is known about the author but *The Magus* details the use of natural magic and herbs and gemstones; magnetism; talismanic magic; alchemy; numerology; elemental law; ceremonial magic and biographies of famous **Adepts** from history. The original book passed unnoticed for years until Eliphas **Lévi** rediscovered it. (2) An esoteric novel of the same name, written by John Fowles in 1966.

Maiden: Coven title conferred upon the **Lady**, or sometimes the Lady's daughter if appropriate.

Maiden Castle, Dorset: Probably the best known hill fort in England, this Iron Age fort was built on the site of a much earlier causewayed camp. Neolithic defenses have been discovered below the Iron Age ramparts, and there is a late Neolithic long barrow on the hilltop. The fort was captured and reduced by Vespasian's 2nd Roman Legion. Artifacts from the site can be seen at the Dorset County Museum.

Maiden Stone, Aberdeen: An exceptionally fine and well preserved Pictist symbol stone. It is of red granite, carved in relief with a variety of men, fish and monsters.

Maid Marion: A **Morris** dance, or the boy in the Morris called *mad morian*, from the 'morian' or headpiece that he wears on his head. Maid Marian

is a corruption first of the words, and then of the sex according to *Brewer's Dictionary of Phrase & Fable*: '*A set of morrice dancers danced a maid marian with a tabor and pipe.*'

Ma-Ion: A term coined by Frater Achad (Charles Stansfeld Jones) to denote the formula of Manifestation and the nature of the New Aeon, which he claimed to have inaugurated in 1948. SOURCE: *Cults of the Shadow*, Kenneth Grant.

Maju and **Mari:** Divine spirits of the **Basques**. When the two meet, there is a mighty thunderstorm. Maju appears in the form of a snake, while Mari is represented by a sickle. The belief that a house can ward off lightning by placing a sickle in front of the building is still widespread.

Malediction: The act of cursing; the words with which the curse is laid.

Maleficia: The name given to misfortunes, injuries or calamities suffered by persons, animals or property, for which no immediate explanation could be found and so they were attributed to witchcraft.

Male Mysteries: Rarely written about or discussed in modern pagan circles but there have always been male **Mystery** Traditions. SOURCE: *The God Year: Festival Days of the Sacred Male*, Nigel Pennick and Helen Field.

Malkuth: The tenth and final sephirah of the Tree of Life and represents the sphere of Earth. From its molten core to the outermost reaches of its atmosphere, Malkuth represents the Earth-soul – the 'subtle, psychic aspect of matter' and the elemental energies of Earth. The **Names of Power** are those appropriate for earth and grain deities,

Magic – What is it?

Broadly speaking, magic employs the use of ritual, symbol and ceremonial as a means of representing and communicating with forces underlying the universe and man – the macrocosm and the microcosm. The ritual aspect is the process of dramatizing the focus of what is being expressed so that the whole person (body, emotions and mind) is channeled into bringing about 'the total experience'. This type of ritual working draws on all the five senses, using all the methods of drama and all the techniques of religion – without focusing on any particular religious belief. The magician directs his/her attention on *symbols* that are keys to the subconscious. These symbols or correspondences make it possible to communicate concepts and ideals *beyond* religious philosophy or intellectual understanding since the roots are buried deep within the collective (or universal) unconscious.

It is important to understand, however, that although a magician is not required to follow a specific religion or devotional observance, s/he does believe in a 'Higher Power' on which s/he calls during a ritual – but it is more than likely to be the deity that 'corresponds' with the *natural* energies of the cosmos, not a deity perceived for devotional purposes. This explains why much of what was originally made public concerning magical practice was seen as satanic and/or devil worship, since the magician was just as likely to call on a demon as an archangel.

Much is made of this penchant for working with the demonic – but what exactly are these 'demons' of which we hear so much in connection with magic? If we examine the characteristics of those in Aleister Crowley's *Goetia*, for example, each one represents the exaggerated aspects of the things most people strive for under normal circumstances: knowledge, wealth, ambition or a loving partner. If these desires become distorted to the point of obsession, the thirst for them becomes a corruptive and insatiable desire for magical understanding, fabulous wealth, unlimited power and licentious sex. The 'evil' spirits or demons of *Goetia* are thereby recognized as portions of the human brain; the correspondences are methods of stimulating or regulating these particular areas.

In many cases, the misrepresentation has grown from modern academic interpretations of old *grimoires* and histories taken from the likes of John Dee, Paracelsus, Eliphas Lévi and Crowley, but written by those with no formal magical training, or actual belief in the practice of magic itself. Magic, and especially ritual magic, by its very nature is obtuse – it is also the last great adventure – so what hope do non-initiates have in understanding the cosmic mysteries that the Adept strives to explore?

For example, Professor Elizabeth Butler might have been a Faust scholar but it was scant qualification for her to write on the subject of *Ritual Magic* with any real degree of *understanding*. From the historical perspective, however, she is worthy of note as her introductory observations show: *'That so-called 'black' magic is rarely as black as it has been painted is one of the conclusions to which I have been irresistibly drawn by a close scrutiny of the texts available; but folly is on the whole more prevalent than vice, as the 'black' rituals abundantly prove.'* Nevertheless, this did not prevent her from stating that Crowley *'did his ineffective best to set the myth of Satanism in circulation again in a positive spate of pagan, gnostic, pantheistic, Qabalistic and generally speaking synthetic ritual processes'* to demonstrate that she had learned little about *practical working* magic from her research.

It is generally accepted that magic is an art and can be learned – but it cannot be taught – and unlike science it has the power to experience and fathom things that are inaccessible to human reason according to Paracelsus: *'For magic is a great secret wisdom, just as reason is a great public folly.'*

EXTRACT FROM *THE INTRODUCTION TO MAGIC FROM THE FOURTH YEAR STUDY COURSE : THE TEMPLE OF KHEM*
MÉLUSINE DRACO

male and female (see **Earth**).

Mallard: The traditional 'wild duck' made famous on the many inn signs throughout the country. The male is extremely promiscuous and abandons his 'mate' as soon as she is settled on her eggs; by contrast the female is reputed to be a good mother. The feathers are appropriate for use in sex or relationship magic as appropriate.

Malleus Malificarum: *The Hammer of Witches* has been described as 'a perfect armory of judicial murder'. First printed in 1486, its authors were Dominicans Jakob Sprenger and Heinrich Kramer; it was frequently republished in the 16th and 17th centuries being generally accepted as the most authoritative work on the behavior of witches and demons, and on methods of interrogating, torturing and convicting witches. There is a modern English translation by Montague **Summers**. SOURCE: *The Encyclopedia of Witchcraft & Demonology*, Rossell Hope Robbins; *Malleus Satani: The Hammer of Satan*, Suzanne Ruthven.

Mallow: Native to Britain and Europe, the mallow was known to the Greeks, Romans, and Anglo-Saxons, being listed by **Aelfric**. Both the common and marsh mallow were used medicinally for many of the same ailments. The modern sugary confection known as 'marshmallow', which contains no herbal extracts, originated from a soothing sweet recipe made from the powdered root of the marsh mallow. Ruling planet: **Venus**.

Mam Tor, Derbyshire: An Iron Age hill fort of 16 acres and the largest in the Peak District (see **Shivering Mountain**).

Mana: Originally a Polynesian concept of spiritual power deriving from a long line of ancestors, and present within all things and beings descended from them. The idea of a power or energy underlying all things is a common theme within contemporary paganism, but the reverence for the **Ancestors** is generally confined to the more traditional branches of British witchcraft.

Mandala: A Sanskrit word meaning 'circle'; used in both Hindu and Buddhist rituals to denote a mystical diagram charged with occult significance, and although it is usually circular, other symmetrical shapes are occasionally used. Psychologist Carl Jung recognized in the mystic circle used in Eastern magic and meditative practice an archetypal image from the depths of the mind expressing the soul itself. SOURCE: *Man, Myth & Magic*, ed Richard Cavendish.

Mandrake or **Mandragora:** The best known of all aphrodisiacs of the ancient world was the mandrake (or mandragora), a purple-flowered tuber with roots that often resemble a human body. Known also as 'Circe's Plant', it has been used in the form of a love potion from very early times. **Pliny** the Elder wrote that, *'when a mandrake root in the shape of a male genital organ was found, it secured genital love.'* This plant, which was said to emit a terrifying scream when dragged from the earth, was also used in medicine. Ruling planet: **Mercury**.

Manes: To the Romans they were the deified souls of their ancestors, or *di manes*. In the month of February the festivals of *Parentalis* and *Feralia* were held in their honor. Taken collectively, they were considered as hostile, but euphemistically known as the 'kindly ones'.

Manheim: In Scandinavian mythology this is the abode of man. Vanirheim is the abode of the **Vanir**; **Jotunheim** the abode of giants; Gladsheim the abode of Odin; Helheim the abode of **Hela** (goddess of death). Muspellheim is the abode of elemental fire; Niflheim is hell and Svartalheim is the abode of the dwarves.

Manifestation: The physical appearance of a spirit or discarnate entity.

Man in Black: In Traditional Craft this is an enigmatic figure and always a member of the parent coven. His function is to observe, inform and report on the activities of covens that have hived off from the parent group; he may if he wishes take part or stand apart and to the north, during the ritual. His token of office is the raven's feather and, as far as possible, his identity should remain concealed from those not of the parent coven. SOURCE: *Witchcraft – A Tradition Renewed*, Evan John Jones.

Manitou: The term used by the Native American Algonquin Indians for spirit beings and for supernatural and magical power contained within the whole phenomena of Nature. It was the responsibility of the medicine men, to make contact with the world of the manitous, and the 'secret society' of these shamanic practitioners was believed to have been founded by the manitous. A manitou might also be the guardian spirit of an individual, perhaps taking the form of an animal and revealing itself in a dream or under

unusual circumstances. SOURCE: *Hiawatha,* Henry Wordsworth Longfellow.

Man, Myth & Magic: The definitive encyclopedia on the occult. It was available during the 1970s in weekly parts that built up into a seven-volume collection. Because of its popularity, an abridged version was later published but rare sets of the original are still available – at a price!

Manthras: Referring to 'sacred words' in **Zoroastrianism** and also the term used for all prayers.

Mantic Art: Most mantic arts are known by their Greek or historical root name, ending with *mancy*. It is a system of asking a question silently or aloud and to receive a response in a manner that reveals the hidden answer (see **Divination**).

Mantike: A form of Greek divination, the aim of which was not to predict the future, as to seek advice concerning a future action.

Mantra: The vibration of subtle sound in the form of a word(s) constantly reverberated to transform consciousness. It is a form of words or sounds that have a magical effect when uttered with intent.

Maple: Pollen records trace the maple back to the Neolithic period but despite the tree being around for a very long time, there is little recorded about it in British folklore. Maple wood tables were valuable collector's items in the Roman world, one being sold for its weight in gold.

Mara: The 'evil one' in Buddhist mythology. Literally, the name means 'the killer'.

Marga: A Sanskrit term meaning the

'way' or 'path'.

Margaritomancy: Solving the question of guilt or innocence using pearls.

Marigold: A yellow-flowered plant ruled by the **Sun** and used in fumes and potions to obtain solary influence.

Marjoram: Brought to Britain by the Romans, this herb has many social uses, as well as numerous medicinal and culinary ones. Sweet marjoram was introduced into England during the Middle Ages. Ruling planet: **Mercury** in **Aries**.

Marriage Knot: The custom of binding the hands (or thumbs) of the bride and groom at pagan weddings. The Carthaginians bound the thumbs of the betrothed with a leather thong.

Mars: (1) The Roman god of war, identified with the Greek **Ares**.(2) Astrologically speaking, Mars activates the signs it governs – **Aries** and **Scorpio** – with both signs showing strong, aggressive qualities. (3) The planet has some spectacular features. There is tantalizing evidence on the planet's surface of erosion by flowing waters or lava some time in the past; Olympus Mons, an enormous volcano, which is larger than any mountain on Earth; and the Valles Marineris, a canyon system up to four miles deep, stretching 2,500 miles across the planet. (4) The alchemical symbol for Mars is iron, manifested in the Sword. (5) Represented by (the four fives of the **Minor Arcana**) and the **Tower** in the **Major Arcana** of the **Tarot**, and **Geburah** in the **Qabalah**.

Martial Arts: Oriental martial arts are as much a spiritual discipline as fighting techniques, drawing on the cosmic energy known as **ch'i** or **prana**. In the West the focus is predominantly on the physical at the expense of the spiritual.

Martinmas: The 11th November was the feast of St. Martin and the time in the agricultural calendar when surplus livestock was killed and salted down for the winter, hence the old saying that our slaying time (death) will come as surely as that of a hog at St. Martin's tide. According to the old **Julian** Calendar, Samhain would have also coincided with this festival and some Old Craft covens continue to observe this day instead of 31st October.

Mascotte: One who brings good luck and possesses a 'good eye', as opposed to Jettatore of the **Evil Eye**, who always brings bad luck. *'I tell you he was a Mascotte of the first water,' The Ludgate Monthly*, No 1, vol ii: *Tippitywitchet*, Nov 1891.

Masloth: [Qabalah] The Sphere of the Fixed Stars. A name given to the second cosmic power-zone, **Chokmah**, the realm of the **Magus**.

Masks: As ritual objects, masks are often used as part of elaborate ceremonies where the dancers or performers use them to suggest a link with the world of animal or spirit; a form of channeling by which humans can tap the forces possessed by these beings. SOURCE: *Man, Myth & Magic*, Richard Cavendish.

Masque of Queens, The: A court performance, possibly written to demonstrate the depth of Ben **Jonson's** classical learning and curry favor with **James I** of England.

Mass of St. Secaire: see **Black Mass**.

Master: In occult terms, **Adepts** who have achieved the 'summit of perfection' but who have chosen to remain on earth, usually unknown to the majority of mankind but guiding humanity in wisdom by inspiring gifted individuals. They include the founders of the great religions and are known by a wide variety of titles: Mahatmas, the Great Ones, the Secret Brotherhood, the Great White Lodge, the Watchers, the Light-bearers, Urshu, etc.

Materia Medica: The fifth book by Dioscorides in his series considers some 200 'stones' from a medicinal point of view, and though the majority are oxides and other minerals, a few authentic gems are also included, i.e. *'sapphire' (that is lapis lazuli) against the bites of serpents; of selenite against epilepsy. And of coral for skin troubles, sore eyes and spitting blood.'*

Mathers, Samuel Liddell MacGregor: Together with his wife **Moina** they were the driving force behind the **Golden Dawn**, although their autocratic behavior eventually caused considerable resentment among the members. The Mathers' took themselves off to Paris and founded the Ahathoor Temple and gave semi-public performances of the Rites of Isis. There is some evidence to suggest that Samuel Mathers was verging on the borders of madness. Nevertheless, it was while he was translating occult texts in Paris that he located and translated a medieval grimoire, *The Sacred Magic of **Abra-melin** the Mage,* regarded by some (including Aleister **Crowley**) as one of the most powerful texts in the entire Western magical tradition. Among his other notable translations is *The Kabbalah Unveiled.*

Matres: In the Celtic Tradition, the 'Divine Mothers', often represented in groups of three in Gaul and Britain. They are accompanied by fertility symbols such as horns of plenty, fruits, leaves, loaves or children, and in Gaul by dogs, birds and trees.

Matralia: Mater Matuta, an old Italian goddess of dawn and birth; this was the matron's festival at Rome, held on 11th June.

Mātrōnālia: In the Roman religion, the festival of **Juno** on 1st March, the old New Year's Day. It was a sort of *Saturnalia* for women, when the 'matrons' served food to their slaves and married women received presents from married men – not their husbands.

Matsuri: The names given to **Shinto** ceremonies and festivals, which invoke the presence of the *kami* in order to obtain their approval. Combining early shamanistic practice with agricultural rituals, these marked the seasonal changes, aided fertility and warded off plagues. The harvest festival (*Niiname-sai*) was traditionally the most important, when the male celestial *kami* descended to unite with the female terrestrial *kami*, terminating in the sacred feast.

Mausoleum: One of the **Seven Wonders** of the World and the tomb of Mausolus at Halicarnassus. Parts of this sepulcher are now in the British Museum.

May Day, Rood Mass or **Beltaine:** Celebrates the inauguration of the second half of the pagan year. The central symbols of the festivities was the dance of the **Morris** men, the maypole or the may-tree, the **Hawthorn**, which possessed supernatural powers and symbolized the transition from spring to summer. Under Oliver Cromwell, the traditional maypoles were banned, since to the Puritan mind the sight of 'rustics capering around an upright pole was all too reminiscent of pagan worship'. SOURCE: *Root and Branch* and *A Witch's Treasury of the Countryside*, Mélusine Draco..

Maze: A symbolic spiral operation known as 'walking' or 'running the maze' and probably has its roots in the sacred spirals dating from the Bronze Age. From the Middle Ages, the concentric pathways were used to represent the contemporary view of the universe, with the earth at its center, surrounded by the orbits of the sun, moon and planets. Turf mazes have their roots in British antiquity, one of the most enduring being the Shepherd's Race, a spiral-circular grass maze formerly at Boughton Green in Northamptonshire. It dated from at least 1353 when it was mentioned in a charter given by Edward III, as a feature of a three-day June fair: it was destroyed around 1916. SOURCE: *Goddess of the Stones*, George Terence Meaden.

Mazikeen or **Shedeem:** A species of beings in Jewish mythology resembling the Arabian Jinn, and said to be the agents of magic and enchantment. According to the **Talmud** they are the offspring of Adam and **Lilith**.

Meadowsweet: One of the **Three Sacred Herbs** of the Druids. Used in medieval times as a strewing herb, and for flavoring mead and beer. Ruling planet: **Venus**.

Measure: A traditional Craft cord used to measure the length of the would-be Initiate's body. Blood was smeared on it and it was kept to exercise a 'measure'

of control over the person to whom it belonged.

Medea: In Greek mythology, a witch who fell in love with Jason and used magic to enable him to steal the Golden Fleece; she was the niece of **Circe,** another famous sorceress. There were three classical tragedies of the legend by Euripides, Seneca and Ovid.

Medea's Kettle: Medea cut an old ram into pieces and put them in her magic kettle and it came out a young lamb. The daughters of Pelias thought to restore their father to youth in the same way, but Medea refused to speak the magical words and the old man died. Similar to the **Cauldron** of Rebirth in Celtic myth.

Medicinal Days: According to Hippocrates, these were the 6th, 8th, 10th,12th, 16th, 18th, etc, of a disease, because it was believed that no 'crisis' occurred on those days, and that medicine could be safely administered.

Medicinal Hours: According to Quincy, the proper hours for taking medicine: morning fasting, an hour before dinner, four hours after dinner and bedtime.

Medicinal Leech: (*Hirudo medicinalis*) Used medicinally since ancient times and in certain types of surgery today. At one time they were common in ponds close to old monastery sites and collecting them provided an income for the humble. It is now a rare and protected species.

Medicine Bundle: A sacred Amerindian pouch containing objects representative and evocative of power, such as eagle feathers, shells, animal parts, tobacco or herbs. The pouch was usually received as a talisman as a tangible sign of the supernatural power conferred on him by his guardian spirit. The bundle then served as an individual emblem, symbolizing the relationship between the seeker and his guardian spirit.

Medicine Man: The general designation for a **Shaman**, healer or diviner among the **Amerindians**. Those whose visions indicate a potential career undergo a period of apprenticeship wherein ritual and curing techniques are learned. He is responsible for the community's religious affairs, for communicating with the supernatural, for divination and healing the sick, and for protecting the community against supernatural attack.

Medicine Wheel: A Native American concept of a sacred circle which is the focal point of the ceremonial observances of the tribe.

Medieval Magic: The ideas about magic that flourished in medieval Europe came from a wide variety of sources. Magical beliefs and practices from the classical cultures of the Mediterranean blended with those of the Germanic and Celtic people from northern Europe. Medieval Christians absorbed notions about magic from the migrant Jews and the Arab world. As a result it is often difficult to distinguish precisely where a specific belief first arose. SOURCE: *Conjuring Spirits*, Claire Fanger; *The History of Magic*, Kurt Seligmann; *Magic in the Middle Ages*, Richard Kieckhefer.

Meditation: A method of enhancing the quality of inner peace through a series of mental and physical exercises. The mental transition from the mundane to the spiritual level or plane, it is common to nearly all forms of religious worship. In the East meditation is seen as a means to union with the Absolute, while in the West it is the mystic's path to God; both routes are beset with perils which can only be countered by the use of proven disciplines. SOURCE: *365 Tao: Daily Meditations*, Deng Ming-Dao; *Magic – White & Black*, Franz Hartmann; *Meditation*, David Fontana; *Principles of Meditation*, Christina Feldman; *Teach Yourself to Meditate*, Eric Harrison.

Meditrinalia: Celebrated when a libation of a new wine was made in the honor of Meditrina, Roman goddess of healing. A day (11th October) for special religious observance.

Medium: The name given to a person whom is believed to act as a medium of communication between the living and the dead. Although the term used in this context is relatively recent, there is evidence of the phenomena in the **Sibyls** of ancient Greece. SOURCE: *Man, Myth & Magic*, Richard Cavendish.

Medmenham Abbey: The ruins of a 12th century Cistercian abbey, made notorious by Sir Francis Dashwood as a meeting place for his **Hell-Fire Club** in 1745.

Meet or **Moot:** The traditional name for an informal gathering of witches.

Megalasia: The six-day (4–10th April) festival to celebrate the arrival from Phrygia of the sacred stone of the goddess **Cybele**, or Mater Magna.

Megaliths: see **Stone Circles**.

Meigle Museum, Perthshire: A small museum containing a fine collection of 25 Pictish symbol stones, showing a wide range of different types.

Meini Gwyr, Carmarthenshire: The Preseli mountains run parallel to the coast and on the fringe of its southern slopes are many isolated monuments. Among them this circle is unique in design because the stones are not set directly into the ground, but in a raised ring made especially for them.

Melancholy: [Greek, *melas cholē*] A lowness of spirits, supposed at one time to arise from a redundance of black bile.

Mell Supper: Harvest supper from the French *meler* (to mix together), where the master and the servants sat together at the harvest board.

Memento Mori: Something to put us in mind of the shortness and uncertainty of life.

Menat: A piece of ancient Egyptian ritual jewelry worn as a necklace. It was associated with Hathor, and with the rites of birth, rebirth and every critical rite of passage.

Mendes, the Goat of: Herodotus noted the sacrifice of goats at Mendes, in contrast to the use of sheep elsewhere in Egypt. It is believed that he mistook the sacred ram for a goat and, as a result, the 'goat' has passed into occult history and is often identified with **Baphomet**.

Menorah: The seven-branched golden candlestick said to have stood six feet high, which Antiochus removed from the Temple in Jerusalem and destroyed. The seven branches are said to represent the seven planets, with the Qabalistic implication that the Jewish God claimed the powers of the planetary gods of Mesopotamia.

Menstruation: Beliefs in the harmful potency of a menstruating woman are common is one form or another all over the world. Menstrual blood will dull the edge of a knife, make plants barren, and turn new wine sour. It can also cause impotency when given in a potion. In occult terms, menstruation can often be used to enhance a magical working, especially when calling upon positive female energy.

Mephistopheles: The name of the demon to whom **Faust** sold his soul; he is next in rank to **Satan** and appears in the literature of **Necromancy** and magic in the late Middle Ages.

Mercia: The eighth and last kingdom of the Heptarchy between the Thames and the Humber. It was the *merc* or boundary of the Anglo-Saxons and the free Britons of Wales.

Mercury: (1) Mercury was a Roman deity – the god of commerce, who is commonly identified with the Greek god **Hermes**, the messenger of the gods, and **Tahuti** (**Thoth**), the Egyptian god of magic and wisdom. (2) In astrological terms Mercury is the governing influence over the signs of **Gemini** and **Virgo**. (3) Even though Mercury is the planet that orbits closest to the Sun, it has one of the coldest nights in the Solar System. (4) It is the only metal that is liquid at or near room temperature and of prime importance in traditional alchemy. (5) Mercury is identified with the sphere of **Hod** on the magical **Qabalah**, and with the **Magus** of the **Major Arcana** (and the four eights of the **Minor Arcana**) of the **Tarot**.

Meridians: In Chinese medicine the channels through which vital energy (*qi*) is believed to flow through the body.

Merlin: The guide and mentor of **Arthurian** legend, who first takes shape in the works of Geoffrey of

Monmouth, who published some alleged prophesies around 1135, which he afterwards inserted in his *History of the Kings of Britain*. In Geoffrey's *History*, Merlin makes his entry as a boy in Carmarthen and later uses magic to help transport the stones of Wales to Salisbury Plain (see **Black Book of Carmarthen**). Professor R.J.C. Atkinson has shown that behind the mythical marvels Geoffrey may well have tapped into an authentic, oral tradition about Stonehenge and the transporting of the 'blue stones' from the west. *'If so, Merlin is in some degree a projection of a Britain older than Christianity – older, indeed, than the Celtic population that produced Arthur and the mythology surrounding him.'*

Merfolk: The merfolk were supposed to live in an underwater world of great splendor, to which they lured their victims. This theme occurs again and again in the lore of the sea, with a constant emphasis on the presence of a mermaid as foreshadowing some calamity – a storm, shipwreck or drowning. SOURCE: *Folklore, Myths & Legends of Britain*, Reader's Digest.

Mermaid's Purse: The egg-case of a dogfish or skate that can be used for spell-working on the beach. SOURCE: *Sea Change: Practical Magic for the Sea Witch*, Mélusine Draco.

"Merry Meet": The shortened form of *'Merry meet, and merry part, and merry meet again,'* which is the traditional witches' greeting.

Meru: A fabulous mountain in the center of the world; the home of **Vishnu** and a perfect paradise. It may be termed as the Indian Olympus.

Mesmer, Friedrich Anton: (1733–1815) German scholar, astrologer, healer and doctor best known for his development of therapeutic hypnosis and magnetism.

Mesoamerican Religions: Includes those civilizations that developed in central America between 2300BC and 1521AD, such as the Toltec, Maya, Huastec, Mixtec and Aztec, who shared many similarities in cultural and religious features.

Meso-paganism: A people that has been influenced by a conquering culture but has in turn had an influence on that incoming culture. It usually succeeds in maintaining a separate culture and a separate religious practice. Many Native American nations have succeeded in doing this.

Mesopotamia: The Sumerians and their successors in Mesopotamia developed a complex pantheon of deities, together with an equally complex system of demonology and magic that had its roots in prehistory.

Metals: Seven metals are traditionally linked with the seven planets known in antiquity, and these were thought to develop in the earth under the influence of its planet. Gold – **Apollo** or the **Sun**; Silver – **Diana** or the **Moon**; Quicksilver = **Mercury**; Copper – **Venus**; Iron – **Mars**; Tin – **Jupiter**; Lead – **Saturn**. Alchemy was the art of perfecting metal and indicates why those with metalworking skills (such as **Blacksmiths**) were thought to have powerful magical skills.

Metamorphosis: see **Shape-shifting**.

Metaphysics: The study of that which is acceptable as real without visible evidence of its existence; or the study of cosmic consciousness.

Metaphysics, Laws of: The principles of psychic and mystical sciences that are known to occur time and again. The following are the main headings:
• The Law of Free Will – everyone has the freedom of choice.
• The Law of Good – there is only good in the universe.
• The Law of Infinite Universe – each person sees the universe in a different way.
• The Law of Karma – to be responsible for all personal actions.
• The Law of Omnipresence – the universe is within every particle of the universe.
• The Law of Personal Return – everything in the universe is cyclic.
• The Law of Readiness – everything will happen in its time.
• The Law of Uncertainty – the universe exists in all possible states at the same instant of time.

Metempsychosis: The transmigration or passage of a human or animal soul into a new body after death. The new body may be of the same species although in some cultures the belief developed that souls pass from one form of life to a higher or lower one as a result of their conduct in their previous life. In many parts of the world, the human soul may be reborn into the same kin-group.

Meteors: The words meteor and meteorite both come from the Greek *meteora* (literally 'things up in the air'), a term used by Aristotle. A meteor is an object seen as a shooting star that is burned up as it falls; a meteorite is one that survives its plunge and actually hits the earth.

Meteorites: Have provided the meteoric iron used to make ancient sacred objects and have always been interpreted as portents of disaster. Any amulet made from the stone or metal that has fallen to Earth will protect from witchcraft, storms, disease and accident.

Metonic Cycle: A cycle of 19 years, at the end of which period the new moon falls on the same days of the year, and eclipses recur. Discovered by Meton in 432BC.

Metopomancy: In 1658, Jerome Cardan published *Metoposcopia*, a guide to reading and divining the future by observing the lines on a person's forehead.

Mezuzah: A Jewish talisman made from a small scroll of parchment inserted inside a metal or wooden case and hung on the doorpost of the house. The pious touch their fingers to it and then to their lips when entering or leaving the house. A small silver amulet or pendant representing the sacred image of any faith can be utilized in much the same way.

Microcosm: see **Macrocosm**.

Middle Pillar Exercise: One of the most famous of ritual magical exercises that is now used in witchcraft.

Midewiwin: Literally meaning 'mystic doings' from an occult-medicine society primarily found among the Ojibwa and Chippewa Indians.

Midsummer Eve: Falls on or around 21st June, and marks the **Summer Solstice**, although the Christian calendar had moved it back three days to coincide with the Feast of St. John on the 24th June.

Midwinter Festival: The traditional name for the revels that take place around the **Winter Solstice** on 21st December (see **Christmas**).

Mighty Ones, The: A term used to mean the **Watchers**; the ancestral dead; the elemental guardians of the Circle; or the Hidden Company.

Miko: Female shaman in **Shinto**, formally called *kamiko* and *ichiko*; these are young women who are dedicated to the service of the **Kami** and carry out duties at the Shinto shrines.

Mikveh: A pool of natural water for ritual purification in Judaism.

Milarepa, Jetsun: (1052–1135) Considered to be one of the leading Tibetan mystics of all time and a national hero.

Milking Charm: It was believed that a cow would low in a peculiar manner if it were being milked invisibly by magic. One way to prevent this was to bind a twig of rowan with red thread and place it across the threshold of the barn.

Milky Way: Viewed by the ancients as a river of souls, the Milky Way is actually a glowing maelstrom of some 200 billion suns and about 150,000 light years across. Our **Sun** is no more than a minute speck in one of the **Galaxy's** spiral arms.

Mill, The: Part of a magical operation where 'Treading the Mill' raises the power for magical purposes with the **Circle**. SOURCE: *Witchcraft – A Tradition Renewed*, Evan John Jones.

Milton, John: (1608–1674) It was Milton who gave a surprising new dimension to his literary **Lucifer**, depicted in *Paradise Lost* and written after the Restoration. This fictitious archfiend is so magnificently proud, so full of courage, eloquence and arrogant defiance that the loyal angels of heaven pale into insignificance beside the flamboyant anti-hero. SOURCE: *Malleus Satani*, Suzanne Ruthven.

Mimer: The Scandinavian god of wisdom, who presided over a well at the root of the sacred **Ash** tree, in which all wisdom lay concealed.

Mimetic Masked Dance: The figures of the masked dancers in animal disguises suggesting the hunter impersonating the 'spirit' of the particular animal embodied in the costume/mask.

Min: An indigenous Egyptian deity of great antiquity, whose totem, a thunderbolt, appeared at the top of prehistoric standards. He was worshipped at Coptos as the god of roads and protector of travelers in the desert. His image is invariably shown with an enormous erect phallus, and as the harvest god, the first sheaf to be cut was offered in his name.

Mind, Body & Spirit or **MB&S:** A modern generic term for all things 'pagan', particularly within mainstream publishing, that avoids using the word '**Occult**'.

Ming Shu: Chinese astrology based on the Four Pillars of Fate, the Five Elements and the Twelve Branches.

Minerva: Roman goddess of craftsmen and teachers, who was equated with the Greek goddess **Athena**. She was also goddess of war.

Minervalia: A five-day celebration starting on 21st March as this was regarded as the goddess **Minerva's** birthday, and came to be thought of as a festival in her honor.

Minotaur: Comes from classical mythology and was part-man and part-bull. It is the prototype of such creatures that live deep in the subconscious of the cultures that followed the Bull, exalted it and sacrificed it. In Mesopotamia, for example, the creature with a bull's head on the body of a man is a benevolent figure. SOURCE: *The Power of the Bull*, Michael Rice.

Mint: The many different varieties of mint have been used since ancient times. Listed by **Aelfric**, mint was grown in monastic gardens from at least the 9th century. Water mint was one of the three most sacred herbs of the **Druids**, the others being meadowsweet and vervain. Ruling planet: **Venus**.

Miolnier or **Mjolnir:** [pron *youl-ner* = The crusher] The magic hammer of Thor.

Mirror Magic: An application that can trace its origins to the old **Grimoires** and texts on angel magic where the use of such a mirror or 'shew stone' is recommended. The powerful influence of mirror magic is referred to in the story of Vulcan's mirror that revealed the past, present and future; the magic mirror of Merlin, which gave warning of treason; the mirror of Cambuscan in Chaucer's *Canterbury Tales*, which told of misfortunes to come; or Lao's mirror in Goldsmith's *Citizen of the World* which reflected thought itself; while in the *Arabian Nights* there is the all-seeing mirror of Al-Asnam. Mirror magic of one kind or another has been practiced down the ages and in Britain has continued to the present day.

Mirror of Hathor: Mirrors had both a functional and symbolic use for the Egyptians. They consisted of a flat disc, usually of polished bronze or copper, attached to a handle. Hathor was a common image used for the handle, and in the modern Egyptian Tradition this type of mirror is used for **Skrying** (see **Mirror Magic**).

Misericords: Carvings beneath seats in medieval churches and cathedrals depicting country life of the times. They include remarkable everyday scenes that were popular in books of the period, where they were often used to illustrate calendars.

Mistletoe: *The Golden Bough*, which is the title of Sir James Frazer's classic work on magic and religion, is also a name for the mistletoe. The most magical mistletoe grows on oaks and if cut for magical purposes a knife or sickle of sacred gold had to be used. According to **Pliny**, the **Druids** did this, taking great care that it should not touch the ground. In addition to its own medicinal properties, mistletoe was reputed to possess those of the host plant. Ruling planet: Sun. SOURCE: *Root & Branch*, Mélusine Draco..

Mithraism: Practiced in the remotest provinces of the Roman Empire for more than three centuries. This colorful religion of Mithra, the 'Unconquered Sun', originated in Persia and enjoyed such an immense popularity in the valleys of the Danube and Rhine, and in Britain (where alone there are five temples), that for a time Europe almost became Mithraic. The **Mysteries** appealed to both the Roman soldiers and officials, but exactly how an ancient Persian god found his way to Rome, to be adopted by high-ranking army officers, is still not fully known. SOURCE: *Julian*, Gore Vidal; *Man, Myth & Magic*, Richard Cavendish: *A Mithraic Ritual*, G.R.S. Mead; *The Mysteries of Mithra*, Franz Cumont; *The Mysteries of Mithra*, G.R.S. Mead; *The Path of Enlightenment in the Mithraic Mysteries*, Julius Evola; *Penguin Dictionary of*

Religions, John R. Hinnells.

Möbius Strip: The one-sided surface formed by joining together the two ends of a long rectangular strip, one end being twisted through 180 degrees before the join is made.

Mola Salsa: In Roman religious practice, a cake or meal, made by the **Vestal Virgins** for sacrificial purposes. It was gathered, roasted and ground before being mixed with salt.

Mole: Various parts of a mole can be used for ingredients in magical spells.

Moly: In Greek mythology, a magical herb given by **Hermes** to Odysseus to protect him against the enchantments of **Circe**. It is described as having a black root, a flower like milk, and being hard to uproot; it has not been convincingly identified with any real herb, though mandrake, garlic and rue have been suggested. *Brewer's Dictionary of Phrase & Fable* suggests it was wild, or sorcerer's garlic. SOURCE: *Odyssey*, Homer.

Molybdomancy: Divination by interpreting the hisses and patterns made by dropping molten lead into water. According to *Discoverie of Witchcraft* published in 1584, the practice was in use at that time for discovering whether someone was bewitched.

Moneywort: A native of Britain, the plant grows in moist meadows, along riverbanks, and in damp woodland clearings and hedgerows. It was highly valued by old herbalists as a wound-herb. Ruling planet: **Venus**.

Monk's Hood: see **Aconite**.

Monotheism: The doctrine that there is only one god.

Montelban, Madeline: (1912–1982) Described during her life time as 'one of the best ceremonial magicians in London'. She taught her students that, first and foremost, magic was a science or art, based on natural laws and principles – and that they should '*Accept nothing. Question everything.*' Unfortunately, she did not write any books on the magical arts although she was highly respected by those who belonged to her Order of the Morning Star, founded in 1956.

Montu: Apart from **Neith**, who was identified as a hunter/warrior goddess, the only other war god of the Egyptians was Montu. The first record of him is from Thebes around 2000BC, being depicted as a falcon-headed man, crowned with a solar disc. He eventually became fused with the sun god as Montu-Re.

Moon: (1) The Moon is usually identified with a goddess (usually **Diana** or **Artemis**) although the ancient Egyptians attributed its power to the male deity, **Thoth** (**Tahuti**), the god of magic. (2) In astrological terms, the Moon governs the more subtle side of human nature. (3) The Moon is our nearest neighbor, and as it orbits the Earth its appearance to us changes from new to full and back; the gravitational pull causing the tides. (4) The term given by alchemists to silver was Luna (Moon). (5) Associated with **Yesod** in the **Qabalah**, and the eighteenth card in the **Major Arcana** of the **Tarot** being the archetypal symbol of **Illusion**; often representing the standing on the brink of change. (6) There are widely held rural superstitions governing the phases of the Moon and crop planting.

Moonraker: (1) A Wiltshire tale of how

smugglers, surprised by the Excisemen, explained that they were trying to rake the reflection of the moon out of a pond. Mocking the idiocy of the locals, the patrol rode away and the smugglers fished their ill-gotten gains out of the pond. (2) There was a Moonraker coven in Warwickshire in the 1960s close to **Long Compton**.

Moots: (1) Debates that formerly took place in the halls and libraries of Inns of Court. (2) Now used as a description for an informal gathering of pagans, i.e. pub moots.

Mora Witches: Possibly one of the most amazing accusations of witchcraft came from Sweden in 1669, which resulted in the burning of 85 people accused of bewitching 300 children into flying to a sabbat. The original documents of the trial were printed by Balthasar Bekker in his *World Bewitched*, and translated from High Dutch into English by Dr. Anthony Horneck (1641-97), as an appendix to Glanvill's *Saducismus Triumphatus*.

Morgan le Fay: In Arthurian legend, she is the sister of **Arthur** but her earliest persona is quite different. (1) She is first heard of as the daughter of Avallach, king of the enchanted island of Avalon, which gives her an otherworldly setting, derived from pagan mythology. (2) As a literary character she seems to have been linked to Arthurian legend during the 12th century as a 'good fairy' but as Arthurian became a 'good and Christian knight', so Morgan's detractors see her fairy origins as evil. (3) The name given to the principal character in two of Dion Fortune's novels, *The Sea Priestess* and *Moon Magic*.

Morrigan: In Irish mythology, one of the three war goddesses, the other two being Neman and Macha. The Morrigan was the Mighty Queen with a triple aspect. Robert **Graves** gave the three aspects of the Morrigan as Ana, Babd and Macha.

Morris men or **Morris dancers:** Known for centuries as the 'luck-bringers, life-dispensers and medicine men' of pre-Christian England. The dance is a ritual, performed traditionally by young men (and now women) at seasonal festivals, which has survived despite discouragement by the Church. Much of the faith in the magical powers of the ritual folk dances has weakened, so that it may now be regarded as rural entertainment rather than healing or propitiatory rites. Its origins are obscure but it was regarded as an ancient tradition in the reign of **Elizabeth I**.

Morte d'Arthur: Compiled by Sir Thomas Malory from the French originals of the **Arthurian** romances.

Mortuary Mass: A sacrilegious mass celebrated to bring about the death of a living person and performed by a disenfranchised priest (see **Black Mass**).

Moses Rod: A divining rod for the discovery of water or mineral treasure.

Moth: Most moths are nocturnal and, as a result, rarely display the brilliance of their markings. Usually night-loving creatures shy away from light, yet the expression of 'moths to a flame' has become a euphemism for irresistible attraction.

Mother-Goddess: A being in whom opposites combine: human love and child-rearing is one of her areas of influence, but so is the urge that leads men into war; the giver of life, she is also the deity who takes it away. SOURCE: *The Cult of the Mother Goddess*, E.O. James.

Mother Goose: A name associated with nursery rhymes. Mrs. Goose used to sing the rhymes to her grandson, and Thomas Fleet (her son-in-law) printed the first edition in 1719. A valuable collection of traditional rhymes relating to witchcraft and its connecting folklore. SOURCE: *Earth, Air, Fire, Water*, Robin Skelton and Margaret Blackwood.

Mother Redcap: An English generic name commonly given to brothel keepers, wise women and witches.

Mother Shipton: A 15th century witch, Ursula Southeil, whose predictions were published in 1667 under the title of the *Strange and Wonderful History of Mother Shipton*.

Mound, The: As the waters of **Nun** receded, the hill that emerged was an important concept in Egyptian religious thought and imagery. The emergence of the Mound was symbolized every year by the **Inundation**. As the Nile waters receded, leaving rich, fertile soil in its wake, so the Mound was held to have risen out of the primeval waters to provide a birthplace for the gods. Although there were several different creation myths the overall 'original hill' legend continued to influence the design and layout in temples and tombs.

Mountain: Seen as a source of inspiration and strength, mountains have been the dwelling places of the gods in various cultures from around the world.

Mu: A legendary lost continent beneath the Pacific Ocean, sometimes identified with **Lemuria**.

Mudra: [Sanskrit] A mystic attitude or gesture that usually accompanies the vibration of a **Mantra**.

Mugwort: A plant with leaves that turn towards the north which is frequently used as an ingredient in various magical preparations. Pick it before sunrise saying: *'Tollam te artemsia, ne lassus sim in via.'* One of the **Nine Sacred Herbs** of the Anglo-Saxons. Ruling planet: **Venus**.

Mulberry: Introduced into Britain by the Romans and listed by **Aelfric**. It had more culinary uses than medicinal although **Culpeper** claimed it was an antidote for 'those that have taken aconite.' Ruling planet: **Mercury**.

Mule: Because a mule is sterile, its hair and/or ear wax was believed to be a contraceptive. To break or hinder love charms, make a potion from the dust in which a mule has lain.

Mullein: A weed with coarse leaves and yellow flowers that is worn as protection against witchcraft and sorcery. Hang it above the door to keep away ill-wishing, demons and nightmares. It has certain medicinal properties but the country name of 'hag's taper' refers to the plant's use in the rites, potions and spells of witches. Ruling planet: **Saturn**.

Mummers: Actors in folk plays, especially the **Midwinter** and **Yule** mumming plays, which preserve pagan fertility themes and symbolism in the actions and dances. Intricate dance steps, each of which had some symbolic meaning, played a large part in mumming; mumming plays, whose origins are believed to be rooted in the oldest of pagan ceremonies, were a traditional part of the medieval court (see **Morris men**).

Mummification: The preservation of dead bodies – sometimes as part of the funerary rites or preserved by the dry sand or peat bogs of the indigenous landscape.

Murray, Margaret: A distinguished Egyptologist with an interest in the anthropological side of archeology when she began her study of witchcraft. She was President of the **Folklore Society** between 1953–5, and died in 1963 a few months after her 100th birthday. Her findings were published in *The Witch-Cult in Western Europe, The God of the Witches, The Divine King in England.* SOURCE: *Malleus Satani: The Hammer of Satan,* Suzanne Ruthven; *Witchcraft Today,* Gerald B. Gardner.

Murrell, James: The last and most famous 'witch-doctor' in Essex, he was born the **Seventh Son of a Seventh Son**, and known as 'Cunning Murrell'. His equipment included a magic mirror for discovering lost or stolen property, a telescope for looking through walls, and a copper charm that could distinguish between honest and dishonest folk. He had the power to banish spirits and counter-spells, often by the use of one of his iron **Witch Bottles**, containing blood, urine, nails and hair of the afflicted person. The day before his died on 16th December 1860, he predicted the time of his death to the minute. He was buried in an unmarked grave in Hadleigh churchyard.

Muses: In the earliest Greek traditions the Muses were goddesses who inspired poetry and song; gradually they came to be thought of as presiding over the arts and sciences in general. Originally three in number, they later increased to nine: Calliope (epic poetry); Clio (history); Erato (erotic poetry and mime); Euterpe (lyric poetry); Melpomene (the singer); Polyhymnia (hymn); Terpsichore (choral dance and song); Thalia (comedy and idyllic poetry); Urania (astronomy).

Museum of Witchcraft: The Museum houses the world's largest collection of artifacts relating to folklore, witchcraft, Wicca and ritual magic and is based in Boscastle, Cornwall. Cecil **Williamson** moved from the Isle of Man having sold the original building to Gerald **Gardner** in 1952 and brought the exhibits back to England, opening another museum in Windsor but the local residents objected and he was forced to move again. This time to Bourton-on-the-Water, but local pressure forced him out and he relocated to Cornwall, finally settling on the present site in Boscastle. In 1996, he retired and sold the museum and most of its contents to Graham King – the deal was completed at midnight Samhain 1996. The collection continues to grow as many witches bequeath their working tools and books to the museum in their wills, in order to ensure that their possessions do not fall into the wrong hands. SOURCE: *The Encyclopedia of Witches & Witchcraft,* Rosemary Ellen Guiley.

Mushroom: More appropriately called 'fungi' and people throughout history have been dying from poisoning (accidentally or otherwise) after eating them. Different varieties of mushroom had medicinal properties according to **Culpeper** and **Gerard**. Ruling planet: **Mercury** in **Aries**. SOURCE: *Mushrooms and Toadstools of Britain and*

Europe, Edmund Garnweidner.

Music: *'At its best music can heighten holy word and ritual action alike; and can point beyond itself.'* The drumbeats of primitive societies and the chanting of Gregorian plainsong are aspects of music's essential role in religious rituals, and there are few religions in which music has played no part at all. SOURCE: *The Ancient Egyptians*, J. Gardner Wilkinson; *The Oxford Companion to Classical Literature*, ed Sir Paul Harvey.

Music of the Spheres: A concept developed by **Pythagoras** relating planetary orbits to the mathematical relationship between the tones of the musical scale.

Musk: A strong-scented secretion of the male musk deer that is used in magical perfumes and is a powerful ingredient in love potions.

Mustard: Listed by **Aelfric**, and in medieval times one of the main centers of mustard production was in the Vale of Gloucester. Shakespeare mentions 'Tewkesbury mustard' in *Henry IV, Part II*. With its long list of medical uses, **Culpeper** wrote: *'Whenever a strong, stimulating medicine is wanted to act upon the nerves, and not excite heat, there is none preferable to mustard seed.'* Ruling planet: **Mars**.

Mut: Although identified as the consort of Amun-Re, this is an ill-defined deity, whose name signified 'Mother'. She is usually represented as a woman wearing a headdress in the form of a vulture – the hieroglyphic for her name. With Amun, and the boy moon god Khonsu, she featured as the female aspect of the Theban sacred **Triad**.

Myddfai, The Physicians of: A remarkable group of herbal doctors, believed to belong to the same family, and who passed healing knowledge down from generation to generation for many hundreds of years. Although some of their secrets were written down in the 12th or 13th centuries, the manuscripts were not translated from Welsh into English until the mid-19th century.

Myomancy: Divination by observing the behavior of rats or mice.

Myrrh: A gum resin originating in Somalia and southern Arabia. The earliest samples of myrrh that can be assigned a date appear to stem from the Egyptian New Kingdom. Used in fumes to contact the **Mighty Dead**.

Myrtle: The best myrtle grew in Egypt according to Pliny, where it never grew wild but was cultivated in gardens. Myrtle leaves from wreaths or garlands have been found in excavations of Graeco-Roman date and a plant identified as myrtle occurs in Egyptian medical texts. Ruled by the planet **Venus**.

Mystère Lycanthropique: A term used to denote magical transformations resulting from the assumption of god-forms as practiced by the **Golden Dawn,** and the formula of Atavistic Resurgence used in **Zos Kia Cultus**. SOURCE: *Cults of the Shadows*, Kenneth Grant.

Mysteries or **Mysteria:** A modern adaptation of the classic Mystery Schools of **Elesuis**, **Mithra**, **Cybel**, etc. A mystical initiation, mirroring the experiences of death, descent into the Underworld and rebirth. Examples abound in the ancient Mediterranean world of religious societies, outside the 'civic' or official religion, which imparted their secrets only to Initiates. SOURCE: *The Book of the Hopi* (Amerindian), Frank Waters; *Celebrating the Male Mysteries*, R.J. Stewart; *The Mysteries of Mithra*, Franz Cumont; *The Oriental Religions in Roman Paganism*, Franz Cumont; *The Oxford Companion to Classical Literature*, ed by Sir Paul Harvey; *Penguin Dictionary of Religion*, ed John R. Hinnells; *The Sacred* (Amerindian), Peggy V. Beck, Anna Lee Walters and Nia Francisco.

Mystery-Cult: Devotion, often to a single god or goddess, in which secret rituals and doctrines have a place. Examples abound in the ancient world, of religious societies outside the official religion, where their secrets were only imparted to initiates [Greek *mustae*]. SOURCE: *The Penguin Dictionary of Religions*, ed John R. Hinnells.

Mysticism: An umbrella term for practices, experiences and writings in which direct awareness of and/or union with 'god' or ultimate reality is the main focus. The modern, eclectic view that mysticism and the mystical experience are essentially the same in all traditions is mistaken; on the contrary, there are important differences between, and within, the Eastern and Western traditions. SOURCE: *The Complete Guide to World Mysticism*, Timothy Freke and Peter Gandy; *Man, Myth & Magic*, Richard Cavendish; *The Elements of Mysticism*, R.A. Gilbert; *Mysticism in the World's Religions*, Geoffrey Parrinder; *Mysticism in World Religions*, S. Spencer; *The Oxford Companion to Classical Literature*, ed by Sir Paul Harvey.

Myth: A narrative, usually traditional, in which events are described as deeds of the gods, heroes, or other super-human beings; events in the realm of pre-history.

Mythology: The science that examines myths or legends of cosmogony and of gods and heroes; it is also the term for the legends themselves. These ancient myths contain two elements: the rational and what to modern minds seems irrational. The rational myths are those that represent the gods as good and wise, but the real difficulty of mythology springs from the irrational elements, which to modern thinking appears brutal, senseless or repellent. SOURCE: *The Complete Dictionary of European Gods & Goddesses*, Janet and Stewart Farrar, with Gavin Bone; *Dictionary of Gods & Goddesses, Devils & Demons*, Manfred Lurker; *Egyptian Mythology*, Paul Hamlyn; *Ancient Egyptian Myths & Legends*, Lewis Spence; *Encyclopaedia Britannica*; *The Golden Bough*, Sir James Frazer; *The Masks of God* (5 vols), Joseph Campbell; *The Oxford Companion to Classical Literature*, ed by Sir Paul Harvey.

Mythos (peri Theon): Myths concerning the individual gods in Greek religion.

"From time immemorial the seasonal sequence has arrested the attention of mankind and aroused an intense emotional reaction in all states and stages of culture and types of society ..."
E O James
[*Seasonal Feasts & Festivals*]

N

Nadi: [Sanskrit] Nerve center related to sound or vibration. The Nadis are the ramifying network of nerve centers in the human psychosomatic organism. The reception of transmissions from 'outside' depends on the Nadis being maintained in a state of hypersensitivity and clarity. This has not necessarily to do with any state of physical health.

Nadir: An Arabic word, signifying that point in the heavens that is directly opposite to the **Zenith**. Also used for a representation of the planetary system. *'We then lost* (c1091) *a most beautiful table, fabricated of different metals... Saturn was of copper, Jupiter of gold, Mars of iron, the Sun of latten* [sic], *Mercury of amber, Venus of tin, and the Moon of silver... It was the most celebrated nadir in all England,"* Ingulphus.

Naga: [Sanskrit] A serpent, usually depicted as a cobra and symbolically linked to the **Ophidian** Tradition.

Nail: Using nails from an old coffin, or horseshoe nails, to cast a spell is common in Old Craft workings. It may have its roots in the Roman custom of driving a nail into the wall of the temple of **Jupiter** on 13th September each year to ward off calamity from the city, or driving nails into the cottage walls to ward off plague.

Names or **Words of Power**: European magic frequently makes use of 'words of power', which are the names of gods and spirits; the power of a supernatural being is tapped by the use of the name as automatically as turning on an electric light. It is not enough, however, merely to say a Name of Power; it must be correctly resonated. In occult-lore, an individual's magical name must be kept secret to prevent it being used against them. In Egyptian mythology, Isis took the power of the sun god by discovering his real name; and in European fairy lore the belief is if the name of the fairy is revealed, then their power is at an end. SOURCE: *The Magical Arts*, Richard Cavendish; *The Hollow Tree*, Mélusine Draco.

Nantwich, Cheshire: An ancient town famous for its brine springs. The origins of the settlement date to Roman times when salt from Nantwich was used by the Roman garrisons at Chester (Deva Victrix) and Stoke-on-Trent as both a preservative and a condiment. Rock salt was laid down in this region some 220 million years ago, during the Triassic geological era when seawater moved inland from an open sea, creating a chain of shallow salt marshes across what is today the Cheshire basin. As the marshes evaporated, deep deposits of rock salt were formed. *Wich* and *wych* are names used to denote brine springs or wells.

Napoleon's Book of Fate: One of the most popular of the oracle-style fortune-telling books – *The Book of Fate, formerly in the Possession of Napoleon, the Late Emperor of France*, was published in London in 1822. The romance surrounding it claims that the book was found in a mummy's tomb during the Egyptian campaign, and used extensively by the Emperor in planning his military and political career... and lost after his defeat at the Battle of Leipzig, with only one copy surviving! SOURCE: *Napoleon's Book of Fate: Its Origins and Uses*, Richard Deacon.

Natal Horoscope: A chart showing the placement of the planets at the time of a birth for prediction purposes.

Natal Stone: Although lists of gemstone amulets goes back a long way in history, it was only at a comparatively late date that there is any evidence for wearing such stones as natal stones. The custom appears to have originated in Poland in the late 18th century. Even so, there is no definitive listing and the sources can vary considerably between cultures and sources (see **Birthstone**).

Native Americans: see **Amerindian Religions.**

Narwhal: Drinking cups made of the bone of the narwhal were greatly prized because of the belief that they counteracted the fatal effects of poison.

Natural History: There is growing realization that terrestrial life is controlled by astral phenomena, and that 'biological clocks' are built into the nature cycles of life on the Earth. SOURCE: *The Cosmic Clocks*, Michel Gauquelin; *Supernature*, Lyall Watson.

Natural History Museum, London: These lofty halls provide nearly four acres of gallery space and include the products of early man from the Stone Age onwards.

Natural Theology: The understanding of the nature and existence of God, and the duty, freedom and immortality of mankind.

Natural Tides: The natural energies that influence daily happenings on the Earth; the energies harnessed in order to perform magical working. [SEE PANEL]

Nature: The power that creates and regulates the world, often personified in the guise of Mother Nature (see **Gaia**).

Nature Sprites: Include sylphs, gnomes, undines and salamanders. These are not usually evil, although they can sometimes prove troublesome to mankind.

Naturopathy: The healing power of nature – a holistic system of medicine that emphasizes the need to assist the body in resisting disease rather than attacking the disease itself.

Nazi Occultism: Speculation about the subject has become part of popular culture since 1959 when the first examples of this literary genre appeared in the occult milieu in France and England. The recurring element is the allegation that the Nazis were directed by occult agencies of some sort (see **Neo-Paganism**).

Near Death Experience: The experience of those who have died briefly and then revived, or come close to death through accident or illness. The common denominators taken from many different cultures are remarkably similar.

Nebo: The Babylonian god of science and literature, said to have invented cuneiform writing. His temple was at Borsippa, but his worship was carried out wherever Babylonian letters were written or carved.

Nectar: In Greek mythology this sweet liquid was the drink of the gods and, along with ambrosia (food), kept them immortal.

Necromancy: A form of divination by means of summoning the spirits of the dead to interpret omens and predict the future. In classical Greece literature, Homer tells us that Odysseus made sacrifice at a *necromanteion* to obtain information relating to his journey. The most famous instance is the **Witch of Endor** calling up Samuel. SOURCE: *The Book of Black Magic & of Pacts*, A.E. Waite; *Dictionary of Demons*, Fred Gettings; *The Magical Arts*, Richard Cavendish; *Magic In The Middle Ages*, Richard Kieckhefer.

Necronomican, The: The **Grimoire**, *Al Azif*, supposedly composed in 730AD at Damascus and translated into Greek as the *Necronomican* (*The Book of Dead Names*) in 950AD. The original was alleged to have been burned in 1050 but various secret copies were rescued and further translations found their way into publication in Germany (c1440) and Italy (c1500). There is a stronger belief that the book can be attributed to Howard Phillips **Lovecraft**, an American author who created it, although many people now believe it to be real.

Need-Fire or **Elf-fire:** A ritualized form of fire-lighting, which was used during times of distress or poor harvest. The need-fire, or 'living-fire' cannot be taken from an existing flame but must be re-kindled anew. The nine sacred woods used were ash, birch, yew, hazel, rowan, willow, pine and thorn. SOURCE: *Root and Branch* and *A Witch's Treasury of the Countryside*, Mélusine Draco .

Negative Confession: The ancient Egyptian dead were required to address their declaration of innocence – or the 42 negative confessions – first to **Osiris** and then to 42 other deities who will sit in judgement. These are the 42 representatives from the 42 nomes (or districts) of Upper and Lower Egypt. The confession must be completed to assure the assembly that the deceased has committed no moral offences that would prevent them from entering the **Duat** or **Amenti** (see **Judgement**).

Neith: An Egyptian creator-goddess dating from the beginning of the dynastic period. She has a double role in Egyptian religion: as a warrior-hunter goddess, and as a woman skilled in the domestic arts.

Nekhbet: Together with **Wedjet**, the vulture goddess Nekhbet was one of the dual protectors of the Egyptian kings, and usually shown with wings spread, grasping the symbols of eternity in her claws. The vulture and the cobra together became the symbol of the unification of Lower and Upper Egypt; known as the 'two ladies', the epithet indicated the two protectresses.

Nemesis: According to Hesiod, a child of Night and the Greek personification of the gods' resentment at, and consequent punishment of, insolence (*hubris*) towards themselves.

Nemoralia: Festival in the honor of the Roman Diana as a celestial goddess (13th August).

Nennius: A 9th century Welsh writer was the first to mention **Arthur** by name as a historical war leader against the Saxon invaders in his *Historia Brittonum*.

Neo-Pagan: see **Paganism – modern**.

Neo-Paganism: The first Neo-Pagan religious sects emerged in Germany at

Natural Tides

Since the beginning of time, when man first stood on the shoreline and wondered at the vastness of the ocean, it has been recognized that the periodic rise and fall of great stretches of water had something to do with the moon. Nowhere else on earth was Nature's power and glory so much in evidence.

The tides are due to the moon's gravitational pull on the water, lifting it to form a bulge resembling enormous wave-crests: one on the side of the earth facing the moon, and the other on the earth's far side, for there the moon's pull draws the earth away from the water. The friction between the water and the rotating earth slows the movement of these bulges, and for this reason *high tide*, as the bulge is called, does not occur exactly when the moon is overhead, but somewhat later.

The sun's gravitational pull raises similar tides, but less powerful than those caused by the moon. At full and new moon, when the sun and moon are in a straight line with the earth, they produce an especially powerful *spring tide*. This has nothing to do with the season: spring tides occur throughout the year.

This means that we need to tear ourselves away from the stereotypical moon goddess concept and think in terms of the natural interaction of the Sun *and* Moon, moving in a cosmic rhythm of perpetual motion. Some may be reluctant to accept this idea but it is a scientific fact that, despite its impressive gravitational pull, the moon is a dead, barren place, reflecting the sun's light, not its own.

Although the ancients had no scientific understanding, this is what is known magically as 'old wisdom' – the true interpretation recorded in folklore and logged into our collective subconscious – not the modern 'fake-lore' currently in vogue. Without coming to grips with this ancient knowledge, our own modern magic will be stunted.

So, let us return to the sea... in mid ocean, the tides are simply a rhythmic rise and fall of the water. On the continental shelf, they act like the waves on a beach, and become a bodily rush of the water towards or away from the land, producing the tide's ebb and flow, and in between, when the tide is almost at a standstill, there are brief periods of slack water. This rise and fall takes place twice every day and the sea witch recognizes the importance of knowing about them from both a magical and safety point of view.

Besides the familiar tides of the *ocean tides*, there are also two other examples to take into account: *earth tides* and *atmospheric tides*. Earth tides refer to the alternating slight change of shape of the Earth due to the gravitational action of the sun and moon, and atmospheric tides of the alternating slight motions of the atmosphere, which have the same effect. The moon draws away the envelope of air that surrounds the Earth to produce the daily atmospheric tides.

Recent research has revealed more evidence of the effects of these earth-tides: parts of western Britain and Ireland, for example, 'bounce' by four inches and that the movement is caused as tides ebb and flow twice daily! Again, we have scientific proof of cosmic influences on the earth on which we stand, so magical working can be timed to coincide with these natural movements for greater effect.

- **High tide**, just before the water pressure is at its greatest, would be the best time for positive or drawing magic.
- **Low tide**, when the tide has turned and the earth is about to 'bounce' back, is the time for banishing or reducing magic.

Calendars and almanacs give the dates of the moon's phases, but for the sea witch it is essential to also consult local tide tables (usually given in local newspapers) so that we always know the actual times of high and low tide for our area.

Magical synchronicity is the secret key-word.

EXTRACT FROM *SEA CHANGE: PRACTICAL CRAFT FOR THE SEAWITCH*
MÉLUSINE DRACO

the beginning of the 20th century. All of them were by-products of the German *völkisch* movement, a confused and complicated ideological phenomenon, stemming from the ideas of the late Romantic movement and German nationalism, according to the entry in *Man, Myth & Magic*.

Neophyte: A beginner or novice; one who is newly entered (i.e. converted) into a magical, religious or mystical Order.

Nephelomancy: Divination using the patterns and images seen in cloud formations.

Nephthys: A rather shadowy Egyptian deity who was the sister of Osiris, Isis, Horus (the Elder) and Set.

Neptune: (1) Originally Neptune was the Roman god of fresh water with a shrine near the Tiber river – it was only in historical times that he became a sea god and identified with the Greek god, **Poseidon**. (2) The planet Neptune does not appear in classical astrology. (3) Neptune's relationship with the sea turned out to be highly appropriate, as the planet is a deep blue disk with bright clouds of methane ice crystals. (4) and (5) The planet does not feature in traditional Tarot or the Qabalah since it was not discovered until 1846.

Neptunalia: In Rome's oldest civil calendar the feast of Neptune was observed on 23rd July.

Neter: (1) The gods of ancient Egypt. (2) In an occult context it suggests the ultrasexual nature of the Creative Force.

Nettle, Common or **Stinging:** Native to Britain, the plant has been praised and cursed by man since prehistoric times. Listed by **Aelfric, Pliny, Culpeper** and

Gerard for its medicinal and culinary qualities, it was also one of the **Nine Sacred Herbs** of the Anglo-Saxons. Ruling planet: **Mars**.

Netzach: The sphere of Victory on the Tree of Life and the seventh Path of 'occult intelligence', because it represents intellectual virtues and love in all forms. The **Names of Power** are all the deities associated with Love (**see Venus**).

New Aeon: A term used by Aleister **Crowley** to denote the current cycle or era, which will endure for approximately 2000 years, and which is under the aegis of the god Horus. The Aeon of Horus commenced in 1904 when *AL* was transmitted to Crowley by an extra-terrestrial Intelligence named **Aiwass**.

New Age: The 'new age' refers to the dawning of the Age of Aquarius, and encompasses the whole gamut of alternative beliefs and ways of life. It has attracted an eager following and is expanding its influence throughout the world, regardless of culture or creed.

Newbury Witchcraft: An incident during the Civil War gives a rare example of lynch law in England, and the unusual execution of a witch by shooting. A contemporary text on the case (1643) is now in the British Museum.

Newgrange: The most famous megalithic passage grave in Ireland, situated in the Boyne Valley Cemetery (see **Brugh na Boinne**). The chamber with three cells and the approach passage are walled with huge upright slabs; the north cell contains one of the finest and intricately carved ceiling slabs.

New Isis Lodge: A Lodge of the OTO operated by Kenneth **Grant** for seven years (1955-62), for the purpose of transmitting magical knowledge.

New Year Celebrations: Rites in celebration of the New Year take place all over the world, irrespective of differing cultural systems or methods of computing time. The Jewish New Year is a moveable feast, while in ancient Egypt it coincided with the annual Inundation of the Nile around the **Summer Solstice**. Until the introduction of the **Gregorian** calendar in 1752, the official New Year in the British Isles began in March, although as far as ordinary folk were concerned, they celebrated on 1st January. Many of the pagan traditions recognize **Samhain**, **Winter Solstice** or Old **Yule** as the beginning of the New Year, while the Chinese celebrate **Yuan Tan** in February.

Nganga: Probably the most widely extended of all African religious terms. It refers to a religious expert who can control evil forces and who has the ability to 'sniff out' witches and sorcerers, despite the fact that s/he uses fetishes, herbalism and divination as part of their 'witch-hunts'. If, among the Africans, witchcraft is seen to be the greatest force of evil, then the *nganga* is above all the anti-witchcraft expert. It was against this African-Azande yardstick that sociologists and anthropologists measured European witchcraft in the early 20th century. SOURCE: *Witchcraft & Sorcery*, Max Marwick.

Nibelungen-Lied and **Nôt**: A famous German epic of the 13th century and divided into two parts: one ending with the death of Siegfried, and the other with the death of his widow, Kriemhild.

Niflheim: (pron *mist-home*) The region of endless cold and everlasting night, ruled over by **Hela** in Scandinavian mythology. It consists of nine worlds, to which are consigned those who die of disease or old age.

Nightingale: One of the most celebrated of birds, immortalized in music, poetry and literature but with very little in the way of folklore.

Nightmare: Comes from the Old English word *mare* (spirit or night hag). According to Gettings, the etymology of the word has frequently been misunderstood and is now used to refer to the equine 'mare' and gives rise to the folklore belief that witches or the **Faere** Folk would steal horses for a frenzied night-ride. The most famous painting depicting the terror of the night is *The Nightmare* by Fuseli, and it was said that the artist used to eat raw beef and pork chops for supper to produce nightmares, so that he might draw his horrible visions. SOURCE: *Dictionary of Demons*, Fred Gettings; *White Horse: Equine Magical Lore*, Rupert Percy.

Nigromancy: Communicating with the dead to interpret omens or provide information about future events on a psychic level, whereas **Necromancy** summons the dead to speak. Often erroneously used to mean 'black magic'.

Nine: (1) Consists of a trinity of trinities. According to Pythagorean theory, man is a full cord, or eight notes, and deity comes next. Three being the **Trinity**, represents a perfect unity, twice three is the perfect dual, and thrice three is the perfect plural. This explains the use of nine as a mystical number. (2) Number

IX equals the **Hermit** in the **Tarot** (or the four Nines of the Minor Arcana), **Yesod** in the **Qabalah** and is governed by the **Moon**.

Nine Sacred Herbs: see **Lacnunga**.

Nine Woods of the Balefire: The ash, birch, yew, hazel, rowan, willow, pine, thorn and any other indigenous trees recognized as being traditionally sacred may be used, with the exception of the oak or elder. SOURCE: *Root and Branch* and *A Witch's Treasury of the Countryside*, Mélusine Draco.

Nirvana: The state of union with 'godhead' within Hindu, Buddhist and yoga practice. Attaining nirvana obliterates the ego and discharges all karmic debt, thereby removing the need for **Reincarnation**.

Nomos: The Law. Greek laws were man-made but considered to be divinely sanctioned, since unwritten laws and customs had been given by the gods in the past, and **Zeus** was said to watch over law and justice. Impiety (*asebeia*) was an offence punishable in law and following the notorious Athenian impiety trial in 399BC, the philosopher Socrates was condemned to death and executed.

Normanton Down: One of the most remarkable barrow groups, mostly of the Early Bronze Age, are graves of people of importance of the 'Wessex culture'. It is probable that the site was chosen to be near Stonehenge, which is surrounded for miles by concentrations of fine barrows.

Norna: The well of Urda in Scandinavian mythology, where the gods sit in judgement. It was near the 'fair building' of the Norns called 'Doomstead'.

Nornir or **Norns:** The three fates of Scandinavian mythology Urda, Verdandi and Skulda (Past, Present and Future). They spin the events of human life sitting under the ash tree **Yggdrasil**. It was also believed that each person had a personal Norn of Fate.

Norse or **Northern Tradition:** A contemporary Tradition based on legends contained in the Icelandic poems, the *Eddas*, and the worship of the old Scandinavian deities. It has a structure unlike any other pagan religion, but at the same time retains a 'sort of nomadic looseness at worshipper level' (see **Aesir, Asatru** and **Vanir**). SOURCE: *European Myth & Legend*, Mike Dixon-Kennedy; *Magic In The Middle Ages*, Richard Kieckhefer; *The New Believers*, David V. Barrett; *Norse Magic*, D.J. Conway; *Northern Mysteries & Magick* (formerly *Leaves of Yggdrasil*), Freya Aswynn; *The Odin Brotherhood*, Prof. Mark Mirabello; *Practical Magic in the Northern Tradition*, Nigel Pennick; *Songs of Yggdrasil*, Freya Aswynn.

North: (1) Considered by many pagan cultures to be the 'Place of Power'. (2) Christian doctrine considered it to be the dark side of the earth, and some old churches still have the Devil's Door in the north wall. The poor of the parish objected to being buried on the north side of the churchyard, the ecclesiastical reason being that the east is God's side; the west is man's side; the south the side of the angels and the sun; the north is the devil's side, where his legions lurk to catch the unwary. '*As men die, so shall they arise, if in faith in the Lord, towards the south; if in unbelief... towards the north.*' Coverdale, *Praying for the Dead.*

North Berwick Witch Trials: A unique and contemporary tract, *News From Scotland* (1591), now in Lambeth Palace Library, reveals how these trials mushroomed out of seemingly miraculous cures wrought by a serving girl, to implicate some 70 people, including the Earl of Bothwell, on charges of high treason.

Northern Gate of the Sun: The zodiacal sign of **Cancer** or **Summer Solstice** and so called because it marks the northern tropic.

Northern Lights: The **Aurora Borealis** was thought to be the 'merriment of ghosts'.

Northern Wagoner, The: **Ursa Major:** also called the Plough, the Big Dipper, Charles' Wain or wagon, is a constellation containing seven bright stars. Charles' Wain is a misnomer for the 'Churls' or Peasant's Wain. *'By this the northern wagoner has set/His seven fold team behind the steadfast star* [the Pole Star].'

Northways: Anticlockwise, **Widdershins**, against the sun.

Norwegian Witchcraft: Probably less than two dozen witch trials took place in Norway, although the earliest recorded was in 1592 when Oluf Gurdal was sentenced to death in Bergen. Belief in sorcery and demons was well established and drew on the seafaring traditions of the country.

Norwood Gypsies: Once a heavily wooded area where five London boroughs meet and where the gypsies became so widely known in the 17th and 18th centuries that the place became synonymous with fortune-telling. It is not known when the gypsies settled there but as early as 1668, Samuel Pepys recorded a visit in his famous *Diary*. Hundreds of London girls made the trip to Norwood to have their fortunes told. One character, Margaret Finch, purported to be the Gypsy Queen, became nationally known in her time and died in 1740, at the reputed age of 108 or 109.

Nostradamus: aka Michel de Nostre Dame (1503–1566) was the favorite astrologer to Catherine de Medici. His book, *The Centuries* – better known as *The True Prophecies or Pronostications of Michael Nostradamus* – which has appeared in numerous editions since 1555 purports to include prophesies for the world up to its end in 1999. SOURCE: *The Complete Prophecies of Nostrodamus*, edited by Henry C. Roberts; *Nostradamus*, J.H. Brennan.

Nottingham: The Romans ignored the original hamlet, which the Angles later called Snot or Snotta, but the Danes made it a borough called Nottingham. The Normans built a castle and for some forgotten cause there was a continuous feud between the Saxon townspeople and the Normans, crystallized in the legend of **Robin Hood** and his men, who used nearby Sherwood Forest as their base. The medieval Goose Fair, once a prolonged week of merrymaking, as now been reduced to three days in the first week of October, with amusements rather than trade as its motif.

NOX: [Gnostic] Night, and the counterpart of **LUX**; the Unconscious Will that has its roots in the Night of **Pan**.

Nuit: Goddess of the night sky, depicted in the form of a woman arched over the earth, her body strewn with stars (see

Nut). This representation is of vital importance in **Thelemic** teaching.

Numbers, Magical: Ascribed to some demons in demonology, and derived from the used of magical squares, relating to the corresponding planets (see **Squares**). Pythagoras, however, looked on numbers as influential principles, i.e. 1 = Unity, and represents Deity, which has no parts; 2 = Diversity and disorder, the principle of strife and evil; 3 = Perfect Harmony, or the union of unity and diversity; 4 = Perfection, being the first square (2 x 2 = 4); 5 = The Prevailing number in Nature and art; 6 = Justice; 7 = the Medical Number, the climatic number found in all diseases, etc. SOURCE: *Dictionary of Demons*, Fred Gettings.

Numen: In the ancient Roman religion, the power or spirit dwelling in each natural object – a tree, a fountain or spring, the earth – and also in each man, controlling the phenomena of nature, and the actions of man himself.

Numerology: Draws much of its inspiration from the 6th century philosopher **Pythagoras**, who believed that numbers represent the essences and qualities of things. This attribution of mystical or symbolic meaning to numbers is probably universal. Jewish students of the **Qabalah** had their own numerological system, *gematria*. SOURCE: *Applied Magic*, Dion Fortune; *Guide to the Supernatural*, Raymond Buckland; *Liber 777*, Aleister Crowley; *The Magical Arts*, Richard Cavendish; *Modern Numerology*, John King; *Numerology for Beginners*, Gerie Bauer; *The Numerology of Names*, Laurel Blyth; *Principles of Numerology*, Sonia Ducie.

Numinous: The state of mind aroused by the mysterious, uncanny and supernatural; the state of religious awe or dread, the sense of the presence of the *mysterium tremendum*, the 'overpowering mystery'. A term coined by German theologian, Rudolf Otto that refers to the mystical, the sacred and mysterious; magic and religion are both parts of the numinous world.

Nun: The personification of the primeval waters from which the ancient Egyptian creation myths derived. It was believed that if the correct precatory observances were not carried out, then the waters of Nun would re-envelop the world and everything would plunge back into **Chaos**.

Nursery Rhymes: The persistence of the seemingly innocent childhood rhymes down the centuries has preserved the references to mythology, folklore and witchcraft (see **Mother Goose**).

Nut: (1) The pre-dynastic Nut was the personification of 'Our Lady of the Starry Heavens' and, in primeval belief, the destination of the king's soul – the imperishable stars. As the Egyptian pantheon developed she became identified as the mother of **Osiris, Horus, Set, Isis** and **Nephthys**. (2) In more modern times, she is identified as Nuit in Aleister **Crowley's** *The Book of the Law*.

Nutcracker Night: All **Hallows** Eve, when it was customary in some places to crack open nuts in large quantities and leave for any spirits that may walk abroad.

Nymphs: Belonging to the oldest and deepest layers of Greek popular religion, mythology and folklore, nymphs were believed to be the personification of seas, rivers and springs, caves, trees and mountains – in fact *Nature* in all its aspects. They are divided into:

- Dryads – of the oak trees
- Hamadryads - of trees and tree cults
- Naiads – of running water, rivers and springs
- Napaeae – of valleys, prairies and groves
- Nereides – of seas and oceans
- Oreads – of the mountains

"*The belief in the virtues of rare stones passed into scientific knowledge of the Babylonians and hence found a place in their astrological cosmos.*"
Joan Evans
[*Magical Jewels*]

O

Oak: Probably the most sacred tree in the world's mythology with some ancient pagan societies enforcing the death penalty for anyone found damaging an oak tree. According to **Frazer**, the offender's navel was cut out and nailed to the wound in the tree; he was then driven round the tree till his intestines were wrapped round the trunk – a wound for a wound, a man's death for the tree's life. Ruling planet: Jupiter. SOURCE: *Root & Branch* and *A Witch's Treasury of the Countryside*, Mélusine Draco; *The Golden Bough*, Sir James Frazer.

'Oak and Ash': The tradition is, if the oak comes into leaf before the ash a fine and productive year may be expected; if the ash precedes the oak in foliage, a cold summer and unproductive autumn may be anticipated.

Oath: In magical terms, an oath involves calling upon a god or gods, or upon the psychic force contained in some ritual object, or symbol of power. *'The oath, which is sworn by or on some sacred or even dangerous authority, is intended to establish contact with its power, which can then be turned against the one who violates his or her given word.'* SOURCE: *Witchcraft – A Tradition Renewed*, Evan John Jones.

Oats: Introduced into Britain during the Iron Age, they were a staple food of medieval times and had many medicinal uses. Ruling planet: Venus.

Obeah: An African and Caribbean form of sorcery, which involves the worship of the Serpent (Ob) and the projection of the Astral Light for magical purposes. Obeah utilizes objects as 'containers' of occult energy: balls of earth mixed with feathers, hair or rags, tied up with string and sometimes decorated with beads. In some cases parts of human or animal bodies will be included, together with soil from graves, eggshells, rum, blood and broken glass. Practitioners are called obeah men or women.

Obelisk: A tall, four-sided pillar usually associated with the solar temples of ancient Egypt.

Object Link: Material sample impregnated with magnetism of a proposed victim, or subject of magic (as opposed to a **Power Object**).

Object Reading: By doing no more than hold some personal object – a photograph, piece of clothing or jewelry – psychometrists can often give the most detailed information concerning the person, and the circumstances, with which the object is connected.

Oblation: An offering or sacrifice.

Obsidian: A natural glass of volcanic origin, which has been used for thousands of years in the making of tools, weapons and ornaments. An obsidian mirror, which seemed to smoke when the diviner looked into it was the symbol of Tezcatlipoca in the Aztec religion, and is often used for skrying purposes today. Also known as Apache Tears.

Occult: Literally means 'hidden' but it has developed sinister connotations within Christian propaganda to suggest evil and devil worship. Within occultism it suggests secret or esoteric knowledge that can only be imparted to Initiates of the Western **Ritual Magic** Traditions. It is now appears unfashionable to use the term, especially within the 'mind, body and spirit' publishing genre.

Occult Sciences: Magic, alchemy and astrology – so called because they were occult or mysterious.

Ocher: A native pigment composed of fine clay and an iron oxide (limonite in yellow ochre; hematite in red). Red ocher was used in funerary rites as far back as the Stone Age.

Octinomos: The Master Magician having the eight-lettered name, i.e. **Baphomet.** Aleister **Crowley** assumed this title within the **OTO.**

Oculomancy: Observance of the eye to discern the health of a person.

Od: A term coined around c1850 by Baron von Reichenbach to name the hypothetical force that was believed to be at work in animal magnetism, mesmerism, crystals and other pseudo-scientific phenomena. He maintained that in humans, the force streamed from the fingertips of suitably sensitive persons (see **Energy**).

Odin: The dominant figure in Scandinavian mythology, he was an old man with one eye, who dressed in a cloak and a broad-brimmed hat. He is usually depicted with two ravens at his shoulders and two wolves at his feet. His influenced was multi-dimensional: being the god of battle, the guide of the dead whom he conducts to Otherworld, and the inspiration for poetry, oratory and learning. He is also a shape-shifter and expert in magic. SOURCE: *Gods & Myths of Northern Europe*, H.R. Ellis Davidson.

Odinism: see **Northern Tradition.**

Odium Theologicum: The bitter hatred of rival religionists. *'No wars so sanguinary as holy wars; no persecutions so relentless as religious persecutions; no hatred so bitter as theological hatred.'*

Odyllic Force: The energy that issues from every substance in the world. It may be used to create great power in magical workings.

Odyssey: A Homeric epic poem describing the adventures of Odysseus on his ten-year journey home following the fall of Troy.

Offa's Dyke: The northern end of this great earthwork lies at the seaward end of the Dee estuary and passes through the western counties to end at the mouth of the river Wye opposite Chepstow. All evidence points to it having been constructed to the orders of Offa, the king of Mercia in the second half of the 8th century to define the boundary between his kingdom and that of Wales.

Officer: A **Magister's** lieutenant; can also be the **Man in Black**, **Verdelet**, or the **Summoner** within the traditional **Coven** system.

'O Fortuna': see *Carmina Burana.*

Offerings: see **Sacrifice**.

Ogham: Known as the Irish tree alphabet and originally used by the Celts and Picts for inscriptions. It came to prominence in 1948 with the publication of Robert **Graves'** *The White Goddess: A Historical Grammar of Poetic Myth,* which included two chapters on the spiritual meaning of the Ogham. SOURCE: *Ogham & Coelbren: Keys to the Celtic Mysteries*, Nigel Pennick; *Ogam Stones & Inscriptions*, A. Gorham.

Oil, Ointments and **Unguents:** The substances that have been used for anointing purposes have been many and various, including vegetable oils, often perfumed and containing gums, resins and balsams, animal fat, blood, honey and mud. The use in ritual is both ancient and widespread; they might be employed in the worship of a deity, as a means of consecration, for the unction of the sick, or the burial of the dead, or to impart special powers. A magical factor is present in all forms of anointing. SOURCE: *Magic: An Occult Primer*, David Conway; *Sacred Luxuries*, Lise Manniche.

Oimelc: see **Imbolc**.

Oinomancy: Divination and omen interpretation used since Roman times, by studying and evaluating the color, consistency and taste of wine.

Ointment: see **Oil**.

Ojas: [Sanskrit] Electromagnetic energy peculiar to the **Chakras**, or power zones, when vitalized by the **Fire Snake**.

Olcott, Colonel Henry Steel: (1832–1907) A co-founder of the **Theosophical** Society with Madame **Blavatsky**, and when the organization moved to India he became interested in **Buddhism** and **Hinduism**. He was author of a number of books on the occult: *People From the Other World*; *Theosophy, Religion and Occult Languages*; *A Buddhist Catechism*; and a three-volume *Old Diary Leaves*.

Old Craft: Usually conspicuous by its lack of representation in pagan circles. It is not a 'gentle' belief in that its adherents are committed to the **Horned God** energy, which is often empowered by the **Wild Hunt**; the feminine principle is not the Goddess as portrayed in modern paganism and **Wicca**. SOURCE: *Coarse Witchcraft*, Gabrielle and Rupert Percy; *Coven of*

the Scales, A.R. Clay-Egerton; *What You Call Time*, Suzanne Ruthven; *A Witch's Treasury for Hearth & Garden*, Gabrielle Sidonie. [SEE PANEL]

Ol' Lad and **Lass:** Familiar Old Craft names for divinity.

Old Moore's Almanac: Francis Moore (1657–1715) was an English astrologer who published the annual *Francis Moore's Almanac* containing predictions for the year ahead, together with medical and herbal remedies. It was so popular, that it has been published annually to this day.

Old Ones: The **Mighty Dead** and archetypal deities deriving from the legends of the **Watchers**.

Old Sarum, Wiltshire: Here on the hill are the multiple earthworks of the forerunner of modern Salisbury but only the outermost bank dates back to the Iron Age. Because it stood at the crossing of important roads, it became the Roman Sorviodunum. Centuries later the Normans quickly realized its strength and the inner earthworks are from that period. Here a small town grew and an early cathedral was built. Not until the 12th century, when Salisbury Cathedral was built in the valley, below did the people of Sarum colonize the new site by the river.

Old Style Dates: An Act of Parliament, to reconcile the differences between the Julian and Gregorian calendars, altered the official calendar in use in Britain in 1752. Under the new law, September 1752 was shortened by 11 days, with the 2nd being followed by the 14th although many people refused to recognize the new calendar in calculating the dates of festivals and seasonal customs, i.e. celebrating

Traditional British Old Craft

Contrary to what many modern pagans choose to believe, it should be understood that there *is* a system of witchcraft older than modern Wicca that has never left the shadows. These groups have never been part of the publicity machine to popularize 'paganism', and have always muttered darkly that the mass publicity of the past 20 years would destroy Craft — not preserve it.

Traditional British Old Craft covens usually pre-date the repeal of the Witchcraft Act (1951), or can prove their antecedents as having direct contact with these older strands of witchcraft. The concept behind their teaching is that behind one set of Mysteries, is only another set of Mysteries – which may often conflict with those previously learned! The rituals are almost impossible to define because there are no set patterns and the group relies solely on spontaneous reaction to channel magical energies.

There is little altruistic about traditional Old Craft. It can best be described as having a tribal mentality in that it believes in protecting its own, but with no obligation to mankind in general. In view of the historical backlash, even in more modern times, it is not surprising that *'Trust None!'* is the creed of Old Craft, and it has preserved its Mysteries by *not* divulging its rites and practices. No matter what a publisher's blurb may claim, there are no genuine Old Craft rituals, rites of passages, spells, charms or pathworkings in print, for one simple reason...

Any Old Crafter committing any of these to paper for public scrutiny would be in breach of their own Initiatory Oaths – and this still carries the ultimate penalty for treachery and betrayal. Admittedly, there are 'smokescreens' that may offer a *parody* of the genuine thing – but the gnarled roots of Old Craft remain firmly in the shadows, where they belong. Nowadays, there are an increasing number of people claiming their antecedents stem from this branch of witchcraft, but a few moments of conversation is enough to reveal that *their* roots are very modern indeed!

Although there may be a variation in formulae from region to region, the underlying Mysteries remain the same, and the only way to know about the Mysteries is to have experienced them first hand. In the past, there have been those who have used these 'regional disparities' to excuse any breach of etiquette, or lack of familiarity of the rites within Craft circles. In fact, there are so many undercurrents and overtones that any 'pretender' stands little or no chance of passing themselves off as a genuine traditional Crafter, no matter how well read or extensively published.

There should be no doubt about it – although witchcraft is NOT a religion (and never has been), it *does* have an overriding spirituality that is extremely profound in its concepts and perceptions. Research shows that traditional Old Craft appears to be as strong and healthy as it has ever been, and it should not be assumed that its natural orientation is nature-worship, as with contemporary Wicca or paganism. Old Craft *interacts* with Nature and this means acceptance in *all* its guises.

These seemingly insurmountable obstacles do not necessarily mean that the doors to Old Craft are permanently barred. The road may be long and arduous but the true seeker will get there in the end – and will not regret the struggles and hardship. Or, in much simpler terms, and to quote that old adage of Evan John Jones: *'If one who claims to be a Witch can perform the tasks of Witchcraft, i.e. summon the spirits and they come, can divine with rod, fingers and birds. If they can also claim the right to the omens and have them; have the power to call, heal and curse and above all, can tell the maze and cross the Lethe, then you have a witch.'*

This is as it should be.

EXTRACT FROM *WHAT YOU CALL TIME: A GUIDE TO MODERN WITCHCRAFT AND RITUAL MAGIC*
SUZANNE RUTHVEN

Christmas Day on 6th January. This created alternative dates throughout the year, which became known as 'old style' dates and has had a profound effect on the traditional year with many anomalies becoming apparent in later years. Many Old Craft festivals are still aligned with the old Julian calendar.

Old Ways or **Old Religion:** Any form of witchcraft that is followed by worshipping the pre-Christian gods of that particular Tradition.

Olive: Tradition has it that the olive tree was a gift of **Athena** to the Athenians in order to settle a dispute with **Poseidon**. It was later adopted by the Christians as a symbol of peace and reconciliation.

Olympus: A mountain on the borders of Thessaly and Macedonia and the home of the Greek gods.

Om: The most sacred syllable in **Hinduism**, and believed to be the primal sound from which all things were created. It is placed at the beginning and the end of most sacred writings, and also used as a mantra: *Om mani padme hum.*

Omens and **Auguries:** see **Divination**.

One: In the whole phenomena of existence there is One, which is also the Whole; a belief found in many religions and mystical traditions. Mystics wish to become One with God, and as a result the number One has been revered as combining the opposites of odd and even, and all the other opposites in the universe. The One is shown in the **Yin** and **Yang** symbols and the serpent eating its tail (see **Uroboros**) Number I equals the **Magician** (or the four Aces of the Minor Arcana) in the **Tarot, Kether** in the **Qabalah** and governed by the **Primum Mobile.**

Oneiromancy: Interpretation of visions experienced during the deepest levels of sleep.

Onimancy: Divination using olive oil was widely used until the Middle Ages, when it came to be considered witchcraft.

Onion: A widespread and firm belief that an onion, sliced in half, will keep illness at bay. Many of the numerous applications of onions in folk medicine have a very long history. The remedy has also been used in kennels to keep away kennel-cough. Onions were also used as a charm against witchcraft and the Evil Eye, both on the person and in the home. Ruling planet: **Mars**.

Onomancy: Divination by using the letters, or numbers of the letters of a person's name for divinatory purposes.

Onychomancy: An ancient Arabian method of divination by studying a person's fingernails.

Oomancy: Interpretation of the patterns made by dropping an egg white into a bowl of water.

Ooser: According to *Folklore, Myth & Legends of Britain,* most Dorset villages had an ooser, a horned mask that was believed to be the representative of the **Horned God.** By the beginning of the 20th century only one was left at Melbury Osmond but this has now been lost.

Opal: From the Greek *ops* (the eye). Considered unlucky for the same reason that peacock's feathers in a house are said to be unlucky. A peacock's feather being full of eyes acts as spies in the house, prying into one's privacy. Similarly, it is unlucky to introduce the eye-stone or opal into a house, because it will interfere with the sanctity of domestic privacy. *'Not an opal/Wrapped in a bay-leaf in my left fist,/ To charm their eyes with,'* Ben Jonson.

Opet, Festival of: A huge public festival that took place annually when the ritual procession of the divine images from Karnak traveled to Luxor. The religious purpose of the festival was to celebrate the divine 'marriage' between the god Amun and the mother of the reigning king.

Ophidian Current: Refers to the sexual energies used in connection with magical or mystical rites, i.e. for causing change to occur in the physical world.

Ophimancy: Derives from the Greek *ophis*, meaning serpent, and refers to observing the behavior of snakes for divinatory purposes.

Optalia: The festival of Ops, the Roman goddess of the harvest, held on the 9th December.

Oracle: A person or place of divination, usually a shrine or temple dedicated to the worship and consultation of a prophetic god.

Oracle Bones: Chinese Shang period (1523–1027BC) divination bones using 5,000 different characters concerning ritual, military, agricultural and domestic matters.

Orchis: Generally thought of as an aphrodisiac and the name *orchis* comes from the Greek for testicles. According to **Culpeper**, the root had various medicinal properties; **Gerard**, however, wrote: *'There is no great use of these in physic...'* Ruling planet: **Venus**.

Ordeal: (1) A trial of courage, strength and belief, frequently imposed on candidates for initiation. (2) The medieval trial by ordeal was a method of proving guilt or innocence by subjecting the accused to the test in the belief that God would preserve the innocent.

Order of the Garter: see **Garter**.

Ordo Templis Orientis or **OTO:** The Order of the Temple of the East – the East being the place of ascending solar-phallic power – the OTO was founded by Theodor Reuss and Carl Kellner around 1902. SOURCE: *Rituals & Sex Magick,* Theodor Reuss and Aleister Crowley; *Confessions,* Aleister Crowley; *The Magical Revival,* Kenneth Grant.

Orgy: In a religious or magical context, the belief that the release of animal and irrational impulses brings about an ecstasy in which man is raised to the level of the divine. The word derives from *orgia,* the rites of worship of the Greek god **Dionysus**.

Orientalism: The study or interest of Eastern religious/mystical beliefs, including Japanese Shinto, Tibetan Bon, Hinduism, Buddhism, Taoism, Confucianism, and the traditional deities of China. SOURCE: *Chinese Gods,* Keith Stevens; *Eastern Religions,* ed Michael D. Coogan.

Orion: This constellation has been recognized as a distinctive group of stars for thousands of years. In the northern hemisphere The Hunter arrives to herald the start of the hunting season, and departs in the spring when it ends. It contains the Great Nebula, which is clearly visible as the central star of Orion's sword hanging from the three belt stars. This star nursery is one of the marvels of the night sky.

Orisha: The many divinities of the Yoruba religion, partly comparable with

Vodun. Probably the most complex pantheon in Africa, their number is asserted to be hundreds, although the principal deities are few.

Ornithomancy: Divination by the observance of bird flight or song.

Orphic Mysteries: A mystic Greek cult, connected with Orpheus as the legendary source of the sacred poems from which the Orphic doctrines were derived. It explained the mixture of good and evil in human nature and departed from the primitive Greek religion in making the guilt and punishment of the individual the center of its doctrine. It taught the transmigration of souls. SOURCE: *The Orphic Mysteries in Syria & Early Christianity*, V. Burch; *The Orphic Pantheon*, G.R.S. Mead; *The Oxford Companion to Classical Literature*, ed by Sir Paul Harvey.

Osiris: Originally a fertility god, Osiris is always shown with the green skin that he inherited from his father, **Geb**. It would appear that as early as the *Pyramid Texts*, that he was considered primarily a god of the dead. It was not until much later (when the priesthood had reattributed some of Re's functions) that he, **Isis** and **Horus** became the chief deities with which the later Pharaohs identified themselves.

Ostara: The **Spring Equinox.**

Ostrich: The stone from the gizzard of an ostrich arouses lust, cures impotence, and enables a man to make love with great power when powdered and taken in a potion, or hung around the neck.

Otherworld: A generic term to cover the spirit realms but not necessarily the **Underworld** – as in the 'abode of the dead'. Also applies to different levels of consciousness, realities and dimensions.

Otter: An animal, especially its skin, was endowed with many magical properties.

Ouija Board: Although the messages that 'come through' the Ouija board can often be traced to the participant's subconscious, there are many instances when they do appear to emanate from some source that is outside the normal spheres of understanding. It has been suggested that the name derives from the French and German words for 'yes' – *oui* and *ja*.

Ouspensky, Peter Demianovich: (1878–1947) Russian author and mathematician who was already committed to an attempt to reconcile Western logical thought with Eastern mysticism when he met **Gurdjieff** and discovered that many of his teachings complemented his own. From then on he devoted his life to the development of Gurdjieff's ideas.

Out of the Body Experience: A not uncommon sensation where the subject appears to view the external world from some position other than that of his physical body.

Over-look: The ability to travel in the astral body to watch or spy on another.

Overton Hill: The Sanctuary is a henge monument terminating the Avenue, leading from **Avebury**. In its present form it consists of two circles of sarsens dating from the very beginning of the Bronze Age and apparently replaced a previous timber structure of Neolithic times.

Owls: Almost everywhere in the world owls have been associated with strange powers, although not necessary sinister ones. It was the emblem of Athena and Athens; and the only bird to be shown full face in the Egyptian hieroglyphic system. In the early Egyptian period it symbolized 'black' and used to represent 'Khem' as the black land. There is also an old country saying: *I live too near a wood to be scared by an owl* – meaning 'don't try to frighten me with something so familiar'. SOURCE: *The Folklore of Birds*, E.A. Armstrong; *A Witch's Treasury of the Countryside*, Mélusine Draco.

Owl-light: Twilight.

Oyster: According to *Fauna Britannica*, there is no more famous, fabled and celebrated mollusk in the world. They have inspired artists and poets, songwriters and novelists; cherished and eaten since ancient times and provide pearls and mother-of-pearl for ornamentation.

"Egypt is the most ancient of all nation states. When virtually all the rest of the world was locked in the immemorial and seemingly unchanging life of the stone-age hunters and scavengers, a civiliasation at once majestic and totally assured rose on the Nile's banks."

Michael Rice

[*Egypt's Legacy*]

P

Pact: Pacts with the Devil were considered the very essence of witchcraft because this pinpointed sorcery as heresy, and brought witchcraft under the jurisdiction of the **Inquisition**; take out the pact, and the heresy disappeared. Allegedly written in the witch's own blood, the pact provides the most spectacular aspect of the charge, and the Faust legend, in all its variations, has perpetuated it as fact. SOURCE: *The Book of Black Magic & of Pacts*, A.E. Waite; *Dictionary of Demons*, Fred Gettings; *A Dictionary of Devils & Demons*, J. Tondriau and R. Villeneuve; *The Encyclopedia of Witchcraft & Demonology*, Rossell Hope Robbins; *Malleus Malificarum*, trans Montague Summers.

Paddock: Believed to be a diminutive of the Anglo-Saxon word for a toad.

Pæan: (1) A hymn to Apollo and applied to the god himself. The hymn began, '*Io Pæan...*' (2) Homer applies it to a triumphal song in general.

Pagan Federation: An international organization founded in 1971 to provide information on paganism and to counter misconceptions about pagan beliefs. It arranges members-only and public events, with conferences and regional gatherings held throughout the UK and other countries. The Federation also publishes a quarterly journal, *Pagan Dawn* (formerly *The Wiccan*, first published in 1968).

Paganalia: A celebration (24th January) in the *pagi* (divisions of rural areas) of sowing, and associated with the earth goddesses **Ceres** and Tellus.

Paganism: [pre-Christian] Originally referred to country-dwellers with their attendant rural beliefs and practices; the sophisticated, cosmopolitan, educated Romans applied the term to anyone (usually on the fringes of the Empire) who held on to these strange customs; and there is a surprising amount of genuine pagan tradition contained in medieval Irish and Welsh literature. Pagan simply means someone who follows the old native religion of their land and can today apply to other beliefs such as **Shinto** and **Hinduism**, as readily as the modern Neo-Pagan movement. SOURCE: *Paganism Today*, Graham Harvey and Charlotte Hardman; *The Pagan Religions of the Ancient British Isles*, Professor Ronald Hutton; *The Pattern of the Past*, Guy Underwood; *The Roman Book of Days*, Paulina Erina.

Paganism: [modern] Used as an umbrella term for an eclectic borrowing from all creeds and cultures, although it is largely '*a revival and reconstruction of ancient Nature religions adapted for the modern world,*' according to Oberon Zell, of the Church of all Worlds. SOURCE: *Beginners Guide to Paganism, Wicca, Witchcraft & Shamanism*, Sorcerer's Apprentice; *The New Believers*, David V. Barrett; *Pagan Pathways*, Graham Harvey and Charlotte Hardman; *Pagan Rites of Passage*, Pauline Campanelli; *Principles of Paganism*, Vivianne Crowley; *What You Call Time*, Suzanne Ruthven.

Pālēs: In the Roman religion, a rustic spirit, whose festival the *Parilia* held on 21st April, and a ritual purification of shepherds and their flocks. The animals were driven through the flames of blazing straw as an invocation of prosperity for the coming season. Similar rituals have been performed at about the same time of the year in various parts of Europe right down to modern times (see **Beltaine**).

Palindrome: A word that reads the same forwards as backwards; some Magic Squares were arranged to read the same in all directions, which was believed to give them magical power.

Palladism: An alleged cult of Satan-Lucifer in certain Masonic lodges towards the end of the 19th century, reported in a volume entitled *Le Palladisme*, published in 1895 by Domenico Margiotta.

Palladium: Something that affords effectual protection and safety. The Palladium was a colossal wooden statue of **Pallas** in the city of Troy. It was believed that so long as it remained within the city, Troy would be safe; but if removed, the city would fall to the enemy. The statue was carried away by the Greeks, and the city was burned to the ground.

Pallas: A name of **Athena**. It has been suggested that it was the name of a foreign goddess whom the Greeks identified with Athena.

Palmistry or **Cheiromancy:** The belief that an individual's destiny is imprinted on his hands has a long history; even today it is commonly accepted that an accurate interpretation of the configurations of the hand can enable a man to recognize and change his fate. SOURCE: *Book of Divining the Future*, Eva Shaw; *The Book of the Hand*,

Fred Gettings; *Guide to the Supernatural*, Raymond Buckland.

Pan: Comes from the Greek word meaning 'All'. (1) Pan had no part in the traditional Olympian pantheon but he was revered in his native Arcadia long before his cult spread into other parts of Greece. (2) Magically speaking, it is a cosmic power popularly conceived of in a goatish or goat-footed form, the goat being symbolic of the lonely leaper in high places, i.e. the aspiration and consequent exaltation of the soul to high and holy places. Symbolized by the 'Devil' card in the **Tarot**.

Panacea: A universal cure. The word comes from the daughter of **Asclepius** (god of medicine).

Panathenaia, The: A Greek summer festival to honor the traditional birthday of **Athena**, celebrated by musical competitions, athletic and gymnastic exercises that included coxing, wrestling, horse and chariot racing, concluding with a torchlight procession and sacrifices.

Pandaemonium: A word derived directly from the Greek meaning 'all the demons'.

Panegyric: An eulogy, especially a public and elaborate one.

Pangaea: [pan- and Greek *gē*, the Earth] The postulated supercontinent that began to break up, forming the present continents of the **Earth**.

Panhellenic: Pertaining to all things Greek – religion, history, art, literature, etc.

Panic: A sudden and contagious fear; a great terror, often without any visible reason or foundation.

Pantacle: [Greek] The same as *pentalpha*; the triple triangle of **Pythagoras**. In esoteric philosophy the *pentalpha* is the symbol of the Ego. Should not be confused with the **Pentacle** or **Pentagram**. The most well-known example is the one made in wax by Dr. **Dee**, now in the British Museum.

Panth: The Sanskrit word for 'path' or 'road' and used to designate different groups following particular teachers or doctrines.

Panthea: Statues or medals carrying the symbols of several deities.

Pantheism: The worship of all gods and the doctrine that god and the universe are identical, and the belief that the whole of reality is divine.

Pantheon: (1) The famous domed temple in Rome that was dedicated to all the gods. (2) The collective term for all the divinities of a nation.

Papus: The pseudonym of Dr. Gérard Encausse (1865–1916) who was responsible for the widespread interest in occultism in France during the late 1880s. He was the influential author of a number of books on the **Qabalah**, the **Tarot** and **Astrology**. Serving with distinction in the French army medical corps during WWI, he died of a pulmonary infection aged 51. Although his magical career only spanned 30 years, he gave thousands of French the opportunity to acquire at least a superficial knowledge of occultism.

Papyrus: A number of Egyptian papyri containing what was believed to be alchemical references have been preserved, the oldest being found at Luxor in 1873 by Georg Ebers, and thought to date from around 1550BC, with text referring back even further to Imhotep of the 3rd Dynasty. It was thought that the hieroglyphics were the script of the **Mysteries**.

Paracelsus: Born Phillipus Aureolus Theophrast Bombast von Hohenheim in Switzerland in 1493. Although he was detested by orthodox physicians of his time, he has since been recognized as the first modern medical scientist; he was also a mystic whose writings and personality have fascinated generations of occultists. His non-medical works, *De Occulta Philosophia* and *Archidoxis Magica* are hermetic writings reflecting his theory that Nature heals and man can only assist the course of Nature. SOURCE: *Alchemy: An Illustrated A-Z*, Diana Fernando; *The Archidoxes of Magic*, Paracelsus; *The Hermetic & Alchemical Writings of Paracelsus* and *Selected Writings*.

Parables: Stories, usually drawn from ordinary life, to illustrate some religious or ethical principle.

Paradise: The **Avalon** of **Arthurian** legend; the Greek **Elysian Fields** and the Norse **Valhalla** are all pagan concepts of paradise.

Paranormal and **Parapsychology:** Refer to the scientific study or investigation of psychic phenomena under controlled conditions. In the past, the paranormal was explained in supernatural, occult or miraculous terms but today it is scientifically divided into a number of general, often overlapping categories: ghosts, divination, ESP (the 'sixth' sense), comprising of clairvoyance, telepathy, precognition and retrocognition; PK (psychokinesis – the action of the mind on matter without the agency of any known physical force), whose effects include metal-bending, table-turning, direct writing and teleportation.

SOURCE: *Experimental Psychical Research*, Robert H. Thouless; *Mysteries*, Colin Wilson; *The Occult*, Colin Wilson; *The Paranormal*, Brian Inglis.

Paraphernalia: [Greek, *parapherne*, beyond dower] Means all that a woman can claim at the death of her husband beyond her jointure. Under Roman law her paraphernalia included the furniture of her chamber, her wearing apparel, jewels, personal attire, fittings, generally anything for show or decoration.

Parc Cwm: An interesting Neolithic long barrow – or more correctly, cairn – standing near the center of the Gower peninsular, that has been the cause of some controversy. It has a 'horned' forecourt leading to a gallery with two pairs of transeptal chambers, like those found in the Cotswolds; but the mound is oval, like those of the Western Atlantic type. Examples of both types are known on Gower and it is possible that the monument is a hybrid form. SOURCE: *Facing the Ocean*, Barry Cunliffe.

Parchment: Writing material made from the skins of animals, usually sheep or goats. Between the 8th and 14th centuries it replaced papyrus, until its use was superseded by paper. It is recommended in the **Grimoires** as the appropriate material on which to inscribe magical symbols and talismans.

Parc Le Breos, Glamorgan: One of the best preserved passage-graves in Wales and demonstrates the ritualistic planning of this type of tomb. When the mound was excavated in 1869 the remains of 24 skeletons were found.

Parc-y-Meirch: The remarkable hill fort of Dinorben stands not far from the sea, on a hill skirting the west side of the Vale of Clwyd. The fort was certainly occupied long before the Roman invasion; it was then abandoned for a time, to be restored and reoccupied in the Dark Ages.

Paregoric: A camphorated opium tincture that was used in magic unguents in medieval Europe.

Parentalia: The days set aside to honor Roman ancestral dead: 13th–21st February. During this period temples were closed, marriages forbidden, and each family carried out rites at the family tombs.

Parian Chronicle: A chronological register of the chief events in the mythology and history of ancient Greece during a series of 1,318 years, beginning with the reign of Cecrops, and ending with the archonship of Diognetus. It is engraved on Parian marble, and was found on the island of Paros; it is one of the Arundelian Marbles.

Parilia: A festival to honor the old Italian pastoral goddess, **Pālēs** (also called Palila) and observed by driving livestock through burning straw as part of the purification rites held on 21st April.

Paris Witch Trial: It is possible to read the verbatim record, preserved in the manuscripts from the Grand Châtelet, the criminal court of Paris, of the first secular trial in Europe for witchcraft. It took place in Paris in 1390 after the Parlement [sic] of Paris decided that witchcraft was a civil as well as an ecclesiastical offense.

Parnassos: A mountain near **Delphi** that has two summits, one being consecrated to **Apollo** and the **Muses**, the other to **Bacchus**. It was formally called Larnassos, from *larnos* (an ark), because **Deucalion's** ark stranded there after the **Deluge**. After the oracle of Delphi was built at its foot, it received the name of Parnassos.

Parsley: (1) The Greeks decked tombs with parsley because it keeps green for a long time. Hence the saying: *'He has need now of nothing but a little parsley,'* – i.e. he is dead. (2) Listed by **Aelfric**, there are numerous superstitions about parsley mostly concerning bad luck if it is transplanted. In folk medicine it is recommended for a variety of ailments and was used in witches' ointments. Ruling planet: **Mercury**.

Parting Cup: Drunk by the Romans in honor of the god Mercury at the end of an evening and to insure sound sleep – perhaps the original of 'one for the road'.

Passing Bell: It now means the bell tolled to announce the death of someone in the parish. Originally it meant the bell that announced that the person was *in extremis*, or passing from time into eternity.

Past-Life Regression: The apparent recovery, under hypnosis, of details relating to a 'previous life' and taken by some to be proof of **Reincarnation**.

Path: (1) In occult terminology, all Paths lead to a single divine or cosmic destination and the chosen Path can be any form of religious or magical application. The term comes originally from India, where *panth* refers to a reading of any portion of the sacred scriptures. (2) There are also 22 Paths in the astral Otherword of modern Western occultism, corresponding to the 22 cards of the **Major Arcana** of the Tarot. These Paths are shown as lines running from one **Sephira** to another on the **Tree of Life**.

Pathworking: A form of guided meditation, the subject being helped by storytelling of a related situation or mystical encounter, during which the mind begins to interact independently. SOURCE: *The Pathworkings of Aleister Crowley*, J.F.C. Fuller.

Paviland or **Goat's Hole Cave:** This is probably the most sacred ancestral site in the British Isles. Originally, the cave opened onto a coastal plain but today it is a cleft in the sea cliffs of the Bristol Channel and visitors must be mindful of the tides. Discovered early in the 19th century, it revealed the first British Paleolithic burial – a human skeleton associated with the bones of extinct animals by the last Ice Age – but scholars of the time refused to accept this evidence of the antiquity of man. Further excavations showed that above these ancient traces, the cave was still being used as late as Roman times. SOURCE: *Britain BC*, Francis Pryor.

Pea: Cultivated in England at least since Roman times, peas were also a staple diet in medieval times, used in soups, pottages, porreys and many other dishes. **Culpeper** said they were 'good to sweeten the blood' and tradition maintained that drinking the water the peas had been boiled in would cure measles. Ruling planet: **Jupiter** in **Aries**.

Pear: Although pear charcoal has been found dating from Neolithic times, as well as being mentioned in medieval documents, there is very little available by way of folklore. It appears in Anglo-

Saxon charters, and was listed by **Aelfric**. Ruling planet: **Venus.**

Pearl: Hidden within the heart of the oyster, the pearl became an emblem of the soul, i.e. the precious jewel concealed within the rough exterior of the body. Superstition often connects pearls with tears but magically an amulet of pearl brings longevity and good fortune.

Pearl Mussel: Buries itself in the bed of clean, fast-flowing rivers, generally in acidic areas; Britain has been known since Roman times for its fine quality 'freshwater' pearls.

Pebble: Tiny stones or pebbles may be scattered on the floor to keep away witches. Kidney-shaped pebbles, especially black ones, are potent charms against the **Evil Eye**. White pebbles are used for divination.

Peddars Way: A prehistoric trackway that crosses Norfolk.

Pegomancy: Interpreting the images created as water runs from a fountain (see **Hydromancy**).

Pelagianism: A view that humanity is basically good and in possession of libertarian free will; a doctrine incompatible with biblical writ and historically opposed by Augustine (354–430), leading to its condemnation as a heresy at the Council of Carthage in 418AD. The doctrine was primarily recognized in Britain and Gaul.

Pellar: A term in traditional English folk-magic and witchcraft for a healer, diviner and maker of spells and charms.

Penates: Household gods of the Romans. They were venerated, together with the **Lares**, at the household hearth.

Pendle Witches: The second great 'witch-hunt' (see **Lancashire Witches**) took place in 1633 and saw over 30 people arrested, and 17 convicted of witchcraft. One of the accused was Jennet Device who, 20 years earlier, had been the key child witness in the first Lancashire trial.

Pendragon: According to *Brewer's Dictionary of Phrase & Fable*, a title conferred on several British chiefs in the time of great danger, when they were invested with dictatorial power. *'So much for fact, and now for the fable…'*, which comes from Geoffrey of Monmouth's *History*, books viii, xiv, xvii.

Pendulum: A suspended weight used in dowsing. A weight suspended from a thread or piece of string so that the pendulum can swing freely. SOURCE: *Pendulum Dowsing*, Tom Graves; *The Power of the Pendulum*, T.C. Lethbridge; *Practical Pendulum Book*, D Jurriaanse.

Penetralia: (1) The private rooms of a house; the secrets of a family. (2) Part of a Roman temple into which the priest alone had access. Here were the sacred images, the responses of the oracle and where the sacred **Mysteries** were performed. The Holy of Holies was the *penetralia* of the Jewish Temple.

Pen Dinas, Cardigan: An unusual double Iron Age hill fort with a considerable history of remodeling.

Penfound Manor, Cornwall: The oldest inhabited manor in Britain, part Saxon and Norman with Elizabethan and Stuart additions. It was mentioned in the Doomsday Book.

Pentacle: (1) Interestingly, *Brewer's Dictionary of Phrase and Fable* states that this refers to a five-sided head-dress of fine linen, meant to represent the five senses, and worn as a defense against demons in the act of conjuration. *'The Holy Pentacles numbered forty-four, of which seven were consecrated to each of the planets Saturn, Jupiter, Mars and the Sun; five to both Venus and Mercury; and six to the Moon. The divers figures were enclosed in a double circle, containing the name of god in Hebrew, and other mystical words.'* In this instance, no source is given for the information. (2) In modern occultism it is the symbol of the five-pointed star usually in the form of a disk made from wood, clay, wax, pottery or metal that is placed on the altar as part of the ritual equipment. It is often inscribed with a pentagram and other magical symbols. In *Magick*, Aleister Crowley wrote: *'All pentacles will contain the ultimate conceptions of the circle and the cross, though some will prefer to replace the cross by a point, or by a Tau, or by a triangle...'* SOURCE: *Techniques of High Magic*, Francis King and Stephen Skinner.

Pentagram: 'Drawn' – either by hand or performed by making the sign in the air, or on corresponding parts of the body. The methods of drawing opening and closing pentagrams are precise and vary according to the purpose of the ritual. The inverted pentagram has been used to represent evil or negative energy. SOURCE: *The Complete Golden Dawn System of Magic*, Israel Regardie.

Pentre Ifan: The finest example of the Pembrokeshire burial chambers, on the slopes of the Preseli mountains. Not only do the great uprights carry their capstone, estimated to weigh some 17 tons, but the upright slabs which formed the forecourt of the mound still stand to show that it was semi-circular in plan; the stones appear to be more carefully graded than usual.

Peony: Although the common peony was listed by **Aelfric**, it is not known how or when it was introduced into England. In the Middle Ages the seeds were used as a spice and a substitute for pepper. **Pliny** recommended taking fifteen black grains (seeds) in wine to prevent *'the mocking delusions that Fauns bring on us in our sleep.'* Ruling planet: **Sun** in **Leo**.

Pepys, Samuel: (1633–1703) English naval administrator and Member of Parliament, famous for the diary he kept for a decade while still a relatively young man. The detailed private diary, kept from 1660 until 1669 was first published in the 19th century, and is one of the most important primary sources for the Restoration period. It provides a combination of personal revelation and eyewitness accounts of great events, such as the Great Plague of London, the Second Dutch War and the Great Fire of London.

Perfume: The burning of perfumes has been a feature of worship for some 5000 years. The fragrance was thought to render the sacrifice more acceptable to the deity (see **Aromatherapy**).

Periwinkle or **Sorcerer's Violet:** Listed by **Aelfric**, the plant was a symbol of immortality and sometimes worn by those about to be executed. Medicinally it was used to check internal bleeding and **Culpeper** said, *'it is a great binder, and stays bleeding at the mouth and nose, if it be chewed.'* Ruling planet: **Venus**.

Persephone or **Kore:** In classic literature she is the daughter of **Zeus** and **Demeter**, who was carried off by **Hades** to the underworld. Homer calls her 'dread Persephone' and makes her the wife of the lord of the underworld, who is terrible and a sender of terrifying ghosts and apparitions, like **Hecate** with whom she is sometimes identified. The myth of her abduction and the angry grief of Demeter appears for the first time in the Homeric *Hymn to Demeter*. The **Eleusian Mysteries** reflect this story.

Perth Witch Trial: The report from a trial in Perth in 1623 is valuable for showing some of the allegations, which in Scotland would bring about an arrest for witchcraft: simple folk charms (generally of a beneficent nature), and washing and bathing! The basic pact with the **Devil** was automatically assumed.

Pessomancy: Divination using pebbles cast onto the ground and interpreting the patterns formed.

Petro: A **Voodoo** term that distinguishes the rites of the 'infernal' **Loa** from those of the more acceptable kind of Rada rites.

Peyote: The native **Amerindians** say that unless a man is morally upright he cannot use peyote because the cactus that produces visions is regarded as a teacher, healer and savior of their race. The cult surrounding the use of the drug appears to have begun around 1870 but only documented from 1890, the year of the great **Ghost Dance.**

Phallic Symbolism: The reproductive organs of both male and female were often modeled in disproportionate size to stress their power and importance. These images were treated with reverence and not considered at all smutty or disgusting. The most well-known phallic symbol within traditional witchcraft is the fashioning

of the handle of the besom.

Phantasm: see **Phantom.**

Phantasmagoria: A fantastic series of illusory images.

Phantom: From the Greek word *phantasma*, meaning an apparition, or spectre.

Pharaoh: Term regularly used by modern writers to refer to any Egyptian monarch. The word is the Greek form of the ancient Egyptian phrase *per-aa* ('great house'), which was originally used to refer to the royal palace rather than the king. Only from the New Kingdom (1550–1069 BC) onwards, was the term used to refer to the king himself.

Pharmacopoeia: [Greek *pharmakopoiiā – pharmakon*, a drug, *poieein*, to make.] A book or list of drugs with directions for their preparation. The first known dated work of this kind published under civic authority appears to have been that of Nuremberg in 1542; a passing student named Valerius Cordus showed a collection of medical receipts, which he had selected from the writings of the most eminent medical authorities, to the physicians of the town, who urged him to print it for the benefit of the apothecaries. A work known as the *Antidotarium Florentinum* was published under the authority of the college of medicine of Florence in the 16th century. The term *Pharmacopoeia* first appears as a distinct title in a work published at Basel in 1561 but does not appear to have come into general use until the beginning of the 17th century. Until 1617 such drugs and medicines as were in common use were sold in England by the apothecaries and grocers. In that year the apothecaries obtained a separate charter, and it was enacted that no grocer should keep an apothecary's shop. The preparation of physicians' prescriptions was thus confined to the apothecaries, upon whom pressure was brought to bear to make them dispense accurately, by the issue of a pharmacopoeia in May 1618 by the College of Physicians. This, the first authorized *London Pharmacopoeia*, was found to be so full of errors that the whole edition was cancelled, and a fresh edition was published in the following December.

Phenomenology: The science of observing or a description of phenomena; the philosophy of Edmund Husserl (1859–1938), concerned with the experiences of the Self.

Phenomenology of Religion: The orderly study of religious (or spiritual) phenomena, setting aside all assumptions about the truth or falsity of specific beliefs and reality of putative objects of religious experience.

Pheromone: A natural chemical substance secreted by an animal that influences the behavior of others of its species.

Philosopher's Stone: Refers to the **Great Work** of the alchemist, which is to find or make the Stone that could transmute impure substance into a rarefied state. Alchemical texts were not written to provide outsiders with information, and directions for making the Philosopher's Stone were frequently couched in symbolic language so deliberately obscure that it has largely defied interpretation ever since.

Philosophia: In so far as it seeks an ultimate explanation of the cosmos, a great deal of Greek philosophy can be viewed as philosophy of religion, constructing physical/metaphysical counterparts to religious belief. Some thinkers associated natural or metaphysical entities with traditional divinities. SOURCE: *The Penguin Dictionary of Religions*, ed John R. Hinnells.

Philter: A magic potion to inspire or destroy love. SOURCE: *Magic: An Occult Primer*, David Conway.

Phlegethon: [Greek *phlego*, to burn] A river of liquid fire in **Hades**.

Phoenix: The archetypal alchemical bird, rising from the ashes, demonstrates the alchemical process of life and death (see **Bennu Bird**). An image of the recurring symbol of time.

Phrātriā: ('brotherhood') At Athens in primitive times, a clan, consisting of a noble family and its dependants, who shared in the family cult. This later developed into various religious organizations and their great festival was the *Apaturia*, held annually in October.

Phrenology: Divination by interpreting the bumps on a person's head is a relatively modern method, dating from 18th century when Dr. Franz Gall (1756–1828) published the definitive work on the subject, *The Physiognomical System*.

Phyllomancy: Divination by examining the shape, pattern, veins and color of leaves, believing to be a Druidic method of foretelling the future.

Phyllorhodomancy: Supposedly an ancient Greek method of divining the future by placing the petal of a rose in the palm of the right hand, and then firmly slapping the hands together. A burst petal meant the answer was 'yes' and if the petal remained intact, the answer was 'no'.

Physiognomy: Divination of the future by reading a person's face according to the first book on the subject published in China, *Ma Yee Shang Fa = The Simple Guide to Face Reading*.

Physicians of Myddfai: see **Myddfai**.

Picardy Stone: Aberdeen: A Pictish symbol stone that stands in a small enclosure close to a byroad near Insch. Its designs are those of the abstract symbol series, such as Z-rod, serpent, mirror and double-disc.

Picatrix: An 11th century Arabian compendium of magic based upon much earlier Greek sources, which contains a vast amount of esoteric cosmology, astrology, talismans and incantations. The text has not been available in any modern form until the publication of a German version in 1962.

Pickingill, George: (1816–1909) The leader of a group of witches in Canewdon, Essex during the late 1800s, from which the East Anglian Pickingill Craft originates. SOURCE: *The Pickingill Papers*, W.E. Liddell, ed by Michael Howard.

Pig: In cultural and religious thought, the pig is revered by some and loathed by others. It is the Buddhist symbol of indolence and in Europe of license; it was worshipped in Crete, and in Greece sacrificed to the gods. For both the Arabs and the Jews the meat is taboo; the ancient Egyptians looked at the animal from both sides, on account of the pig representing **Osiris** at sowing time and **Set** at the harvest; pig meat was only eaten by them at the **Midwinter** feast, and a pig could only be sacrificed at the full moon. The pig was prone to witchcraft and ill-wishing as were all farm animals.

Pigeon: Widely feared as a pagan death omen, they were nevertheless extensively used in a last ditch attempt to save someone who was dying. Pigeon hearts were sometimes used as an integral part of spellcasting, either as counter-magic or in a love charm. Pigeons have been domesticated since 4000BC and for centuries were used as message-carriers – in Beach House Park, Worthing, there was a drinking pool and stone memorial to the 'warrior birds', carrier pigeons killed in the war. The wild variety known as wood pigeons have a wide range of culinary and medicinal uses.

Pike: No other freshwater fish *'conjures up such an aura of raw ferocity and naked sharp-toothed aggression'*, as this voracious predator that lies in wait for its prey among aquatic vegetation. The teeth of the fish are useful ingredients in magical working.

Pillar: Refers to the two columns that flank the doorways to the inner world, through which the magician passes when entering his temple on the astral or mundane planes. The left-hand pillar is black and the right-hand silver. Also refers to the three columns on the Tree of Life – Severity, Mildness and Mercy. SOURCE: *The Hollow Tree*, Mélusine Draco; *The Mystical Qabalah*, Dion Fortune.

Pin: A common tool used in spells for **Cursing** and **Bottling**. Old-fashioned hat pins were also used to 'spike' wax images.

Pine: A symbol of longevity and immortality (see **Scots Pine**).

Piper: A minor office held in an **Old Craft** coven, and one connected specifically to the **Dame** rather than the **Magister** (see **Officer**).

Pisces: (1) The last sign in the zodiac – 19 February–21 March – in Graeco-Roman mythology the fishes are identified with **Aphrodite** and her son, Heros. (2) The ring of stars in the western fish, which is beneath Pegasus, is called the Circlet; and the eastern fish is beneath Andromeda.

Pixies: Small fairy-like spirits from the West Country in England, who are amused by leading travelers astray.

Planchette: A variant of the Ouija board with a pencil attached for receiving automatic writing.

Plancy, Collin de: (1793–1887) Regarded as an authority in the occult sciences, his *Infernal Dictionary* went through six different editions between 1818 and 1863. Among the other works ascribed to him are: *The Devil's Self-Portrait* (1819), *Critical Dictionary of Relics* (1821), *Dictionary of Occult Sciences* (1846–1852), *History of Ghosts & Demons* (1819), *History of Vampires* (1820), and numerous works on myths and legends.

Planets: In esoteric terms, the heavenly bodies believed by astrologists to influence events on earth, and particularly the personalities and fortunes of mankind. The best source for **Planetary Influences** is Aleister Crowley's *Liber 777* and *Magic: An Occult Primer* by David Conway (see **Astronomy** and **Astrology**).

Planetary Hours: Each hour of the day and night is aligned with a planetary influence and is an integral part of all magical working. Planetary hours are divided into two parts – sunrise to sunset and sunset to sunrise – and calculated by the exact rising and setting of the sun.

Plantagenet: An English ruling family, descended from the Angevin nobility. They were often described as 'the Devil's Brood' on account of their ancestress being Mélusine the enchantress and because of their long, turbulent reign and ruthlessness.

Throughout the medieval period the belief in witchcraft and sorcery was an important element in the intellectual climate of the period. Accusations of witchcraft were leveled (at times successfully) in every reign against members of the royal family. The most famous cases were those brought against Eleanor Cobham, Duchess of Gloucester and Jacquetta, Duchess of Bedford. SOURCE: *Witchcraft and the Sons of York*, W.E. Hampton (*The Ricardian*, March 1980); *Who's Who in Late Medieval England*, Michael Hicks; *The Conquering Family*, Thomas B. Costain.

Plantain: One of the **Nine Sacred** Herbs of the Anglo-Saxons. The leaves were used to poultice wounds, blisters and bites. Internally it was used for gastric ulcers, catarrh and sinus problems. Ruling planet: **Mars**.

Plant Medicine: see **Folk Medicine**.

Pliny: (1) Pliny the Elder (23–79AD) a Roman author of *Natural History* of which little importance is attached today, and (2) Pliny the Younger (62–112AD), his nephew, who provided valuable information on plants and the layout of Roman gardens.

Plough Monday: The day farming resumed after the **Yule** holidays, when ploughs were blessed and accompanied by traditional **Mummers** and **Sword Dances**, echoing the death and rebirth theme of the agricultural year.

Plum: Listed by **Aelfric**, plums were plentiful in the wild and seldom grown in gardens. They had both culinary and medicinal uses and **Culpeper** prescribed the gum or leaves boiled in vinegar for skin disease and ringworm. Ruling planet: **Venus**.

Pluto: (1) Also called **Hades**, the Greek god ruled the kingdom of the underworld with his queen **Persephone/Kore**. (2) There is no association in classical astrology. (3) The Solar System's most distant planet, it loops around the Sun in a strange orbit, accompanied by its unusually large moon, Charon. Its status as a planet is an ongoing dispute in scientific circles. (4) and (5) There are no alchemical or magical associations with the planet, as it was only discovered in 1930.

Pneuma: The Greek word for air, breath and spirit, which raised a great deal of physiological and philosophical debate in the ancient world, concerning the similarity between air and breath (without which mankind cannot live) and the spirit (which animates the body).

Podomancy: An ancient Eastern method of divination by studying the lines on the feet.

Pointing: Witches and sorcerers from many different cultures are believed to have the power to kill by pointing, often using bones as a pointer.

Poison: Poisoning has always had a close connection with witchcraft and the powers of darkness, despite the fact that there were dozens of highly toxic plants in rural fields and hedgerows 'readily available to anyone with murder in mind'. The most highly publicized case of mass poisoning associated with witchcraft was known as the **Chambre Ardente Affair** in the 17th century. It has also been suggested that because in classical times 'witch' and 'poisoner' were often synonymous, the biblical translation should have read: 'Thou shalt not suffer a *poisoner* to live.' SOURCE: *Compendium Maleficarum*, Guazzo; *The Encyclopedia of Witchcraft & Demonology*, Russell Hope Robbins.

Poison Detectors: It is said that: **Opals** turn pale; Peacocks ruffle their feathers; Venetian glass will shiver; and if poison is put into a cup made of Rhinoceros horn, the liquid will effervesce.

Poison Tree: see **Proving Tree**.

Politike: The state-cult, with its monumental temples and spectacular festivals, was used in ancient Greece to manipulate the promotion of certain cults.

Poltergeists: More often than not, pockets of psychic energy normally associated with adolescents. The word comes from the German, meaning 'noisy ghost'. SOURCE: *Dictionary of Demons*, Fred Gettings; *The Encyclopedia of Witchcraft & Demonology*, Rossell Hope Robbins; *Man, Myth & Magic*, Richard Cavendish.

Polytheism: The belief in, or worship of, many gods who preside over different departments of life.

Poplar: An indigenous British tree with plenty of medicinal benefits. Poplar leaves were one of the ingredients used in making the 'witches' flying ointment'.

Poplifugia: A significant religious

festival that honored Jupiter (5th July). It was a day of feasting and celebration but the ancient rites were obscure even to the Romans.

Poppet: A waxen image or doll of a person used for cursing or hexing.

Poppy: Symbol of sleep, death and the soothing of pain because it yields opium. The flower was associated with the Roman goddess **Ceres**, because it grew in wheatfields; and with the Egyptian god, **Set**. There was a widespread belief that the poppy sprang from the blood of fallen warriors and since WWI it has been the symbol of remembrance of those killed in battle. The plant was listed by **Aelfric** and a syrup made from poppy seeds was given to relieve coughs, throat infections, chest complaints, insomnia and whooping cough. Ruling planet: Moon.

Portents: Signs foretelling future events, especially calamitous ones.

Poseidon: Greek sea god who Homer rates as one of the most powerful gods along with **Zeus**, lord of heaven and **Hades**, lord of the underworld. He often appeared in the shape of a horse, and was venerated as the patron of horse breeding; in Corinth horse races were held in his honor. His Roman counterpart is **Neptune**.

Possession: As defined by the Christian Church, i.e. the existence of the demonic, is more than often based on myth. According to psychologist, Marc Cramer, the overwhelming majority of all reported cases are the result of hysteria or fraud. Demonical possession is exceedingly rare. A leading authority on parapsychological issues, Cramer acted as an advisor

to BBC Cymru and is a member of the **Society for Psychical Research.** SOURCE: *The Devils of Loudon*, Aldous Huxley; *The Devil Within*, Marc Cramer; *Dictionary of Demons*, Fred Gettings; *The Encyclopedia of Witchcraft & Demonology*, Rossell Hope Robbins.

Posset: A hot drink made from ale, honey and herbs. Refined people spooned their posset out of a silver pot; the less refined sipped it from the spout of an earthenware one.

Potion: A dose of liquid medicine or poison.

Powders: Poisons in powdered form, which women bought from witches in the 16th century in order to make themselves widows.

Power Objects: Personal items which have magical properties, a psychic battery. Material objects charged with witch-power and transferred into a subject's presence to effect a certain result.

Power of Mythos: The importance of linking the correct mythological correspondences to magical working. [SEE PANEL]

Prana: In Hindu yoga, a universal energy associated with the breath, absorbed into and used by the human body to maintain health and fitness. Sanskrit for 'life force'.

Pranava: The mystic syllable or primal vibration OM.

Pranayama: The control or direction to magical or mystical ends of **Prana**.

Prayer: An entreaty, petition, or communication with a god or spiritual power.

Prayer Flag: A strip of cloth on which is written a prayer or request. Usually tied to a tree or bush and represents a

The Power of Mythos

All magical energy should be looked upon as dangerous, if the magician fails to understand what it is that he is calling upon. 'God'-power can be equally as destructive as demonic-energy if we haven't bothered to find out *exactly* what it is that we're channeling for magical purposes. Any problems stemming from this lack of recognition are the result of sheer arrogance on the part of the magician, who believes he can control something that he isn't even on nodding acquaintance with.

For the reasons of self-protection, we must be fully conversant with the nature of the energies we encounter on the astral levels. We need to differentiate between the *individual* god-power represented by Aphrodite (Greek), Venus (Roman), Hathor (Egyptian), Ishtar (Babylonian) or Astarte (Phoenician). In eclectic paganism, all these energies would be identified as having one source, i.e. the Goddess — which is why much of what passes for modern magic is often sterile.

To understand the true god-power emanating from each source, we have to understand what the indigenous peoples who worshipped them called upon, not what we read in dumbed-down, quasi-magical books. If we read genuine magical material from the Golden Dawn or Aleister Crowley, for example, we are instantly struck by the wealth of classical references in the texts. These were not scattered through the text at random; they were carefully controlled and contrived in order to produce the maximum effect in a particular working.

It may also come as a surprise to learn that myth, folklore and legend are now recognized as a vital part of the development of the human race, rather than just a confused jumble of ancient cultural stories. Myths that might, at first glance, seem merely products of fancy are very far from being merely fanciful, and are the means by which ancient peoples expressed their fundamental notions of life and nature. These enduring myths are the *actual methods* by which they expressed certain ways of viewing the 'rules' of life, and which were brought into existence by the manner in which life was regulated in their society. **The myths reflect the morality according to the lights of their time.**

When we talk about the 'mythology of Egypt' for example, we are referring to the whole body of Egypt divine, heroic and cosmogonic legends, together with the various attempts that have been made to explain these ancient narratives for the benefit of *modern* thinking. The real function of these myths, however, was to strengthen the existing tradition and endow it with a greater value and prestige by tracing it back to a higher, more 'supernatural' reality of ancient events. What men have thought throughout history about the supernatural *is* important not only for what it may tell us about the Mysteries of life and death as the ancients viewed it, but for what it tells us about human beings today. If nothing else, it shows what we have lost!

Very early in the history of conscious thought, the priesthood awoke to the reality that their religious stories (i.e. those that concealed the Mysteries) were much in need of public explanation. As a result, popular versions took over and the esoteric became exoteric. The myths of civilized peoples: the Aryans of India, the Celts, the Egyptians and the Greeks thus contained two elements: the rational and what to modern minds sees the irrational. The rational myths were those that represented the gods as beautiful and wise; but the *real* difficulties presented by mythology spring from the irrational elements, which to modern minds appear unnatural, senseless or even, at times, repellent.

It is to these *irrational* elements that the magician must turn if he wishes to reconnect with the ancient Mysteries, which still lie at the very heart of the Great Work. For the true seeker, the great classic myths remain 'true' stories; not because we think they really happened but because they contain certain 'universal truths' about humanity and life. Truths which cannot be translated into plain statement.

EXTRACT FROM THE TEMPLE OF KHEM STUDY COURSE
MÉLUSINE DRACO

very old method of entreaty.

Prayer Wheel: Tibetan prayer wheels convey a blessing when turned to the right, the side of good, but a curse when the movement is to the left.

Preseli Mountains: From this area about 80 five-ton 'blue stones' were transported the 240 miles to **Stonehenge**, where they were erected to form the inner horseshoe and middle ring enclosed by the circle of large sarsen stones. To the east of the 'quarry', on the summit of the eastern-most knoll of the Preselis, is the 11-acre Iron Age hill fort known as Moel Trigarn.

Precession: A term that frequently occurs in magical texts (see **Calendar**). Because of the tidal effects of the Sun and Moon, the Earth 'wobbles' like a spinning top, causing the direction of the vernal equinox to shift in the sky. The wobble is called precession and takes place over 26,000 years. The Vernal Equinox is now in **Pisces**, but over the full wobble it will move through all the signs in the zodiac: in 200BC the **Vernal** Equinox was in **Aries**. The celestial poles also move, so **Polaris**, our northern pole star, will be of little use to us in 1,000 years time. SOURCE: *Calendars & Constellations of the Ancient World*, Emmeline Plunkett.

Precognition: A received message in the form of a symbol or sign as to what is going to happen in the future.

Predestination: A doctrine that states whatever is to happen has been unalterably fixed by Fate from the beginning of time.

Prediction: Psychically obtained information.

Prehistoric Religion: Cultural remains from pre-recorded history suggest that early man developed an, all be it primitive, religious view of burial and ancestral worship (see **Cave Art**).

Premonition: Knowledge of what is going to happen in the future, usually in the form of intuition or insight.

Pretani: The indigenous people of the British Isles from a Celtic word meaning the 'painted people' or the 'tattooed ones'. SOURCE: *The Tribes of Britain*, David Miles.

Priapus: An old Phrygian god of fertility, he was represented as an ugly, satyr-like creature with exaggerated genitals. He was also the Greek patron of fishermen and sailors.

Pricking: Linked to the theory of **Witch's Marks**, supposedly confirming the victim's branding by **Satan**. Matthew **Hopkins** was suspected of using false bodkins with retractable blades so that the accused witch would feel no pain when it was put against her flesh. SOURCE: *The Encyclopedia of Witchcraft & Demonology*, Rossell Hope Robbins.

Priddy Circles, Somerset: This complex consists of four circles, each about 200 yards across and set in a straight line almost a mile long. There are numerous round barrows close to the site of the circles, probably the burials of the people who used these sacred sites.

Pride of the Morning: An early mist or shower that promises a fine day.

Priest: The priesthood, medicine men or shamans are 'specialists in the supernatural', who provide a channel of communication between humans and the divine. Members of different priesthoods may have little in common except for their ability to establish contact with gods and spirits.

Priestess or **High Priestess:** (1) A rank within the **Coven** system in contemporary **Wicca**. (2) The third card in the standard **Tarot** deck and the archetypal priestess of the hidden Mysteries.

Primeval Mound: The hill that emerged from the primeval waters was an important element in ancient Egyptian thought and imagery (see **Mound**).

Primitive Astronomy: The connection between megalithic monuments and their prehistoric alignment with the stars (see **Astronomy** and **Astro-archeology**). SOURCE: *Starchild*, Mélusine Draco; *Prehistoric Astronomy & Ritual*, Aubrey Burl; *Astronomy before the Telescope*, ed Christopher Walker.

Primrose: A native of Britain, the plant had various medicinal uses. In folklore it was said that by eating the flowers children could see fairies; they were also used in love potions, and in charms to protect against evil. Ruling planet: **Venus**.

Prímum Móbile: In the Ptolomaic system of astronomy, this was the tenth (not the ninth) sphere, supposed to revolve from east to west in 24 hours, carrying with it all the other spheres. The eleven spheres are: (1) **Diana** or the **Moon**, (2) **Mercury**, (3) **Venus**, (4) **Apollo** or the **Sun**, (5) **Mars**, (6) **Jupiter**, (7) **Saturn**, (8) the starry sphere or that of the fixed stars, (9) the crystalline, (10) the prímum móbile, and (11) the empyréan. Ptolemy himself only acknowledged the first nine; the latter two were devised by his followers. The motion of the crystalline, according to this system, caused the precession of the equinoxes, its axis being that of the ecliptic. The motion of the prímum móbile produces the alternation of night and day; its axis is that of the equator, and its extremities the poles of the heavens.

Prodigia: Signs received by the Romans to indicate that the normal order between gods and men (*pax deorum*, 'peace of mind') had been disturbed. The signs took the form of unusual or extraordinary events such as buildings struck by lightening, abnormal births, wild animals penetrating cities, rains of blood, milk or stones. The priests identified the deity who had been offended and recommended appropriate measures (*remedia*) be taken to restore the balance.

Profane: To treat holy or sacred objects or places with scorn or desecration. To the Romans it referred to the uninitiated, meaning literally 'before the temple', Latin *pro fanum*.

Prometheus: Having made images of men out of clay, he stole fire from heaven to animate them. In punishment, **Zeus** had him chained to Mount Caucasus, where an eagle daily tore at his liver.

Prométhean Fire: The vital principle; the fire with which Prometheus quickened into life his clay images. *'I know not where is that Promethean heat/That can thy life relume.'* Shakespeare, *Othello*, v.2.

Promethean Unguent: Made from an herb on which some of the blood of Prometheus had fallen. **Medea** gave Jason some of this unguent in order to render his body proof against fire and warlike instruments.

Prometheans: The first invention that developed into Bryant & May's 'safety matches'. They were originally made in 1805 by Chancel, a French chemist, who tipped cedar splints with a paste of chlorate of potash and sugar. On dipping one of these matches into a little bottle containing asbestos wetted with sulfuric acid, it burst into flame on drawing it out. It was not introduced into England until after the battle of Waterloo.

Promise of Odin: The most binding of all promises to a Scandinavian. In making this promise the person passed his hand through a massive silver ring kept for the purpose, or through a hole in a sacrificial stone, like the one called the Circle of Stennis.

Prophecy: (see **Divination**).

Prophesy Upon Velvet: To prophesy what is already a known fact because it *'goes on velvet slippers without fear of stumbling'*.

Prospero: In Shakespeare's *The Tempest*, he is the rightful Duke of Milan. Deposed by his brother and exiled to a desert island where he practices magic and raises a tempest in which his brother is shipwrecked.

Protection: In magical terms, measures taken to preserve the well-being of a person, thing or building, and keep negative energies at bay.

Proteus: Neptune's herdsman, an old man and a prophet. He was the archetypal **Shape-shifter** and could transform himself in an instant into any form he chose.

Providence: Power that determines the course of all events, distinguished from **Fate** because it is regarded as benevolent.

Proving Tree: During the Middle Ages, through the Renaissance and up to the French Revolution, the royal banqueting table had a curious object of tableware. A metal stand often

attached to the salt dish that had from five to fifteen different stone pendants hanging from its branches. Each stone was believed to detect different poisons, and it was the chamberlain's job to dip the stones, one by one, into the monarch's food and wine as it was brought from the kitchen.

Psi: An umbrella term used by parapsychologists to describe paranormal phenomena.

Psyche: From the Greek meaning life, soul, spirit or mind and in classical mythology the mortal girl with whom Cupid fell in love. The story, told in Apuleius's *The Golden Ass*, illustrates the parable of the union between the human soul and divine love. The modern dictionary meaning: the principle of mental and emotional life, conscious and unconscious.

Psychic: That which is of the mind or psyche; sensitive to or in touch with that which has not yet been explained physically.

Psychical Research: In the last 150 years scientific examination has been used to investigate ghosts, mediumship and other paranormal phenomena, including ESP and telekinesis, although it is not a term that is easy to define. The stated purpose of the **Society for Psychical Research** is to 'examine without prejudice or prepossession and in a scientific spirit those faculties of man, real or supposed, which appear to be inexplicable'. SOURCE: *The Founders of Psychical Research*, A. Gauld.

Psychic Attack: A mental attack by one magical practitioner on another in order to cause illness, harm or accident. An extremely debilitating method for both parties. SOURCE: *The Magical Arts*, Richard Cavendish; *Psychic Self-Defense*, Dion Fortune; *Mastering Witchcraft*, Paul Huson.

Psychic Power: A collective term for what are seen as supernatural or paranormal abilities such as **Levitation** (raising the body from the ground without perceptible means of support); **Psychokinesis** (moving objects without physical contact); **Precognition** (knowledge of future events); **Telepathy** ((knowledge of others' thoughts); **Clairvoyance** and **Clairaudience** ('seeing' and 'hearing' beyond the range of sensory perception) etc. The last four are often classified as **Extrasensory perception (ESP)**.

Psychic Vampire: A person who drains another's energy on a continuous basis but not necessarily via psychic means. Overdemanding family or friends can produce the same debilitating effect (see **Vampire**).

Psychodrama: Commonly known as 'the bells and smells' approach to magical practice. Usually refers to the methods used by those who need the hype of ritual before being able to get on their contacts.

Psychokinesis: The ability to influence or control physical matter through mental concentration.

Psychometry: (see **Object Reading**).

Psychopomp: A term used for the conductor of souls of the dead to the Otherworld, or a spirit guide or 'one who can move between the worlds'. The archetypal psychopomp is Anubis, the jackal-headed god of the Egyptians as part of the Mysteries. SOURCE: *The Setian*, Billie Walker-John.

Ptah: The principal Egyptian god of Memphis, who was the protector of artisans and artists, and the inventor of the arts. Worshipped from the earliest time, he is usually represented as a mummified figure, with his skull encased in a tight headband.

Puck: Derives from the Old English *pucca*, or mischievous sprite, better known in English folklore as Robin Goodfellow. It is also another name for the nightjar. SOURCE: *The Anatomy of Puck*, K.M. Briggs.

Purification: A cleansing of impurities and negative influences from people, objects or places by the means of prayer and/or magical application.

Purulli Festival: The principal Anatolian festival known as *Purulliyas*, a term meaning 'of the earth', and celebrated in the spring.

Pwyll: [Welsh = understanding, judgement] An ancient Welsh god of the underworld, whose son, Pryderi, brought pigs from the underworld to Wales.

Pyramid: (1) A solid figure on a triangular square, or polygonal base, with triangular sides meeting in a point. (2) The pyramidal structures of ancient Egypt and Central America.

Pyramidology: The attempt to prove a theory first proposed by John Taylor in 1859, and developed by the Astronomer Royal, Charles Piazzi Smith in 1864. This theory held that the Great Pyramid was built with supernormal knowledge. SOURCE: *Our Inheritance in the Great Pyramid*, Charles Piazzi Smith; *Pyramidology*, Adam Rutherford; *Supernature*, Lyall Watson.

Pyramid Texts: The earliest Egyptian funerary texts, comprising some 800 spells or 'utterances' written in columns on the walls of the corridors of

funerary temples and burial chambers.
SOURCE: *The Ancient Egyptian Pyramid Texts*, R.O. Faulkner.

Pyromancy: Divination using flames.

Pyrrhic Dance: The most famous war-dance of antiquity; it was danced to the flute and its time was very quick. Julius Caesar introduced it into Rome and the *Romaika*, still danced in Greece in modern times, is supposed to be a relic.

Pythagoras: Greek philosopher and mathematician, who was also a mystic, teaching the importance of contemplation and meditation. His doctrine placed a special emphasis upon the significance of numbers as symbols of cosmic principles.

Python: Originally the name of the serpent slain by **Apollo** at **Delphi**. It has been suggested, however, that the legend relates to the existence of a telluric or chthonic mystery cult at Delphi that was displaced by the solar mysteries associated with Apollo. The Pythoness was a woman with the gift of prophecy.

Q

Qabalah: Has as its central motif the Tree of Life and probably more than any other magical system or mystical philosophy, has had a profound influence on the development of Western occultism. Qabalistic learning focuses on the levels of consciousness between man and the Divine, where the magician begins with his present level of 'earth consciousness' and attempts to reconnect with the Absolute via the ten sephiroth of **Malkuth, Yesod, Hod, Netzach, Tiphareth, Geburah, Chesed, Binah, Chokmah** and **Kether**. SOURCE: *The Anatomy of Fate*, Z'ev ben Shimon Halevi; *The Complete Golden Dawn System of Magic*, Israel Regardie; *The Essence of the Practical Qabalah*, Frater Achad; *The Garden of Pomegranates*, Israel Regardie; *The History of Magic*, Kurt Seligmann; *The Hollow Tree*, Mélusine Draco; *An Introduction to the Mystical Qabalah*, Alan Richardson; *The Kabbalah Unveiled*, S. MacGregor Mathers; *The Kabbalistic Prayer*, Eliphas Lévi; *The Magical Arts*, Richard Cavendish; *Magic: An Occult Primer*, David Conway; *The Middle Pillar*, Israel Regardie; *The Mystical Qabalah*, Dion Fortune; *The Qabalah*, Will Parfitt; *The Shining Paths*, Dolores Ashcroft-Nowicki. [SEE PANEL]

Qabalistic Cross: A magical gesture referred to repeatedly throughout the **Golden Dawn** system of working and **Crowley's Thelemic** writings. SOURCE: *The Complete Golden Dawn System of Magic*, Israel Regardie; *The Equinox*, Aleister Crowley.

Qadosh: [Hebrew] Holy, primitive, ancient, original, first cause. This term has a highly technical significance in occultism. SOURCE: *Aleister Crowley and the Hidden God*, Kenneth Grant.

Qesheth: (1) A rainbow. (2) In esoteric terms it is associated with the alchemical symbolism for putrefication.

Qliphoth: (singular form *Qlipha* = harlot) The name given to a world or plane of soulless entities that are not truly living, but merely lingering shells of once conscious humans. Each sephirah of the **Tree of Life** has its corresponding qliphoth, which is the reflection of the energies that it represents. SOURCE: *The Hollow Tree*, Mélusine Draco; *The Mystical Qabalah*, Dion Fortune; *The Magical Revival*, Kenneth Grant.

Quaker Witchcraft: The founder of the Society of Friends, George Fox, never questioned 'the spirit of witchcraft', but ridiculed such superstitions as witches raising storms, and telling seafaring men not to be deluded. As a result, the Quakers often found themselves abused and linked with witchcraft. Pennsylvania had only one trial ,in 1683, of an old Swedish woman accused of bewitching animals but this was quickly dealt with. The presiding magistrate asked her: *'Art thou a witch? Hast thou ridden through the air on a broomstick?'* The confused woman said she had, and the magistrate replied that she had a perfect right to do so, as there was no law against it, and ordered the trial dismissed!

Quadrivium: The four higher subjects of scholastic philosophy up to the 12th century. It embraced music,

Qabalah

Upon first introduction, the Qabalah appears to baffle the student with a blanket of pseudo-magical science and nonsensical imagery. Indeed there are dozens of incomprehensible tomes on the subject that do little to shed light on this ancient philosophy. Modern occultists of all types have been influenced by the power of the Qabalah, although strictly speaking it is a system of Hebrew mystical thought which originated in southern France and Spain in the 12–13th centuries; there are Rabbinic references to much earlier influences, probably Chaldean. The word means 'receiving' or 'that which is received' and by the 2nd–3rd century AD, it had been reinterpreted as a mystery tradition — especially one handed down by word of mouth – although it was a long way removed from the esoteric connotations that surround its modern usage.

The 'magical' version familiar to 20th century occultists is that expanded and revised by Eliphas Lévi in the 19th century, and by Dion Fortune and Aleister Crowley in the 20th.

The fundamental idea of the Qabalah is that the Universe may be regarded as an elaboration of the numbers 0–10, arranged in a certain geometric design and connected by 22 'paths'. Qabalistic study claims to reduce all possible ideas to combinations of comparatively few originals, the ten numbers, in fact; these ten numbers being, of course, interrelated. The problem for the novice is the acquisition of perfect comprehension as to the essential nature of these numbers.

The entry in *Man, Myth & Magic* states that the backbone of the Qabalistic system is its doctrine of deity, which distinguishes between the inaccessible and the unknowable, *deus absconditus* (the hidden god) on the one hand, and the self-revealing dynamic god of religious experience on the other. Of the former not even existence can be predicted. This is the paradoxical fullness of the great divine Nothing.

In simplistic terms the Tree of Life comprises of three columns, which are positive, negative and neutral; its ten *sephiroth* (spheres) which correspond to a planet and are seen as a diagram of the way in which the universe came into existence. Each *sephiroth* is attributed with certain key symbols and qualities but the student quickly learns to make his own associations 'until eventually he will relate to every aspect of his existence, every happening within him and without, with the interrelated symbolism of the spheres upon the Tree'.

Conversely, it is also seen as a diagram of the way in which man can unite himself with, or become the One by rising up through the spheres—spiritually climbing the ladder of the ten *sephiroth* to reach 'God'. The twenty-two Major Arcana of the Tarot symbolize the twenty-two paths that link the ten *sephiroth* together, and provide mystical pathways along which the magician travels.

Perhaps the most accessible works on the subject are Alan Richardson's *An Introduction to the Mystical Qabalah*, which was first published in 1974 and not been out of print since; Mélusine Draco's *The Hollow Tree*, a thorough yet elementary guide to working with the Qabalah and Tarot as a practical introduction to the roots of Western ritual magic techniques; Dion Fortune's *The Mystical Qabalah*, which focuses on the correspondences, which in turn are based on the *otz chaim*, of the Tree of Life. The simple system of the latter has been described as the 'mighty all-embracing glyph of the Universe and the soul of man' capable of infinite interpretations on an infinite number of levels. Alan Richardson, writing on Fortune's approach to the subject in *Priestess*, added: 'Once planted within the psyche it grows and grows, almost impossible to uproot. It links heaven and Hades, and leads mankind up or down, only to find that one is the same as the other. We can make it grow exactly how we want, give it any slant and make it bear any fruit.'

EXTRACT FROM *WHAT YOU CALL TIME*
A PRACTICAL GUIDE TO MODERN WITCHCRAFT & RITUAL MAGIC
SUZANNE RUTHVEN

arithmetic, geometry and astronomy. The *quadrivium* was the 'fourfold way' to knowledge; the *trivium* was the 'three-fold way' to eloquence – both together encompassed the seven arts or sciences.

Quarters: The four cardinal points of the **Circle** (see **Compass**).

Quartz: The most common rock-forming mineral; composed of silica, and occurring in hexagonal crystals (clear and colorless when pure). The traditional **Crystal Ball** and **Shewstone** were made from polished quartz.

Quartz Crystal: A disc or rod cut in certain directions from a piece of piezoelectric quartz and ground so that it vibrates naturally at a particular frequency.

Quasar: A point-like source of brilliant light of all colors. In **Astronomy**, quasars are very distant, primeval objects, deep in Look-back Time, near the limit of the visible universe.

Quasi: [Latin] Something that is not the real thing, but may be accepted in its place.

Queen of the Witches: A derogatory term for someone publicly claiming high rank within witchcraft. A silly appellation often given by the media to anyone giving interviews and claiming to speak on behalf of the entire Craft community.

Querant: One who asks; a seeker.

Question, Put to the: Subjected to torture to extract a confession for witchcraft or heresy.

Question de la Strie: Published in 1505, this was one of the few works prior to 1550 to refute the idea of witchcraft. Written by a Franciscan friar, Samuel de Cassini, only two copies are extant:

one in Milan and the other in **Cornell University Library**.

Quetzalcoatl: The feathered or plumed serpent god of the Aztecs. He had a multi-dimensional aspect being god of the wind and the breathe of life; he was also a culture hero and divine king – the first ruler of the Toltecs, who taught men the calendar, arts and crafts. There was a legend that he would return and when Cortez, the conquistador, arrived in Mexico in 1519, the people thought he was Quetzalcoatl.

Quicksilver: In medieval Europe, quicksilver (or **Mercury**) was believed to have magical properties because of its luminous appearance and its unique fluid properties.

Quinquantria: A festival of **Mars** (18th March) at which the sacred shields were purified, followed by a luxurious banquet.

Quinta Essentia: The quintessence, fifth element or **Philosopher's Stone**. Several alchemists have written books of this title.

Quintessence: The 'fifth essence' – a term used in alchemy, and in ancient and medieval philosophy for a fifth element, additional to the normal four. It was thought to be the material of which the heavenly bodies were made and to exist in latent form in all earthly things. SOURCE: *Starchild*, Mélusine Draco.

Quirinalia: A festival (17th February) in honor of **Quirinus**, a local deity (possibly a war god) of the Sabine community. When these people became part of Rome, Quirinus was associated with **Mars**.

Quirin Stone: A stone found in the nest of either the lapwing or hoopoe that is said to produce the truth.

Quirinus: Revered along with **Jupiter** and **Mars** as the third member of an ancient divine **Triad**. He appears to have had a military function in connection with defensive rather than offensive engagements. His sacred plant was the myrtle, which was regarded in antiquity as the symbol of bloodless victory.

Quisquiliae: (1) Light, dry fragments of things, i.e. small twigs and leaves that fall from trees. (2) The detritus from magical workings.

Qur'an: The sacred book of Islam.

Quzah: An ancient Arabian god of storms and thunder, who was worshipped in the neighborhood of Mecca. His weapon is a bow that he uses to shoot arrows of hail.

"Animals, and even humans, were not slaughtered in these rituals to be offered as a gift to the gods but rather to release the life-blood which had a unique and mysterious sacrificial efficacy."

I Bradley
[*The Power of Sacrifice*]

R

Rada: In Voodoo, Rada is usually equated with benevolent magic, as opposed to Petro's more malignant aspects. The Rada rhythms are in strict tempo compared to the 'off-beat' meter of **Petro**.

Radionics or **Radiesthesia:** Medical use of dowsing to detect changes in the radiation in the human body relating to illness. Also used to locate missing objects.

Radon: A gaseous radioactive element in the Earth; the first disintegration product of radium.

Radish: The plant was used by the Anglo-Saxon and listed by **Aelfric**. Because they were plentiful in the wild, radishes were seldom cultivated in medieval gardens. They were used medicinally for coughs and respiratory complaints, while **Culpeper** said they 'provoke urine and is good for the stone and gravel'. Ruling planet: **Mars**.

Ragnarok: The Doom or **Twilight of the Gods** in Scandinavian mythology refers to the destruction of the gods and the world by the forces of chaos. The myth is told in the medieval Icelandic poem *Völuspa*.

Ragwort: Although lethal when eaten by cattle, the astringent juice is used for wounds, ulcers, sores, burns and inflammation in humans. Its country name 'cankerwort' refers to its use in the treatment of cancerous ulcers. Ruling planet: **Venus**.

Rāhu: The Indian demon of eclipses in cosmogony; the ascending lunar path. He drives a chariot drawn by eight black horses, and pursues the sun and moon with his jaws open. Whenever he succeeds in swallowing one or the other, there is an eclipse.

Rain: Rain gods and rituals play an important part in many cultures around the world. Rain-making or averting magic ranges from dropping small objects into the Tiber to bring rain to Rome; to the simple children's chant: *'Rain, rain, go away. Come again another day.'*

Rain Bird: A bird such as the green woodpecker and various kinds of cuckoo, supposed to foretell rain when it calls.

Rainbow: A colored arch in the sky caused by refraction and internal reflection of light in raindrops.

Raining Tree: The Til, a linden-tree of the Canaries, mentioned in a wide number of sources including *History of the Canary Islands*. Mandelolo describes it in some detail, and states that the water that falls from this tree provides a plentiful supply for the inhabitants and livestock of the whole island of Fierro, which has no river.

Rain-maker: A person in tribal societies who professes to bring rain by magical means.

Rama: [The dark colored one] He corresponds to the seventh incarnation of the Indian god **Vishnu**. In iconography, his attributes are a bow and arrows. Several north Indian dynasties claimed Rama as their divine progenitor.

Ramayama: The epic story of **Rama**, which also contains a great deal of ancient Indian folklore.

Ram Feast, The: A May Day observances at Holme, near Dartmoor, where a ram is roasted whole, with its skin and fleece, close to a granite pillar. At midday there was a scramble for a slice of the meat, which was supposed to bring luck to those who got one. The close proximity to the granite pillar suggests the event is a pagan relic.

Rampa, Lobsang: A highly controversial author of the 1960s whose real name was Cyril Hoskin from Dublin. His book *The Third Eye* became an international best-seller.

Rasputin, Gregori: (1871–1916) A Russian peasant and mystic who moved in court circles. Tsar Nicholas and Alexandra were haunted by constant anxiety for their son Alexis, the heir to the throne, who suffered from hemophilia, and Rasputin's influence with them stemmed from his mysterious ability to stop the bleeding. When he was murdered in 1916, the Empress had his body buried in a special chapel, to which she went for spiritual comfort.

Rat: According to folklore, rates (and mice) respond well to civility and/or legal formulae, and a time-honored method of getting rid of them is to ask them to politely leave – either verbally, or written on a piece of paper which is put down their hole or pinned up nearby.

Rath: An elven or **Faere** dwelling, usually an earthen ringfort or under a mound with a **Hawthorn** tree on top.

Raven: see **Crow**.

Re or Ra: The old Egyptian name of the sun god, whose cult was well established at an early date. His name was later fused with other sky gods and the orb of the sun was taken to be the visible body of the god – but it was also regarded as his eye. From the 4th dynasty onwards, the kings described themselves as 'sons of Re'.

Reach: The part of a river that lies between two points or bends, so called because it reaches from point to point.

Reculver, Kent: [Regulbium] The earliest fort of what later became the series known as the Saxon Shore. It was first occupied in the 3rd century AD and guarded the northern entrance to the Wantsum Channel, now represented by the drained flats on the east side. In the center of the enclosure stands a remnant of an early Saxon church, although the encroaching sea is eating away at the low cliff on which it stands.

Red: The color of blood, aggressiveness and love in magical correspondences. In the Middle Ages dark red was symbolically the color of the **Devil** and many **Grimoires** were written in red ink, or bound in red leather. *'Red is the color of magic in every country, and has been so from the very earliest times."* Yeats: *Fairy and Folk Tales of the Irish Peasantry.* Red was also the color associated with death in the Celtic world, and red horsemen are seen to be an omen of death. For the ancient Egyptians, it was the color of Set. SOURCE: *Pagan Celtic Britain*, Anne Ross.

Red Hair: Red-headed women, especially those with very white skin, were considered likely to be witches, a belief expounded in Christopher Fry's play, *The Lady's Not For Burning*. In the Middle Ages, henna was associated with witchcraft and a woman faced imprisonment for its use. This notion persisted as late as the 16–17th centuries, and any woman who altered her appearance was considered to be practicing witchcraft. An Act of Parliament of 1770, as cited in *The Magic of Herbs* by Mrs. C.F. Lyell, states: *That all women of whatever age, rank, profession or degree, whether virgin maid or widow, that shall from and after such Act impose upon, seduce and betray into matrimony any of His Majesty's subjects by means of scent, paints, cosmetics, washes, artificial teeth, false hair, Spanish wool (red wool used for painting the face), iron stays, hoops, high-heeled shoes or bolstered hips, shall incur the penalty of the law now in force against witchcraft and like misdemeanours, and that the marriage upon conviction shall stand null and void.* There is even an account of an arrest made as late as the 1800s because some henna was found in an Essex woman's house.

Red Man: In French folklore a red man commands the elements, and wrecks the ships off the coast of Brittany of those he condemns to death. The legend says that he appeared to Napoleon and foretold his downfall.

Red Tincture: A preparation that alchemists believed would convert any base metal into gold (see **White Tincture**). It is sometimes called the **Philosopher's Stone**, the Great Elixir and the Great Magisterium.

Reed: Listed by **Aelfric**, the plants grow in sediment at the edges of rivers, lakes and brackish waters throughout Britain. The long stems were used for thatching, matting and fuel. The roots, shoots and seeds of the common reed were eaten in times of famine; the roots and rhizomes were used to treat fevers, coughs, phlegm and lung complaints.

No ruling planet is given by **Culpeper**.

Regalia: The trappings and insignia of the priesthood within witchcraft and ritual magic, including the magical weapons. SOURCE: *Witchcraft – A Tradition Renewed*, Evan John Jones; *Coven of the Scales*, A.R. Clay-Egerton; *Magick*, Aleister Crowley.

Regardie, Israel: Born in England (1907–1985) but lived most of his life in America where he practiced as a Reichian psychotherapist. He is best known as one of the major occult writers on magic, mythology and the rituals of the **Golden Dawn**. In 1928 he became Aleister **Crowley's** personal secretary, and in 1937 published the first of four volumes providing full details of the magical rituals of the Golden Dawn and Stella Matutina. Although many occultists feel that he had broken his magical oath, he has preserved for future generations accessible guides to magical practice and philosophy. SOURCE: *The Eye in The Triangle; The Complete Golden Dawn System of Magic*, Israel Regardie.

Regifugium: An obscure ceremony that is only a symbolic inclusion in the Roman calendar. It appears to have been a festival for men only. SOURCE: *The Roman Book of Days*, Erina Paulina.

Regression: The process of pushing the unconscious memory back towards childhood.

Reiki: A Japanese form of energy transfer to promote healing and well-being.

Reimkennar: A sorceress or pythoness; one skilled in numbers. The Anglo-Saxon *rimstafas* means charms or conjuration, and the Norse *reim-kennar* means one skilled in numbers or charms.

Reincarnation: A predominantly Hindu and Buddhist belief that the human soul or consciousness continues to be reborn through a series of lifetimes. The idea is becoming more and more popular in the West, and is being absorbed into both Christian and pagan beliefs. SOURCE: *Applied Magic*, Dion Fortune; *Exploring Reincarnation*, Hans TenDam; *Karma & Reincarnation*, Dr. Hiroshi Motoyama; *Magic – White & Black*, Franz Hartmann; *Reincarnation*, A.T. Mann; *The Scales of Karma*, Owen Rutter.

Relics: Three major religions have attached importance to relics: Buddhism, Greek paganism and Christianity. These exist in the form of identifiable bones or ashes, garments or other possessions that have been preserved with high honor and religious awe.

Religion: When talking about religion, it is easy to become confused about what it really is and the more we delve, the more we come to realize that there is always some essence that is common to all. SOURCE: *Daily Life of the Egyptian Gods*, Dmitri Meeks and Christine Favard-Meeks; *The Oxford Companion to Classical Literature*, ed by Sir Paul Harvey; *Phases in the Religion of Ancient Rome*, Cyril Bailey; *The Penguin Dictionary of Religions*, ed John R. Hinnells; *Eastern Religions*, ed Michael D. Coogan; *The World's Religions*, Ninian Smart.

Renaissance: The art and culture of the Renaissance contained powerful strands of paganism and magic, drawn from the civilizations of late antiquity to which scholars and artists longingly looked back. One of the themes that fascinated artists and scholars was the reconciliation of opposites in a higher unity. For example: love and violence, two opposites united in the famous painting *Mars and Venus,* by Botticelli. The goddess has put the war god to sleep, and baby satyrs use his weapons as toys, but the element of hostility remains present in the wasps round his head.

Renenutet: Egyptian goddess of agriculture and the harvest. When the crops were being gathered in and the grapes were being pressed, offerings were made to her.

Rennes-le-Chateau: A French village that provided the 20th century with an ancient **Mystery** that involved the **Cathars,** the **Templars,** hidden treasure, lost esoteric wisdom and the Sangreal (or **Grail**). SOURCE: *The Holy Place*, Henry Lincoln; *The Holy Blood and the Holy Grail*, Michael Baigent, Richard Leigh and Henry Lincoln.

Repercussion: A phenomenon of reproduction of injuries received by a projected wraith form on an entranced parent body.

Reprobacion, The: The first book on witchcraft (by Pedro Cirvelo) to be printed in Spanish (1539), and considered a classic for well over a century. A 1551 edition from Medina del Campa is now in **Cornell** University Library.

Restall Orr, Emma: Together with Philip Shalcross, she has helped to popularize the Druidic revival across the globe. TITLES: *Druid Priestess, Principles of Druidry, Ritual* and *Spirits of the Sacred Grove*.

Resurrection Men: Grave robbers. The term was first applied to Burke and Hare in 1829, who rifled graves to sell the bodies for dissection, and sometimes even murdered people for the same purpose.

Retrocognition: Knowledge of past events through psychic means.

Reynoldston: The Gower peninsular has many fine monuments, of which Arthur's Stone (burial chamber) is outstanding. Its remarkable feature is the size of the capstone – a huge rock estimated to weigh no less than 25 tons.

Rhabdomancy: see **Dowsing**.

Rhapsodomancy: see **Bibliomancy**.

Ribchester: The Roman fort of Bremetennacum, on the north bank of the River Ribble, where it guarded the crossing of the road from Ilkley to the Fylde with the main highway from Manchester to Carlisle. The museum relates to life in the garrison in a wild part of the country and contains altar stones and a tombstone.

Richborough, Kent: Rutupiae was the key Roman fort of the Saxon Shore defenses, built in the last decade of the 3rd century. In its last days it was garrisoned by a detachment of the 2nd Legion brought from **Caerleon** in South Wales and guarded the south entrance to the Wantsum Channel (see **Reculver**).

Reuss, Theodor: Succeeded as head of the *Ordo Templi Orientis* (OTO) in 1905. It was he who invited Aleister **Crowley** to join the organization and in 1922, after a stroke, Reuss resigned from his post and handed over to Crowley.

Revelation: In most religions it is claimed that supernatural knowledge has been revealed to man through divine intervention. The Christian work in this tradition, which also crops up repeatedly in occult literature, is the *Book of Revelation*; teeming with vivid imagery, it was for many centuries the most popular book of the Bible. SOURCE: *Interpreting Revelation*, M.C. Tenney.

Rhyming to Death: The Irish at one time believed that children and cattle could be 'eybitten', that is bewitched by an **Evil Eye,** and the the 'eybitter' or witch could 'rime' them to death according to Scot in *Discoverie of Witchcraft*.

Richardson, Alan: One of the most underrated of British esoteric authors, who studied magic under the watchful eye of W.G. (Bill) **Gray**, and wrote *An Introduction to the Mystical Qabalah* when still in his teens. His many other titles include *The Old Sod* (biography of Bill Gray), *Priestess* (biography of Dion Fortune), *The Inner Guide to Egypt* (with Billie Walker-John) and *The Google Tantra*.

Riddles: The most famous of all riddles was the one asked by the **Sphinx**: *'What has four feet in the morning, two at midday, and three in the evening?'* If travelers were unable to give the correct answer, they were strangled on the spot. Oedipus replied, 'Man – because a baby goes on all fours, a man in the prime of life stands on two legs, and an old man in the evening of his days leans on a stick.' At this the Sphinx leapt from the mountainside and killed herself.

Ridgeway, The: A prehistoric track that runs across England from the coast near Dover to Ilchester in Somerset.

Right Foot: *Put the shoe on the right foot first.* The twelfth symbol of the

Protreptics of **Iamblichus.**

Right Foot Forward: In Rome a boy was stationed at the door of a mansion to caution visitors not to cross the threshold with their left foot first, which would have been a sign of ill-omen.

Right-hand Path: An erroneous magical term widely popularized in the occult novels of Dennis Wheatley as being the benign side of magic.

Rings: Rings have long been associated with magical properties and inscriptions were thought to increase the supernatural power. A ring was also in itself a symbol of power and often carried the ability to heal. William Jones wrote in his *Finger-Ring Lore* (1877): *'The use of galvanic rings for the cure of rheumatism belongs to our own time, and is by now means extinct.'* A gold ring rubbed against a stye was also supposed to be effective.

Risis: [seers] In Vedism, the singers of holy songs before the dawn of time: holy ones raised to supernatural status who form the seven stars of **Ursa Major.**

Rite: A ceremonial form of religious observance.

Rites of Passage: The transition from one state to another; a way of entrance or exit either spiritual (initiation or advancement) or temporal (birth, death, marriage, etc) Rituals relating to both religious and social rites of passage have been shown to follow a consistent pattern and were meant to ensure the effective completion of the transition or changeover.

Ritual or **Rite:** A prescribed manner of performing divine rites or ceremonies, especially in an elaborate or excessive way. In ancient times sacrifice was the central rite performed on almost every cultic occasion but contemporary rituals still conform to a patterned behavior, often communal, consisting of prescribed actions performed periodically and/or repetitively. There is a difference between rites of passage (transition rites, e.g. of initiation or at puberty); intensification rites (promoting or celebrating joint activity); and piacular rites (to do with cleansing, purification, forgiveness or expiation). SOURCE: *Elements of Ritual*, Deborah Lipp; *First Steps in Ritual*, Dolores Ashcroft-Nowicki; *Magic: A Occult Primer*, David Conway; *Witchcraft – A Tradition Renewed*, Evan John Jones.

Ritual Magic: A method that employs ritual, symbols and ceremonial as a means of representing and communicating with forces underlying the universe and man. To attain a complete understanding of what ritual magic entails, it is necessary to look at the subject in its historical context, not just from a contemporary standpoint. The summoning of a powerful supernatural, entity, energy or force is the principle aim of Western ritual magic. SOURCE: *The History of Magic*, Kurt Seligmann; *An Introduction to Ritual Magic*, Fortune and Knight; *The Magical Arts*, Richard Cavendish: *Ritual Magic*, Elizabeth M. Butler; *Ritual Magic in England*, Francis King; *The Ritual Magic Workbook*, Dolores Ashcroft-Nowicki; *The Secret Lore of Magic*, Idries Shah; *Techniques of High Magic*, Francis King and Stephen Skinner; *What You Call Time*, Suzanne Ruthven.

***Rituale Romanum, The*:** The Roman

Catholic Church's manual containing the only formal rites of exorcism, sanctioned by an established church. Written in 1614 at the time of Pope Paul V, the ritual remained unchanged until several minor revisions were made to the text in 1952. The *Ritual* provides instruction for both exorcism of people possessed by evil spirits and exorcism of places infested by demons.

River: (1) Rivers share the same symbolism as water as the source of life and the bringers of fertility. (2) Rivers of the **Underworld**. Besides the Styx and Acheron, three other rives intersect **Hades** – Phlegethon ('the fiery'), Cocytus and Lethe (forgetfulness).

Robes: Can vary in the manner of style and color from coven to temple although the most popular modern style is black, cut in the shape of a T or the Tau. To put on the robe is a sign of assuming a frame of mind suitable to the ceremony to be performed.

Robigalia: A day (25th April) sacred to the Roman god, Robigus, god of ergot, mildew and rust.

Robin: Despite the bird's popularity and strong traditions protecting them from harm, robins can often be seen as death omens. They have inspired a wealth of folklore, literature and poetry and despite their friendly approach to humans, they are fiercely territorial.

Robin Goodfellow: Capricious but not unfriendly, this nature entity is **Puck** by another name.

Robin's Pincushion: These remarkable flower-like, hairy red galls on roses are caused by a gall wasp, and named after **Robin Goodfellow.**

Robin Hood: A living part of British tradition, the first certain reference to him in English literature is made by William Langland in his revised edition of *The Vision of Piers Plowman* (1377). The oldest existing ballad is the *Lytell Geste of Robin Hode and his Meiny,* which was printed by Wynken de Worde at the end of the 15th century.

Rock Paintings: see **Cave Art.**

Rollright Stones: Legend tells how an army was turned to stone by the protective powers of a local witch. An ambitious warlord was told: *'Seven long strides thou shalt take! If* **Long Compton** *thou canst see, King of England thou shalt be!'* Knowing the village was just over the hill, he took seven strides forward but a mound obscured his view. The witch responded: *'As Long Compton thou canst not see, thou and thy men hoar stones shalt be.'* The stones consist of a circle about 100 ft in diameter, the Whispering Knights (that form a separate group), and the King Stone standing apart from the others. There are 72 stones in total but they defy attempts to count them: *The man will never live who shall count the stones three times and find the number the same.*

Roman Tradition: Draws on the identity of the Roman pantheon and has much stronger links with British paganism than the more frequently used Greek associations. Most ancient Romans left the celebration of the civil gods to the state priesthood; at home private worship of the **Penates** (gods of the food cupboard – *penus*), **Lares** (hearth deities) and **Genius** (the domestic procreative force) continued unabated for centuries. Many aspects of the Roman religion were imported into Britain. SOURCE: *Arcana Mundi: Magic & the Occult in the Greek & Roman Worlds,*

Georg Luck; *The Calendar of the Roman Republic*, A.K. Michels; *The Decline & Fall of the Roman Empire*, Edward Gibbon; *Discovering Roman Britain*, David E. Johnston; *The History of Magic*, Kurt Seligmann; *A History of Roman Religion*, F. Altheim; *I, Claudius* and *Claudius, the God*, Robert Graves; *Julian*, Gore Vidal; *The Oxford Companion to Classical Literature*, ed Sir Paul Harvey; *The Pagan Religions of the Ancient British Isles*, Ronald Hutton; *The Roman Book of Days*, Paulina Erina. [SEE PANEL]

Romany or **Gipsy:** Gipsy women are popularly believed to be exceptionally gifted in the art of magic and divination; gipsy fortune-tellers divine future events by using a crystal ball, tea leaves and playing cards, as well as astrology and palmistry. Gipsies can charm away warts and cure horses by magic, and are skilled in making highly potent herbal medicines, love potions and aphrodisiacs. Superstition, coupled with a strong belief in the supernatural, occupies a vital role in the gipsy community. Although they have remained aloof from conventional society, their language 'Romany' has blended with English. They also have a secret sign language, using grass and leaves, called *patrin*. SOURCE: *Gypsy Magic*, Patrinella Cooper; *A Roman Tapestry* and *The Eildon Tree: Romany Language & Lore*, Michael Hoadley; *Secrets of Gypsty Fortune Telling*, Ray Buckland.

Romulus: The founder of Rome who, along with his brother Remus, was suckled by a she-wolf and raised by a herdsman. He killed Remus and became the first king of the city. At his death he was raised to heaven and

revered as the god **Quirinus**.

Rook: see **Corvinus**.

Rooky Wood: Not a wood where rooks congregate, but a misty or dark wood. *'Light thickens, and the crow/Makes wing to the rooky wood.'* Shakespeare, *Macbeth*, *iii.2*.

Rosary: A string of beads found in a number of religions where it is used as an aid to meditation and prayer.

Rose: In the language of flowers, many different associations are given to the rose. It was probably introduced into Britain by the Romans and listed by **Aelfric**; and by medieval times, the warring factions of York (white rose) and Lancaster (red rose) had plunged England into the War of the Roses. The plant has several medicinal and culinary uses (see **Briar**). Ruling planet: **Moon** (white rose) and **Jupiter** (red rose).

Rose Cross: [*rosa crux*] Emblem of the **Rosicrucians**, the rose and cross have a rich symbolism and together can be interpreted in many ways: male/female; unclean/purified; material/spiritual; sensual love/spiritual love. According to the entry in *Brewer's Dictionary of Phrase & Fable*, however, it should be *ros crux* – dew cross – because dew was considered by alchemists as the most powerful solvent of gold; and *cross* in alchemy is the symbol of light.

Rosebay Willowherb: According to **Culpeper**, all the species of willowherb have the same virtues; **Gerard** recorded that a fume of the herb drove away flies and gnats. The plant was prescribed for a variety of medicinal purposes, while the shoots were boiled and eaten like asparagus. Ruling planet: **Saturn**.

Rosemary: According to an ancient

tradition, this herb strengthens the memory, while its list of medicinal and culinary uses is endless. A piece of rosemary may be worn to drive away evil spirits, or placed over the bed to prevent nightmares. Ruling planet: **Sun**.

Rosetta Stone, The: The vital clue to Egyptian **Hieroglyphic** translation was a broken slab of black basalt that was discovered by French troops during Napoleon's Egyptian campaign in 1799. The text was written in Greek, hieroglyphics and demotic script but it took a further 23 years before the Stone was finally decoded by Jean-Francoise Champollion.

Rose, Under The: [*sub rosa*] In strict confidence. Cupid gave Harpocrates (the god of silence) a rose, to bribe him not to reveal the affairs of **Venus**. The flower became the symbol of silence or trust. It was for this reason the rose was sculptured on the ceilings of banqueting rooms – to remind guests that what was spoken *sub rosa* was not to be made public.

Rose Window: Gothic circular windows, shaped like a rose with 12 petals of refracting stained glass. Designed by the master craftsmen of Chartres or Cluny, the glass was made from a secret recipe using antimony. The windows have a curious transformational effect on those contemplating them. SOURCE: *Chartres: The Making of a Miracle*, Colin Ward.

Rosewood: So called because when cut it yields a perfume like that of roses.

Rosicrucianism: Refers to several different mystical Orders based on the legendary teaching of Christian Rosencruz who was born in 1378,

traveled in the Middle East, and died aged 106 in 1484. He set up a fraternity, the *Spiritus Sanctum*, or House of the Holy Spirit, dedicated to the well-being of mankind, social reform and healing the sick; this reformation of the whole world was to be accomplished by men of secret, magical learning. Two classic sources are *The Brotherhood of the Rosy Cross* (1887), and *The Real History of the Rosicrucians* by A.E. Waite. SOURCE: *The Complete Golden Dawn System of Magic*, Israel Regardie; *The Hidden Symbols of the Rosicrucians*, Harold Bayley; *Magic – White & Black*, Franz Hartmann; *Man, Myth & Magic*, Richard Cavendish: *The New Believers*, David V. Barrett; *The Rosicrucians*, W. Westcott; *A Rosicrucian Primer*, Ashley McFadden; *Rosicrucian Symbols*, Franz Hartmann.

Rosslyn Chapel: Dating back to 1446, this building is one of the most enigmatic sacred sites in the British Isles. The wealth of carvings are of special significance to the initiated; many portray biblical scenes but others are obvious pagan symbols – there are over a hundred **Green Man** images – together with emblems of the **Knights** Templar and **Freemasonry**.

Rote: [Latin *rota*, a wheel and Old French, *rote*, road, have been conjectured] (1) Learning by mechanical memory, repetition or performance without regard to the meaning. (2) Performing ritual or magic without having an understanding of the roots or antecedents.

Rough Music: A ceremony that takes place after sunset, when neighbors assemble outside the house of a man or woman who has outraged propriety,

The Influence of Roman Gods in Britain

When the Romans arrived in Britain, they brought their gods with them — not just the images of the great State gods but also those of the soldiers, many of whom were not native Romans. Neither were they slow to assimilate foreign deities with their own vast pantheon, both indigenous and imported.

As the Empire grew and expanded so did the number of deities who were honored in Rome. The Roman religion was constantly growing and changing, and becoming ever more complex and many-layered. The influence of Greek culture had altered and augmented the prehistoric religious traditions of Italy, and while Graeco-Roman concepts affected the native cults of the Roman provinces, the inhabitants of the provinces in turn made their own distinctive contributions. Furthermore, during the early empire and even before, Egyptian and other Eastern cults were becoming increasingly popular in Rome.

This was the state of affairs when the Romans arrived in Britain following Claudius's campaign and, regardless of the people they had conquered, both natives and settlers alike, the fundamental principal of religious belief focused upon fertility — and the most basic concept of this element of faith was the honoring of the mother-goddess.

Most goddesses in the Roman pantheon had some maternal characteristics and the triple form found in Gaul, the Rhineland and Britain would have been familiar to them. In Roman Britain, some fifty dedications to the 'mothers' are recorded in stone inscriptions, in addition to numerous un-inscribed sculptures and other objects that show the importance of the cult among the Celts, foreign soldiers serving in the army and the Romans themselves.

Religious artifacts from all over the Empire found their way to Romano-Britain. Such as the white pipe-clay statuette of a mother-goddess, seated in a wickerwork chair; this mold-made terracotta was manufactured in Gaul and found at Welwyn, Hertfordshire. Or the statuette of the Celtic horse goddess Epona discovered in Wiltshire. Or the small bronze statuette of Priapus, bringer of good luck and fertility that was buried in Fakenham, Suffolk. That Epona appealed to the auxiliaries of the Roman cavalry is borne out by the altar from Scotland that is dedicated to her along with Mars, Minerva, the goddesses of the parade ground, Hercules and Victory.

Various hordes of treasure that have been found in Britain reveal the diversity of religious worship that flourished during this period, in addition to the Celtic gods that were predominant at the time of the conquest. The Thetford treasure included spoons inscribed with dedications to the god Faunus. The sun wheel, often paired with a crescent moon, is found on wholly Roman objects such as jewelry from Italy and in Britain, the gold necklaces and bracelets from the Backworth hoard; from Dolaucothi in West Wales; Snettisham and Felmingham in Norfolk give a tantalizing glimpse of the religious beliefs of the Romano-British period. The latter contains fragments of headdresses, perhaps items of priestly regalia, part of a scepter, a bronze rattle, together with heads of Jupiter and Minerva and a small mask of Sol.

At Brigstock in Northamptonshire, and from Brough in Nottinghamshire, images of a rider god, identified with Mars, have been found. In fact, inscriptions to Mars and representations of him are very common in Roman Britain, such as the altar from Bisley in Gloucestershire. At other sites it is Mercury, rather than Mars, who represents the local deity and the Temple to Mercury at Uley was undisturbed when it was accidentally discovered in the late 1970s. At Bath Spa, the Roman goddess Minerva was honored as Sulis-Minerva, while Mithra had his own *mithraeum* in London.

It is impossible to say how widespread family religious observance went in this far-flung outpost of Empire, but the many small statuettes that have been found in great numbers may have come from household shrines; statuettes of *lares* have been found in Britain, and these will certainly have come from domestic shrines, having been brought from Italy to help keep the faith in a distant land.

EXTRACT FROM *THE ROMAN BOOK OF DAYS*
PAULINA ERINA

and make an appalling din with bells, horns, tin pans and other noisy instruments. It has been known for this to happen when a person has been accused of witchcraft.

Rough Tor, Cornwall: Within a radius of about a mile of Rough Tor on Bodmin Moor are two stone circles, a ruined stone fort, and groups of enclosed fields with remains of their owner's circular huts, believed to belong to the second half of the Bronze Age.

Round Church: The legacy of the **Knights** Templar are the four surviving 'round' churches in imitation of the church of the Holy Sepulchre at Jerusalem: Temple Church in London, Cambridge, Northampton and at Little Maplestead, Essex.

Round Table: The most famous was that of King **Arthur** but the concept was common to all ages of chivalry. In Castle Hall, Winchester, is a Round Table alleged to be that of King Arthur and his Knights, which was almost certainly put there in the 12th century by Henry de Blois. Researchers now believe Arthur's stronghold of Camelot was built on the site of a recently discovered Roman amphitheatre in Chester: a vast wood and stone structure which would have allowed more than 1,000 of his followers to gather.

Rowan or **Mountain Ash:** In folklore there is apparently no situation in which a piece of rowan wood wasn't successful in keeping away witches! In *Witchcraft – A Tradition Renewed*, Evan John Jones lists it under 'sacred woods and trees: *'Sprigs of this tree are considered to bring good luck, and to protect from black magic and the evil eye. Hence an old Celtic salutation was 'peace be here and rown tree'.'*

Ruby: Considered to be the 'king of precious stones' with many magical properties. The rare 'phenomenal gem' of the Star Ruby (see **Star Sapphire**) is considered to be a bringer of good fortune.

Ruddock: see **Robin**.

Rue: *'To rue the day'* is a curse thrown in the face of a rival or enemy, together with a handful of the herb. Listed by **Aelfric**, the plant was used in perfumes and cosmetics, as well as having numerous medicinal uses. Ruling planet: Sun in Leo.

Rufus Stone: see **William Rufus**.

Rufus, William: King William II of England, see **William Rufus**.

Runes: (1) Used by the Germanic and Scandinavian peoples from the 2nd century AD until after the Viking Age, sometimes for straightforward messages, recorded verses, or inscriptions, but often for magical purposes. **Odin** was said to have taught men runic lore and the symbols, representing sounds, each with a special name, were arranged in sets of eight to form a **Futhark** or alphabet. Unlike the **Ogham** symbols used in Ireland, they were not based on the Latin alphabet. (2) Ancient magical script or hieroglyphic alphabet. SOURCE: *Magic In The Middle Ages*, Richard Kieckhefer; *Principles of the Runes*, Freya Aswynn; *Rune Magic*, Nigel Pennick; *Way of the Runes*, Bernard King; *Understanding Runes*, Michael Howard.

Runic Wands: Willow wands with mystic characters inscribed on them, used by the Scandinavians for magic ceremonies.

Running Water: There is a belief that no

enchantment can subsist in a running stream and that any tainted object can be cleansed by holding it in running water.

Rupert, Prince, of the Rhine: (1619–49) Charles I's brilliant cavalry commander during the Civil War. His Puritan opponents ascribed his skill and success to the aid of witchcraft, and claimed that his beloved dog, Boy, which went everywhere with him, was his familiar spirit. The dog was killed at the Battle of Marston Moor in June 1644, Rupert's first serious defeat, which helped to compound the belief.

Rush or **Bulrush:** Listed by **Aelfric** and an integral part of medieval life, rushes were strewn on the floors to 'soften the tread and freshen the air'. The pith inside the stems was made into wicks for candles and lamps; dipped into animal fat, rushes were an economical source of domestic lighting. **Pliny, Culpeper** and **Gerard** all cite the medicinal use of the rush. Ruling planet: **Saturn.**

Russell, G.W.: Irish esoteric poet and painter (1867–1835), better known as 'A.E.' and a lifelong associate of **W.B. Yeats**. He left the **Theosophical Society** in 1898 to form the Hermetic Society and although he discouraged his own students from experimenting with the occult, he insisted on the practice of meditation. His amazing paintings were far ahead of their time and one of his last prose works was *The Avatars*.

"Magic has the power to experience and fathom things which are inaccessible to human reason. For magic is a great secret wisdom, just as reason is a great public folly."
Parscelsus
[*De Occulta Philosophia*]

S

SS Collar: The collar consisted of a series of the letter S in gold, either linked together or set in close order, on a blue and white ribbon. *'On the Wednesday preceeding Easter, 1465, as Sir Anthony was speaking to his royal sister... all the ladies of the court gathered round him and bound to his left knee a band of gold, adorned with stones fashioned into the letters SS (souvenance, or remembrance) and to this band was suspended an enamelled forget-me-not.'* Lord Lytton: *Last of the Barons*, bk.iv.5

Sabbat: According to academic sources this observance appears to have been fabricated during the 14th and 15th centuries, largely by the investigators and judges connected to the Inquisition, and by the 16th century, the sabbat was an established part of witchcraft. Some later writers linked witchcraft to the two traditional Druidic festivals, 31st October and 30th April; while *grand sabbats* were supposed to take place on the four pagan **Seasonal Festivals** which had been incorporated into the Christian calendar: the winter festival of February 2nd (**Candlemas**); the spring festival of 23rd June (Eve of St. John the Baptist); the summer festival of 1st August (**Lammas Day**) and the autumn festival of 21st December (St. Thomas). It is interesting to note just how much the seasonal alignments and the calendar itself have altered since then and that the spring and autumn equinoxes were not included. The word *sabbat* is possibly derived from Old French. SOURCE: *A Dictionary of Devils & Demons*, J. Tondriau and R.

Villeneuve; *Encyclopedia of Witchcraft & Demonology*, Rossell Hope Robbins; *Witchcraft – A Tradition Renewed*, Evan John Jones; *The Witch-Cult in Western Europe* and *The God of the Witches*, Margaret Murray; *What You Call Time*, Suzanne Ruthven.

Sabeanism: An ancient religious sect worshipping the sun, moon, and host of heaven [Chaldee, *tzaba*, a host]. The Arabs were chiefly Sabbeanists before their conversion to Islam.

Sacerdotes: Roman priests belonged to a number of different colleges, with defined spheres of action, which could not be interchanged. These covered matters of sacrifice, temples, festivals and the calendar; the **Augurs** for the *auspicia*; and the *fetiales* for the rituals of declaring war and making treaties. Each college had its own body of law and kept its own books and records; typically, the priests acted as advisers on problems relating to sacred law.

Sacrament: The performance of the sacramental ritual in the quest for supernatural power is found in many religions, both ancient and modern, and is closely akin to magic. One of the oldest examples is the 'Opening of the Mouth' ritual of the Egyptians, a compound of symbolic and practical action to restore the dead to 'life' in the **Otherworld**. The word was originally a military oath taken by Roman soldiers not to desert their post, turn their back on the enemy, or abandon their general.

Sacred Animals: Animals held to be sacred as living manifestations of various gods. **Pythagoras's** doctrine, for example, was that a white cock should never be sacrificed because it was sacred to the moon. The Greeks said: *'Nourish a cock, but sacrifice it not,'* because all cockerels were sacred to either the sun or the moon as they announced the hours.

Sacred Geometry: The artistic representation of sacred subjects in 'the virtue of numbers'; a belief that numbers are endowed with some occult power. This doctrine came from the genius of Pythagoras, in that divine wisdom is reflected in the numbers impressed on the construction of the physical and moral world, as expressed in the geometric symbolism of the Gothic cathedrals. SOURCE: *Chartres: The Making of a Miracle,* Colin Ward.

Sacred Mountain: Widely thought of as being the source of inspiration and strength, mountains have always been the awesome dwelling places of the gods. Often shrouded in cloud or snow, the inhospitable peaks have been regarded as sacred throughout the world.

Sacred Space: (1) Refers to places that have been dedicated to a particular god, or group of gods, either permanently or for the duration of a magical/spiritual working. (2) It also refers to those places with an unexplained aura that is only detectable to certain people, and not necessarily with any particular historical or spiritual significance. SOURCE: *Gardens of the Spirit,* Roni Jay; *The Pattern of the Past,* Guy Underwood; *Secret Places of the Goddess,* Philip Heselton; *Witchcraft – A Tradition Renewed,* Evan John Jones.

Sacrifice: A word that causes a lot of controversy within occultism but refers to gifts or offerings made to deity during a ritual in the form of food, libation and/or incense. The action may be undertaken for thanksgiving or divination; as a means of renewing life or of continuing a seasonal or cosmic cycle; to secure favor or ward off evil; or as a ratification of agreement between human and deity. Sacrifice, from the Latin *sacrificium* ('making sacred'), generally means the surrender to the deity of something belonging to the worshipper. It was a central act of the ritual of worship among the Greeks and Romans and always accompanied by prayer. SOURCE: *Dying for the Gods,* Miranda Green; *The Oxford Companion to Classical Literature,* ed by Sir Paul Harvey.

Sacrificial King: The obligatory death of the existing old king as his powers were failing, so that his people could be governed by the new young king, who would bring strength and vigor to the kingdom. In historical times it has been suggested that the death of **William Rufus** was such a sacrificial killing.

Sacrilege: Profanation of anything holy, or extreme disrespect of anything regarded as worthy of extreme respect.

Sæhrimnir: The boar served to the gods in **Valhalla** every evening; by next morning the part eaten was miraculously restored.

Saffron: A native of the Middle East, the plant was grown commercially in England from at least the 14th century. It is estimated that it took over 4000 flowers to produce one ounce of spice. Tradition tells that it was brought from the Holy Land by a pilgrim or Knight of St. John, at the risk of being punished by death if he were caught. It has its uses in medicine and, ruled by the Sun in Leo, it is a powerful ingredient in solary recipes and spells.

Saffron Walden, Essex: A settlement of the ancient Britons, 'Waledana'; remnants of the extensive earthwork fortifications remain to the west and south of the town. A Saxon burial ground has also been discovered there. Nearby is a series of circular excavations – the best surviving earth **Maze** in England. Such mazes were once numerous and although their precise origin and use are obscure, they are undoubtedly pre-Christian and connected with the sacred rites of 'the maze'.

Saga: The northern mythological and historical traditions chiefly compiled in the 12-15th centuries. *'All these legends are short, abrupt, concise, full of bold metaphor and graphic descriptions,'* according to *Brewer's Dictionary of Phrase and Fable.*

Sage: (1) Old man revered for his profound wisdom and a classic figure in legend and literature. An archetype described by Carl **Jung** and represented by the **Hermit** in the **Tarot**. (2) A herb that features widely in folk medicine and cookery, introduced into England by the Romans. Ruling planet: **Jupiter**.

Sagittarius: (1) The ninth sign of the zodiac is the archer in the form of the centaur Chiron, who at death was placed among the stars – 22 November– 21 December. (2) The constellation of Sagittarius is located on the Milky Way in the direction of the center of the galaxy. It is a treasure trove of galactic and global clusters, plus bright and dark nebulae.

Sailing Under False Colors: Pretending to be what you are not. The allusion is to pirate vessels, which hoisted any colors (i.e. naval flags) to elude detection.

Saint: Many traditional charms and spells call upon the Christian saints for aid (see **Santeria**).

St. David's Head: This small promontory fort is one of the most beautifully cited in Wales, being at the extreme end of St. David's Head, with a magnificent view of Ramsey Island and Sound to the south-east. Inside there are a number of stone huts and rock shelters, while the whole area between the fort and Carn Llidi is rich in prehistoric remains. St. David's Cathedral, close by, is built of purple sandstone from local quarries.

St. Elmo's Fire: A natural electrical discharge seen playing about the masts of ships during stormy weather.

Saint-Germain, Count de: Popularly known as the aristocratic 18th century Freemason and Rosicrucian 'who did not die' thus intimating that he was one of the ageless *Illuminati*. Whatever the real truth, it is acknowledged that Saint-Germain produced one of the most remarkable occult manuscripts in his *Most Holy Trinosophia*, a collection of alchemical-mystical visions. This work was reissued in the USA in the early 1970s.

St. John's Wort: In his herbal of 1525, Banckes wrote that if the plant was put in a house, no wicked spirit would be able to enter. It was also believed to give protection against enchantment, against 'second sight', the **Evil Eye** and even death! A native of Britain, the plant has numerous medicinal uses. Ruling planet: Sun in **Leo**.

St. Osyth Witches: Dr. Hope Robbins in his *Encyclopedia* raises the issue that, with its psychologically interesting informers, this case was the 'barometer of English witchcraft' falling between the famous **Chelmsford** trial (1566) and **Warboys** trial (1593). It highlighted the formation of a *'specifically indigenous tradition of sorcery, without transvection, metamorphosis or sabbats,'* which were not recorded in trials prior to 1612.

Saint-Sécaire Mass: A form of **Black Mass** performed by a forsworn priest, over the body of a naked woman, in a ruined church. The purpose behind the rite was to bring about the death of an enemy.

St. Vitus' Dance: Ergot poisoningsee **Dance of St Vitus**).

Saitan: The Arabic form of the name **Satan**. In pre-Islamic writings the name is synonymous with **Jinn.**

Salamander: A creature of Elemental Fire. Spirits made from the atoms of fire in which they live.

Salamander's Wool: see **Asbestos.**

Salary: The salt rations served to the Roman army and civil servants.

Salem Witch Trials: Notable for their wealth of detail over how a small, insular community of religious suppression could erupt into one of the most infamous periods in American history. The hysterical accusations of two young girls triggered off the witch-hunt in New England in 1692, which resulted in more than 200 people being arrested under the suspicion of being witches and 19 being executed. SOURCE: *The Crucible*, Arthur Miller; *The Encyclopedia of Witchcraft & Demonology*, Rossell Hope Robbins; *Witchcraft At Salem*, Chadwich Hansen.

Saliens, The: A college of 12 priests of **Mars** and custodians of a sacred shield. The legend tells how the shield fell from heaven and the nymph Egēria predicted that wherever it was preserved those people would be the dominant race. To prevent the shield from being stolen, Numa, the King of Rome, had 11 others made exactly like it and appointed 12 priests as guardians.

Saliva: According to *A Dictionary of Devils & Demons*, by J. Tondriau and R. Villeneuve, in contagious magic saliva is treated to either heal or harm the individual from whence it came. In sympathetic magic, when casting an *envoutement*, saliva is applied to the effigy of the intended victim, while saying a magic spell. The saliva is believed to give the 'doll' the life substance of the intended victim.

Salmon: In both its natural and supernatural aspects the salmon has always been a fish of mystery; it is the 'fish of wisdom' and occurs up in this guise frequently in ancient and modern traditions.

Salt: (1) The symbol of incorruptibility and therefore eternity; in magical terms salt is considered a powerful defensive weapon against the powers of evil. It is erroneously stated in many texts that witches cannot eat food containing salt, since it features strongly in many Craft applications. (2) It has alchemical associations with mercury and sulfur, and the **Empress** card of the **Tarot**. (3) To eat salt under someone's roof creates a sacred bond between host and guest. No one who has eaten of another's salt should speak ill of him, or do him an ill turn. Thackeray observed: *'One does not eat a man's salt… at these dinners. There is* *nothing sacred in … London hospitality.'*

Salt Burning: The power of a witch is supposed to be destroyed by sprinkling salt into the fire nine mornings in succession. The person who sprinkles the salt must be the one affected by the suspected spellcasting.

Salting the Beer: In Scotland it was customary to throw a handful of salt on top of the mash to 'keep the witches from it'. In fact, salt has the effect of moderating the fermentation and refining the liquor.

Salt in the Coffin: It was a custom to put salt into a coffin to keep Satan away from the soul of the departed, because it was the symbol of incorruption and immortality.

Salt, Maldon: Produced in Britain since Roman times, these characteristic pyramid-shaped crystals are perfect for magical use. Available worldwide from any good delicatessen store. SOURCE: *Sea Change*, Mélusine Draco.

Salve: From the Latin *salvia* (sage) and one of the most popular of medieval remedies. *'To other woundes, and to broken armes/Some hadde salve, and some hadde charms.'* Chaucer: *Canterbury Tales*, line 2,715.

Samael: In Jewish demonology, the prince of demons who, in the guise of a serpent, tempted Eve; also called the angel of death.

Samadhi: A state of super-consciousness, which is the supreme goal of yogic meditation; a condition of unqualified blessedness, of contemplation of and participation in the bliss of the Absolute, and apprehension of the oneness of the self and the Infinite.

Samhain (or **All Hallows Eve** in the church calendar): The time of the year when the way to Otherworld remains open until **Yule** – the **Winter Solstice**. For the Celts, Samhain marked the beginning of winter and was the time when the cattle were brought in from pasture to spend the winter under cover. It was also the beginning of a new year, although there was no formal calendar in existence in ancient times. Modern Samhain is observed on 31st October.

Samedi, Baron: [Voodoo] A form of Baron Cimitière, Lord of the Dead.

Sanctuary: A holy place, area or building set aside for the worship of a god; or a particularly sacred inner area with a temple.

Sanctum Regnum: The name given to a system of ceremonial magic derived from the writings of Eliphas **Lévi** and including Qabalistic and **Tarot** reading. SOURCE: *The Book of Ceremonial Magic*, A.E. Waite; *The Magical Ritual of the Sanctum Regnum*, Wynn Westcott.

Sanctum Sanctorum: A private room into which no one uninvited enters.

Sanders, Alex: The flamboyant Wiccan leader whose character is probably best summed up by Bob **Clay-Egerton**, who knew him well: *'In fairness, no one who really knew Alex Sanders considered his powers in his final years as affectation – it was his overt dedication to tasteless showmanship that non-Alexandrians found offensive. It should be noted, however, that he had been responsible for some of the most adverse publicity ever aimed at the Craft during the 1960s and did more to harm embryonic paganism than anything its enemies could have invented.'* SOURCE: *King of the Witches*, June Johns; *The Truth About Witchcraft*, Hans Holzer; *Coven of the Scales*, A.R. Clay-Egerton.

Sangreal: The cup supposedly used at the Last Supper and mingled with the **Grail** legends of King **Arthur**. The story of the Sangreal (or Samgraal) was first written in verse by Chrétien de Troyes in the 10th century, and turned into French prose by Gautier Map on the order of Henry III.

Sanicle: In medieval England it was valued as one of the great wound herbs. So powerful were its healing properties, that it was said: *'He that hath sanicle, needeth no surgeon.'* Ruling planet: **Mars**.

Santería: Similar in practice to **Vodun** and centers around the worship of the African gods who have been assimilated as Catholic saints. Like Vodun, Santería arrived in the Americas with the beliefs of million of slaves, mostly taken from the Yoruban tribes along the Niger River, in West Africa. Forced to convert to Catholicism, the slaves continued their native beliefs in secret, passing along their ancient oral traditions, or in handwritten notebooks referred to as *libretas*. SOURCE: *Santeria*, Joseph Murphy; *Santeria*, Donna Rose; *Power of the Orishas, Santeria: African Magic in Latin America* and *Santeria: The Religion*, Migene Gonzalez-Wippler.

Sarcophagus: A stone, according to Pliny, that consumed the flesh, and therefore chosen by the ancients for coffins. Greek, *sarx*, flesh; *phagein*, to eat or consume.

Sardonyx: An orange-brown cornelian. According to **Pliny** it is called 'sard' from Sardis in Asia Minor, where it is found; and 'onyx', the nail, because its color resembles that of the skin under the nail.

Sarsen Stones: According to *Brewer's Dictionary of Phrase & Fable*, the early Christian Saxons used the word *saresyn* as a synonym of pagan or heathen, and as these stones were popularly (if erroneously) associated with **Druid** worship, they were called *saresyn* or heathen stones.

Satan: Originally an angelic entity, whose job it was to test man's fidelity to God. He was not evil, but became evil by identification with his functions and power to inflict suffering. Much of his satanic identity was the result of mistranslation rather than his turning against God's authority. In Islam the Devil is called *Iblis* or *al-Shaitan* in the *Qur'an*, and identified as being an angel who refused to acknowledge God's creature Adam as his superior, for which he was cast out of paradise. Like his Christian counterpart, he perpetually seeks to lead mankind astray with his insidious suggestions. SOURCE: *Dictionary of Demons*, Fred Gettings; *A Dictionary of Devils & Demons*, J. Tondriau and R. Villeneuve; *The Encyclopedia of Witchcraft & Demonology*, Rossell Hope Robbins; *What You Call Time*, Suzanne Ruthven.

Satanic Bible, The: A formal presentation of the philosophy and outlook of the Church of Satan. SOURCE: *The New Believers*, David V. Barrett; *The Satanic Bible*, Anton LaVey.

Satanic Child Abuse Myth: The term given to the anti-occult campaign that took place over a period of 1989–1994, when hundreds of children were taken away from their families following the accusations of devil worship and human sacrifice, instigated by evangelical Christians and social workers (see **Anti-Occult Campaign**).

SOURCE: *The New Believers*, David V. Barrett; *Malleus Satani, The Hammer of Satan*, Suzanne Ruthven.

Satanic School, The: A name given to Lord Byron and his imitators, who defied the generally received notions of religion. Of English writers, Byron, Shelley, Moore and Bulwer are the most prominent; of French writers, Rousseau, Victor Hugo, Paul de Kock and George Sand.

Satanism: Always interpreted as the worship of evil, and a belief founded on the very principles that Christianity rejects. In effect, it is an offshoot of Christianity and no one but a disenfranchised Christian could follow its philosophy because the belief in the Devil or Satan is confined to the Christian Church and has no place in any of the pagan beliefs despite the claims made in books such as the Dennis **Wheatley** novels and *The Black Arts* by Rollo **Ahmed**. By this definition, there have been very few genuine Satanists throughout history. SOURCE: *Coven of the Scales*, A.R. Clay-Egerton; *The Magical Arts*, Richard Cavendish; *Malleus Satani, The Hammer of Satan*, Suzanne Ruthven; *The New Believers*, David V. Barrett; *The Satanic Bible*, Anton Szandor LaVey; *The Satanic Mass*, H.T.F. Rhodes; *The Secret Life of a Satanist*, Blanche Barton.

Saturn: (1) Identified with the Greek **Cronus**, Saturn is generally regarded as a cruel and gloomy god, although his festival, the *Saturnalia*, was a time of revelry. (2) His sinister aspects are perpetuated in the astrological significance of the planet Saturn, which governs **Capricornus** and **Aquarius**. (3) With its magnificent system of rings,

Saturn's image is always breathtaking. (4) For the alchemists, Saturn designated lead. (5) Represented in the Major Arcana of the **Tarot** by the **Universe** (the four threes in the Minor Arcana) and **Binah** in the **Qabalah**.

Saturnalia: The Roman religious festival that was held between the 17th and 19th December to celebrate the sowing of crops. It was a period of general festivity, license, exchanging gifts, lighting of candles and prototype, if not the origin of the combined European festivals of midwinter, **Yule** and **Christmas**, having lost its primitive Italian character of an agricultural festival.

Satyr: An attendant of **Dionysus**, the satyrs were minor Nature spirits, part human and part animal, sensual, lascivious and pleasure-loving.

Savory: The Romans classed this plant as a spice and introduced it into Britain; it was known to the Anglo-Saxons and listed by **Aelfric**. Both summer and winter savory possess similar healing properties. Ruling planet: **Mercury**.

Saxifrage: A native of Britain, the plant was held in high esteem by ancient herbalists for the treatment of digestive and respiratory infections, kidney and urinary complaints, and protection against the plague. Ruling planet: **Moon**.

Scallop: The scallop has figured in the affairs of man from earliest times, permeating all cultures and all periods of history. It has existed in its recognized form for about 150 million years, with some geologists tracing its remains in rocks 300 million years old. The almost round outline, with ribs radiating like a Roman comb, caused

Pliny to call them *pecten*. SOURCE: *Sea Change*, Mélusine Draco.

Scandinavia: Classical paganism survived until about 1000AD in Denmark, Norway and Iceland, and even later in Sweden. This has meant that far more material has survived than in Anglo-Saxon England and Germany. There is a rich heritage from the Scandinavian pagan past, such as the *Elder Edda* and the *Prose Edda* (see **Edda** and **Northern Tradition**).

Scapegoat: A person or animal made to take the blame for any wrongdoing of the family or tribe. The allusion is to the Jewish custom of driving a goat out into the wilderness to carry away the sins of the people.

Scarab: An Egyptian symbol of the creative life force. Amulets were worn to combat all anti-life forces, including old age.

Scarlet Woman, The: A term that has a special connotation within Thelemic teaching for a woman medium with outstanding abilities.

Scatomancy: Divination by interpreting the pattern in a person's feces.

Scepticism: One who thinks for himself and denies that there are grounds for reasonable belief in religious matters.

Schultheis, Heinrich von: A notorious German witch-finder, his *Detailed Instructions how to proceed in the inquisition against the horrible vice of witchcraft*, published in 1634, has been described as the most gruesome in all the gruesome literature of witch persecution. There is only one known copy of this book in the world, now in the **Cornell** University Library.

Sciomancy: Interpreting the meaning of the size and shape of a shadow.

Scoring Above the Breath: This involved scratching or cutting a witch's forehead so that the blood flowed, in order to nullify her magical powers.

Scorpio: (1) The eighth sign of the zodiac in the form of a scorpion – 23 October–22 November – the creature that killed **Orion**. (2) The two constellations are set at opposite sides of the sky, to avoid further trouble between them.

Scorpion: Often found in amulets to ward off evil (see **Scorpio**).

Scot, Reginald: see *Discoverie of Witchcraft*.

Scots Pine: Apart from the **Yew** and **Juniper**, this is the only native conifer of the British Isles. The tree has a long history of spiritual and inspirational significance that can be traced back to pre-Christian cultures. The **Pine** is associated with the **Winter Solstice** and the rebirth of the Sun. Pine resin was used in ointments and plasters for wounds, skin irritations and muscular aches and pains. Ruling planet: **Mars**.

Scottish Folklore: Although nominally Christian the lives of the early Scots were still ruled by other, older beliefs. Fairies, water-beasts, witches and spirits of the dead were always lying in wait and the Christian faith was itself riddled with memories of pagan ritual. Springs, caves and standing stones all had their supernatural guardians.

Scottish Witchcraft: According to Dr. **Hope Robbins**, Scotland was second only to Germany in the barbarity of its witch trials. Various estimates have been made of the number of witches executed in Scotland, and although the Presbytery of Scotland admitted to burning some 4,000, the actual number is thought to be higher.

Scourge: A small whip used ceremonially within some areas of traditional Craft.

Scrying: (see **Skkrying**).

Scythe: Symbol of death and time: death is frequently represented as a skeleton carrying a scythe with which he mows down the living. Father Time is an old man with a scythe, derived from the sickle of the Roman god, **Saturn**.

Sea: From the sea came the first form of life and, like the land gods, the sea gods demanded and received tribute from those who used their resources. Japanese fishermen still pay tribute to the god of the sea with gifts of cloth and rice. SOURCE: *Sea Change*, Mélusine Draco; *Secret Places of the Goddess*, Philip Heselton; *The Way of the Sea*, Timothy Freke; *Facing the Ocean*, Barry Cunliffe.

Seahenge: An ancient circle of wooden stumps found on a beach in Norfolk in 1998. Carbon dating has shown the trees to be over 4,000 years old. SOURCE: *Seahenge*, Francis Pryor.

Seal: (1) The folklore of the seal owes much to the animal's resemblance, in some respect, to a human being (see **Selkie**). (2) A summoning diagram or **Sigil**.

Séance: A French word for 'sitting', commonly used for a meeting of a group of people with a medium via whom messages from the dead are received.

Seasonal Rites: In Greek mythology, the Seasons (or *Hōrai*) were three in number – spring, summer and winter; the Egyptian calendar also observed three seasons – while for the Celts there were only two – summer and winter. Contemporary pagans usually observe the traditional four seasons. SOURCE: *Seasonal Feasts and Festivals*, E.O. James; *The Egyptian Book of Days*, Mélusine Draco; *The Oxford Companion to Classical Literature*, ed by Sir Paul Harvey; *Root and Branch, A Witch's Treasury of the Countryside*, Mélusine Draco; *Witchcraft – A Tradition Renewed*, Evan John Jones. [SEE PANEL]

Sea Witch: Superstitious sailors voyaged in fear of the witches of the sea, who had the power to control a sailor's fate out on the ocean. Most dreaded was the storm witch, who not only had power over the winds, she had the ability to drive a vessel on to a dangerous shore. SOURCE: *Sea Change*, Mélusine Draco; *Facing the Ocean*, Barry Cunliffe.

Second Sight: The ability to perceive things not visible to ordinary sight, in the future or at a distance. Modern psychical research suggests that some people have this ability to a marked degree, and that it may be latent in all human beings and possibly in some animals.

Secret Chiefs: A term used by several occult schools for a group of entities of superhuman intelligence and power, and transmitters of secret knowledge. Used by Adepts of the **Golden Dawn** and, later, by Aleister **Crowley** to denote Intelligences beyond the Abyss, that are beyond the comprehension of human consciousness. They include the minions and messengers of the **Old Ones**, and numerous other entities considered by humans to be 'extra-terrestrial'.

Sect: A body of followers, especially of an extreme political or religious movement; a subdivision of one of the main religious divisions of mankind. SOURCE: *The New Believers*, David

Seasonal Celebrations

Sometimes it's a good idea for the seasons to be celebrated without any 'witchy' overtones to the festivities, so that friends, family and children can participate.

Winter Solstice (21st December)

Coinciding with Yule and Christmas, arrange a party to suit everyone without compromising personal beliefs because evergreens, log fires, decorations and feasting all hark back to the days of our pagan ancestors. Traditional fare for rich cakes, mincemeat and puddings can be found in old cookery books.

Candlemas or Imbolc (2nd February)

Although still in the depths of winter, it's a celebration of new beginnings. Formal dinner parties may have gone by the board, but small supper parties are still the best way of entertaining friends at home and repaying hospitality. Your guests may not necessarily be of pagan persuasion but this is a time for a ritual gesture of friendship.

Spring Equinox (21st March)

Easter is the only moveable feast in the Christian calendar: falling on the first Sunday following the full moon after the Spring Equinox. Originally celebrating the festival of Eostre, the personification of spring – and what better day to celebrate than at the Vernal Equinox. Consider a formal Sunday lunch or supper party to share with family and friends – when even the most jaded of adults can be persuaded to take part in a treasure hunt for small cream eggs wrapped in gold and silver foil.

Beltaine or May Day (31st April)

To celebrate 'bringing home the may' and we shouldn't overlook the more sensual overtones of this festival. Ideally, it's an evening spent with your partner for a special meal. On the other hand, if you live alone, this festival could present the opportunity to hold a traditional fire festival with a bonfire or candles in the garden.

Summer Solstice (21st June)

Time for a summer garden party complete with lanterns and bonfires. If you're not into barbeques then try a variation on the Scandinavian open sandwich. Make up a selection to hand around to give people the idea; then invite them to help themselves from a wide selection of ingredients and make up their own. The party can be as lavish or modest as you choose.

Lammas or Lughnasadh (1st August)

The traditional start of autumn and six weeks of intense labor in the fields; in the kitchen there is also plenty going on in terms of bottling fruit, pickles and jams for the coming winter, and to give away as small gifts. Utilize the natural harvest and be busy drying herbs and preparing potions for the months ahead when the fresh ingredients won't be available.

Autumn Equinox (21st September)

Time for a traditional 'Harvest Home' – a supper that offers all the things that would be waiting in a farmhouse kitchen after a long day in the fields. The supper should be eaten around the kitchen table, as this would have been a 'working' meal. Before the end of the evening, make sure everyone's glass is full and propose a toast to the bounty of the 'harvest'. If you've made your own jams or pickles, give each guest a small jar in a gesture of sharing.

Samhain or Hallowe'en (31st October)

Calls for the traditional Hallowe'en party rather than the ancestral rites observed in private. Decorations are as important as the food, with the rooms dimly lit by candle and firelight; plenty of evergreen foliage with black and silver ribbons can look extremely effective. Many seasonal games are associated with fortune-telling but this doesn't mean compromising your integrity. Devise a bran tub or wheel of fortune with suitable 'omens' that the reader can interpret for themselves.

Witchcraft is a way of life but it may not always be possible to celebrate the traditional days with ritual observance. In the old days, the wheel of the year would have been celebrated with festivity and celebration because it would be seen as a form of thanksgiving in a natural and pleasurable way.

EXTRACT FROM *A WITCH'S TREASURY FOR HEARTH AND GARDEN*
GABRIELLE SIDONIE

V. Barrett; *The Penguin Dictionary of Religions*, ed John R. Hinnells.

Sed Festival: A royal Egyptian rite held for the purpose of rejuvenating the reigning Pharaoh by a re-investiture to confirm his rule.

Seemurgh: In Persian mythology, a fabulous bird that could speak all languages of the world and whose knowledge embraced past, present and future events.

Seer: Someone who has the psychic ability to see into the future.

Se'irim: Mentioned in the Old Testament as demons in the shape of a goat. In Leviticus 17:7, the children of Israel are forbidden to make sacrifice to the Se'irim (goat-spirits).

Sekhmet: The most difficult and unpredictable deity in the whole Egyptian pantheon, whose name means 'powerful'. When mankind rebelled against Re, the gods called down retribution in the form of the mighty lion goddess who began to systematically massacre the human race, and could only be stopped by making her drunk. By contrast, she is also the patron of doctors and healers.

Selago: According to *The Complete Book of Magic & Witchcraft*, the **Druid** name for club-moss; it should be picked with the right hand, covered, and removed with the left, in a meadow before sunrise.

Selenomancy: Studying celestial conditions, particularly the Moon for favorable signs.

Selfheal: A native plant that flourished in grassland, pastures and open woodland throughout Britain. Although it has various medical uses, including being a traditional cure for sore throats, in medieval England it was primarily regarded as a wound herb. Ruling planet: **Venus**.

Self-Initiation: A rite of passage following intense spiritual and magical instruction by a mentor or guru, whereby the initiate undertakes to go through the gateway to the Mysteries alone and unsupported by other members of the Order. It is not a DIY form of initiation for novices and is extremely dangerous. SOURCE: *Techniques of High Magic*, Francis King and Stephen Skinner; *Liber Pyramidos*, Aleister Crowley.

Selket: An early Egyptian scorpion goddess who had a protective role around the throne of the king, and was patron of 'magicians-medics' dealing with poisonous bites.

Selkie: Also known as the Seal-Folk, they are seals by day and human-like creatures at night. In this form they are said to be extremely beautiful with shining black hair and bewitching eyes.

Semnocosus: A northern Hispanic war god whose cult became popular among Roman troops. Prisoners, horses and goats were sacrificed to him.

Sensei: Japanese for teacher.

Sensitive: Another term for a psychic or medium.

Sephiroth: The ten spheres or emanations of cosmic consciousness located on the Tree of Life (see **Qabalah**).

Serpent: There is probably no creature that is more widely distributed in the mythologies of the world than the serpent. The snake or serpent is generally thought to have **Otherworld** connections and is, by no means, always an evil one. It is a powerful magic symbol; and stands for wisdom and the knowledge of good and evil that is a prerequisite of magical power. The Tree of Life of the **Qabalah** is often represented with a serpent twining through the branches; and a serpent swallowing its tail (see **Uroboros**) symbolizes the **Great Work**, the transformation of something into a higher form that is inherent within it.

Serpent Formulae: A description of the magical forces of the four elements as they circulate around the North Pole.

Serpent Power: The **Kundalini** or cosmic magical power.

Servants of the Light: Founded in 1973 by W.E. **Butler** and based in Jersey; the Helios Course which led to the foundation of SOL was constructed by Butler and Gareth **Knight**. Both were former members of Dion **Fortune's** Society of the Inner Light and Butler's successor as SOL's Director of Studies is Dolores **Ashcroft-Nowicki**. SOURCE: *The New Believers*, David V. Barrett.

Servitor: A Familiar.

Sesha: In Hindu mythology, the king of the serpent race, on which **Vishnu** reclines on the primeval waters. It has a thousand heads, on one of which the world rests. The coiled up *sesha* is the emblem of eternity.

Set: (Lit. Black) The primordial god of the ancient Egyptians and no earlier named deity exists in recorded human history. He is also the most complex of all the Egyptian deities since his name and reputation underwent some drastic character assassination during the march of history. He is rarely dealt with in depth in popular renditions of Egyptian mythology, often being merely given as the evil murderer of his brother Osiris. SOURCE: *The Setian*,

Billie Walker John; *Starchild*, Mélusine Draco.

Sethlans: An Etruscan god of fire and blacksmiths.

Seven: A holy number that occurs frequently in occult matters and generally thought to be lucky. With its uncanny and mysterious power it is linked with the **Moon**, and so with the underlying cycles and rhythms of life in the universe. Number VII equals the **Chariot** (or four Sevens of the Minor Arcana) in the **Tarot**, **Netzach** in the **Qabalah** and is governed by **Venus**.

Seven Barrows, Lambourn: This famous barrow group is one of the finest in England. 'Seven' is a misnomer since there are 26 in the whole group, which sit either side of a minor road. The barrows are of various types, including bowl, disc, bell and saucer, as well as an earlier long barrow.

Seven Bodies in Alchemy: Sun is gold; Moon silver; Mars iron; Mercury quicksilver; Saturn lead; Jupiter tin; and Venus copper.

Seven Deadly Sins: Pride, avarice, lust, wrath, gluttony, envy and sloth.

Seven Virtues: Faith, hope, charity, temperance, prudence, fortitude and justice.

Seven Wonders of the World: The most famous were of the ancient world –

The Pyramids first, which in Egypt were laid;
Then Babylon's Garden, for Amytis made;
Third, Mausolus's Tomb of affection and guilt;
Fourth, the Temple of Dian, in Ephesus built;
Fifth, Colossos of Rhodes, cast in brass to the sun;
Sixth Pharos of Egypt, last wonder of old;

Or the Palace of Cyrus, cemented with gold. E.C.B.

Brewer's Dictionary of Phrase & Fable also lists seven wonders from the medieval world:

The Coliseum of Rome

The Catacombs of Alexandria

The Great Wall of China

Stonehenge

The Leaning Tower of Pisa

The Porcelain Tower of Nankin

The Mosque of St. Sophia at Constantinople

Seventh Son of a Seventh Son: Believed to have the gift of healing and if born into a witch-family, his spells are more powerful than other witches (see **James Murrell**).

Sex Magic: The conscious use of sexual energies, with or without physical contact, to achieve a specific end result. Since ancient times sex has been linked to magico-religious rites but most texts focus on the titillating aspects rather than the genuine use of sexual energies within magical practice. SOURCE: *The Art of Sexual Magic*, Margo Anand; *The Enochian world of Aleister Crowley: Enochian Sex Magic*, Christopher S. Hyatt; *The Magical Revival*, Kenneth Grant; *Modern Sex Magick*, Donald Michael Kraig; *Secrets of the German Sex Magicians*, U.D. Frater; *Sex and the Supernatural*, Benjamin Walker; *Sex & the Occult*, Gordon Wellesley; *Sexuality, Magic & Perversion*, Francis King; *The Tree of Ecstasy*, Dolores Ashcroft-Nowicki; *What You Call Time*, Suzanne Ruthven; *Mastering Witchcraft*, Paul Huson.

Shakti: Female creative power. She is allotted to **Shiva**, the male creative principle, as a consort. The Tantric symbol of Shakti is the yoni, which unites with the lingam of Shiva to express the unity of all opposites.

Shade: An earth-bound spirit of the dead, a ghost.

Shadow: In many parts of the world it is believed that a person's shadow is an integral part of themselves. Can also refer to a ghost, as Macbeth says to the murdered Banquo: *'Hence, horrible shadow!'*

Shaft: *I will make either a shaft of it or a bolt of it.* Meaning I will make use of it one way or another. The bolt was the crossbow arrow, the shaft was the arrow of the longbow.

Shaitan: The god worshipped by the Yezidi in Lower Mesopotamia, and the ancient source of the **Sumerian** Tradition. The fundamental Christian corruption of the name is **Satan**.

Shamanism: In the strict anthropological sense is restricted to Siberia where the shaman is a magician or healer who interacts with the gods and spirits sacred to his people. The term is now applied to native 'medicine men' from both South and North America and has passed as a fashionable occult practice into the West. SOURCE: *Beginners Guide to Paganism, Wicca, Witchcraft & Shamanism*, Sorcerer's Apprentice; *A Dictionary of Devils & Demons*, J. Tondriau and R. Villeneuve; *The New Believers*, David V. Barrett; *Of Water & Spirit* (African), Malidoma Patrice Somé; *The Principles of Shamanism*, Leo Rutherford; *Shamanism*, Nevill Drury; *Shamanism: Archaic Techniques of Ecstasy*, Mircea Eliade; *The Shamans of Siberia*, Dr. Ronald Hutton; *The Shaman & the Magician*, Nevill Drury; *The Way of the Shaman*, Michael Harner.

Shape-Shifting: The idea that it is possible, in certain circumstances, for magical practitioners to change their natural bodily form and assume, for a time, that of an some other non-human creature, is very old and was once practically worldwide. Witches were believed to have the ability to turn themselves into a **Hare** or **Bat**.

Sheela-na-gig: The opposite pagan number of the **Green Man** and representation of the spirit of fecundity. Her rather graphic images can, rather surprisingly, also be found adorning medieval ecclesiastical buildings as a way of warding off evil.

Shells: Symbols of protection and frequently used as amulets.

Sheol: The Hebrew word that has the closest approximation to the Greek **Hades**, although it is often wrongly interpreted as meaning 'Hell' in the Christian sense. It was a place of 'silence and forgetfulness, dust and darkness, worms and maggots, to which all the dead go to live in shadowy and powerless obscurity – good and bad alike.'

Shepherd's Sundial: The scarlet pimpernel, which opens at a little past seven in the morning, and closes at a little past two. When rain is forecast, or the weather is unfavorable, it does not open at all.

Shewstone: A polished quartz crystal used for skrying. John **Dee's** shewstone is now in the British Museum.

Shiatsu: A Japanese system of massage therapy meaning 'finger pressure'.

Shibboleth: The password of a secret society; the secret sign by which those of a group know each other.

Shichi Fukujin: The seven gods of good luck in Japan.

Shinto: The religion indigenous to Japan, which is probably the purest form of 'paganism' on the planet. With its roots in pre-historical agricultural ceremonies, Shinto interacts with the *kami*, the powers of nature 'for benevolent treatment and protection' as well as having a highly developed form of ancestor-worship. Community ceremonies take place at fixed times during the year and focus on sites of natural beauty, although Shinto lacks any definite account of the origins of the gods. SOURCE: *The Great Religions*, Floyd H. Ross and Tynette Hills; *Penguin Dictionary of Religion*, ed John R. Hinnells; *Eastern Religions*, ed Michael D. Coogan; *The World's Religions*, Ninian Smart.

Ship: The black-sailed 'ship of death' travels over the land and sucks in the souls of damned seamen; the belief that the dead are transported to their final destination by boat is common to many religions. Superstition also surrounds the life of a ship, from the time of its building until it reaches the breaker's yard. SOURCE: *Sea Change*, Mélusine Draco.

Ship Burial: The ship has been a funerary symbol for ancient peoples, even those not normally connected with the sea. For example: the magnificent Sutton Hoo treasure was placed within an entire 90-foot long ship under the Suffolk burial mound; or those excavated in the Pyramid complex of Khufu at Giza (one of which has been reconstructed and displayed in situ), were intended to carry the deceased king on his final journey through Amenti.

Shipton, Mother: A 15th century

English psychic and contemporary of Nostradamus, although it is not clear whether she was an actual person.

Shi-tenno: The name applied to the four Shinto deities who guard the heavenly quarters. Their Indian counterparts are the Lokapales.

Shivering Mountain: Mam Tor in the Peak district of Derbyshire and so called because of the breaking away of its mass in small 'shivers' or small pieces. This shivering has been going on for ages, as the hill consists of alternate layers of shale and gritstone. The former, being soft, is reduced to powder, and as it crumbles away small 'shivers' of gritstone break away through lack of support.

Shiva: Pure Consciousness (see **Shakti**).

Shooting Stars: Tiny particles, usually the residue of comets, that sweep into the Earth's atmosphere from space. Annual meteorite showers can be spectacular and it is customary to make a wish when seeing a 'shooting star'.

Shrine: Originally a chest or cabinet. A casket for relics or an erection surrounding it – a place hallowed by association.

Shu: The Egyptian god of air and sunlight who, with his sister-wife **Tefnut**, goddess of moisture, were the first two gods created by **Atum** according to the creation myth of Heliopolis.

Shudder: A sudden shiver will often be followed by the comment: *someone is walking over my grave.*

Shugal: [Hebrew] The desert fox; a wild dog synonymous with Sagal, the twin of the Dog-Star, Sirius. SOURCE: *Aubrey's Dog:Practical Canine Magic*, Mélusine Draco.

Sibyls: The prophecies of the Sibyls were manifestations of a power to which they felt they were enslaved, and usually referred to disasters such as war, plague and famine. Although Sibyls do not appear in Homer, many allusions to them are scattered through Greek and Latin texts; the celebrated legend of the **Sibylline Books** demonstrate that the 'renown of the Sibyls in later literature and art is Roman rather than Greek'. The books were kept in a chest in a stone vault under the Temple of the Capitoline Jupiter and were consumed in the burning of the Capitol in 670AD.

Sibylline Verses: When the Sybylline Books were destroyed, all the floating verses of several Sibyls were collected and deposited in the new temple of Jupiter in Rome. Augustus had some 2000 of these verses destroyed as spurious, and placed the rest in two gilt cases under the base of the statue of Apollo in the temple on the Palatine Hill. They were finally destroyed when the city was burnt in the reign of Nero.

Siddhi: [Sanskrit] Magical or occult power; *siddha* – one who possesses same.

Sideromancy: Studying the twisting and smoldering of straw placed on a red-hot surface.

Sidorite: A witch amulet of lodestone.

Sieve and Shears: A complex procedure used to discover thieves or lost items. Scot's description in 1584 is the earliest known reference but it was in everyday use in 1602 when two Shetlanders were accused of witchcraft after using this method of divination.

Sigil: The occult application using a graphic representation of a spiritual idea. In Western ritual magic symbols linked to ideas by which means entities can by evoked and controlled. Following his research for *Dictionary of Occult Hermetic & Alchemical Sigils*, Fred Gettings estimated that there were over 15,000 basic forms of sigil relating to astrology, alchemy and general occult sciences.

Sigillum Diaboli: The mark or seal of the Devil.

Silbury Hill: One of the most remarkable monuments in the British Isles and built several hundred years before Stonehenge was erected. Dating from the Stone Age, recent excavations have revealed that the man-made hill in Wiltshire had a spiral processional walkway encircling the mound, which gave access to the flattened summit. Built from chalk, it was originally brilliant white and surrounded by a large shallow lake. SOURCE: *Goddess of the Stones*, George Terence Meaden; *Historical Atlas of Britain*, ed Nigel Saul.

Silures: The Welsh tribe of King **Arthur** (see **Ute**) who were later subjugated by the Romans (see **Caerwent**).

Silvans: Originally ancient Roman divinities of the forests and fields. In later times the silvans became the minor deity Silvanus; one of the finest Roman altars discovered in Britain is dedicated to this god. SOURCE: *The Archaeology of Roman Britain*, R.G. Collingwood.

Silver: Metal of the moon and, according to some alchemical texts, a stage in the work was the making of the White Stone, which turned all things to silver and which connected with the white stone referred to in Revelation 2.17. In occult lore there is a widespread

tradition that a silver bullet will kill supernatural creatures such as vampires and werewolves. SOURCE: *Liber 777*, Aleister Crowley.

Silver Cord: The connecting link between the physical and the astral body.

Silver Star, The: see **A.A.**

Silver Water: A regular remedy for any person or livestock suffering from the effects of the **Evil Eye** consisted of placing a piece of silver in water and using the 'silver water' to effect the cure.

Simon Magus: A 2nd century magician and teacher whose cosmology was reflective of **Gnostic** ideas opposed by the early church; regarded as the founder of the Christian heresy. SOURCE: *Simon Magus: The Gnostic Magician*, G.R.S. Mead.

Simple: A philter derived from a single herb.

Simulacrum: An image projected as a thought-form, intended to be seen (and sometimes felt) by the intended victim. Dion **Fortune's** discriptions of the phenomena are the most well-known.

Sin: (1) An essentially religious concept since it applies to an offense with regard to a religiously or supernaturally conceived reality, or a set of taboos possessing supernatural sanctions. There is also the difference between 'sinning' and 'wrongdoing' and even within a single culture there can be different degrees of sin. For example in Japanese Shinto *ama-tsu-tsumi* refers to sins relating to heaven and *kuni-tsu-tsumi*, sins relating to earth. (2) Hebrew for the lunar current.

Sinister: [Latin – on the left hand] In augury, signs appearing on the left-hand side foretell ill-luck. For example:

corva sinistra (a crow on the left-hand) is a sign of ill-luck that belongs to English superstition as much as to the ancient Romans or Etruscans.

Sirens: Originally characters in Greek mythology, who first appeared in Homer's *Odyssey*, they have also become part of **Voodoo** belief: the consort of Agoué, the *loa* or spirit of the oceans, is the Lady of the Sirens.

Sirius: Canis Major, the Dog-Star and the brightest star in the sky, which was cited by Homer as being the hound of **Orion**, the hunter (see **Shugal**). The Egyptians called it **Sothis**. It would rise just before dawn in late summer (heliacal rising), heralding the annual flooding of the Nile and marking the beginning of the year. Sirius has more magical lore surrounding it than any other star in the heavens.

Sistrum: A musical rattle from ancient Egypt as depicted in tomb paintings showing women shaking the sistrum while participating in religious rites.

Sitra Achra: A term used in the **Qabalah** for the powers of evil, meaning literally 'other side' since evil has no life of its own, and must derive life-giving energy as a parasite on holiness.

Six: Represents all or nothing; the only 'perfect' number in the first ten because six is the number of love. A perfect number is one that equals the sum of its divisors other than itself: $6=1+2+3$. The number VI in the **Tarot** equals the **Lovers** (or four sixes – Emperors or Princes of the Minor Arcana), **Tiphareth** in the **Qabalah,** and is governed by the **Sun.**

Six-six-six or **666:** The number of the 'Beast' or the anti-Christ according to the book of **Revelation**. It is commonly associated (rightly or wrongly) with the Devil, Satanism and Aleister Crowley.

Skald: An old Norse poet attached to the court, whose aim was to celebrate living warriors or their ancestors. Few complete Skaldic poems have survived, but a multitude of fragments exist.

Skara Brae: A Neolithic settlement of stone houses on Orkney, preserved under blown sand. The houses are closely grouped and each contains furniture of stone planks built into the main structure, which include box-beds, wall-cupboards and dressers that may have served as a family altar.

Skirophoria, The: A Greek summer festival held at the time of threshing and celebrated by very young girls of noble birth.

Skrying (or sckrying): A form of divination by meditation using the play of light on a shiny surface or object – a ball of rock-crystal, a mirror, a pool of ink or other liquid. Future events may reveal themselves as pictures or symbolic images. John **Dee** used this method to communicate with spirits in the 16th century and his 'shewstone' is on display in The British Museum. SOURCE: *Book of Fortune Telling*, Sybil Leek; *The Complete Golden Dawn System of Magic*, Israel Regardie.

Skull: According to the entry in *Man, Myth & Magic*, two beliefs that are found the world over, and which are shared by humanity past and present, are that bones are centers of psychic energy, and that the head (skull) is the dwelling places of the soul. The discovery of numerous horse skulls dating throughout the ages also suggest that these were powerful protective totem significance. SOURCE: *Design* *for Death*, Barbara Jones; *Witchcraft – A Tradition Renewed*, Evan John Jones.

Skull & Crossbones: Usually seen as the pirate flag known as the Jolly Roger, but it was originally the maritime flag of the **Knights Templar**. The image is often found in carvings at sites associated with the Templars.

Sky: In many traditions the Afterlife is seen as being in the sky, among the stars. The Pharaohs of Egypt were buried with rites to enable them to join the sun god in the heavens; and throughout history, various heroic mortals have been taken up into the sky by Creator gods. There are different sorts of sky gods and the god of the storm is not always the same as the supreme power of the sky itself. The supreme sky god is the cosmic master of all things, which he himself generally created.

Skyclad: A modern Wiccan term meaning to work naked during a rite. SOURCE: *What You Call Time*, Suzanne Ruthven; *Coven Working*, Philip Wright and Carrie West.

Sky Father: The consort of the **Earth Mother** in the earliest folk-religions of the ancient world.

Skylark: The fluting song of the skylark is the true sound of an English summer. In some parts of the country it was considered a sacred bird and any disturbance to its nest would bring a curse.

Slade, Paddy: An English village witch, or wise woman in the hereditary tradition. She believed that any would-be witch should take a couple of years to become familiar with the elements and rhythms of Nature before even attempting to learn magic. She also made the point that many who follow modern **Wicca** as a religion are well intentioned, but do not know what they are doing because they have not taken the time or trouble to educate themselves to the ways of **Nature** which she refers to as 'Old Wild Magic'. TITLES: *Seasonal Magic: Diary of a Village Witch* and *Natural Magic*, Paddy Slade.

Sleepers: The connection between Death and Sleep occurs in both magical practice and the legends of bygone heroes, who are not truly dead but lying in a deathlike trance, ready to rise up in time of national danger. King Arthur and Sir Francis Drake have this legend surrounding them. The Seven Sleepers of Ephesus in the Koran are watched over by the faithfulll dog Katmir, who will be one of the nine animals that will be allowed into Paradise.

Slieve na calliagh: The long ridge of low hills south-east of Oldcastle, Co Meath is surmounted by a remarkable series of 30 passage-graves (chambered tombs in which the chamber and passage leading to it form two distinct structural units). Many of the stones have Bronze Age ornament. There is also a ringfort, a rectangular earthwork, a pillar-stone and a cross-stone.

Smith: The village blacksmith was formerly revered as a 'master of fire' and possessor of secret knowledge, acting as healer, charmer and practitioner of the occult. Indispensable to the community, the smith was nevertheless regarded with a mixture of respect and fear. The smith-cult plays an integral part in the indigenous beliefs of the British Isles and Old Craft in particular. SOURCE: *The Forge & the Crucible*, Mircea Eliade.

Smoke: Smoke from the sacred fires

(including incense, joss, etc) carries the prayers and supplications from the petitioners to the gods.

Snail: Used extensively in cures and minor divination procedures. They were eaten, sometimes for medical purposes but also for food. SOURCE: *The Penguin Guide to Superstitions of Britain & Ireland*, Steve Roud; *Fauna Britannica*, Stefan Buczacki.

Snake: see **Serpent**.

Snakestone: A stone from a snake, which the **Druids** believed would float against the current and not sink. It has been described as small and glassy, usually green but sometimes blue, and streaked with white and red.

Sobek: The Egyptian crocodile god who was depicted as a crocodile with a crown of plumes, or as a man with a crocodile's head. His temples were provided with a pool containing sacred crocodiles, and in the form of Sobek-Re he was seen as another manifestation of the sun god.

Society of Inner Light: Founded by Dion **Fortune** in 1927, the society has changed some of the emphasis of its teachings over the years and although Fortune's books are still read and recommended today by both esoteric and non-pagan organizations, the Society plays down the 'pagan' aspects of her work. SOURCE: *Dion Fortune & the Inner Light*, Gareth Knight; *The Forgotten Mage: The Magical Lectures of Col. C.R.F. Seymour*, ed by Dolores Ashcroft-Nowicki.

Society for Psychical Research: Founded in 1882, SPR is the oldest organization still in existence that is dedicated to the scientific investigation of claims of the supernatural.

Sokar: The Egyptian hawk-headed god of Memphis. His annual feast was celebrated on a grand scale in Thebes where there is evidence that it almost rivaled the annual festival of **Opet**.

Sol: [Latin] (1) The Sun. (2) The term given by alchemists to gold; silver was Luna. (3) In the *Eddas* and Scandinavian mythology, Sol was so beautiful that at death she was placed in heaven to drive the sun-chariot.

Solar Barque: Just as images of the Egyptian gods were carried in ritual procession in ceremonial barques, so Atum-Re was believed to travel through the **Otherworld** in a solar-barque. There were two distinct types of barque, and it has been suggested that those excavated in the Pyramid complex of Khufu at Giza (one of which has been reconstructed and displayed in situ), were intended to carry the deceased king on his final journey through Amenti.

Solar or **Sun Cults:** The Sun was universally seen as the presiding male deity and came to represent the Creator in many different forms. Powerful animals such as the lion or bull were usually associated with him. SOURCE: *The Mysteries of Mithra*, Franz Cumont.

Solitary: The generic term for witches who work alone (or with a selected partner) rather than with a group or coven.

Solomon: King of Israel in the 10th century BC and builder of the Temple. Renowned for his wisdom, wealth and longevity, he flourished in legend as a master magician who controlled all demons by the power of his magic ring; the *Key of Solomon* and other magical *grimoires* were attributed to him.

Solomon's Ring: According to rabbinic legend, Solomon wore a ring in which was set a chaste stone that told the king everything he desired to know.

Solomon's Seal: (1) The six-pointed star of David or **Magen David**. (2) A plant cultivated for ornament and medicine. Gerard said the root *'taketh away in one night, or two at the most, any bruise, black or blue spots gotten by falls or woman's wilfulness, in stumbling upon their hasty husband's fists, or such like.'* Ruling planet: **Saturn**.

Solstice: see **Summer** and **Winter Solstice.**

"So Mote It Be": The traditional affirmation made at the completion of a rite or spellcasting.

Song: All over the world people raise their voices in song as a musical instrument to supplicate or thank their gods.

Sons of the Sorceress: A biblical reference meaning those who study and practice magic. Isaiah 57:3.

Soothsayer: A person who can foretell the future by means of divination or augury.

Sorcerer: [O.Fr. *sorcerie*] One who practices magic and divination with the aid of spirits (see **Sorcery**).

Sorcerer's Apprentice, The: Possibly the most famous occult shop in the world. Founded in 1974, it has survived paint and firebombing by Christian fundamentalists but still remains in pole-position when it comes to magical supplies and hard to find books. Located in Leeds, it can supply almost anything by mail order.

Sorcerer's Violet: see **Periwinkle**.

Sorcery: According to academic sources, this is a timeless and worldwide phenomena, 'whereas witchcraft is specifically limited to approximately three centuries from 1450 to 1750 and to Christian Western Europe (with the exception of Salem)'. SOURCE: *A Dictionary of Devils & Demons,* J. Tondriau and R Villeneuve; *The Encyclopedia of Witchcraft & Demonology,* Rossell Hope Robbins; *Magic In The Middle Ages,* Richard Kieckhefer; *The Book of Black Magic & of Pacts,* A.E. Waite; *The Encyclopedia of Witchcraft & Demonology,* Rossell Hope Robbins; *The New Believers,* David V. Barrett.

Sorrel: A native of Britain, the plant has been valued for its medicinal and culinary properties since ancient times. Ruling planet: **Venus**.

Sortes Virgilianæ: Tell a person's fortune by consulting the *Æneid* of Virgil. Take up the book, open it at random, and the passage you touch with your finger is the oracular response.

Sothis: see **Sirius.**

Soul: The belief in a spiritual element of the human personality distinct from the visible and tangible body. The idea of the soul as an entity that can exist outside or independently of the body occurs among many different faiths, some of whom believe that each person has more than one soul.

Southern Gate of the Sun: The sign **Capricornus**, or **Winter Solstice**, because it is the most southern limit of the sun's course in the ecliptic.

Southways: see **Deosil.**

Sow Thistle: A native of Britain, the plant was a common weed of waysides, waste and cultivated ground. Listed by **Aelfric**, it was believed to possess various magical properties, including the power to repel witches. It had a wide variety of medicinal uses and the leaves were eaten raw in salads, or cooked in soups, or as a vegetable. Ruling planet: **Venus**.

Spanish Witchcraft: Sorcery and witchcraft were clearly defined in Spain, the former was prosecuted vigorously for centuries, while the latter was only relatively restricted. The reason for this moderation resulted from the Spanish Inquisition's complete control over the country, and although it burned the greatest number of heretics in Europe, actual witchcraft persecutions suffered the least. SOURCE: *The Encyclopedia of Witchcraft & Demonology*, Rossell Hope Robbins.

Spare, Austin Osman: (1886–1956) Known as a 'great trance artist-magician' who won a scholarship to the Royal College of Art when he was only sixteen. He developed an interest in magic, Egyptian mythology and the teachings of Aleister **Crowley**, and began incorporating these images into his work, giving it an increasingly menacing impression. Spare also developed a system of sigils, which were symbols of meditation used for unleashing the potencies of the subconscious mind. His work is best known for its atavisms, the almost tangible primeval forces drawn from previous levels of existence and the deepest layers of the human psyche. TITLES: *Book of Pleasure, The Focus of Life, Ethos, Anathema of Zos*. SOURCE: *Cults of the Shadows*, Kenneth Grant; *Mystery of An Artist, Stealing the Fire From Heaven* and *From the Inferno to Zos* (3 vols), ed by A.R. Naylor; *Images & Oracles of Austin Osman Spare*, Kenneth Grant; *The Search for Abraxas*, Drury and Skinner.

Spectre: From the Latin *spectrum*, 'vision', a ghost or apparition, especially one that is terrifying. The Spectre of the Brocken is a huge shadow, often accompanied by rings of colored light, cast by an observer on top of a hill on the upper surfaces of clouds that are below him.

Spectrum: [Latin, *specto*, to behold] (1) The image of a sunbeam beheld on a screen, after refraction by one or more prisms. (2) Spectra are the images of objects left on the eye after the object has been removed from sight.

Speculum: A mirror, often made of polished metal and used for skrying.

Spell: A word, set of words or procedure believed to have a magical effect.

Sphere: One of the hollow transparent concentric globes formerly believed to revolve around the earth, carrying with them the sun, moon and planets; their motion was thought to produce a harmonious sound – the **Music of the Spheres**. Allotting one sphere to the Prime Mover, the fixed stars, and each of the seven planets, gave a total of nine, with the earth at the center; or the earth itself could be allotted a sphere, making ten, as in the **Qabalah**.

Sphinx: A hybrid creature combining human and animal parts, the most famous being the Great Sphinx at Giza in Egypt. In Greek mythology the woman-headed Sphinx of Thebes strangled passers-by when they failed to answer the riddle she put to them (see **Riddle**). SOURCE: *Riddles of the Sphinx*, Paul Jordan.

Spider: Routinely used in cures for various ailments, while cobwebs were, and still are, used to stop bleeding.

Spiders are believed to be lucky to have around and it is thought unlucky to harm one. The earliest fossils of spiders date from the famous 300 year old beds of Devonshire chert in Scotland.

Spikenard: Oil extracted from the plant.

Spinning: An activity symbolically connected to Fate, as in classical mythology the three Fates spin the thread of life, weave it and sever it. The fact that **Spiders** spin webs to catch their prey has contributed to their place in folklore and symbolism.

Spiral, The: (see **Maze** and **Labyrinth**) Of all the basic symbols associated with primitive ancestral beliefs, the spiral is the most difficult to draw, yet it became the most dominant art motif of prehistoric times. Spirals have a hypnotic effect on the eye, drawing it in decreasing circles towards the center; and then back out again – and in again – in alternating rhythms. SOURCE: *The Goddess of the Stones*, George Terrence Meaden.

Spirit: From the Latin *spirare*, 'to breathe', and the animating principle in living things; a being or intelligence that has no earthly body.

Spirituality: A respect and/or affinity for the spiritual without a formal commitment to a religion.

Spiritualism: The basic ability to communicate with the dead is not confined to Western society, although the term is generally used to refer to the activities of the modern Western Spiritualist movement. SOURCE: *Modern Spiritualism*, F. Podmore; *Principles of Spiritualism*, Lyn de Swarte; *Spiritualism & Society*, G.K. Nelson.

Spittle: A vital ingredient when casting spells as a means of concentrating magical energy. Spitting without purpose was considered a waste of magical force and could expose the 'spitter' to the malevolent attentions of enemies who capture the **Saliva**.

Spodomancy: Placing a 'wish' on a piece of paper, setting it alight, and then studying the smoke and flames consuming it.

Spring Equinox: Falls on or around the 21st March each year.

Springs and **Wells:** Sacred springs and wells play an important part in the folklore of all cultures, and is one of the most ancient and universal forms of worship. Well-dressing is a rural custom that has survived from pre-Christian times, and focuses on the belief that each well had its own guardian who had to be propitiated every year if the crops were to flourish. SOURCE: *English Shrines & Sanctuaries*, Christina Hole; *The Holy Wells of Wales*, Francis Jones.

Spring Tide: The sea tide that springs or wells up. These full tides occur at the new and full moon, when the attraction of both the sun and moon act is a direct line (see **Natural Tides**).

Sprout-kale or **Kale-month:** The Saxon name for February. Kale is colewort, the great pot-wort of the ancient Saxons, which began sprouting in February.

Squares (Magical): Numbers and letters are containers of magical power and, if arranged in a square following certain rules, they are believed to make powerful talismans. Francis Barratt's *Magus* and Eliphas **Lévi's** *Transcendental Magic* reproduce the squares of the planets given in Agrippa's *Occult Philosophy*.

Stable Keys: Stables and byres frequently

have a perforated flint **Hagstone** or horn attached to the keys to guard the livestock from harm by evil spirits. The flint is to propitiate the witches, and the horn to obtain the good graces of **Pan**, the protector of cattle.

Staff: see **Stang**.

Stag: The rock painting of a man wearing antlers, in the cave of Les Trois Frères in southern France, suggests that the stag was of ritual importance way back in the Stone Age. The stag was also widely regarded as a supernatural animal and among some people was thought to be connected with the **Underworld**. The Celtic divinity, **Cernunnos**, was depicted as wearing antlers as shown on the Gundestrup cauldron found in Jutland; while **Artemis/Diana** has close association with the stag.

Stang or **Staff:** Rarely seen outside Traditional or Old Craft. On an individual level, the stang is a symbol of faith and acts as a personal altar, representing the Old God energy and all it represents. Bearing this in mind, the choice of wood is left to the individual, although ash shod with iron is traditional. The coven stag is usually a garlanded ash and, on very rare occasions, a blackthorn stang will be brought into Circle should the coven or one of its members need to defend themselves. SOURCE: *Witchcraft – A Tradition Renewed*, Evan John Jones.

Stanton Drew, Somerset: Three circles of standing stones. From the largest, an avenue runs east to join another from the north circle; the remaining circle lies to the south-west. In addition there is also a structural remnant standing behind the Druid's Arms, whose precise significance remains a mystery.

Stanton Moor, Derbyshire: Within a radius of some 600 yards there is a concentration of monuments dating from the Middle Bronze Age. Near the north end of the area is the embanked circle known as the Nine Ladies, with the isolated King Stone close by. To the west is Doll Tor, a free-standing circle with many of the stones remaining upright. There are 70 or more cairns in the area.

Star: (1) From a magical and mystical perspective the star is a reoccurring theme of mystery, particularly those that were visible to the ancients, as a home of the gods. (2) The seventeenth card in the **Major Arcana** of the **Tarot** and the archetypal symbol of timeless Mystery and the ever-turning cosmos.

Star Carr: The most famous Mesolithic site in Britain that was occupied around 7500BC by a hunting community on the edge of a postglacial lake. Remarkable for having domestic dogs (which were presumed to have been used for hunting), and for the antler headdresses that may have had ritual use. SOURCE: *Britain BC*, Francis Pryor.

Star Charts: Maps of the stars according to how the ancients saw the constellations. Claudius Ptolemaeus made the first scientific maps of the heavens, while Hipparchus produced the first star catalogue and discovered the precession of the equinoxes. SOURCE: *Skywatching*, David Levy.

Star-crossed: Not favored by the stars. Unlucky.

Star Flower: see **Borage**.

Starling: The old Welsh name of 'bird of the snows' harks back to the time when the bird was a winter visitor. The images formed by the huge, wheeling flocks of the birds can be used for divination. SOURCE: *Mean Streets Witchcraft*, Mélusine Draco.

Star Sapphire: One of the rarest and most precious of stones – and one of the most potent – it is the stone of the **Initiate**. SOURCE: *The Equinox*, Aleister Crowley.

Star Ruby: Like the Star Sapphire, it is known as a 'phenomenal gem' and brings good fortune to the wearer. SOURCE: *The Equinox*, Aleister Crowley.

Star-worship: The sun, moon, planets and stars have been worshipped as gods in a number of cultures, evolving from the awe felt at the beauty, regularity, mystery and power of the heavenly bodies. Star-worship usually accompanies the early development of astronomy, calendrics and astrology. SOURCE: *Starchild*, Mélusine Draco; *The Penguin Dictionary of Religions*, ed John R. Hinnells.

Starry Sphere: The eighth heaven of the Peripatetic system; also called the **Firmament**.

Steiner, Rudolf (1861–1925) Esotericist, philosopher and founder of the Anthroposophical Society has been described as the 'most remarkable occultist of the present century' [20th]. The extraordinary originality of his mind led him to establish a philosophy that linked up the world of natural science with the world of spirit. His revolutionary ideas took form in a number of projects, ranging from art and architecture, to education and farming. SOURCE: *Dictionary of Demons*, Fred Gettings; *Knowledge of the Higher Worlds* and *Occult Science*, Rudolf Steiner.

Stella Matutina: An off-shoot of the **Golden Dawn** of which Israel **Regardie** was a member.

Stellar or **Star Cults:** A primitive form of star-worship probably underlies the prehistoric megalithic sites of northern Europe and similar sites in North America. While it is doubtful whether the stars have ever been worshipped purely for themselves, they have been associated with divine beings from a very early period, often as a form of manifestation or dwelling place. SOURCE: *Starchild*, Mélusine Draco.

Stenness, Orkney: Three stone rings – The Ring of Bookan, a cairn with a surrounding ditch; the Ring of Brodgar, a henge monument originally of 60 stones; and the Ring of Stenness, also a henge.

Stevington, Bedfordshire: Under the churchyard's east wall there is a little spring called the Holy Well that was visited by pilgrims in medieval times. It was probably a pre-Christian sacred spring that was incorporated into the church complex.

Stichomancy: Reading of random selections of passages or verses from a book. Unlike **Bibliomancy**, this does not have to be a holy book.

Stigmata Diaboli: see **Witches' Mark.**

Stoat: Possesses a vitality and reputation for aggressiveness that are out of all proportion to its size. The fur turns white in winter, when it is known as ermine. The traditional symbol of purity was ermine, and there is the famous portrait of Elizabeth I at Hatfield House, wearing an ermine on her sleeve.

Stolisomancy: The significance of the way and manner in which a person dresses themselves.

Stone: Ordinary stones and pebbles have long been accredited with magical or healing properties. Any unusual shape or image within the stone may give it magical properties.

Stonecrop: A native of Britain, the plant grew wild on roofs, rocks, walls, sand dunes and dry grassy slopes. Its botanical name, *Sedum*, is thought to be derived from the Latin 'to calm' or 'to settle', a reference to its soothing properties. Among its reputed magical uses, the plant was said to repel witches. Ruling planet: **Moon**.

Stone of Destiny: Irish kings sat on this stone on the hill of Tara at their coronation and according to tradition wherever the stone might be the people would be dominant. It was removed to Scone in Scotland, and moved from Scone Abbey to London by Edward I. It is kept in Westminster Abbey under the royal throne, on which the English sovereigns sit at their **Coronation**.

Stone Heads: The hundreds of stone heads that have been found in the West Riding of Yorkshire have presented archeologists with a fascinating problem. Do they date from Celtic times, or are some of them only a few hundred years old? The Celts that lived in the area 2300 years ago revered the human head, and severed heads of their enemies were treated with respect. Large numbers of these stone heads have been found in Scotland, Ireland and on the Continent, but in the Bradford area, where many of them were placed in drystone walls and above cottage doors, some are no more than 100 years old. There is a theory that they were still serving their original purpose and that an Iron Age cult had survived into the reign of Queen Victoria. SOURCE: *Folklore, Myths & Legends of Britain*, Reader's Digest.

Stonehenge: Described as Europe's greatest prehistoric monument, because as a circle of huge standing stones it is in a class of its own. Despite various theories about its purpose it remains an enduring enigma. SOURCE: *From Stonehenge to Modern Cosmology*, Fred Hoyle; *The Pattern of the Past*, Guy Underwood; *Stonehenge Decoded*, G.S. Hawking; *Historical Atlas of Britain*, ed Nigel Saul.

Stone Circles and **Megaliths:** Mark the important magico-religious sites of our Neolithic ancestors, which can be located all over the British Isles. The most important being Arbor Low (Derbyshire); Avebury (Wiltshire); the Castlerigg Circle (Cumbria); Kingston Russell (Dorset); the Rollright Stones (Oxfordshire) and the Stanton Drew Circles (Avon). SOURCE: *The Goddess of the Stones*, George Terence Meaden; *The Pagan Religions of the Ancient British Isles*, Ronald Hutton; *Prehistoric Astronomy & Ritual* and *Prehistoric Stones Circles*, Aubrey Burl; *The Secret Country*, Janet and Colin Bord.

Storm: Believed to be an expression of anger from the sky god, his voice being thunder and his weapon lightning. The oldest manifestation of this thought is in the ancient Egyptian concept of their storm god **Set**. In medieval times, church bells were rung to ward off evil spirits of the storm, and various plants were thought to give protection against lightning. That witches could raise storms is another popular folklore belief

SOURCE: *The Dictionary of Omens & Superstitions*, Philippa Waring; *Folklore, Myths & Legends of Britain*, Reader's Digest; *Superstitions of the Countryside*, E. & M.A. Radford.

Storm Petrel: Birds of the open ocean, they only come ashore at night or to nest. Their association with storms is genuine enough because in extreme weather they can be blown ashore and inland. To the sailor, their presence means storms, which is one reason why they were disliked and known as 'witches' or 'waterwitches'. The more familiar name is Mother Carey's chickens.

Straw: Dolls used in image magic are often made partially or wholly of straw. It is used in many charms to cause death, injury, impotency and infertility.

Strawberry or **Wood Strawberry:** A native of Britain, wild strawberries were known to the ancient Britons, the Romans and the Anglo-Saxons. The name comes from the Old English 'to strew', and refers to the plant's spreading creepers. It has a variety of medicinal uses and according to the **Doctrine of Signatures**, the color and shape of the fruit suggested that it was a cure for heart disease. Ruling planet: **Venus**.

Strawberry Tree: Of all the native British trees, the strawberry tree is one of the rarest in the wild, and can only be found still growing naturally in a few isolated areas in southern Ireland. There is little folklore surrounding it but the leaves and flowers were said to be an antidote to poison and plague.

Strega: An Italian hereditary witch or sorceress, coming from a family in which the Craft has been practiced for generations. Charles **Leland** believed that in many instances the line could be traced back to 'medieval, Roman, or Etruscan times'. Strega is the root of Italian pagan belief that gave rise to Leyland's **Aradia**. SOURCE: *Aradia, or Gospel of the Witches*, Charles Leyland; *Hereditary Witchcraft*, Raven Grimassi; *Italian Witchcraft* (formerly *Ways of the Strega*), Raven Grimassi.

Strega, La: The first work on witchcraft to be printed in Italian by Pico della Mirandola (1555). Also called *Strix* [*The Witch*], the text shows that the theory of witchcraft was fully developed by the beginning of the 16th century.

Strength: The eleventh card in the **Major Arcana** of the **Tarot**; although in the Thoth Tarot this is called Lust, the meaning is similar. The archetypal symbol of inner Strength that can unexpectedly come to the surface in the most unlikely of persons or situations.

Strigae: [sing. *striga* = she who screeches] In Roman popular belief, birdlike demons who stole children. Sometimes they were said to be old women who had turned into birds.

Stygian: Pertaining to the Styx, the fabled river of hell. It was said to flow nine times around the infernal regions.

Sub Jove: [Latin] Under Jove – in the open air. **Jupiter** (or Jove) being the deified personification of the upper regions of the air.

Sub Rosa: see **Rose.**

Succession Powder: The poison said to have been used by the Marquise de Brinvilliers in her poisonings, for the benefit of 'successors'.

Succubus: A female night demon that can trace its legendary roots from ancient Assyria to medieval Europe (see **Incubus**). SOURCE: *The Encyclopedia of Witchcraft & Demonology*, Rossell Hope Robbins; *Magic – White & Black*, Franz Hartmann; *What You Call Time*, Suzanne Ruthven.

Sul: A Celtic goddess worshipped at Bath (see **Bath Spa**). Eternal fire burned in her temple; her name means 'the sun'. During the Roman occupation she was identified with **Minerva**.

Sullt: [Starvation] The knife that the goddess Hel is accustomed to use when she sits down to eat from her dish 'hunger'.

Sulphur: According to early alchemists, the element in a substance which enables it to burn and regarded as one of the basic components of all matter: the others being **Mercury** and **Salt**.

Summer: the **Second** or **Autumnal**: Said to last 30 days and begins about the time that the sun enters **Scorpio** (23rd October). It is variously called St. Martin's summer; All Saints' or All Hallow Summer and St. Luke's little summer (see **Indian Summer**). Shakespeare refers to them as: *'Expect St. Martin's summer; halcyon days,'* in *Henry VI, 1.2* and *'Farewell, All Hallow summer,'* in *Henry IV, 1.2*.

Summerland, The: (1) More than 1300 years ago, West Saxon farmers used to fatten their cattle in a place where pastures were so rich that they called it the Summer Land. (2) In contemporary **Wicca**, this term has now become a euphemism for the **Otherworld**, or afterlife.

Summers, Montague: A fanatic whose numerous books on Satanism, demonology, witchcraft and black magic was accepted by the establishment as

'expert testimony', openly advocating the reintroduction of the death penalty for witchcraft. He was generally referred to as 'The Reverend' or even 'Father' and dressed in elaborate clerical attire, although whether he had any claim to such titles is a matter for conjecture. He frequently mixed with various occult personalities of the early part of the 20th century and translated the infamous *Malleus Malificarum* into English. TITLES: *The History of Witchcraft & Demonology, Witchcraft & Black Magic*.

Summoner: An officer in traditional Craft, whose task it is to 'summon' members from hived-off groups to attend the 'Mother Coven'. This summons cannot be ignored as it is made on the behest of the **Magister**.

Summer Solstice, or **Midsummer Day:** (1) When the sun is above the horizon for the longest period of the year on or around 21st June. It is a day of importance for both historical and traditional Craft. (2) The Church moved Midsummer Day to 24th June to coincide with the Feast of St. John.

Sun: (1) In classical mythology the Sun is associated with Apollo. The ancients recognized that it provided the heat and light necessary for existence, and so it was worshipped in many guises in nearly every culture, the most well-known being Amun-Ra, sun god of the Egyptians (see **Solar Worship**). (2) The Sun in astrology is associated with the specific area of the heavens that establishes the zodiacal sign under which an individual was born. (3) The Sun rules our Solar system and is responsible for life existing on Earth. It's visible surface with its dark spots and looping prominences. Deeper down, energy streams out from the nuclear powerhouse at the core. (4) The Sun or *Sol* [Latin] was the term given by alchemists to gold. (5) The nineteenth card in the **Major Arcana** of the **Tarot** (the archetypal symbol of Light, warmth and strength) and **Tipareth** in the **Qabalah**.

Sun Dance: A sacred ritual observed by the Plains tribes of Native Americans.

Sunflower: Ruled by, and symbolizes the **Sun**; a powerful charm against evil spirits.

Supernatural: The unexplained or hidden world that genuine occultists must seek in order to gain knowledge.

Superstition: Detrimental to true occult working since it relies on blind faith in something, as opposed to a questioning/enquiring creed, or a degenerated magical teaching relegated to folk memory. Mankind reverts to irrational beliefs whenever its faith wilts and it becomes afraid; superstition is a form of personal magic that is used for coming to terms with the unknown. SOURCE: *The Dictionary of Omens & Superstitions*, Philippa Waring; *The Psychology of Superstition*, Gustav Jahoda; *Superstitions of the Countryside*, E. & M.A. Radford; *Superstition & the Superstitious*, Eric Maple; *The Penguin Guide to the Superstitions of Britain & Ireland*, Steve Roud.

Supplicātiō: A solemn rite of humiliation or thanksgiving, carried out on the occasion of some Roman success.

Supplication: (1) A word that has changed from its original meaning – the Romans used it for a thanksgiving after a successful event. The word means the act of folding the knees (*sub-plico*). (2)

We now use the word for begging or entreating.

"Surest Way to Peace is a Constant Preparation for War": Advice given to Henry VIII by the Bishop of Hereford. [In Latin: *Si vis pacem, para bellum.*]

Surname or **Sirename:** For a long time people had no family name and were known by a personal name – sometimes 'son of' would be added. Surnames are not traced back farther than the latter part of the 10th century. *'In ford, in ham and ley and ton/The most of English surnames run'* or *'In Tre, Pol and Pen, you can trace the Cornishmen.'*

Suttee (or **Sati**): To perish in the flames of her dead husband's funeral pyre as an act of purification was the duty of the high-case Hindu widow; a practice that survived in remote areas in defiance of the law, until as recently as the 1940s. There are accounts of this ancient practice dating from the time of Alexander the Great's invasion of India (327–325BCE).

Swallow: In Roman superstition it was considered lucky for a swallow to build about the property. The bird was sacred to the **Penates**, or household gods, and to injure one would be to bring wrath upon your own house. This belief obviously passed into British superstition: *'Perhaps you failed in your foreseeing skill,/ For swallows are unlucky birds to kill,'* Dryden: *Hind and Panther,* part iii – and exists to the present day. Ointment with a swallow's feather in it is used to secure universal love and affection. In Ireland and Scotland, however, the swallow is sometimes thought of as one of the Devil's birds.

Swan: Since men have recorded anything about birds, they have had many things to say about swans, much of which has been preserved in folklore. Although the flesh was prized by the nobility, it was considered unlucky to kill a swan; in Gaelic and Celtic myth, virgins were turned into swans after death. SOURCE: *Fauna Britannica*, Stefan Buczacki.

Swastika: A word derived from the Sanskrit, *svastika*, which means well-being, good fortune or luck. Although the sigil has been used as a mystical symbol in many parts of the world from prehistoric times onwards, it is the negative connotations of the Third Reich with which it is associated today. Chosen on the mistaken belief that it was a Nordic emblem, the swastika came to stand for Hitler's Germany (see **Nazi Occultism**).

Swear: Now means to take an oath, but in the original sense it merely meant to *aver* or *affirm*; when to affirm on oath was required, the word *oath* was appended – as *'I swear by oath'*. Shakespeare also uses: *'I swear by my sword.'*

Sweat Lodge: Originally an **Amerindian** rite of purification as a prelude to a **Rite of Passage.**

Sweet Cicely: Introduced into Britain by the Romans, the herb has a wide variety of medicinal and culinary uses. **Gerard** said the roots were 'very good for old people that are dull and without courage.' Ruling planet: **Jupiter.**

Sweet Track, The: A carefully constructed prehistoric linear platform or causeway running for 2km across the Somerset fens. A wide variety of votive offerings dating back to prehistoric times have been found there.

Swimming: The ordeal by immersion in water is a very ancient means of determining innocence or guilt. The last recorded instance of the 'swimming' of a suspected witch in England was in 1863, when an 80-year old man, a deaf-mute, was accused of bewitching a Mrs. Smith and making her ill. Villagers dragged the old man from the bar of the Swan Inn at Sible Hedingham and threw him into a stream. Some of the villagers hauled him out but he died several days later in the local workhouse. Mrs. Smith and a man named Stammers were charged with manslaughter and sentenced at Chelmsford in 1864 to six month's hard labor.

Sword: Regarded with mystical reverence in the Dark Ages, the sword was credited with a personality and power of its own and the oldest known specimens date from the Bronze Age. It has become part of Wiccan regalia but according to **Crowley** in *Magick*, the sword is only an important weapon in the lower forms of magic. SOURCE: *The Archaeology of Weapons*, R.E. Oakeshott; *Coven of the Scales*, A.R. Clay-Egerton; *Magic: An Occult Primer*, David Conway; *Magick in Theory & Practice*, Aleister Crowley; *Man, Myth & Magic*, Richard Cavendish; *Techniques of High Magic*, Francis King and Stephen Skinner; *Witchcraft – A Tradition Renewed*, Evan John Jones.

Sword Dance: The origins of sword dancing, like those of **Mumming** plays and **Morris** dancing, are obscure. The dances vary from area to area but all involve the mock decapitation of a leader with a long sword. It is believed that all three disciplines are relics of pre-Christian paganism.

Sycomancy: A leaf (originally a fig) is selected from a tree and the question written on the leaf, which is placed in the sun to dry. If it immediately begins to shrive and dry, the answer is 'no'; if it remains fresh for some hours, the answer is 'yes'.

Sycorax: A witch, whose son was Caliban in Shakespeare's *The Tempest*.

Sylphs: A creature of Elemental Air. Spirits made from the atoms of air in which they live.

Symbol: An object or activity representing or standing for something else. The symbols (and **Correspondences**) used in magical practice from arbitrary or intrinsic signs, through gestures and words, to those kinds of language, imagery and actions that embody the meaning and interpretation they convey. SOURCE: *Man & His Symbols*, Carl G. Jung; *Liber 777*, Aleister Crowley.

Sympathetic Magic: A term coined by Sir James Frazer, in *The Golden Bough*, for the principle that *'things act on each other at a distance through a secret sympathy'* and combining two basic assumptions of magical thinking: mimicry and contact. SOURCE: *A Dictionary of Devils & Demons*, J. Tondriau and R. Villeneuve.

Synastry: The technique of comparing horoscopes.

Syncretism: The formation of new cults by the merging of elements from different traditions.

Syncreto-paganism: Similar to **Meso-paganism**, this defines a group that has submerged itself into a dominant culture and adopted the external practices and symbols of that culture's religion. **Voodoo** and **Santeria** adopted many of the Christian saints as part of its belief.

"... there are in Italy great numbers of Strega, fortune tellers or witches, who divining by cards, perform strange ceremonies in which spirits are supposed to be invoked, make and sell small amulets and in fact comport themselves generally as their reputed kind are wont to do ..."

Charles Leland

[*Aradia, or the Gospel of the Witches*]

T

Taboo: [Polynesian] A restriction or ban on potent and sacred things, which can refer to religion or what is seen as a social / cultural taboo; to break it would mean automatic punishment.

Tabla Rasa: [Latin] A clean slate on which anything can be written.

Table Turning: The art of turning tables without the application of force. Claimed to be the work of departed spirits as a means of communication.

TabulæToletanæ: The astronomical tables composed by order of Alphonso X of Castile, in the middle of the 13th century, were so called because they were adapted to the city of Toledo. *'His Tables Tolletanes forth he brought,/ Ful wel corrected, ne ther lakked nought,'* Chaucer: *Canterbury Tales*, 11,585.

Tace: Latin for candle, and a candle symbolizes light. The phrase *tace* means 'keep it dark', do not throw light upon it. Reference is made to it by W.B. Yates in *Fairy Tales of the Irish Peasantry* and Sir Walter Scott in *Redgauntlet*.

Taghairm: A bizarre means of Scottish divination. A person wrapped in the hide of a freshly killed bullock was placed beside a waterfall, or at the foot of a precipice, and left there to meditate on the question requiring an answer. Whatever their fancy suggested to them passed for inspiration. Sir Walter Scott refers to it in *Lady of the Lake*, iv, 4.

Tahuti or **Thoth:** The Egyptian god of the moon, wisdom and magic and often referred to as 'the magician's magician'.

Tai Chi Ch'uan: For centuries this ancient Chinese system of exercise and meditation has offers practitioners a 'natural, holistic way to achieve a healthier, happier life'. Tai Chi offers relief from stress, breathing disorders, muscular ailments etc, as well as having a calming effect on emotional problems. SOURCE: *The Healing Art of Tai Chi*, Martin and Emily Lee; *Principles of Tai Chi*, Paul Brecher; *Tai Chi*, P. Crompton; *Tai Chi Ch'uan*, Wei Yue Sun and William Chen.

Tailtiu: An Irish goddess, embodying **Tellurian** and natural forces. In Irish myth she is the nurse of Lug and after her death a festival was inaugurated for her – the **Lughnasadh**, i.e. the espousal of the god, Lug. *The Dictionary of Gods and Goddesses, Devils and Demons* suggests that this festival represents the *hieros gamos* between the god of light and the earth goddess.

Tai-sui-xing: 'The star of the great year' refers to **Jupiter**, which takes 12 years to complete its orbit, and regarded as the god of time in China.

Takamimusubi: ['High and sublime begetter'] The Japanese progenitor god of the royal family. As a sky god he rules the world together with the sun goddess **Amaterasu**.

Taliesin: The Welsh legend surrounding a bard of the 6th century, who attracted almost as many myths as **Merlin**.

Talisman: A talisman can be defined as an object that has been magically endowed with the power of attracting good fortune, or deflecting bad fortune. In Arab countries a talisman is still used in the form of a piece of paper on which are written the names of the Seven Sleepers and their dog, to protect the house from ghosts and evil spirits. SOURCE: *Book of Charms & Talismans*, W.G.O. Sepharial; *The Book of Magical Talismans*, Elbee Wright; *The Complete Golden Dawn System of Magic*, Israel Regardie.

Talmud: The main text of rabbinic Judaism.

Tamarisk: From a Hebrew word meaning 'to cleanse'. The Romans wreathed the brows of criminals with it.

Tangie: A water sprite of the Orkneys, from Danish for *tang* (seaweed) with which it is covered. The tangie sometimes appears in human form, sometimes as a small horse (see **Kelpie**).

Tansy: A native plant of Britain, it was known to the Anglo-Saxons and listed by **Aelfric**. Apart from its wide range of medicinal and culinary uses, in the Middle Ages it was a popular herb for strewing, and an insect repellant. Ruling planet: **Venus**.

Tantra: The term applied to certain Hindu manuals of ritualized techniques dealing with sexual/yogic and magical practices closely connected with Shakti and performed by small groups of initiates. In Tantric philosophy the interplay of two basic forces, **Shiva** and **Shakti** (male and female), underlies the entire universe: the female principle is the dominant one and the male the subordinate. SOURCE: *Ecstasy Through Tantra*, Dr. John Mumford; *Hindu World*, Benjamin Walker; *The Tantric Experience*, Osho; *Tantric Sex*, Cassandra Lorius; *The Google Tantra*, Alan Richardson.

Taoism: Tao is the uncomplicated essence of what is right and was founded by Lao Tze in China in the 6th century BC. At the end of his life he inscribed some 5000 characters on bamboo parchment, before leaving for an unknown destination. This small book, the *Tao Te Ching* (see **Book of Change**) is one of the world's great religious classics. SOURCE: *The Great Religions*, Floyd H. Ross and Tynette Hills; *The Penguin Dictionary of Religions*, ed John R. Hinnells; *Eastern Religions*, ed Michael D. Coogan; *The World's Religions*, Ninian Smart.

Tara: The seat of the High Kings of Ireland and the focus of much mythological tradition and ritual practice. Excavations of the site, situated on a low hill in Co Meath, have provided convincing archeological proof of the settlement's importance. The remains consist of various earthworks, and a Neolithic passage grave that was used again during the Bronze Age; this suggests that the Iron Age occupants of the site took over a place that was already considered holy or sacred and applied their own religious traditions to it. SOURCE: *Pagan Celtic Britain* and *Everyday Life of the Pagan Celts*, A. Ross.

Taranis: [Celtic *taran* = thunder] Gallic thunder god and lord of heaven, equated by the Romans with **Jupiter**. It has been suggested that he is the god in Gallic art depicted holding a wheel – a symbol of thunder or of the sun. The Gallic hammer god has also been connected with Taranis, but he usually has a lightning flash in his hand.

Tarantism: A dancing mania that broke out in Germany in 1374, and in France during the Revolution, when it was called the *Carmagnole*. Extremely contagious, priests, lawyers, men and women, even the aged, joined in the mad dance in the open streets till they fell from exhaustion. *Tarantella* were tunes and dances in triplets, that were supposed to cure the dancing mania.

Tarot: More often than not used for divination, although most magicians use the cards of the Major Arcana as gateways to greater cosmic awareness. The esoteric symbolism of each card produces mystical visions related to the imagery of the **Tree of Life.** Much of what is seen as the modern Tarot owes much of its interpretations to the studies of Eliphas **Lévi**, who discovered that the 22 cards of the Major Arcana symbolized the 22 paths leading to the 10 stages (*sephiroth*) of consciousness. The Marseilles or French pack is probably the oldest in design, while the Rider-Waite (designed by A.E. **Waite**) and Thoth (designed by Aleister **Crowley**) packs are the most well-known. Tarot designs are now available for almost any Path or Tradition. SOURCE: *The Complete Golden Dawn System of Magic,* Israel Regardie; *The Hollow Tree,* Mélusine Draco; *The Book of Thoth,* Aleister Crowley; *The Magical Arts,* Richard Cavendish; *The Tarot,* Alfred Douglas; *The Elements of The Tarot,* A.T. Mann; *Techniques of High Magic,* Francis King and Stephen Skinner.

Tartarus: Empire of eternal darkness, the most horrible part of the Graeco-Roman underworld.

Tattoo: The word was introduced to the Western world by Captain Cook and is derived from the Tahitian term *tatau.* In many cultures, including traditional Craft, tattooing has ritual importance as part of an initiation rite. SOURCE: *History of Tattooing,* W.D. Hambly; *The Witch Cult in Western Europe,* Margaret Murray.

Tattva: [Sanskrit] Principle; truth; element; essence.

Tattwa: One of the Eastern elements incorporated in the Golden Dawn system of ritual magic and used in their original Hindu context as symbols for the elements. *Tejas,* a red equilateral triangle = Fire; *Apas,* a silver crescent = Water; *Vayu,* a blue circle = Air; *Prithivi,* a yellow square = Earth and *Akasa,* an indigo eg = Spirit. SOURCE: *The Complete Golden Dawn System of Magic,* Israel Regardie; *Magic: An Occult Primer,* David Conway; *Techniques of High Magic,* Francis King and Stephen Skinner.

Tattwic Tides: From the term *tattwa,* Hindi for 'vibration'. Each level of consciousness has its own vibration or *tattwa.* The rhythms and flow of energies, both in the human body and in the universe, are the tattwic tides.

Tau: The sign of the T-shaped cross and in its upright form it is the symbol of the creative spirit – hence the traditional shape of the magician's or witch's robe is T-shaped. It is the last letter of the Hebrew alphabet and a protective symbol against evil.

Tauret: The popular Egyptian goddess of childbirth. Symbolizing maternity and suckling, she was represented as a pregnant hippopotamus standing upright on her back legs and holding the hieroglyphic sign for protection: a plait of rolled papyrus.

Taurobolium: Part of the rites in the **Mysteries** of **Cybele** and Attis: the initiate descended into a pit and was drenched in the blood of a bull that had been slaughtered above him. After this the initiate was regarded as 'reborn'.

Taurus: (1) The second sign of the zodiac and identified with Zeus's transformation into a **Bull** when he abducted Europa – 19 April–20 May. (2) In the constellation Taurus, only the forequarters of the bull are visible as it emerges from the waves.

Tea Leaves or **Tasseography:** Although telling fortunes by consulting the patterns in the tea leaves was often regarded as harmless drawing room entertainment, it is a legitimate method of divination. The method used is time-honored and simple. The seeker places the cup upside down in the saucer, and turning it round three times taps the bottom three times with the index finger. The leaves are then ready to be read, although all tea leaf readers have their preferred interpretations.

Teanlay Night: The vigil of All Souls, or last evening in October, when bonfires were lighted and rites held for succoring souls in purgatory.

Tears: The absence of tears was considered to be a sure indication that the accused was a witch. This 'truth' was repeated in medieval witch-hunters' guides such as the *Malleus Malificarum*.

Tefnut: The Egyptian goddess of moisture who, with her brother-consort **Shu**, were the first gods created by **Atum**.

Telekinesis: The moving of objects by using the power of the mind.

Telepathy: Communication between one mind and another without the use of speech, gesture or any of the normal methods of communicating: thought transference.

Tellurion: An apparatus representing the earth and sun, demonstrating the occurrence of day and night, the seasons, etc, Tellurian = terrestrial, an inhabitant of the earth.

Temenos: The Greek name for a sanctuary, dedicated to one or more deities and serving a community. It often contained a sacred tree, stone or spring associated with a deity.

Temora: One of the principle poems of Ossian, in eight books, called after the royal residence of the kings of Connaught.

Temperence: The fourteenth card in the Major Arcana of the Tarot. Called Art in the Thoth **Tarot** and heavily laced with **Thelemic** symbolism.

Tempestarii: Medieval folklore cited these mythical witches who raised the wind, thunder and lightning and were seen as the wispy cloud forms that follow a storm.

Temple or **Lodge:** The name given for the room or sacred space where a magical working is carried out and to which outsiders have no access. Usually applies to the working or meeting area of Magical Orders including the **Freemasons** and **Rosicrucians**.

Temple of Khem: Founded in 1996 by a group of magical practitioners for the teaching of the Mysteries and *heka* of ancient Egypt. The Egyptians used the term *Heka* to refer to magical power, in the sense of a divine intervention that could be invoked in order to solve problems or crisis. Another word for magical power is *akhu*, which refers to 'enchantments, sorcery and spells'. SOURCE: *Liber Ægyptius: The Book of Egyptian Magic, Starchild,* and *The Atum-Re Revival,*Mélusine Draco.

Ten: In traditional numerology all two-digit numbers can be reduced by adding the two numbers together: 10 = 1 + 0 = 1 – linking back to the One. Number X in the **Tarot** equals the **Wheel of Fortune** (or the four Tens – Empresses or Princesses of the Minor Arcana), **Malkuth** in the **Qabalah**, and is governed by **Earth**.

Tenri-kyo: [Japanese] Teaches that there is no evil; it is nothing more than types of dust that lodge in the soul and represent hatred, greed, arrogance and other reprehensible dispositions.

Tephramancy: see **Pyromancy.**

Teratology: Study of monstrous creatures, which scientists and demonologists, Bodin (1529), Aldovrande, Pare, Remy (1530) etc, claimed existed, engendered by incubi and demons.

Terminus: Roman god of border markers – his feast, the *Terminalia*, was held on 23rd February.

Terminalia: Popularly thought to be the last day of the sacred Roman year.

Terpsichore: The goddess of dancing and dancers were called 'votaries of Terpsichore'.

Terrestrial Sun: Gold, which in alchemy was the metal corresponding to the sun, as silver did to the moon.

Terricolous: [Latin *terricola*, a dweller upon earth – *terra*, earth, *colêre*, to inhabit] Living in or on the soil.

Testosterone: The chief male sex hormone.

Tetragrammaton: The four Hebrew letters [YHWH] of the name of God in the Old Testament. Regarded with profound awe it was rarely pronounced, and in ordinary services in the synagogue the names Adonai or Elohim were substituted for it. The term passed into Western ritual magic as one of the major '**Names of Power**'. SOURCE: *Tetragrammaton*, Donald Tyson.

Teutonic Knights: An Order that grew out of the Crusades and originally only Germans of noble birth were admitted. Napoleon abolished the Order in 1800.

Thalysia, The: A primitive Greek harvest festival when, according to **Homer**, sacrifices were offered on the threshing floor at the altar of **Demeter** in recognition of her bounty.

Thargelia, The: A primate rite associated with **Apollo** where a central figure was the *pharmakos*, a criminal or scapegoat. He was led through the streets and alternatively fed and flogged with green branches and finally either expelled or executed to rid the city of the evil that has accumulated throughout the year.

Thaumaturgy: Denoting a wonder or miracle healing by 'magical' means.

Theban: A medieval magical alphabet allegedly invented by Pope Honorius and named after the Egyptian city of Thebes. Today it is finding renewed popularity among contemporary magical practitioners. SOURCE: *The Complete Magical Primer*, David Conway.

Theist: Believes there is a God who made and governs all creation; but does not believe in the doctrine of the Trinity, nor in divine revelation.

Thelema: The word means Will and discovery by each man and woman of the True Will; his or her own true purpose, is the central theme of **Thelemic** doctrine. SOURCE: *The Eye in the Triangle*, Israel Regardie; *The Hidden God*, Kenneth Grant; *The Law is for All*, ed Louis Wilkinson. [SEE PANEL]

Thelema

The Book of the Law is where a true study of Thelema actually begins because without it there can be no acceptance or understanding of Aleister Crowley's work or philosophy. Thelema, his *Confessions* inform us, does not merely imply a new religion, but a new cosmology, a new philosophy, a new ethic. The getting to grips with *The Book* means allowing the passages, stanzas and phrases to convey their own personal message to the seeker.

With his inimitable honesty, Crowley wasn't afraid to admit that much of *The Book* was incomprehensible to him. He worked tirelessly in his attempts to interpret its meaning but decided he was too close to the subject and, in the end, entrusted the task to his friend Louis Wilkinson, who wrote that in some one phrase or other of *The Book* there is direct message for every human being. 'The best way for the layman to approach this *Book* is to regard it as a letter written directly to himself. Even though he may not be able to understand some parts of the letter, he is sure to find other parts that are unmistakably addressed, in an intimately personal sense, to him.'

There have been dozens of published versions of *The Book of the Law*, but *The Law is for All*, edited by Louis Wilkinson, offers students the most comprehensive and intelligent approach. Here is 'everything under one roof', so to speak: a facsimile copy of the original in Crowley's hand, a complete version, a concise introduction and an abridged, annotated version broken down verse by verse with commentary.

Of this version, Wilkinson said that he had aimed at making an abridgement that the general reader of 'intelligence and good will can assimilate'. 'But I do not pretend that he will understand this book and make it his own without any difficulty at all; it is only charlatan works that can be so quickly and easily grasped as that...'

Crowley advanced the philosophy that every individual is a

Star — all equal in dignity and spiritual value; all with a true Will to express — **Love Is The Law, Love Under Will** — and that each person can take control of his or her own destiny by liberating themselves from false values, ignorance and hypocrisy. *Do What Thou Wilt…* is a much maligned and misquoted maxim and those translating it as being an instruction to do exactly as they wish have no business calling themselves a Magus. This is a religious faith for the individualist, as is shown by its central text: **Do What Thou Wilt Shall Be The Whole Of The Law.** 'Discover your own true Will is the *real* meaning of this,' explained Wilkinson, 'and then act in harmony with it to the utmost of your powers. Only by so doing will you be shown your own true thought and life.'

That Crowley professed **Every Man And Every Woman Is A Star** demonstrates his belief that man and woman were equal in spirituality, despite the fact that his critics continue to accuse him of the worst excesses of male chauvinism. His own views on sexual equality within the bounds of marriage, so expansively expressed in *Confessions*, show him to be well in advance of his Victorian contemporaries of a more 'respectable' nature. Nevertheless, he taught that each human was a *separate* star — a separate 'god' — a *Starchild* — all equal in dignity and spiritual value; all with a True Will to express; that the modern tendency for herd-instinct 'defiles and destroys the godhead' in both man *and* woman.

Wilkinson's version of *The Law is for All*, giving a thorough commentary for each verse, was very dear to Crowley's heart, but it was a full fifty years before it made its way into print for the benefit of the general reader. *The Book* had already been published in several versions without any explanation but as both Crowley and Wilkinson realized, if it was to reach and influence a wider public, a detailed commentary would be indispensable.

EXTRACT FROM *THE THELEMIC HANDBOOK*
MÉLUSINE DRACO

Thelemic: Pertaining to the teaching and philosophy of **Thelema**.

Theogony: The birth of the gods, an account, myth or theory of the origin, generation and line of descent of the gods – specifically Hesiod's poem on the genealogy of the Greek gods.

Theoi: Gods. Greek deities were anthropomorphic, possessing immortality, extensive powers, knowledge, happiness and beauty. They were neither transcendental nor omnipresent.

Theology: Discourse about god, or the science of religion.

Theomancy: The study of the divine mysteries; a part of the **Qabalah**. Once mastered, theomancy gives the scholar power over angels and demons, the ability to see into the future, and to perform miracles.

Theosophy: Refers to the philosophy of the **Theosophical** Society borrowed from Ammonius Saccas of the 3rd century AD and made popular by Madame **Blavatsky**, whose writings aroused considerable interest and controversy in the late 1800s. It propagates doctrines based on Blavatsky's eclectic, visionary writings drawn from **Hinduism** and **Buddhism**, and all religions are viewed as versions of the one esoteric 'truth' – theosophy. It has been historically important in popularizing Eastern ideas in the West. Caught up in the occult revival, the movement attracted a new influx of adherents in the 1970s. SOURCE: *Isis Unveiled* and *The Secret Doctrine*, Madame H.P. Blavatsky; *The New Believers*, David V. Barrett.

Theriomancy: see **Alectryomancy**.

Therion: [Greek] The Beast. Aleister Crowley assumed the title *To Mega Therion* (The Great Wild Beast) when he attained a further magical grade in New York in 1915, and wrote what has been described as the 'finest modern grimoire', *Magick in Theory & Practice* under this name.

Thesmophoria, The: A Greek festival occurring at the autumn (October) sowing of the new crops in honor of **Demeter**, and performed solely by women.

Thetford, Norfolk: An ancient town with a known history of more than 1000 years. It was the seat of the kings of East Anglia, standing on the **Icknield Way** and surrounded by many relics of Stone Age culture.

Theurgy: An ancient form of spiritualism whereby 'theurists' claim to make direct contact with the gods and convey their wishes to the community. The Emperor **Julian** (called by his detractors as 'the Apostate') was a patron of theory.

Thinit: [An earlier rendering = Tanit] Supreme goddess of Carthage in her triple aspect of the queen of heaven, virgin and mother. Her special symbol is the so-called Thinit emblem: a triangle with horizontal beams placed on it.

Third Eye: A third eye was attributed to the distant ancestors of humanity, which permitted them to see directly into the spirit realms.

Thirteen: That the number 13 is unlucky is one of the most common and persistent of superstitions. In Norse mythology, sitting 13 down to dinner was deemed unlucky, because at a banquet in **Valhalla**, **Loki** arrived uninvited – making 13 guests – and **Balder** was killed (see **Friday 13th**).

Thnetoi Anthropoi: Mortal men. There

is no consistent Greek myth for the creation of the human race, only different tales about individuals.

Thomas the Rhymer: Born around 1220, he grew up to be a poet and prophet, whose gloomy prognostications were first published in 1603. As with the French astrologer **Nostradamus,** there are those who still devote themselves to unraveling his obscure dictums. Sir Walter Scott called him the 'Merlin of Scotland'.

Thor: [Old Saxon *thunar*] Germanic god of thunderstorms and fertility, belonging to the race of the **Aesir**. He drives a chariot drawn by two goats, and possesses the throwing-hammer, **Mjölnir**. His sacred tree was the **Oak**.

Thor, the Hammer of: In the North the hammer of Thor rivaled the cross as a sacred symbol and was a protective amulet against lightning, fire and calamities of all kinds.

Thorn Apple: A poisonous solanaceous plant of the genus *Datura,* used by witches in potions and ointments.

Thoth: The most popular and enduring of all the Egyptian gods, he was the patron of writing and knowledge, and associated with the moon and magic – being thought of as the magician's magician. He invented all the arts and sciences, astronomy, soothsaying, medicine and surgery (see **Tahuti**).

Thrall: [O.E. ON *thræl, thræll*] Slavery, servitude. Used magically to describe an obsession with crystal gazing (crystal-thrall) or Circle-casting (circle-thrall), which is common among beginners.

Three: The number plays a prominent role in universal myth, mysticism, mystery traditions, folklore, alchemy,

ritual and magic (see **Triad**). It is a ruling number that **Pythagorus** calls 'the perfect number' and the symbol of Deity. It is generally considered to be the luckiest of numbers. It equals the **Empress** (or four Threes or Queens in the Minor Arcana) in the **Tarot, Binah** in the **Qabalah** and is governed by **Saturn**.

Threefold Return, Law of: A contemporary Wiccan belief that if a person sends out negative energy to harm or interfere with another, the negativity will return to them threefold.

Three Sacred Herbs: The **Druids** prized three sacred herbs above all others: vervain, meadowsweet and watermint.

Threshold: In his book *Folklore in the Old Testament*, Sir James **Frazer** compared a number of threshold customs and beliefs, taking as his starting point the officials of the Temple in Jerusalem, who were called 'keepers of the threshold'. There are numerous superstitions in Europe relating to threshold customs and magically it remains one of the most important sites for protective magic.

Thuban: (1) A fire-spitting, dragon-like demon in Islamic literature. (2) The star *Draconis* in the constellation of Draco, which was the Pole Star around 2800BC.

Thule: (1) Known to classical writers, it was an island in the northern ocean and thought to be Iceland or Shetland (which is still called the Isle of Thyle by seamen. *'Where the Northern Ocean, in vast whirls,/Boils round the naked melancholy isles/Of farthest thule,'* Thomson: *Autumn*. Ultimate Thule was the end of the world: the last extremity and the most northern point known to the Romans. *'Tibi serviat Ultima Thule.'* Virgil: *Georgics,* i.30. (2) In modern times it has been revived as a **Neo-pagan** tradition.

Thunderbird: A widely recurring theme in Amerindian mythology, of an intermediary, celestial spirit depicted as a great eagle that produces thunder by flapping its wings.

Thunderbolts: Jupiter was depicted by the ancients holding a scepter in his left hand and thunderbolts in his right. Scientifically speaking there are no such things as thunderbolts but many tons of bolides, aerolites, meteors, or shooting stars (of stony or metallic substance) fall every year on the Earth.

Thunder Water: The water in which the farrier (smith) cools hot metal, particularly the **Horseshoes**, which has curative and magical properties.

Thurible: An incense burner on a chain that is used to hold burning charcoal, upon which resin and herbs are burned as part of ritual preparation.

Thyme: An herb introduced into Britain by the Romans and listed by **Aelfric**. Being a favorite flower of the fairies, thyme was reputed to possess the power to make them visible to humans. It has a wide range of medicinal and culinary uses, and was used as incense in temples. Ruling planet: **Venus**.

Thyrsos: An ivy-twined staff with a pine cone, or sometimes garlanded with grapes and vine leaves, was carried by the worshippers of **Dionysus**.

Tiamat: An early personification of the sea in Babylonian mythology; by mingling with fresh water, the first generation of gods were born. She was killed by Marduk, and from her body the universe was born.

Tiberinalia: The day of Tiberinus and **Gaia** (8th December) when rites were performed in honor of the Roman river god and the earth goddess.

Tibetan Tradition: The cult of Tibetan **Buddhism** has caught the imagination of the West because of its esoteric approach to faith and the concepts of karma and reincarnation, not to mention the personal charisma of HH Dalai Lama. Tibetan Buddhism has in many respects preserved the original teachings of Buddha, while exploring more complex issues such as the nature of the mind and the different types or levels of consciousness. SOURCE: *Buddhism & Lamaism: A Study of the Religion of Tibet,* John E. Ellam; *Buddhism in the Tibetan Tradition,* Geshe Kelsang Gyatso; *Death & Dying: The Tibetan Tradition,* Glenn H. Mullin; *Essential Tibetan Buddhism,* Robert A.F. Thurman; *Principles of Tibetan Medicine,* Dr. Tamdin Sither Bradley.

Tides: see **Natural Tides**.

Tiki: A Polynesian carving of a human figure, usually worn around the neck as an amulet; in recent years tikis have become popular in the West as good luck charms.

Time: A concept arising from change experienced and observed, expressed by past, present and future. In magical terms, time is irrelevant as the passage of time between the astral levels and the turning of the earth on its axis cannot be measured. SOURCE: *History, Time & Deity,* S.G.F. Brandon; *What You Call Time,* Suzanne Ruthven.

Tintagel, Cornwall: Located high on the cliff top overlooking the sea, Tintagel is well-known for its association with the Arthurian legend. It was here that Uther Pendragon and Ygraine, **Arthur's** parents, first met. The site became derelict until the interest in Arthurian legend revived in the 19th century. Tennyson's poems popularized the legend and the ruins were repaired in 1852.

Tiphareth: The sixth and central sephirah of the **Tree of Life**, it represents beauty and harmony, called the 'mediating intelligence' because it is the sphere of the **Dying** God and the **Sacrificial** King. The **Names of Power** are those of the **Sun** deities, the Illuminators and the sacrificed gods.

Tirtha: [Sanskrit] A holy place or earthly power-zone usually considered such after having been sanctified by the presence of, or even fleeting contact with, a spiritual being.

Toad: Often have an evil reputation in many parts of Europe, and believed to be in league with the Devil, or to be witches' familiars. De Plancy's fanciful *Dictionnaire Infernal* shows a toad flying to the Sabbath (sic) astride a skeleton but the belief may have its roots in the fact that country people often kept a pet toad in the pantry to get rid of insects.

Toad Bone: A number of traditions claim that there is a particular bone in a toad's body which, if located and removed in the right way, will confer power on its owner. This bone was cited as the key to the **Horseman's Word** and his uncanny mastery over horses.

Toadflax: A native of Britain, the plant flourished in hedges, banks, meadows, waste ground and roadsides; has a variety of uses in folk medicine. Ruling planet: **Mars**.

Toadstone: It was firmly believed, from at least the 15th century, that certain toads had a jewel-like stone in their heads, which could be extracted and worn as an amulet. Shakespeare mentions it in *As You Like It*: 'Which, like the toad, ugly and venomous/Wears yet a precious jewel in his head.' The toadstone prevents boats from sinking and houses from burning (see **Animal Concretion**.

Tofana: An old woman of Naples immortalized by her invention of a tasteless and colorless poison, called by her the *Mana of St. Nicola of Bari*, but better known as *Aqua Tofana*. Over 600 people are believed to have fallen victim to this insidious drug. Tofana died in 1730. Hieronyma Spara, generally called *La Spara*, a reputed witch, about a century earlier, sold a similar elixir. The secret was revealed by the father confessor, after many years of concealment and an alarming number of deaths.

Tomen-y-mur: In the wild mountain country to the south-east of the Snowdon range, this Roman fort stands on a spur of hill some 10 miles from the sea below Harlech. By the path down to the stream are the remains of an amphitheatre, bath-buildings and a parade ground. The small square mounds along this track and beyond the stream are the burial mounds of members of the garrison.

Topaz: A gem of silicate of aluminum worn as an amulet to draw wisdom, wealth and beauty.

Torah: In classic rabbinic teaching, the Torah refers to the Pentateuch, or the Five Books of Moses, and later to the whole range of Jewish teaching.

Torc: A Celtic necklace in the form of a

twisted band, worn as a badge of rank.

Torture: The means of extracting a confession by means of torture is common to nearly all witch trials

Totemism: An animal or plant species, or other natural phenomena, regarded as specifically related to the origin and welfare of an individual or tribe. A person's totem denoted the particular animal, plant or object with which he stands in a special relationship. The totem, by behaving in some unexpected way either in a dream, or in the actual world, warns if danger is near, or turns the mind inwards to receive some revelation. Once a totem has been identified, the individual will neither injure, kill nor eat it unless they are in dire distress. SOURCE: *The Book of Beasts*, Nigel Pennick and Helen Field; *Sacred Animals*, Gordon Maclellan.

Toto Cœlo: An allusion to the **Augurs** who divided the heavens into four parts. When all four parts concurred a prediction was certified *toto cœlo* = entirely. The Romans called the east *Antica*; the west *Postica*; the south *Dextra,* and the north *Sinistra*.

Touching Iron: The most common use for touching iron was when confronted by a potentially dangerous or unlucky person.

Touching Wood: A person will 'touch wood' when they have boasted or tempted Fate in some way.

Tower: The sixteenth card in the Major Arcana of the Tarot and the archetypal symbol of Destruction of all that is important... but not always in a negative form.

Trackways: Prehistoric trackways that ran for a long distance across the landscape, such as the **Ridgeway,**

Icknield Way, Sweet Track, etc, SOURCE: *Medieval Roads & Tracks,* Paul Hindle; *The Old Straight Track,* Alfred Watkins; *Roman Roads,* Richard Bagshawe.

Tractatus de Lamiis: Written by a prominent Italian lawyer, Gianfrancesco Ponzinibio, in 1520 attacking the **Inquisition** and leading theologians for their improper conduct. He was an outstanding opponent of the 'witchcraft delusion' and exerted considerable influence: The book was still being debated in 1672 by the Lord Advocate of Charles II; there is a copy lodged in the **Cornell** University Library.

Tradition: A term used to define a particular magical/mystical Path following preordained antecedents or traditions.

Traditional Witchcraft: Might be termed 'initiatory witchcraft' since those who follow a 'tradition' must go through a period of study and commitment before they are permitted to formally join the group. The main difference between **Old Craft** and Traditional Craft is that the latter tends to be more goddess-oriented and mainly matriarchal. The importance of the initiatory experience is revealed over a series of three grades, or degrees, and only fully-fledged third degree initiates are permitted to run their own coven. Most traditional covens observe the great festivals of **May Eve, Lammastide, Hallowe'en** and **Candlemas,** together with the solstices and equinoxes in a form of group worship. **Gardnerian** and **Alexandrian** groups are now coming under the banner of traditional witchcraft rather than **Wicca,** with which they were once identified. SOURCE: *The Call of the Horned Piper*, Nigel Aldcroft Jackson; *The Complete Book of Magic & Witchcraft*, Kathryn Paulsen; *Lid Off the Cauldron*, Patricia Crowther; *Mastering Witchcraft*, Paul Huson; *What You Call Time*, Suzanne Ruthven; *Witchcraft – A Tradition Renewed*, Evan John Jones;

Trance: Can be induced by drugs, magical or mystical techniques, or by accident; the result is that part of the consciousness is split off from the body / mind. The condition is part of the mystical tradition because it puts man in touch with planes of experience beyond his normal grasp. **Trance Working** is a self-induced condition where the practitioner undergoes a complete cessation of normal consciousness, although the magician retains control of his own individuality, enabling the physical body to remain inert while the astral body or consciousness is free to go on a mystical journey. It is loosely related to astral journeying but involves a much deeper level of shamanistic detachment that can be dangerous if the practitioner is not well versed in the technique. SOURCE: *Divine Horsemen*, M. Deren; *The Middle Pillar*, Israel Regardie; *Trance*, Stewart Wavell.

Transatuaumancy: Chance remarks that reveal something other than their original meaning; also knowing what will be said in a conversation before it occurs.

Transcendental Meditation: Became popular in the 1960s following the publicity surrounding the Beatles and soon became widely practiced in the West. The technique's aim is to improve not only the individual practitioner but also the state of society and the world in general.

Transference: One of the basic principles of folk medicine, everywhere in the world, is that diseases and other medical problems can be transferred to other people, animals or even inanimate objects.

Transmigration or Metempsychosis: The passage of the soul into another body after death. The soul is sometimes thought to be reborn in higher or lower forms of life, depending on its behavior in a part life, or according to its spiritual needs.

Transmutation: The changing of one form, nature or substance into another, especially the transformation of a base metal into gold through alchemy.

Transvection: (1) **Levitation**. (2) The projection of a **Fetch** or wraith-form.

Transubstantiation: In the Eucharist, this refers to the changing of the 'substance' of the bread and wine into the body and blood of Christ, though the outward appearance of the elements remain unaltered. The doctrine is central to the Roman Catholic Mass and marks the fundamental difference between the teaching of the Catholic and Protestant churches; the latter interpreting the 'presence' of Christ in the sacrament in a purely spiritual or symbolic sense.

Traprain Law: Occupied from the Iron Age through into the Dark Ages, this great Scottish hill fort stands on an isolated hilltop north of the Lammermuir Hills. The fort is believed to have been the major settlement of the Votadini tribe.

Tree Alphabet: A Celtic alphabet using the native names of the trees. The most commonly quoted being the version that appears in Robert **Graves'** *The White Goddess.*

Tree of Death: The reverse of the **Tree of Life** to which **Daath** is the Gateway. Erroneously referred to as evil by those not versed in Qabalistic symbolism.

Tree of Life: (see **Qabalah**).

Tree Lore: Trees have a spiritual nature that has remained curiously entwined with humans since mankind's earliest history; to harm or cut down a tree was often punishable by death. The indigenous trees have a rich tapestry of tree-lore, which is an essential part of British folklore and witchcraft. SOURCE: *Celtic Tree Mysteries*, Stephen Blamires; *Magical Guardians*, Philip Heselton; *Ogham & Coelbren: Keys to the Celtic Mysteries*, Nigel Pennick; *Root & Branch*, Mélusine Draco; *The Tree Book*, J. Edward Milner; *Trees in the Wild*, Gerald Wilkinson; *Witchcraft – A Tradition Renewed*, Evan John Jones; *A Witch's Treasury of the Countryside*, Mélusine Draco.

Tregetour: A conjuror or juggler from Old French, *tresgiat* = a juggling trick. The performance of a conjuror was anciently termed his 'minstrelsy'.

Trepanning: A practice common throughout prehistoric Europe, whereby a round piece of human skull was removed from a living person. The most ancient datable examples come from the Neolithic and Bronze Age. SOURCE: *Goddess of the Stones*, George Terence Meaden.

Tre'r Ceiri, Caernarvon: On an isolated hill, overlooking the sea, stands one of the most remarkable Iron Age hill forts in Britain. The inner area, protected by a strong drystone wall, has a long irregular oval plan, and in this are dozens of roughly circular stone huts.

Trevethy Stone: A cromlech at St. Clear, Cornwall. *Trevedi* means a place of graves.

Triad: Three subjects more or less connected formed into one continuous poem or subject. The Welsh triads are collections of historic facts, mythological traditions, moral maxims or rules of poetry disposed in groups of three. The Egyptian triad was the grouping together of three gods who may or may not be identified as a family group.

Triangle of Conjuration: Area for containing demons during ritual magical operations; the demon is confined to the triangle and forced to do the magician's bidding.

Trickster: The global mythological character generically called the Trickster has many dimensions and roles. He is found in various forms in the mythology of nearly every Native American tribe, the most well-known being **Coyote**, while Scandinavian myths feature **Loki**. Trickster survives in Europe as the **Fool, Harlequin** or **Lord of Misrule** of the carnival season before Lent, who cavorts about flouting establishment authority and convention.

Trident: A three-pronged spear especially that of the sea god **Poseidon** or **Neptune. Paracelsus** recommended, as a protection against impotence, a trident fashioned from a cast horseshoe found in the street.

Trigon: The junction of three signs. The zodiac is partitioned into four trigons, named after the four elements. The watery trigon includes Cancer, Scorpio and Pisces; the fiery trigon – Aries,

Leo and Sagittarius; the earthy trigon – Taurus, Virgo and Capricornus; and the airy trigon – Gemini, Libra and Aquarius.

Trimilki: The Anglo-Saxon name for the month of May, because in that month they began to milk their kine three times a day.

Trinity: Tertullian (160–240AD) introduced this word into Christian theology. In fact, the word **Triad** is much older and almost every mythology has a threefold deity. For example, the Iceni of Britain had Got, Ertha and Issus, while the Druids had Taulac, Fan and Mollac according to *Brewer's Dictionary of Phrase & Fable*.

Trinobantes: Inhabitants of what is now Middlesex and Essex, and referred to in Caesar's *Gallic Wars*. This word, converted into Trinovantes, gave rise to the myth that the people came from Troy.

Triple Goddess: see **Fate**.

Trismegistus: The 'thrice-great' epithet that the ancient Hermetists reserved for the Egyptian Hermes,Thoth, to whom is attributed a host of inventions – among others the art of writing in hieroglyphics, the first code of Egyptian laws, harmony, astrology, the lute and lyre, magic, and all mysterious sciences.

Triton: A minor sea god and son of Poseidon; usually represented with a dolphin's tail (sometimes a horse's forelegs) and blowing on a conch-shell.

Trophonios: [Greek] The cave of Trophonios was one of the most celebrated oracles of Greece. The entrance was so narrow that anyone who went to consul the oracle had to lie on their back with their feet towards the cave, where upon they were caught by some unseen force and violently pulled inside the cave. After remaining there some time, they were driven out in similar fashion, looking ghastly pale and terrified. Hence the saying about a melancholy person: *They have visited the cave of Trophonios*.

Trout: A fish often associated with holy wells, and from all over Britain there are folk tales of trout that embody the soul of whoever gave their name to the place. Any trout found in such places must never be taken or eaten.

Trowlesworthy Warren, Devon: A Bronze Age moorland settlement with six walled enclosures and circular huts. Not far way across the moor to the south there is a stone row and a stone circle, both Bronze Age; while across the streams to the east, the slopes of Lee Moor have more hut circles, enclosures and other structures – evidence of extensive occupation of the western valley slopes of Dartmoor during this period.

Tsukuyomi: Japanese moon god. He arose when **Izanagi** washed her right eye in the sea; when she washed her right eye, the sun goddess **Amaterasu** was born.

Tsusano: Japanese god of the winds and lord of the ocean. In his capacity as god of thunder he is associated with snakes and dragons.

Tuatha de Danann: The Irish name for a group of gods; 'peoples of the goddess Danu'. After the coming of Christianity, they were said to retreat into the Sid, the ancient burial mounds of Ireland.

Tuba: [Happiness] A tree of Paradise, of gigantic proportions, whose branches stretch out to those who wish to gather their produce; not only all luscious fruits, but even the flesh of birds already cooked, green garments, and even horses ready saddled and bridled. From the roots of the tree spring the rivers of Paradise, flowing with milk and honey, wine and water, and from the banks of which may be picked inestimable gems.

Tubal Cain: see **Luciferian Tradition.**

Tubilustria: A festival dedicated to **Vulcan** (Volcanus) as the divine smith responsible for making the sacred trumpets (*tubae*). During this time the trumpets were purified for use in religious ceremonies and the entire army would assemble outside the city for a full dress review.

Tubilustrium: A Roman day of special religious observance (23rd March) and sacred to Minerva, the patroness of trumpets.

Tulpa: [Tibetan] A double or magical projection of the magician in a predetermined form.

Tumulus: A prehistoric burial mound dating from the Neolithic and Bronze Age.

Tuneful Nine: see **Muses.**

Tuning Goose: An entertainment given in Yorkshire when the corn at harvest was safely stacked, similar to **Harvest Home.**

Turner, William: The first Englishman to study plants scientifically, whose *A New Herball* was published in three parts in 1551–68.

Turquoise: A blue-green stone worn as an amulet for good fortune and against the **Evil Eye.** Turquoise changes color according to the health of its owner.

Tut: A word used in Lincolnshire for a phantom, as in the Spittal Hill Tut. 'Tom Tut will get you' was used as a threat to frighten children; tut-gotten is panic-struck.

Twilight of the Gods: A final destruction of earth and heaven by evil and the return of **Chaos** when the gods themselves are destroyed.

Two: The evil principle of **Pythagorus** – and so the second day of the second month of the year was sacred to Pluto and deemed unlucky. The number indicates great intuitive powers but may be hampered by insecurity. Sometimes regarded as the number of femininity and the opposite of One. Number II equals the **Priestess** in the **Tarot** (or the four Twos – kings or knights of the Minor Arcana), **Chokmah** in the **Qabalah** and is governed by the Fixed Stars of the **Zodiac.**

Tyburn Gallows: There exists today a stone plaque on a traffic island near Marble Arch, marking the site of Tyburn gallows. One night in 1678, the gallows fell down, it is said 'uprooted by its ghosts'.

Tyche: The Greek personification of fortune or chance; the incalculable element in life, which may bring good or evil. The word means 'that which happens'.

Tylwyth Teg: The 'Fair People' of Wales played such a dominant part in the folklore that they appear to be a parallel population of the country. According to *Myths & Legends of Wales* by Tony Roberts, people believed completely in their existence right up until the rise of popular education.

Typhonian Current: Typhon was the

last of the fearsome old Greek chthonic gods and by writers of the Graeco-Roman period he was identified with the Egyptian Set. In modern ritual magic these energies were used by the **OTO** and by Kenneth **Grant** in his writings.

Tyr: Original form of Tiwaz, a sky god of the early German people, whom the Romans were quick to identify with **Mars**.

"What is life? It is the flash of a firefly in the night. It is the breath of a buffalo in the winter time. It is the little shadow which runs across the grass and loses itself in the Sunset."

Crowfoot, orator for the Blackfoot Confederacy

[*Touch the Earth*]

U

Ubiquity: The ability of being present at the same time in very different and far-apart places.

Uffington White Horse: The figure of a horse cut into the chalk of an escarpment in Oxfordshire – the earliest and largest of the 'Wessex' white horses. The full form can only be appreciated from far across the valley, or from the air. About a mile along the Ridgeway from the White Horse is the Stone Age burial chamber known as **Wayland's Smithy**.

Uji-gami: ['clan-chief'] A Japanese designation for ancestral or progenitor deities.

Uller: In Scandinavian mythology, the god of archery and the chase. No one could outstrip him in his snowshoes.

Ulysses: King of Ithaca, a small rocky island off Greece. He is represented in Homer's *Iliad* as full of tricks, and after the fall of Troy his adventures formed the subject for Homer's other epic, the *Odyssey*.

Ulysses' Bow: Only Ulysses could draw his own bow, and shoot an arrow through twelve rings. By this sign Penelope recognized her husband after an absence of 20 years. The bow itself was also prophetic and at one time belonged to Eurytus of Oechalia.

Unconscious: see **Collective Unconscious.**

Under the Rose: see **Sub Rosa.**

Undine: A creature of Elemental Water. Spirits made from the atoms of water in which they live.

Unction: Anointing with oil as a magico-religious rite, through which a person or object is endowed with supernatural powers, or set apart as sacred.

Underworld: In classical times the place where souls go after death, which is different from Otherworld, which is another dimension of the spirit. [SEE PANEL]

Unguent: see **Oil.**

Unicorn: Created from *'traveler's tales, nurtured by the error of biblical translators and adopted by alchemists, the legend of the unicorn (who combines male and female in one beast) is rich in the symbolism of opposites'.* The unicorn, together with the lion, have long been associated together in legend and heraldry and are the supporters of the shield in the English Royal coat of arms. In magical terms, the demon Amduscias is depicted as a unicorn.

Universe: According to Peripatetic doctrine, the universe consisted of eleven spheres enclosed within each other like Chinese balls. The eleventh sphere is called the empyrean or heaven of the blessed. (2) The twenty-first and last card in the Major Arcana of the **Tarot** and the archetypal representation of the **Macrocosm** and the **Microcosm** – All.

Universal Laws: see **Metaphysical Laws.**

Universal Life Force: An invisible energy that is believed to permeate all things, integrate mind.

Unut: A predynastic Egyptian goddess worshipped in the form of a **Hare** in Upper Egypt.

Urania's Mirror: Sidney Hall (1788–1831) was a British engraver and

Underworld and Otherworld

The predominantly monotheistic Christian concept of Hell or the Underworld, as a place of everlasting torment, is the fictional depiction from Dante's *La Commedia* (or the *Divine Comedy* as it became known some 250 years later). It took the poet around 20 years to write and was divided into three parts: *Inferno, Purgatorio* and *Paradiso*.

After encountering three wild beasts, representing Lust, Pride and Avarice, the deceased passes through the Gates of Hell into the Ante-Hell, devoted to 'those contemptible spirits who lived without blame and without praise', crossing the Acheron to enter the first of the nine concentric circles of Hell proper...

...which is remarkably similar to Hades, the Greek name of the god of the Underworld, and also for the Underworld itself, the word meaning 'the unseen', the position of which varied as ideas of geography changed. In the *Iliad* it was in the far west beyond the river Oceanus that was thought to encircle the earth. Later it was placed underground and approached by various natural chasms where the ghosts of the dead live a vague, unsubstantial existence. This realm of the dead is separated from that of the living by the rivers Styx or Acheron, across which the dead were ferried by Charon; and three other rivers – Phlegethon ('the fiery'), Cocytus and Lethe (forgetfulness).

The fortunate escape to Elysium, while those who were enemies of the gods are removed to Tartarus, an empire of eternal darkness, and the most horrible part of the Graeco-Roman Underworld. Elysium is also known as the Isles of the Blest (*makarōn nēsoi*), where those favored by the gods enjoy a full and pleasant life; the position is vague and quite different from Hades, the Isles being located in the 'stream of Oceanus'.

The ancient Egyptian Underworld was the Duat or Amenti, and the dead moved through this subterranean world with the help of funerary rites. The blessed and the damned coexisted in this strange environment, which provided an arboreal paradise for those who had passed the crucial test of the 'weighing of the heart'. The Field of Reeds was a term used to describe the domain of Osiris, and synonymous with fertility and abundance. In early texts, Amenti was thought to be among the circumpolar stars.

The concept of a form of judgement of the dead and rebirth also comes from these ancient beliefs, as do the Mysteries that require the living to undergo a form of ritual death, to be reborn again. And it is in this area that the differences between Underworld and Otherworld becomes blurred.

Otherworld refers to the astral realms whereby the Adept can commune with the Ancestors and other entities for the purpose of magic and divination. The magician's world has far more dimensions than are available to the normal human existence. They are able to cross dimensional barriers, or to see into other planes, and to draw entities from other dimensions (i.e. Otherworld) into the physical world.

Generally speaking, these are the dimensions of larvae, unformed life force that has not yet grown into a tangible spiritual form; natural elementals and nature sprites; the Mighty Dead and the Ancestors; qliphoth, the residue or physic husks of those who were once living; demons or manifestations of an individual's negative characteristics or psychic vampires. And the more extensively a magician ventures out into Otherworld, the more chance of encountering them.

Although there are certain funerary rites that may require an excursion into the Underworld, it is not something to be undertaken lightly and in a spirit of adventure. The dead should be left alone, unless *they* wish to communicate with us. And should the magician undergo the challenge of initiation into the Mysteries, then a descent into the Underworld *will* be part of that initiatory experience.

Those with genuine psychic gifts, however, may find that they have spent most of their lives with one foot in Otherworld; and that being the case, it holds no terrors for them.

EXTRACT FROM *KICKING OVER THE CAULDRON*
MÉLUSINE DRACO

cartographer well-known and popular for his early nineteenth century atlases and maps of the ancient world. He engraved a series of cards for locating the various constellations by lining up the stars through the holes punched in the cards. The cards were published c1825 in a boxed set called *Urania's Mirror*.

Uranus: (1) The rain that fertilizes the earth is sometimes represented as the seed of the Greek god Uranus, whose name means sky or heaven. (2) In astrology the planet called after him is a harbinger of violence, revolution and upheaval, although it has no significance in classical astrology. (3) The discovery of Uranus in 1781 (and later Neptune and Pluto) wrecked traditional astrological thinking about the order of the universe, in which the seven planets of antiquity corresponded to numerous other groups of seven, and round which so many religious, mystical and magical ideas were associated. (4) and (5) There are no alchemical or magical associations with Uranus and the planet was only discovered in 1781.

Urban Myths or **Legends:** Contemporary popular stories that are sensationalized and have usually happened to 'a friend of a friend'. The term was coined in the 1980s by an American Professor of English, Jan Harold Brunvand.

Urganda la Desconecida: An enchantress similar to **Medea** in the romances of the Amadis and Palmerin series, in the Spanish school of romance.

Urim: [Hebrew] Three stones that were deposited in the double lining of the high priest's breastplate. One stone represented *Yes*, one *No* and one *No*

answer is to be given. When any question was brought to the high priest to be decided by 'Urim', the priest put his hand into the pouch and drew out one of the stones, and according to the stone drawn out, the question was decided. Lev 8:8; 1 Sam 28:6.

Urine: Valued in magical and alchemical preparations because it was thought to retain some of the vital energy of the body from which it came and to provide a magical link with that body.

Uroboros: The serpent that endlessly eats its own tail; whose end is his beginning and who keeps the cosmic waters under control. In the Indian cosmos, the uroboros is the cobra, symbol of eternity.

Uromancy: The use of urine to foretell events. **Pliny** the Elder (23–79AD) wrote about the power of urine to reverse a bad omen and wrote: '*Among the counter-charms are reckoned, the practice of spitting into the urine the moment it is voided.*' In *Discoverie of Witchcraft* (1584) the instruction was that to '*unbewitch the bewitched… you must spit into the pisspot where you have made water.*'

Ursa Major: One of the oldest and best known of the constellations, the Great Bear has numerous legends attached to it. Also known as the Big Dipper, the Plough or Charlie's Wain.

Ursa Minor: Or the Little Dipper as it is a smaller version of the Big Dipper – but it contains the pole star, **Polaris** at the end of its tail.

Urthekau: A personification of the mysterious natural powers that the ancient Egyptians saw as being inherent in the crown.

Usquebaugh: Whisky. [Irish, *uisge-beathe*, water of life] Similar to the Latin *aqua vitae*, and the French *eau de vie*.

Uther: Pendragon (chief) of the Britons. By an adulterous amour with Ygraine (wife of Gorlois, Duke of Cornwall) he became the father of **Arthur**, who succeeded him as king of the **Silures**.

Utgard: [Old Norse, outer ward]. In Scandinavian mythology the circle of rocks that hemmed in the ocean, which was supposed to encompass the world.

Utgard-Lok: A Scandinavian demon of the infernal regions.

Uzume: Japanese goddess of jollity, whose obscene dancing antics entices the goddess **Amaterasu** from her cave, and so ensuring the return of the spring sunshine bringing life and fertility.

"*The moonless time of the month had arrived, which the astronomers called dark time. They regarded dark time in spring as the best time for seeing galaxies, because in spring, the Milky Way lay along the horizon, where it would not interfere with the view straight up into the deep.*"

Richard Preston

[*First Light*]

V

Valhalla: The hall of the slain, ruled by **Odin** in Norse mythology, to which heroes and distinguished warriors went after death, conducted there by the **Valkyries**, Odin's battle-maidens. There they fought all day and those who were slain were restored again in the evening, to join together in the feasting.

Valiente, Doreen: (1922–1999) Well-known for the 'poetic kind of spirituality' she bought to the editing of Gerald **Gardner's** original *Book of Shadows*. Following her death, *The Daily Telegraph* ran her obituary which acknowledged that her own contribution to the body of **Wiccan** ritual could not be overstated., since it was she, perhaps more than Gardner, who established the tone of the modern rites. TITLES: *An ABC of Witchcraft, The Rebirth of Witchcraft, Witchcraft For Tomorrow* and *Natural Magic*. SOURCE: *The Old Sod* (W.G. Gray), Allan Richardson; *Witchcraft – a Tradition Renewed*, Evan John Jones.

Valkyries: The 12 nymphs of **Valhalla** who, mounted on swift horses, selected those destined to die in battle. The name means 'chooser of the slain'.

Vampire: Vampires fall into three categories – (1) the living, (2) the un-dead and (3) the predatory wraith-form. SOURCE: *The Complete Vampyre*, Nigel Jackson; *A Dictionary of Devils & Demons*, J. Tondriau and R. Villeneuve; *The Encyclopedia of Witchcraft & Demonology*, Rossell Hope Robbins; *In Search of Dracula*, McNally and Florescu; *Magic- White & Black*, Franz Hartmann;

The Vampire, Ornella Volta; *The Vampire in Europe*, Montague Summers. [SEE PANEL]

Vampire Vortex: A specific formula of necromantic magick whereby the soul or astral double of a ritually consecrated and 'slain' priestess is made subservient to the will of the magician. SOURCE: *Nightside of Eden*, Kenneth Grant.

Vanir: The old Scandinavian fertility deities, sometimes represented as fair giants dwelling in earth or sea. They were linked with land-spirits of mountains or lakes, and with dead ancestors in the earth to whom offerings were made (see **Northern Tradition, Aesir** and **Asatru**).

Varma Marg: Sanskrit for left/ woman and path, which denotes the worshipping of the female (lunar) principal in the form of erotic ritual. *Dakshina Marg*, which means right/ male and path, is the Path of the Sun.

Vedas: Hindu sacred texts, the word *veda* meaning 'wisdom' or 'knowledge'.

Vegetation Spirits: The decay and rebirth of the seed-corn was personified in a vegetation god, who was invested by ancient man with a deeply religious significance. Foliated heads which can be found in many medieval churches are evidence of the ancestral concern for the spirit of vegetation (see **Green Man**).

Veil of the Abyss: The veil that separates the Triad of the Supernals (Kether, Chokmah and Binah) from the remaining *sephiroth* (see **Tree of Life**).

Vellum: A writing material prepared

Psychic Vampires

Vampires come in all shapes and sizes – although very few fall into the elegant and sophisticated variety popularized by England's 'purplest' literary community, The Gothic Society, where the undead were enjoyed as literary heroes. A genuine vampire can be encountered on several different planes of intelligence but with the single objective of draining the victim of all energy and ability thus feeding in the classical bloodsucking vampire way, i.e. draining the life force from a victim. The *psychic* vampire is doing exactly this.

Some may ask if these creatures really exist and the answer is 'yes' and they are all around you; and 'no' they are not necessarily enemies – *they can be people you know and care about.* Think about it. How many times do you meet or visit someone and feel tired and/or exhausted while in their company? Or you may find being in their company hard work. This is because these people knowingly, or unknowingly, are draining you of energy. This is only one aspect of a psychic vampire.

This 'leeching' of energy can be done by asking continual questions; keeping you talking; demanding your time, or pushing for a meeting. These are all ways of keeping you in their company in order to sap your energy; often they don't understand what they are doing. They are just drawn to you and need to be in your company as it feeds them and makes them feel better – but they often don't know why.

Method: To deal with this type you simply ignore them and keep away. That's the easiest option with this aspect of vampirism and once they are out of your way, your strength will return. The unconscious vampire is merely a pest and can be dealt with easily, providing you make a concerted effort to be unavailable whenever they call upon you for favors or your time. Even telephone calls can be depleting if they go on

for long enough so make yourself unavailable; if it is a family member, ensure that you only see them in the company of other people and make your escape as quickly as you can.

Psychic vampires come from all walks of life, but it's other occultists whom you must watch. This type of vampire is *consciously* after energy or magical strength for its own ends. The real danger is that, if allowed, a conscious vampire feeds on the weak by posing as a strong, intelligent leader whom people are drawn towards – thus ensuring the vampire a continuous feed. Long term they can become extremely powerful and can have devastating effects if allowed to continue to siphon off energy. The sensible magical practitioner should always be on their guard and ensure that protective barriers halt this kind of attention before it can take permanent hold.

More often than not, this kind of psychic vampire will be someone who has professed admiration for an individual's magical ability and may even be more experienced or of a higher 'rank'. Don't be fooled! If there is any illness or infirmity that is hampering their own magic, they will be after a fresh source of energy. One magical practitioner was highly offended when told by another, on whom they had designs, that the only way to deal with a psychic vampire was to destroy it... the predator took the hint and went off looking for easier prey!

Method: Dealing with this type requires more positive action in the form of protective measures. Remember the Count's greeting in *Dracula*: 'Enter freely and of your own will"? It can only be by an act of Will that you will repulse the creature. Make a conscious effort never to agree to help or lend something, keep them away from your home — your acquiescence will scupper any defences you may put in place.

EXTRACT FROM THE TEMPLE OF KHEM STUDY COURSE

from skins, especially of calves, lambs and kids, vellum (or parchment) had a marked advantage over papyrus, being much more durable and scribes were able to write on both sides. The use of vellum is called for in numerous classic occult texts but for modern use the substitute of 'vellum' paper, which can be bought at any stationery shop.

Venus: (1) Roman goddess of love is identified with the Greek goddess Aphrodite, who was the mother of Aeneas and so the 'mother' of the Roman people. (2) In astrology, the planet is said to govern the affairs of those born under the signs of Taurus, and Libra. (3) The planet Venus, the brightest planet in our sky, is both an evening and a morning star. When the planet follows the sun and is an evening star, it is called Hesperus; when it precedes the sun and appears before sunrise, it is called Lucifer, the 'light-bringer'. (4) Alchemy associates Venus with copper. (5) The card assigned to Venus in the **Major Arcana** of the **Tarot** is the Empress (and the four sevens in the **Minor Arcana**); and **Netzach** in the **Qabalah**. (6) It is also an archeological term for the small prehistoric, squat female figurines dating from between 10,000 and 40,000 years ago; the most famous being the *Venus of Willendorf.* Unmistakably pregnant, they reveal the intense primitive concern with birth and fertility.

Verdelet: (1) One who acted as a master of ceremonies in Hell and to be in charge of conducting witches to the Sabbat. It has been suggested that the implication of the 'green one' in the name may suggest some connection with the **Green Man**. (2) In some traditional **Covens** he is one of the officers serving the **Magister**.

Verendum: see **Baculum**.

Verjuice: (1) A culinary additive. (2) A potion used by witches to transform humans into animals.

Vermiculate: An amulet worn to protect from counter-spells.

Vernal Equinox: see **Spring Equinox**.

Ver Sacrum: [Sacred spring] In the old Italian religion, the dedication to the gods in time of great emergency, of the whole of the produce of the following spring, including any children born then.

Vertumnalia: The festival of Vortumnus (23rd August), god of orchards and fruit, who presided over the changes of the year.

Vervane: An herb sacred since ancient times and used in charms, philters and potions. *'Gather the plant at the rising of the Dog Star when neither Sun nor Moon is out.'*

Vesta: Roman goddess of the hearth and worshipped at home as the deity of the family hearth. Her public cult was conducted in a circular shrine, the 'hearth' of the community, where a perpetual fire burned, tended by the **Vestal Virgins**. SOURCE: *The Roman Book of Days*, Paulina Erina.

Vestalia: A festival honoring **Vesta** on 9th June.

Vestal Virgins: The Vestals were chosen as small girls and served for 30 years, during which time they had to remain chaste. Any lapse was punishable by death.

Vetch: Thought to have been introduced into the country by the Romans, and listed by **Aelfric**, during the Middle Ages it was grown for silage and fodder, and the seeds fed to domestic pigeons. **Gerard**, quoting **Galen**, said that although eaten in times of famine, vetch is *'hard of digestion, and bindeth the belly'*. Ruling planet: Moon.

Via Appia: The first of the great Roman roads (c312BC) that ran from Rome to Capua. Ottorino Respighi's awe-inspiring music for *The Pines of the Appian Way*, is a dramatic choice for magical working.

Via Mystica: Latin for mystical way or path

Via Sacra: The approach to the most sacred parts of the city of Rome, the temples of **Vesta** and of the **Penates**, the Forum and the Capitol.

Vibration: *'The universe visible to man can be likened to a web of tiny interlacing octaves of vibrations...'* (1) One source of this analogy is the old Pythagorean theory of the **Music of the Spheres**: that the motions of the heavenly bodies create a harmony of musical sound. That our lives are influenced by mysterious universal vibrations has become a common notion, largely based on the adoption of 19th century scientific theories by occultists and astrologers. (2) In traditional witchcraft it refers to the magical atmosphere around a person, place or thing.

Vigil: A watch by night for the purpose of enlightenment; usually prior to some rite of passage within a magical Order or Coven.

Vikings: see **Northern Tradition**.

Villa of the Mysteries: Cult center of **Dionysus** at Pompeii that contained murals depicting the rituals. The Villa was preserved by ash from the eruptions of Vesuvius in 63 and 70AD.

Vinalia Priora: A festival held in Rome on 23rd April, celebrated by sampling new wine and dedicated to **Jupiter** and **Diana**. The Vinalia takes its name from *vinum* (wine) and was celebrated with wine and fire.

Vine: Introduced to Britain by the Romans, and by Anglo-Saxon times south-east England was famous for its vineyards. Medieval vineyards produced both wine and **Verjuice** (grape vinegar). The plant's numerous healing properties were listed by **Pliny**. Ruling planet: **Sun**.

Vinegar: An acidic liquid that is mingled with history and folklore; it was first mentioned for its preservation and healing powers in ancient Babylon. SOURCE: *Vinegar: Nature's Secret Weapon*, Maxwell Stein.

Violet, Sweet: Although there are about nine British violets, most country folk only recognize two: the sweet violet (with scented flowers) and the dog violet (with no perfume). The ancient Greeks held it in such high esteem that they made it the emblem of Athens. It was also the flower of **Aphrodite** and, as such, was often used in love charms. The plant also has a wide variety of medicinal and culinary uses. Ruling planet: **Venus**.

Viper or **Adder:** The snake has always had a special place in the lives, beliefs and traditions of Britain. Folk remedies for an adder's bite are numerous, with countless herbal brews and incantations being frequently used. Adder bites are rarely fatal and the local cunning man or woman, being the only person who knew this, could be fairly certain of emerging with their reputation for healing enhanced!

Virginity, Magical: A woman chosen

for magical rites is said to be virgin when she is in the dream state or oracular phase of a rite. She is then 'unawakened' or in a magical sleep. SOURCE: *Nightside of Eden*, Kenneth Grant.

Virgo: (1) The only female sign in the zodiac, the Virgin –22 August–23 September – has been associated with a wide variety of goddesses since the beginning of recorded history. (2) The bright white star, Spica is the ear of wheat Virgo is holding. Scattered throughout Virgo and Coma Berenices are more than 13,000 galaxies known as the Virgo Cluster.

Vishnu: In early Hindu mythology Vishnu was relatively unimportant, but through coalescing with other gods he achieved – with **Shiva** – a supreme place in the Hindu Pantheon.

Vision: A term used in religion, magical and mystical spheres to mean an apparition.

Vision Quest: An **Amerindian** practice that involves a quest to acquire spiritual power by means of a vision of a supernatural being.

Visualization: A controlled thought projection of a magical journey or scenario in which the seeker *consciously* takes part. Often used in the early stages of magical learning as a springboard for **Pathworthing** and/or **Meditation.** SOURCE: *Visioning*, Lucia Capacchione; *Visualization – An Introductory Guide*, Helen Graham.

Vital Spark of Heavenly Flame: A belief held by Heraclitus that the soul was a spark of the stellar essence in *Macrobius: In Somnium Scipianis*, I, 14.

Vivienne: An enchantress of Arthurian romance, who entrapped **Merlin.**

Volcanalia: A fire festival of **Vulcanus** (23rd August). Volcanoes, earthquakes and lightening were all the domain of the god, which were taken to have prophetic significance… for the Romans it was highly significant that the eruption of Vesuvius occurred during the *Volcanalia* in 79AD.

Volva: The Icelandic sagas contain accounts of a divination ceremony known as *seid*, over which a *volva*, or female seer, presides. She sits on a high platform and gains hidden knowledge while in a state of trance.

Voodoo or **Vodun:** Refers mainly to the native religion of Haiti in the West Indies, stemming from traditional West African religions, brought to the Caribbean by the slave trade. Wherever the slaves went, they merged their ancestral beliefs with the local religion, employing various magical techniques known as 'obeah'. *'Voodooism satisfies the black man's need for an intensely personal relationship with the otherword, through the medium of the saints or the sainted dead.'* SOURCE: *Cults of the Shadows*, Kenneth Grant; *Divine Horsemen: The Living Gods of Haiti*, Maya Deren; *Famous Voodoo Rituals & Spells*, H.U. Lampe; *Man, Myth & Magic*, Richard Cavendish; *Voodoo & Hoodoo, Their Traditional Crafts Revealed by Actual Practitioners*, Jim Haskins; *Urban Voodoo*, S. Jason Black and Christopher S. Hyatt.

Vör or **Vara:** A Germanic goddess who, according to the Icelandic writer, Snorri, was the patron of contracts. Oaths and pledges are sacred to her, and she is also the guardian of marriage.

Vortex: see **Cone of Power**.

Vortumnus: A Roman god of orchards and fruit, who presided over the seasonal changes of the year. The *Vertumnalia* was celebrated on 23rd August.

Votive Offerings: Both Celtic and Germanic tribes left offerings in sacred places or dropped them into water. Many of the artifacts discovered by the **Sweet Track** are thought to be votive offerings to local gods.

Vulcanus: Roman god of fire and of the blacksmith's craft, his feast the *Volcanalia* was celebrated on 23rd August.

Vulture: Has the magical virtues of the **Eagle**, but not so intense; a sacred bird of kingship in ancient Egypt.

"Science may have found a cure for most evils; but it has found no remedy for the worst of them all - the apathy of human beings."
Helen Keller

W

Wagner, Richard: The Wagnerian operas have exerted a powerful influence on occultists, who have regarded the composer (1813–1883) as a 'natural magician' and even a 'Gnostic saint'. Wagner drew heavily from myth and legend – the cycle of *The Ring*, *Tannhäuser* and *Parsifal* still hold a fascination for those of the **Northern Tradition**.

Waite, Arthur Edward: (1857–1942) The Christian scholar who headed the **Golden Dawn** in its twilight years and who was scornfully referred to by Aleister **Crowley** as 'Dead-Waite' because of the tedious approach of his magical writings. Waite was a reactionary against **Theosophy** and detested the non-Christian aspects of ritual magic because he believed that occult sciences could be incorporated into Christian teaching. In 1910, along with American artist and occultist Pamela Coleman-Smith, he created the best-selling and best known of all **Tarot** cards – the Rider-Waite deck. He should be looked upon as an occult historian of some merit – but not as an occultist. SOURCE: *The Book of Black Magic & of Pacts*, A.E. Waite.

'Waking a Witch': It was believed that the most effective way of obtaining a confession from a witch was by what was termed 'waking her'. For this purpose an iron bridle or hoop was bound across the victim's face with four prongs trust into her mouth. The 'bridle' was fastened behind to the wall by a chain in such a manner that the victim was unable to lie down. She was sometimes kept in this position for several days, while men were constantly nearby to keep her awake. Some of these bridles are still preserved in Scotland.

Waldenses: Originally mendicant preachers, for centuries they were ferociously persecuted by the Roman Church for their unorthodox interpretation of the Bible. The community is generally thought to have been founded at the end of the 12th century by Peter Waldo, a wealthy Lyonnais merchant. In 1215 the Fourth Lateran Council decreed the extermination of the sect, together with the Cathars. In 1233 although thousands of Waldenses had been butchered on the grounds of heresy, the Dominicans were appointed official Inquisitors for the south of France and ordered to destroy the remnants of heresy wherever they found it. Today the Waldensian Church is flourishing throughout Italy, Switzerland and the south of France. SOURCE: *A History of the Inquisition*, Henry Charles Lea.

'Walk not in the Public Ways': The fifth symbol of the *Protreptics* of **Iamblichus**, meaning follow not the multitude in their evil ways. His doctrine was not for the common people but only for his chosen or elect disciples.

Wall, Staffordshire: The remains of the Roman fort and settlement of Letocetum on the Watling Street. The public baths clearly show an exercise hall, surrounded by a corridor with cold, warm and hot baths along its south-west side with hypocausts and furnaces. A museum nearby houses other artifacts found in the district.

Walnut: Introduced into Britain by the Romans, it has a wide range of medicinal and culinary uses. Walnut oil was used in lamps, wood polish and artist's paints. In folklore it was believed that if the nuts were placed under a witch's chair, it would rob her of all power of mobility. Ruling planet: Sun.

Walpurgisnacht: The Old German name for **May Eve** (30th April) when witches and evil spirits were thought to be abroad. The Brocken in Germany was a favorite spot for these revels.

Walton, Charles: A man said to have second sight and known as a witch in his village of **Lower Quinton**. He was murdered in 1945 in what appeared to be a ritual killing. The murder was never solved.

Wand: The most important tool in the magician's regalia, the wand and the rod can be traced back to the staffs of the priest-kings and magician healers of antiquity. There are numerous instructions concerning the correct material to be used but this does depend on the specific Tradition or Path being followed (see **Baculum**). SOURCE: *Magic: An Occult Primer*, David Conway; *Magick in Theory & Practice*, Aleister Crowley; *Techniques of High Magic*, Francis King and Stephen Skinner.

Wanga: [Voodoo] An evil charm or curse.

Wansdyke: One of the finest linear earthworks in Britain, surpassed only by the later **Offa's Dyke** which traverses the Welsh Marches. The best remaining parts of Wansdyke are in Wiltshire.

War, Holy: Some of the world's bloodiest wars have been waged in the name of 'God', even those religions that exalt peace and mercy have put the need to stamp out unorthodoxy before humanitarian considerations.

Warboys Witches: A notorious plot against three innocent people, and the most widely discussed trial for witchcraft in England before 1660. A copy of a contemporary tract (1593) is lodged in the British Museum.

Warham Camp, Norfolk: An almost circular Iron Age fort that lies on the lowland coastal plain, bordered on its west side by the river Stiffkey. It was finally used in the later stages of the Boudicean rebellion.

Warlock: Often used by cowans or outsiders as the term for a male witch. The word is said to stem from the Anglo-Saxon *waerloga*, which means 'traitor'. Traditionally a warlock is a magician or sorcerer and Sir Walter Scott's frequent use of the word gave it 'literary currency'.

Warning Stone: Anything that gives notice of danger. Bakers used to put a 'certain pebble' in their ovens, and when the stone turned white it gave the baker warning that the oven was hot enough for baking.

Warrior Queen, The: Boudicca, Queen of the **Iceni.**

Wart Cures: By far the favorite problem for folk medicine with dozens of remedies ranging from the application of blacksmith's water, to the folklorist's method of the buying and selling of warts and charming them. SOURCE: *The Penguin Guide to Superstitions of Britain & Ireland*, Steve Roud.

Washer at the Ford, The: A sinister crone who may be encountered beside lonely streams washing the blood-stained garments of those about to die. Often identified as the **Morrigan**.

Wassail: (1) A tradition of toasting the fruit trees with cider on Old Twelfth Night. (2) The salutation formerly uttered in drinking a person's health. (3) A liquor usually made from ale with roasted apples, sugar, nutmeg.

Watch: (1) To be on the alert to take advantage of an opportunity; to keep vigil. (2) Keeping guard (or watch) over someone keeping a solitary Vigil as a rite of passage.

Watchers, The: An ancient concept that the Watchers or Light Bearers are semi-divine beings who remained behind after the collapse of the Golden Age to watch over mankind's progress and prevent another **Deluge**/Destruction. Some mated with humans and from this sprung the legend of their descendants having 'elven blood' or 'witch blood'. SOURCE: *The Pillars of Tubal Cain*, Howard & Jackson.

Watch Fire: (1) A fire lit at night as a signal or beacon, or (2) to keep warm those taking part in a Watch or Vigil.

Watchtower: An Enochian term referring to one of the four cardinal quarters.

Watercress: Served as a pottage for cleansing the blood in the spring and 'consume the gross humours winter has left behind'. One of the **Nine Sacred Herbs** of the Anglo-Saxons. Ruling planet: Moon.

Water of Life: Water of chaos, water of destruction – these three principal elements flow and mingle in shifting patterns in the esoteric symbolism of water.

Water-sky: In Artic navigation this refers to a dark or brown sky, indicating an open sea. An ice-sky is a white one, or a sky tinted with orange or rose-color is indicative of a frozen sea.

Watkins, Alfred: A Hereford countryman who discovered ley lines while out riding in the Bredwardine Hills. He published his findings in *The Old Straight Track* in 1925, which has never been out of print since.

Watkins Bookshop: The oldest esoteric bookshop in London. Founded in 1897, it moved to Cecil Court in 1901.

Waxen Image: Damage inflicted upon a wax image by sympathetic magic, produces similar damage upon the body of the enemy it represents (see **Poppet**).

Wayland's Smithy: The smithy was located at a cromlech close to the **Uffington** Horse, close to the **Ridgeway** and the legend of the supernatural blacksmith was told by Sir Walter Scott in his novel *Kenilworth*. SOURCE: *White Horse: Equine Magical Lore*, Rupert Percy; *The Secret Country*, Janet and Colin Bord.

Weapon Salve: A salve believed to cure wounds by sympathy. The salve was applied, not to the wound itself, but to the weapon that caused it. *'Bind the wound and grease the nail'* became a **Rosicrucian** maxim, and is still common when a wound has been caused by a rusty nail.

Weather Lore: The ability to foretell the weather by the observation of Nature has always been one of the 'secrets' of witchcraft. SOURCE: *Weatherwise*, Paul John Goldsack; *Sea Change*, Mélusine Draco.

Weather Magic: There are many

apparently 'magical' methods of forecasting the weather that have since proved to have a scientific basis, but whether medicine men and witches have been able to influence the elements, and how they do it, is very much a matter of belief. SOURCE: *A Witch's Treasury of the Countryside*, Mélusine Draco; *Weatherwise*, Paul John Goldsack.

Wear: *Never wear the image of Deity in a ring.* According to **Iamblichus**'s *Protreptics*, symbol xxiv, God is incorporeal, and not to be likened to any created form.

Web of Life: The thread that links the corporeal body with the spiritual or divine, as a strand of the cosmic web of existence. **Walking the Web** – journeying out onto the astral. **Weaving the Web** – creating a bridge from the earthly to Otherworld to ease the passing of someone *in extremis*.

Wedding Customs: From ancient times there have been superstitions surrounding weddings, with numerous spells and charms to avert ill-luck. SOURCE: *The Penguin Guide to Superstitions of Britain & Ireland*, Steve Roud.

Wedjet: The royal Egyptian cobra goddess whose name means 'the green one'. Usually portrayed as a rearing cobra, she is an integral part of the uraeus, the archetypal serpent-image of kingship that protruded just above the forehead in most royal crowns and headdresses throughout Egyptian history.

Weeping Brides: It was believed that a witch could shed no more than three tears, and those from her left eye only, so a copious flow of tears gave assurance to the husband that the bride had not 'plighted her troth' to Satan, and was no witch!

Weighing of the Heart: The ancient Egyptian judgement of the dead, when the heart of the deceased is weighed against the feather of Ma'at, in the presence of Tahuti and Anubis. A heart found wanting was thrown to the monster Ammet to devour.

Well: A spring. **Wellhead** – the source of a spring or a fountainhead. **Wellspring** – a fountain.

Well-Dressing: The early church found well-worship the most difficult feature of paganism to eradicate and so many forms of it were incorporated into the local calendar of religious observance – hence the large number of 'saint's wells' that can be found the length and breadth of England. Wells and springs were often the focal point of early worship because of their life-giving and healing properties. SOURCE: *Folklore, Myths & Legends of Britain*, Reader's Digest.

Well of Wisdom: In Scandinavian mythology this was the well under the protection of the god Mimir. By drinking from it, Odin became the wisest of all beings.

Welsh Folklore: Traditional Welsh folklore is closely entwined with tales of the *Mabinogion*, the Fair People (**Y Tylwyth Teg**) and Arthurian legend. The Fair People played such a dominant part in Welsh life that they were almost like a parallel community, and this belief persisted until the rise of popular education in the late 1800s. **Arthur** is seen as a great Celtic hero – a military leader against the English – and appears in the earliest tales of the *Mabinogion*.

Wepwawet: An Egyptian jackal-headed god often confused with **Anubis**. A former warrior god, he was also worshipped as a god of the dead and at Abydos he was known as the Lord of the Necropolis

Westbury Horse: A hill figure on Bratton Down in Wiltshire was cut in 1778 over an older horse said to commemorate King Alfred's victory over the Danes. An engraving in Camden's *Britannia*, published in 1772, shows that the original horse was a very different creature from the present version.

Westcott, Dr. William Wynn: A leading **Freemason** and coroner in London when the **Rosicrucian** cipher came into his possession that formed the basis for the rituals of the **Golden Dawn**. He considered himself to be the spiritual master of the Order and contributed a modest volume on Qabalistic symbolism and edited an occult series for the Theosophical Publishing House in the 1890s. TITLES: *Collectanea Hermetica*.

West Kennett Barrow: One of the largest and finest Neolithic long barrows in Britain; a great chalk mound some 350 ft long located near Marlborough.

Werewolf: (1) Northern Europeans generally seem to have viewed the wolf with a fear and hate bordering on hysteria, and the human who turns into a (were)wolf and prowls in search of victims is a persistent figure of folklore and fantasy (see **Shape-shifting**). (2) A predatory wraith-form.

Western Ritual Magic: European magical practices originating in the Renaissance, when older magical traditions were integrated with Hermetism and the **Qabalah** (see **Ritual Magic**).

Weyd-monat: The Anglo-Saxon name for June, *'because the beats did then weyd in the meadow, that is to say, go and feed there'*.

Wheat: One of the oldest and most important of cereal crops, it has been grown in Britain since prehistoric times. In addition to its culinary uses, wheat has a variety of medicinal qualities. From medieval times, the **Corn Dolly** – representing the spirit of the **Harvest** – was plaited from the straw of the last sheaf to be cut. It was believed to contain the Harvest Spirit itself, whose survival was essential to ensure the success of the crop that followed. Ruling planet: Venus.

Wheatley, Dennis: The author who gave the general public an erroneous view of witchcraft and black magic. Despite being occult-illiterate, he wrote novels with occult plots and non-fiction books on magic and the occult. He went to great lengths in his introductions to state that he had never taken any part in black magic or occult ceremonies, although he assured his readers that he had investigated the subject thoroughly via the services of Rollo **Ahmed** and Aleister **Crowley**. TITLES: *The Devil & All His Works* (a study of magic and the occult), *The Devil Rides Out, To the Devil a Daughter, They Used Dark Forces* etc.

Wheel of Fortune: (1) The tenth card in the Major Arcana of the **Tarot**. It represents the introduction of random forces that will bring unexpected and uncontrollable change in a person's circumstances – usually for the better. (2) **Fortuna**, the goddess, is represented on ancient monuments with a wheel in her hand, emblematic of her inconstancy. (3) 'O Fortuna', from Carl Orf's *Carmina Burana*, is a popular piece of evocative music used for magical working.

Wheel of Life: The belief that everyone is shackled to the 'wheel of life', and that they must be reborn on earth until all **Karma** is expended, is a basic concept in **Hinduism** and **Buddhism**.

Wheel of Time: In various Indian myths, the wheel is a symbol of the year, and also of time.

Wheel of the Year: The term used in contemporary paganism for the calendar and the changing seasons marking the solstices and equinoxes, together with the major festivals of **Samhain, Imbolc, Beltaine** and **Lughnasadh**. SOURCE: *Sabbats*, Edain McCoy; *A Witch's Treasury of the Countryside*, Mélusine Draco.

Whin: see **Gorse.**

White: A color having both positive and negative qualities. While it symbolizes good, light, purity and innocence, it also stands for weakness, infirmity and cowardice. The **Druids** and generally the priesthood in ancient times wore white robes.

Whitebeam: Despite being a native British tree, it does not appear to feature in folklore. SOURCE: *Trees in the Wild*, Gerald Wilkinson.

White Harvest: A late harvest when the ground is white with frost in the morning.

White Lady of Ireland: The banshee.

White Magic: Many modern witches erroneously refer to themselves as 'white witches', which demonstrates a lack of understanding of the magical abilities they claim to possess. Magic is neither black nor white since it is morally neutral; it is the magical practitioners themselves who choose the Path they tread. Like magic itself, white has both positive and negative connotations. It might symbolize good, light, purity, peace, modesty and innocence but it is also traditionally the color of weakness, delicacy, infirmity and cowardice. SOURCE: *What You Call Time*, Suzanne Ruthven; *Coven of the Scales*, A.R. Clay-Egerton.

White Stone: An ancient custom of cutting a small stone in two and inscribing the name of the person giving the favor on one piece and the person receiving the favor on the other. This was done so that the receiver, at some future time, might return the favor, if needed, *'and in the stone a new name is written which no man knoweth saving he that receiveth it,'* Rev 2:17.

Whitestone: A traditional teaching coven descended from a genuine Old Craft family. Groups hiving off from the mother-coven use the suffix 'stone' to show their lineage.

White Tincture: A preparation that alchemists believed would convert any baser metal into silver. It was also called the Stone of the Second Order, the Little Elixir, and the Little Magisterium (see **Red Tincture**).

White in the Eye: It was said that the Devil has no white in his eyes, hence the saying: *Do you see any white in my eye?*

Wicca: Often the preferred alternative name for what is seen as contemporary witchcraft although much of the magical aspects have been stripped away in favor of a nature-based religious following with a lot of Eastern influence. Most people now referring to themselves Wiccan have their roots in material taken and adapted from **Gardnerian** and **Alexandrian** schools of witchcraft but without going through the initiatory system, they cannot claim the lineage. In America nearly all witchcraft traditions are referred to as Wiccan. SOURCE: *The Encyclopedia of Witches & Witchcraft*, Rosemary Ellen Guiley; *Lid Off the Cauldron*, Patricia Crowther; *Wicca* and *Living Wicca*, Scott Cunningham; *The New Believers*, David V. Barrett; *What You Call Time*, Suzanne Ruthven; *Wiccan Roots: Gerald Gardner & the Modern Witchcraft Revival*, Philip Heselton; *Wicca: The Old Religion in the New Millennium* and *Principles of Wicca*, Vivianne Crowley; *Witchcraft From the Inside*, Ray Buckland; *A Witches' Bible Complete*, Janet & Stewart Farrar.

Wiccan Rede: The basic creed of contemporary paganism is expressed as: *'Eight words the Wiccan Rede fulfil; An' it harm none, do what ye will.'* Believed to be created by Gerald **Gardner** or Doreen **Valiente**.

Widdershins: Means 'anti-clockwise' and refers to the circular dances or working that runs counter to the Sun's course. An effective method of invoking extremely potent cosmic and elemental forces.

Widow's Curse, The: One of the most powerful of curses if thrown by a widow-woman.

Wildfire: see **Need Fire**.

Wild Hunt, The: One of the most universal pieces of folklore in Western Europe and imported into Britain by the Anglo-Saxons, the Wild Hunt is a terrifying band of spectral riders and hounds led by some divine (or demonic) Huntsman. The Hunt could be heard on dark and stormy nights of midwinter, rushing through the air with a great clamor of hunting horns, galloping hooves and the baying of hounds. People fled to their homes when they heard it approaching and took care not to look out. SOURCE: *White Horse*, Rupert Percy; *A Witch's Treasury of the Countryside*, Mélusine Draco.

Wild Service Tree: In England the presence of this tree is regarded as an indicator of ancient woodland, although there is little written about it in books on the subject. It is mentioned in the traditional herbals but omitted from any texts on folklore.

Wildwood, The: The dark, untamed part of natural woodland where unearthly and potentially dangerous beings are found. Historically, the term 'wildwood' is the name given to the forests as they were some 6,000 years ago, before human interference. SOURCE: *Magical Guardians*, Philip Heselton; *Root & Branch* and *WoodCraft*, Mélusine Draco; *Wind in the Willows*, Kenneth Grahame.

Will: In occult terms, the mental power or faculty by which one initiates or controls one's activities, as opposed to external causation, impulse or instinct. The exercise of the Will is an act of authoritative purpose.

Willow: The earliest record of willow's use comes from the Neolithic period when causeways of willow branches were laid across boggy ground to provide a safe path. In folklore the tree is associated with sorrow and worn as an emblem of being forsaken – *'All around my hat I will wear the green willow'*. It had many medicinal properties and its ruling planet is the Moon.

Willowherb: see **Rosebay Willowherb.**

William Rufus: On 2nd August (**Lammas**) 1100 King William set out with a hunting party in the New Forest. Having become separated from the other members of the party, he was found dead having been killed by an arrow. Legend has it that when the king's body was removed to Winchester, some 20 miles distant, it left a trail of blood all along the way. Today, the Rufus Stone marks the site of his mysterious death on this highly significant date (see **Sacrificial King**).

Will-o'-the-Wisp: Ghostly lights seen hovering or moving about in an eerie manner, especially over fens, marshes and churchyards, which gave rise to numerous superstitions in the countryside. In fact, these lights were caused by atmospheric conditions, or the ignition of gases emanating from decaying plant or animal matter.

Williamson, Cecil: Best remembered as a researcher, occultist and founder of the Witchcraft Research Centre, and the **Museum of Witchcraft** in England. He was acquainted with Gerald **Gardner** and Aleister **Crowley** during the formative years of the witchcraft revival. His study of the occult brought him into contact with a diverse selection of people, among them Wallis **Budge**, Keeper of the Department of Egyptian Antiquities at the British Museum, Montague **Summers** and anthropologist Margaret **Murray**. His expertise involved him in the WWII intelligence network to collect information about **Nazi** occult interests and formed the witchcraft Research Centre for this purpose. Cecil Williamson was also involved in the famous 'witches' ritual' to prevent Hitler from invading England. After the war he set up the museum and continued with his occult research even after his retirement and up to his death in 1996.

Wilmington, Long Man of: A chalk figure in East Sussex, believed by environmental archeologists to be about 400 years old. It was given its present form in 1874; by that date the figure had become so overgrown and was only visible in certain lights or after snow had fallen.

Wilson, Monique: A modern English witch who was the prime beneficiary of Gerald **Gardner's** estate including the **Witchcraft Museum** (the Witch's Mill) on the Isle of Man, his collection of magical tools and regalia, his notebooks, papers and copyright to his books. She initiated Raymond **Buckland** into the Craft in 1963, and he became the chief exponent of the **Garderian** Tradition in America.

Winchester: A tribal center long before the Roman invasion; after which it became the fifth largest city in Britain. King Alfred made the town his capital and in Norman times it was of unrivalled eminence; as late as the 13th century it was second only to London in importance.

Wind: The poetic names for the winds are: The *North* wind, Aquilo or Bóreas; *South*, Notus or Auster; *East*, Eúrus; *West*, Zephyr of Favonius; *North-east*, Argestës; *North-west*, Corus; *South-east*, Volturnus; *South-west*, Aferventus; Africus, Africānus or Libs.

• The Thráscias is a north wind, but not due north.

• The Harmattan – a wind that blows

periodically from the interior of Africa towards the Atlantic in December to February. It is generally accompanied by fog, but is so dry that it withers vegetation and burns the skin.

•The Khamsin – A 50-days' wind in Egypt, from the end of

April to the inundation of the Nile.

•The Mistral – a violent north-west wind blowing down the Gulf

of Lyon and felt particularly at Marseilles and the south-east of France.

•The Samiel or Simoon – a hot suffocating wind that blows occasionally in Africa and Arabia. Its approach is indicated by a redness in the air.

•The Sirocco – a wind from Northern Africa that blows over Italy, Sicily, etc producing extreme languor and menta debility.

•The Solano – a Spanish south-easterly wind, extremely hot and loaded with fine dust.

Wind Flower: see **Anemone**.

Windsor Great Park: see **Herne the Hunter**.

Wine: Used as a libation and poured on the ground at the climax of a ritual as a gesture of thanks.

Wine-month: From the Anglo-Saxon *winmonath*, for the month of October; the time of treading the wine-vats.

Wintergreen: see **Chickweed**.

Winter Solstice: Falls on or around 21st December and heralds the shortest number of hours of daylight in the year. For the Romans this was *Divalia*, a day sacred to **Dia**.

Wint-month: [Wind month] The Anglo-Saxon name for November.

Wise(wo)men: One of the regular names for local practitioners of witchcraft, charmers, and other occult arts.

Wisdom: The second step in the receiving of occult knowledge: Knowledge – Wisdom – Understanding.

Wiseacre: A corruption of the German *weissager* for a soothsayer or prophet. The word has lost its original meaning and is now applied to fools.

Wisest Man of Greece: So the Delphic oracle pronounced Socrates to be, and he modestly made the answer: *"Tis because I alone of all the Greeks know that I know nothing.'*

Wish: A prayer or entreaty, often made silently. The occult adage warns: *Beware of what you wish for, you may just get it!*

Wishbone: A V-shaped bone formed from the clavicles in a bird's breast, pulled apart by two people – the longer part indicates the fulfillment of the wish.

Wish Hounds: see **Yeth Hounds**.

Wishing Well: A spring that is believed to grant wishes if a votive offering is flung into the water.

Witch: One skilled in ancient wisdom and magical craft.

Witch balls: Decorative glass balls often hung in windows to ward of evil spells. Glass fishing floats are often used for this purpose.

Witch bottles: Small glass bottle containing a charm or binding spell, usually containing spittle, urine, hair or nail clippings.

Witch boxes: A small wooden box containing herbs and other relevant material aimed at protecting a house from witchcraft. Popular in the 16-17th centuries, they were sold by the witch-finders while whipping up hysteria about witches in the neighborhood.

Witchcraft Act of 1604: The Act of **James I** repealed the existing statute passed in the reign of **Elizabeth I** (1563) and replaced it with tougher penalties. The most important change was that occult acts aimed at harming another person became punishable by death.

Witchcraft Act of 1736: The Act of George II was a major watershed in the legal treatment of witchcraft and other occult practices because under the new Act it was no longer illegal to indulge in Craft practices, since by implication witchcraft did not exist. It did, however, create a new offence of pretending to practice witchcraft with a penalty of a year in prison and four sessions in the public pillory. The government thereby announced that witches were frauds and should only be punished as such. It was finally replaced by the **Fraudulent Mediums Act** of 1951.

Witchcraft (Hereditary): Usually confined to an extended family and a recognized bloodline. Magical abilities may skip a generation and even those with a great interest in the Craft may not necessarily inherit the intuitive skills required for genuine witchcraft ability. SOURCE: *Witchcraft – A Tradition Renewed*, Evan John Jones.

Witchcraft (Historical): Usually the province of scholarly writers who have no practical, working knowledge of witchcraft and who often refuse to accept that Craft a) still exists in its original form, and b) all magical claims are suspect. Nevertheless it is essential to have a good grounding in the history and politics that have dogged the Craft for hundreds of years. Surprisingly enough, for many years the definitive work on the subject of witchcraft was *Witchcraft & Sorcery* (edited by Max Marwick, 1970), which was based on Professor E.E. Evans-Pritchard's classic study of the Azande tribe of Africa! Books such as *The Devil's Prayerbook*, published in 1972, purported to reveal the complete texts of the witches' rituals and it wasn't until it was reprinted in 2000 as *Rites of Shadow*, that the original author, E.A. St. George could reveal the full story. SOURCE: *The Black Art*, Rollo Ahmed; *The Encyclopedia of Witchcraft & Demonology*, Rossell Hope Robbins; *The Encyclopedia of Witches & Witchcraft*, Rosemary Ellen Guiley; *Europe's Inner Demons*, Norman Cohn; *The God of the Witches*, Margaret Murray; *The History of Witchcraft*, Montague Summers; *The Magical Arts*, Richard Cavendish; *Magic In The Middle Ages*, Richard Kieckhefer; *Religion & the Decline of Magic*, Keith Thomas; *Sex, Dissidence & Damnation*, Jeffrey Richards; *Witchcraft & Black Magic*, Montague Summers; *The Witch-Cult in Western Europe*, Margaret Murray; *Witches & Neighbours*, Robin Briggs.

Witchcraft: (see **Wicca, Traditional Witchcraft** and **Old Craft**).

Witch doctor: Native priests who treat patients for witch-induced illness or misfortune and seek out the culprit for execution. SOURCE: *Witchcraft & Sorcery*, ed Max Marwick.

Witch of Endor: A divining woman consulted by Saul when Samuel was dead. She called up the ghost of the prophet, and Saul was told that his death was at hand. 1 Sam 28.

Witch Finder General: Matthew Hopkins, who, in the middle of the 17th century, traveled through the eastern counties of England to find witches. Traditional has it that, at last, Hopkins himself was tested by his own rule. Being cast into a river, he floated, was declared to be a wizard, and put to death. The last reminder of his reign of terror was discovered in **St. Osyth** in 1921. Two female skeletons were found, pinned into unmarked graves, and with iron rivets driven through their joints. Either Hopkins or one of his associates had made sure that their victims would not return from the grave.

Witching Hour: The hour of midnight on the night of the full moon.

Witch Posts: Several timber-framed houses in Yorkshire and Lancashire still preserve curiously carved oak beams that were once thought to be a defense against witches. These beams were usually fixed upright to support the lintel over the hearth in the living room. It was believed that a witch could not enter beyond the post, nor could she lay a spell upon the hearth that displayed one of these talismans. As the belief in witchcraft faded, the posts were removed and only three or four remain in their original positions. The Rydale Folk Museum possesses examples that originally came from a shoemaker's shop in Danby, a farm in Glaisdale and an old house in Scarborough. SOURCE: *Folklore, Myths & Legends of Britain*, Reader's Digest.

Witch's Bridle: An iron gag and instrument of torture to make obstinate witches confess (*Pitcairn*, vol I, part ii.) There is an example in Forfar Museum, Scotland (see **'Waking a Witch'**).

Witch's Ladder: A cord tied with nine knots and used for spellcasting.

Witch's Mark: According to witch-hunters, this was a permanent mark, always made in 'secret places' and inflicted by the Devil himself on his initiates. All persons accused of witchcraft and brought to trial were thoroughly searched for such marks and any scars, birthmarks, natural blemishes and insensitive patches of skin that did not bleed qualified as witch-marks. Although Margaret **Murray's** theory that the witch-marks were actually tattoos was rejected by historians and academics, she was, in fact, correct; Old Craft witches *do* carry a 'mark' (which always remains covered), as confirmation of their acceptance by their peers.

Witch Trials: The nature of witchcraft in historical terms is best understood by reading court reports of the trials to see how admissions of guilt were secured. The most detailed were those of the 17th century, but the procedures differed little from those of the 16th century. When it is remembered that the accused had to answer, that refusal brought harsher torture, and that the judges or torturers prompted the accused's memory, the uniformity of confession is no mystery. SOURCE: *The Encyclopedia of Witchcraft & Demonology*, Rossell Hope Robbins.

Witch of Wookey Hole: A noted cave system in Somerset where a local witch was supposedly turned stone – but left her curse behind so that local girls rarely find a lover.

Wizard or **Warlock:** Terms used in various periods of history for male magicians, sorcerers or witches but seldom in modern times, except in fiction.

Woad: The leaves of woad were strongly

Words & Names of Power

The magical use of names or sacred words is as important today as it was in ancient and primitive societies. The name or word was seen to contain the essence of the person or 'thing' itself, and the same principle applies to gods, spirits and human beings. Within contemporary ritual magic and witchcraft a person's magical name is kept secret because, if it becomes known to a hostile magician, s/he gains power over them and can destroy them. Those who join magical orders and covens often take new names, to show that they are starting a new life as new people; or adopt a magical name upon attaining a certain rank within the group.

Within magic it is essential that the correct Names are called upon *and in the right context* for them to be magically potent. These are the Names and Words that are so ancient that they are firmly rooted in the universal unconscious as sacred utterances. In this context, we will examine the Names or Words of Power and go back to the points made in Professor Butler's *Ritual Magic*, where she states: *'The ineffable names of the Qabalah were used and misused by the magical confraternity quite as profusely as those of the divinities of Egypt, Greece and Christendom. The holier the names, the more powerful they were supposed to be…'*

What Professor Butler, along with thousands of others who read and write about magical practice, fail to grasp is that the magical usage comes from the *way* the Names or Words of Power are resonated, *not from the name or word itself*. What we are talking about here are what is known in magic as rhythmic sonics and the necessity to chant by rote, spontaneously and without thinking about it. If a witch or magician has poor recall, then the long-winded, full 'bells and smells' orgy of a full-scale ritual will lack impetus if it requires reading from a book. Under these circumstances it is more effective to repeat a two/three/four-line refrain and summon up a fine head of steam, than flounder along trying for the perfect delivery of a four-page ritual.

Even the simple Word of Power – Adonai (meaning Lord) – can

be used for magical effect if the syllables are drawn out into a repetitive chant: *A-don-ayyyyy; A-don-ayyyyy; A-don-ayyyyy...*

Whatever type of god-power/energies a magical practitioner wishes to summon, ideally s/he should either write the lines themselves, or take the time to research those classic poems that use rhymes and rhythmic language appropriate for the ritual. One of the most common is the line taken from Aleister Crowley's *Hymn to Pan* which has been used by all and sundry for years (even Wiccans), simply because it works. The invocation formula is:

IO PAN! IO PAN!
IO PAN! PAN! PAN!
IO PAN! IO PAN!
IO PAN! PAN! PAN!

This should be repeated over and over, gradually increasing the tempo, until the desired energy is built up. Laying down guidelines for what may happen next is pointless, because Pan is the All-principle, *Pangenetir,* who cannot be contained or confined. His energies are equally at home in Chokmah, on the Tree of Life, as the Great God Pan in all his glory, or the earthy Pan of Malkuth. When invoking Pan, we know without a doubt when his energy has descended, but everyone will experience the effects of the ritual in a different way.

Try the ritual in the confines of your Circle and record the sensations in your Magical Journal — remember that from Pan comes panic, so be prepared for an overwhelming sensation of fear. If you live near woods or open places, try the invocation as you walk, timing each word to the rhythm of your step, walking faster and faster in time with the words. This can produce some very interesting experiences...

EXTRACT FROM THE TEMPLE OF KHEM STUDY COURSE

astringent and helped stem the flow of blood, which is probably why the Celts and ancient Britons painted themselves with woad before going into battle.

Wolf: Few European animals surpass the wolf in the richness of its folklore, or in the use of its body parts as magical ingredients in spells and preparations.

Wolf-month: The Anglo-Saxon name for January, because wolves came closer to human habitation to feed on fallen livestock in the depths of winter.

Wolf's Bane: see **Aconite**.

Wood Betony: see **Betony**.

Woodbine: see **Honeysuckle**.

Woodhenge: A Neolithic timber structure near Stonehenge; radio-carbon testing dates this multi-ringed monument to 2300BCE. Recognized from an aerial photograph taken in 1925, the site has a circular bank – 220 ft in diameter – enclosing a ditch and six concentric settings of timber uprights, now marked by rows of concrete pillars. SOURCE: *Goddess of the Stones*, George Terence Meaden.

Wookey Hole Caves: Caves in the Mendip Hills, worn by the river Axe over a period of 50,000 years and evidence of human habitation is displayed in the museum. The famous 'Witch of Wookey' is a massive stalagmite, said by legend to be a petrified old woman.

Wool: To keep away witchcraft and disease, prepare an ointment of black wool and butter.

Words of Power: see **Names of Power**. [SEE PANEL]

Working Tools or **Weapons:** Refers to any consecrated implements used within the Circle for magical purposes: SOURCE: *Coven of the Scales*, A.R. Clay-Egerton; *Magick*, Aleister Crowley;

Techniques of High Magic, Francis King and Stephen Skinner; *Witchcraft – A Tradition Renewed*, Evan John Jones.

Wormwood: A native plant of Europe and Britain, which had a variety of medicinal uses. It was sparsely used in cooking because of its extreme bitterness. Ruling planet: Mars.

Wort: [O.E. *wyrt*, a root, herb] Any herb or vegetable but now used rarely except in plant names. Any localized or popular plant name that contains the suffix, i.e. liverwort, bruisewort, woundwort, etc, indicates that the plant was probably used in **folk medicine**.

Wort-lore: The term used within traditional witchcraft for herbalism.

Woundwort: Several plants renowned for their healing properties for wounds that are caused by external force. (see **Betony**)

Wraith: (1) The double or apparition of someone who is alive, although its appearance is generally taken as an omen of the person's imminent death, or as a sign that he is in serious danger or trouble. (2) Projected astral body or mobile form of witch power 'ensouled by the witch's exteriorized consciousness'.

Wreath: A circle or garland of flowers and/or leaves, bestowed as a mark of distinction, or placed among the funeral regalia to honor the dead. Evergreen wreaths are used as decorations in **Yule** and **Midwinter** celebrations.

Wrekin, The: This great fort crowns an isolated hill commanding a view of the Vale of the Upper Severn.

Wren: Although wrens were considered lucky to have around and it was unlucky to kill one, there was an annual custom of 'hunting the wren' as part of the **Midwinter** celebrations.

Writing on Witchcraft: Up to 1550 some thirty writers chronicled the 'development of the theory of witchcraft', and demonstrated how it evolved as a heresy to be stamped out with all ruthlessness. Nearly all these early works were in Latin and a list of them is given in *The Encyclopedia of Witchcraft and Demonology* by the American scholar Dr. Rossell Hope Robbins under the section of 'Early Writers on Witchcraft'.

Wu: The Chinese term for benevolent magic.

Wych Elm: Giraldus Cambrensis wrote in the 12th century that the Welsh longbow was made of elm, instead of yew as in England. In the 20th century Oliver Rackham, writing in his *History of the Countryside*, devoted a whole chapter on the wych elm as it is *'the most intimately linked to human affairs'*.

Wyrd: The Norse concept of fate or destiny. The 'Web of Wyrd' was woven by the three **Norns**, the Norse goddesses of fate; and the Vikings believed that each one could influence his future. Everyone, without exception, was subject to the cosmic destiny of Wyrd, spun by the Norms with the skein of life (see **Web of Life**).

Wyvern: An early type of heraldic dragon but only having two legs and a forked tail.

"In ancient Rome the sacred fire, personified as the goddess Vesta, was kept by a group of celibate priestesses, the Vestal Virgins ...there were dire penalties for any Vestal who broke her vows of chastity, for her punishment was harsh, as recorded by several ancient authors ..."

Miranda Aldhouse Green

[*Dying for the Gods*]

X

Xanthus: A large shell similar to those used by the **Tritons**. The volutes generally run from right to left but if one is found that runs in the opposite direction, it is considered to be a sacred object.

Xenoglossy: The ability to speak or write fluently a foreign language previous unknown, and which cannot have been acquired naturally.

X-Factor: [SEE PANEL]

Xenophanes: A wandering Greek poet (6th century BC) who attacked the polytheism and anthropomorphism of the traditional Greek religion, and asserted that God is single and eternal. From the presence of fossils of fishes in mountains he inferred that the land and sea had undergone great changes.

Xylomancy: Divination using the arrangement of dry sticks and originally used more than 5000 years age by Hebrew psychics.

The X-Factor

Witchcraft (unlike Wicca) is *not* a religion – it never has been, simply because it's an individual's *natural ability* that distinguishes him or her as a witch. In other words, a witch is born, not made. It just isn't possible to learn how to become a witch if we haven't got these abilities, although it *is* possible to learn how to hone and develop latent or suppressed psychic talents, under the right tuition. And there is no age limit for these discoveries – in either the young, middle-aged or old.

Wicca, on the other hand, is fast becoming accepted as the 'new pagan religion' with its doctrines drawing heavily on an eco-feminine shadow-image of Christianity. This again is nothing new, since Christianity itself absorbed many of the existing pagan festivals and celebrations into the Church calendar (including an identification of the Virgin Mary with Isis), and contemporary paganism is merely reclaiming its own. But in reality, even in the days before the Christian invasion, not all of the pagan populace were skilled in the Craft of witches.

To use a natural analogy, the differences between witchcraft and paganism *per se* is to liken them to the relationship between the domestic and the wild cat. To the casual observer there is little difference. Just as the similarities between the modern wild cat (*felis sylvestris*) and the house cat (*felis catus*) are so great and the differences so few, that it is difficult to establish any authentic genealogy. There is evidence that wild cats have mated with domestic cats and domestic cats can survive in the wild having gone feral, but they don't usually move far from human habitation and will quickly revert if given the opportunity. The wild cat, however, cannot be handled or tamed; even as a small kitten it is extremely ferocious. In appearance it is difficult at a distance to distinguish a wild cat from a large domestic tabby that has gone feral, but (as with witchcraft and paganism), the subtle differences *are* there, if you know where and *how* to look. For example:

Paganism (including Wicca) has developed a very strong com-

munity spirit in recent years, with everyone at public events joining hands to celebrate the festivals, organized around the nearest
weekend coinciding with a formal Wheel of the Year.

Pagans believe that information should be available to all, and that
everyone has the right to access all esoteric knowledge. Many pagans are highly suspicious of witches and some will deny that they
practice any form of magic at all. Paganism caters for teenagers within the community and actively encourages them to attend the fairs,
buy the books and any appropriate accoutrements. Pagans claim to
worship Nature in the persona of 'the Goddess'. **The generally accepted pagan motto is: 'And it harm none, do what you will'.**

Witchcraft is not bound by social rules and conventions, only by
the personal morality of the individual, and is governed solely by the
natural tides. Any form of magical working or spiritual observance
tends to be of a solitary nature, or in the company of tried and
trusted people. Witches believe that esoteric knowledge should
be kept hidden because it is impossible to convey the meaning of
the 'true mysteries' without the appropriate teaching. Traditional
witches are now rarely seen at pagan events, and hold that any
ritual equipment will be acquired as and when it is necessary. The
witch learns his or her Craft along the way, and pays *homage* to
Nature but in a more abstract form that the textbooks will allow,
something along the lines of Blake's *Auguries of Innocence:*

'To see a World in a grain of sand,
And a Heaven in a flower,
Hold Infinity in the palm of your hand
And Eternity in an hour'

**The Old Craft motto is 'Trust None!' although it could well be
taken from the motto of several Scottish clans: 'Touch not the
[wild] cat without a glove'.**
Which path will you ultimately tread?

EXTRACT FROM *MEAN STREETS WITCHCRAFT*
MÉLUSINE DRACO

"How then, you say, will I know when the omens are fulfilled? When all the twined strands of Time weave their final knot, you will know. If you do not know, then you have such a measly knack of magic that you should never have studied it in the first place."

Attrib. Iamblichus

Y

Yamuna: A sacred river of the Hindus, supposed by them to have the power to wash away sin.

Yarrow: Valued for healing wounds, staunching bleeding and reducing fevers. Used as a digestive and cleansing tonic. The stems were used for divination. Ruling planet: Venus.

Year or **Annus Magnus:** The Chaldean astronomers observed that the fixed stars shift their places at a rate of a degree in 72 years – according to which calculation they will perform one revolution in 25,920 years, at the end of which they will return to their original place. This revolution of the fixed stars is the *annus magnus*. The Egyptians made it 30,000 years, and the Arabians 49,000.

Year and a Day: A formal measure of time within traditional Craft, usually applied to contracts, marriages etc.

Yeats, W.B.: The Irish dramatist and mystic who was a disciple and follower of the Celtic mystery tradition and, gravitating towards magic, eventually joined the **Golden Dawn**. He became head of the Order after Samuel MacGregor **Mathers** retired to Paris; and eventually became disillusioned with it and left following the power-struggle between himself and Aleister **Crowley**. Magic continued to influence his work, and he continued to use esoteric imagery in his poetry. The fairy lore of Ireland, that was still a living tradition at the end of the 19th century, was also an important element is his work. SOURCE: *The Collected Poems*, W.B. Yeats.

Yeavering Bell: A large hill fort in Northumberland, with an internal area of nearly 14 acres and stone ramparts encircling the hilltop. There are foundations of numerous circular and oval huts.

Yellow: The symbol of jealousy, inconstancy and adultery.

Yellow Flag: see **Iris**.

Yesod: The ninth sephirah of the **Tree of Life** and the sphere of the **Moon**, the astronomical symbol of Change. The mysteries of sex are particularly attributed to this *sephirah*. The **Names of Power** are those male and female deities linked to the Moon. [SEE PANEL]

Yeth Hounds: A Devonshire superstition that has headless dogs or Wish Hounds, said to be the spirits of unbaptized children, roaming about the woods, making wailing noises. It was from Wistman's Wood on Dartmoor that they began their terrifying hunts across the moorland.

Yew: The English longbow was made from yew and some of the oldest weapons that archeologists have discovered are made from yew and date from Paleolithic times – about 250,000 years ago! According to Cassell's *Trees of Britain and Northern Europe,* on religious sites ancient trees usually predate the current theological use and are often older than the existing buildings. Although poisonous, yew was used as a purgative, and to treat heart and liver disease, gout, rheumatism, arthritis and urinary infections. Ruling planet: **Saturn.**

Yesod: Temple of the Moon

YESOD (Ye-SOD) is the Foundation and the Ninth Path of Pure Intelligence on the Qabalistic Tree of Life — and the *sephirah* **most easily reached from physical manifestation, just as the Moon, its planetary attribution, is the nearest to Earth.**

Yesod is a confusing *sephirah* because of the conflicting messages we find in its symbolism; on one hand it is the Foundation of the Universe, on the other the apparent fluid state of illusion. Many authors also ignore the potent sexual energy that is focused at this level. Not base sexual activity but the more subtle aspects of sex which is only just being rediscovered in the West, having been an important and intrinsic part of Eastern mysticism for thousands of years.

From the magician's point of view, Yesod is of supreme importance in his magical development because this is the level at which he begins to elevate his consciousness and rise in the planes. A word of warning, however, relates to the fact that although this Treasure House of Images offers up a wide panorama of magical images, the neophyte is unable to command or control them, because s/he has not yet learned the words of power.

As Dion Fortune explains in *The Mystical Qabalah*: *'It is truly said in the Mysteries that no degree becomes functional until one has taken the next.'* This means that the true nature of Malkuth cannot be fully understood until the student has ascended to Yesod; the secrets of Yesod will not be revealed until the door to Hod, the Sephirah of Magic, has been unlocked, and so on.

With Hod, and Netzach, Yesod forms the Astral Triangle and these three *sephiroth* form an area of power within the World of Assiah (Elements and Action). The power of Yesod is greatly influenced by the duality of Netzach and Hod, having as it does a dualistic side to its nature. In Qabalistic terms, these magical images symbolize both the rhythmic nature of the Moon and the rhythmic sexual urges in the female, although these are etheric not physical conditions.

Magically these energies will always balance each other *when used correctly*. There are times during magical workings when the polarity of power requires a reversal of focus; on the inner planes the negative energy does the work while the positive energy provides the stimulus. This refers to the male/positive and female/negative energies and the magical partners who have perfected the 'harmony' generate an obvious aura of power to the trained 'eye'.

In human terms, Yesod — the Foundation or Image of the World — is the *sephirah* nearest to us and still represents the world of illusion because we submerge our potential (Kether) beneath a cloak of social, family or professional habits and attitudes.

The word for *persona* is Latin for 'mask', and a rather good description of what we offer to our friends and acquaintances under the guise of our 'personality'. Yesod is the storehouse of library images from the physical and psychological planes and when we sleep we might find we have an action-replay of the day's events; or a completely different scenario with unknown people or places which are transmitted from the other *sephiroth*.

Another important aspect of human action is Yesod's correspondence to the sexual act; this *sephirah* also receives energy, via Tiphareth, from Daath and Kether — and extremely potent energy it is — because only the central *sephiroth* can produce the necessary transformation or conception for a physical or spiritual rebirth.

To reach the **Temple of Yesod** you will have begun in the Temple of Malkuth and traveled the 32nd Path. Sit quietly and visualize the room as shimmering quartz, reflecting the misty violet colors of the veils that line the walls. The floor is veined violet, mauve and purple marble. In the center is a square altar of quartz and on top, a large pearlized sea-shell holding the sacred flame. There are four doors flanked by pillars of violet and silver; the scent of jasmine fills the air...

EXTRACT FROM *THE HOLLOW TREE*
MÉLUSINE DRACO

Yezd: A sect of Persian fire-worshippers, who kept the sacred fire alight on the mountain Ater Quedah for 3000 years, without allowing it to go out for a second.

Yggdrasil or **the World Ash:** The guardian tree of the **Aesir**, which was thought to mark the center of the nine worlds of gods, men, giants, the dead and other supernatural beings. Following the death of the gods at the end of the world, the man and woman who will repopulate the earth will emerge from the World Ash.

Yin-Yang: The ancient Chinese theory of the two opposite and complementary forces in nature. TheYin force is associated with the feminine, the earth, darkness, cold, the night, the moon and passivity. The Yang force is associated with the masculine, the heavens, light, heat, the day, the sun and activity. According to Yin-Yang theory, the seasonal cycle and the whole of the natural order are explained in terms of the progression and alternation of the balance of the two forces. SOURCE: *Yin & Yang*, Martin Palmer.

Ymir: The personification of **Chaos** in Scandinavian mythology.

Yoga: Both a form of **Meditation** and a practical discipline; it is a path to liberation from the bondage of rebirth and the best known form is *hatha* yoga, which charts the course towards mystical union with the **Universal Soul**, through the physical body, in a long series of arduous exercises. SOURCE: *Balanced Yoga*, Dr. Svami Purna; *Eight Lectures on Yoga*, Aleister Crowley; *The Principles of Yoga*, Cheryl Isaacson.

York: One of the leading folk museums in Britain, that also chronicles 340 years of Roman occupation and the Danes, who captured the town in 876. The present cathedral, the largest Gothic church in England, dates from the 13th century.

Yuan Tan: The Chinese New Year.

Yue-Laou: In Chinese mythology, the man in the moon, who unites with a silken cord all predestined couples, after which nothing can prevent their union,

Yule: An old-fashioned term for the Christmas season, taken from the Norse winter fire festival over which the god **Odin** presided. To ensure prosperity for the coming year, the Yule log should be brought into the house at the **Winter Solstice** and lit from a piece of the previous year's log, which has been kept all year to preserve the luck of the household.

Z

Zabian: (1) The world of fashion that worships the stars, or the cult of celebrity in today's parlance. (2) A Zabian is a worshipper of the sun, moon and stars as in the case of the ancient Chaldeans and Persians. *'This is the new meteor, admired with so much devotion by the Zabian world of fashion.'* *Belgravia*, No 1.

Zen: A Japanese form of meditation philosophy with its roots firmly in **Buddhist** teaching. Zen encourages the experience of sacredness in anything and everything we do, from *'stepping on the earth, of standing still a moment, of sitting, or lying down… This ritualization of daily life adds sharpness to experience'*. Zen is one of the paths to enlightenment or *satori*, after a series of enlightening (*kensho*) experiences. SOURCE: *Living by Zen*, D.T. Suzuki; *Zen Flesh, Zen Bones*, Paul Reps; *Zen, A Way of Life*, Christmas Humphreys; *Zen Wisdom*, John Baldock.

Zener Cards: A standard set of cards used in parapsychology experiments. There are openly five symbols: circle, cross, three wavy lines, square and five-pointed star.

Zenith: The point of the heavens immediately above the head of the observer; **Nadir** is the opposite point, immediately beneath the observer's feet.

Zennor Quoit: An unusual megalithic tomb, the style of which originated in Brittany and is also found in the Penwith area of Cornwall. Divided into chamber and antechamber, it was originally covered by a large round cairn, but all trace of this has now disappeared, leaving the internal structure standing free. SOURCE: *Facing the Ocean*, Barry Cunliffe.

Zenobia: Queen of Palmyra who invaded Asia Minor and Egypt in open hostility to Rome in 266AD. She was captured and Palmyra was completely destroyed.

Zeus: The supreme god of the Greeks, who is associated with most aspects of human life. He is the dispenser of good and evil in the destinies of men, but principally of good; he is the father and savior of the human race and giver of laws.

Ziggurat: The stepped temple, built of mud brick that was a notable feature of Mesopotamian cities; the most imposing still surviving at Ur.

Zoanthropy: Divination by observing and interpreting the flames of three lighted candles placed in a triangular position.

Zocho: One of the 'heavenly kings' of Shinto, who protects the world from evil. He is the guardian of the south.

Zodiac: In astrology, a circle in the sky known as the 'zodiacal belt', through which the sun, moon and planets appear to move. A planet's position in the zodiac is believed to affect the way in which it influences people and events on earth (see **Astrology**). The signs of the traditional 'tropical zodiac' are not identical with the actual constellations in the sky and it is also arguable whether a thirteenth sign should be admitted. SOURCE: *Guide to the Zodiac*, Jonathan Cainer; *Magic:*

The Egyptian Zodiac

Despite the historical proofs that Egypt's early religion was stellar-based, there are no authentic records that align the constellations we recognize today with those identified by the ancient Egyptians.

For the Egyptians, the stars 'which grow not weary' had immense significance. The circumpolar stars that never set in the west were identified as 'the Imperishable Ones' and, according to the Pyramid Texts, the kings were raised up to heaven to join their company on death, to be free from change or decay. The association of the stars with the revered dead had a long-standing tradition in Egypt, which was echoed in the ceilings of many tombs being painted with stars, or the arched body of Nut, the sky goddess, depicted on the lids of the coffins.

The hieroglyph of the five-pointed star represented the celestial 'world beyond the tomb' while the star in a circle was the symbol for the place in the sky where the sun and the stars reappeared after having been invisible, according to the Pyramid Texts. In later times it came to represent the Otherworld — celestial or subterranean, i.e. the *dwat* and Amenti.

The constellation Ursa Major suggested a ritual object used ceremonially in 'the Opening of the Mouth' as part of the Osirian funerary rites. It also represented the thigh of a sacrificial animal and therefore connected to Set, while some sources have linked the constellation of Draco with the 'Mother of Set', Nut. The distinctive constellation of Orion was attributed to Sah, 'the glorious soul of Osiris' and held a deep significance in Egyptian belief because of the traditional connection between the stars and the dead.

Sothis (or Sirius, the 'dog star') was originally identified with Sopdet and later Isis; but more importantly, it was associated the annual flooding of the Nile. The ancient Egyptian calendar had been based on the date of Sothis rising near the sun at the summer solstice, which also coincided with the commencement of the Inundation. Ancient texts also assigned the known planets to various gods — Jupiter with Horus ('who limits the two lands'); Mars with Horus of the Horizon; Mercury with Sebegu (a god associated with Set);

Saturn with Horus ('bull of the sky') and Venus ('the one who crosses' or 'god of the morning') either Re or Osiris.

According to astrological reckoning, at the dawn of Egyptian history, the sun would have passed through the zodiacal belt in Aries, at the winter solstice instead of its present day appearance at spring equinox. Between 4000-2000BCE, it was Taurus that marked the spring equinox. Further computer dating shows the sun rising in Leo at summer solstice during the Pyramid Age, and by the reign of Rameses II it had moved to Cancer where it rises to the present day.

The most complete, so-called Egyptian zodiac is the one taken from Hathor's temple at Dendera by the French in 1821 and now on view in the Louvre. The circular zone – the sky – is supported by the four cardinal points – the standing women – and four pairs of kneeling genii with heads of hawks. Around the circumference march the thirty-six genii of the thirty-six decades of the year, for the Egyptian year of 360 days was divided into ten-day periods. Within these are the twelve signs of the Zodiac to which are added symbols of the fixed planets and a number of stars and constellations. The whole appears to be in certain respects a replica of terrestrial Egypt with the same nome divisions. There were more nomes, or provinces, than the twelve Zodiac signs, so they were augmented by the planets and star symbols.

Since the decipherment of hieroglyphic writing was still two years away, there was no way of knowing that the antiquity of the stonework was not as great as the collectors had supposed. The zodiac ceiling at Dendera was a product of the latter end of Egyptian history – the Ptolemaic or even Roman period – hardly Egyptian at all. Nevertheless, the superb drawings made by Prosper Jollis for *Description de l'Egypte* suggest that modern Western astrological symbolism is compatible with that of ancient Egypt from the point of view of magical and astrological working – although we no longer have the hippopotamus and crocodile!

EXTRACT FROM *THE EGYPTIAN BOOK OF NIGHTS*
MÉLUSINE DRACO

An Occult Primer, David Conway. [SEE PANEL]

Zodiac (Chinese): A form of Oriental astrology where the twelve emblems of the year differ from those in the West. The system is based on a table of years that correspond to the signs of the rat, ox, tiger, rabbit, dragon, snake, horse, goat, monkey, rooster, dog and the pig. For many people, the Chinese system appears to be much more accurate than the Western version. SOURCE: *Chinese Astrology,* Man-Ho Kwok; *Chinese Horoscopes,* Lori Reid; *Your Chinese Horoscope,* Neil Somerville.

Zohar, The: The most influential text of the Qabalah, published in the 13th century. Its name 'Book of Splendor' derives from the Hebrew word for radiance or illumination.

Zombie: [Voodoo] A neither living nor dead creature that has had its principle of intelligence (soul) ejected, and whose body has been invaded by alien forces, or by the will of the magician that has generated it.

Zoomancy: see **Alectryomancy**.

Zoroastrianism: From the monotheistic faith with **Ahura Mazda**, the Wise Lord, as its supreme deity, and who revealed himself to the prophet Zoroaster.

Zos: The body considered as a whole – a term coined by Austin Osman Spare to denote the total field of sensation and awareness. The complement of the **Kia**, the Zos is symbolized by the hand. *Zos vel Thanatos* – The magical name of Spare, which has a reference to the 'death posture of the body', *Zos Kia Cultus* – The Cult of the Body. SOURCE: *Cults of the Shadows,* Kenneth Grant.

Zulu: According to this African belief, men become sorcerers by their own choice, but women become witches because they are inherently evil. Yet it is the female whom the ancestral spirits possess, who has the power to heal and make the crops grow.

© **Mélusine Draco (2010)**

Moon Books invites you to begin or deepen your encounter with Paganism, in all its rich, creative, flourishing forms.

Printed and bound by CPI Group (UK) Ltd, Croydon, CR0 4YY